AF411679

CAPITAL PORTRAITS

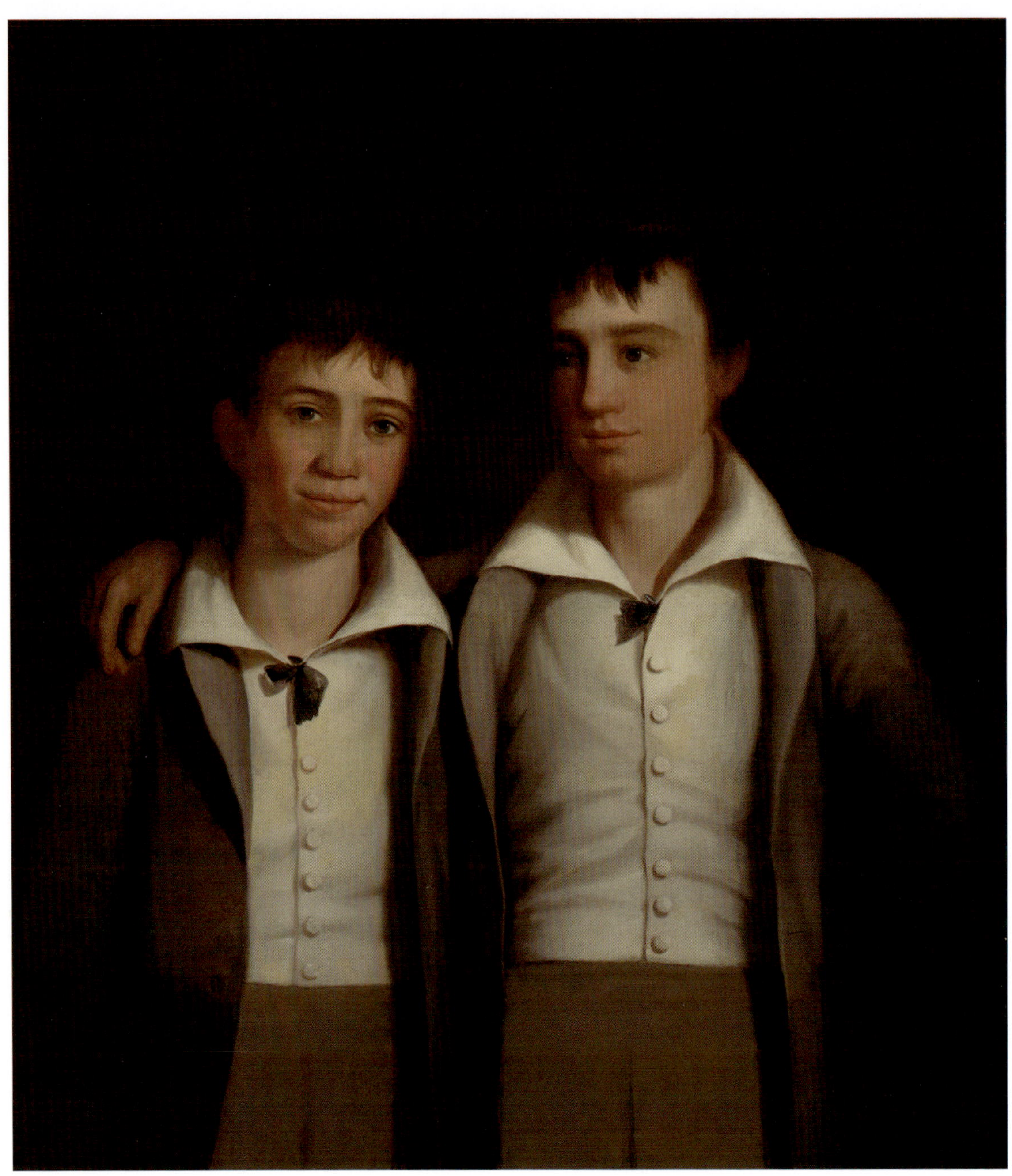

Treasures from Washington Private Collections

CAPITAL PORTRAITS

Carolyn Kinder Carr and Ellen G. Miles
With the assistance of Pie Friendly

Published in cooperation with
ROWMAN & LITTLEFIELD PUBLISHERS, INC.
For the National Portrait Gallery

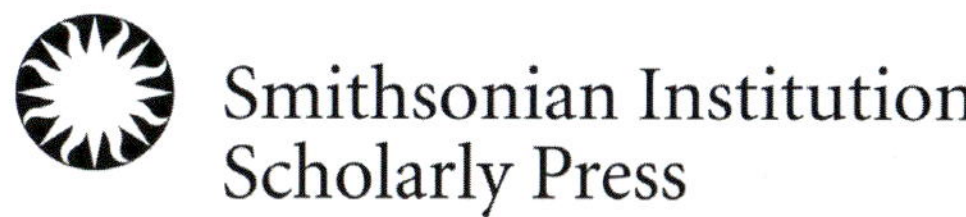

Smithsonian Institution
Scholarly Press

Washington, D.C.
2011

Published to accompany an exhibition at the
National Portrait Gallery, Smithsonian Institution
April 8–September 5, 2011

This publication and the exhibition have been generously supported by the late Robert L. McNeil Jr., in honor of Carolyn Kinder Carr and Ellen G. Miles.

Additional support for the exhibition and publication was provided by
The Mr. and Mrs. Raymond J. Horowitz Foundation for the Arts
Isobel Ellis

Published by SMITHSONIAN INSTITUTION SCHOLARLY PRESS
P.O. Box 37012, MRC 957
Washington, DC 20013-7012
http://www.scholarlypress.si.edu

In cooperation with
ROWMAN & LITTLEFIELD PUBLISHERS, INC.
A wholly owned subsidiary of The Rowman & Littlefield Publishing Group, Inc.
4501 Forbes Boulevard, Suite 200, Lanham, Maryland 20706
www.rowmanlittlefield.com

Estover Road
Plymouth PL6 7PY
United Kingdom

Frontispiece: James Bowdoin Sullivan and George Richard James (Sullivan) Bowdoin by Robert Street. See cat. 16.

British Library Cataloguing in Publication Information Available

Library of Congress Cataloging-in-Publication Data:

Capital portraits : treasures from Washington private collections / Carolyn Kinder Carr and Ellen G. Miles.
    p. cm.
  Includes bibliographical references.
  ISBN 978-1-935623-00-7 (cloth : alk. paper)—ISBN 978-1-935623-07-6 (slipcase edition : alk. paper)
  1. Portraits, American—Exhibitions. 2. Portraits—Private collections—Washington (D.C.)—
Exhibitions. 3. United States—Biography—Portraits—Exhibitions. I. Carr, Carolyn Kinder. II. Miles,
Ellen Gross, 1941–
N7593.C37 2011
704.9'420973074753—dc22   2010034560

Printed in Canada

♾™ The paper used in this publication meets the minimum requirements of American
National Standard for Information Sciences—Permanence of Paper for Printed Library Materials,
ANSI/NISO Z39.48-1992.

This book is dedicated to Robert L. McNeil Jr. (1915–2010) to celebrate his role on the commission of the National Portrait Gallery from 1971 to 1991 and his continued support of the gallery, including his generous donation to this exhibition.

CONTENTS

PORTRAITS IN WASHINGTON PRIVATE COLLECTIONS
A Window on the History of Portraiture in America

Carolyn Kinder Carr and Ellen G. Miles

WASHINGTON, D.C., is well known for the portraits in its public collections. Perhaps the best-known is Gilbert Stuart's portrait of George Washington. Acquired by the federal government in 1800, it was placed on view at the President's House, as the White House was then called. It remains there today as a preeminent symbol of the power of the president and the stability of our political institutions. Every schoolchild knows that Dolley Madison rescued this imposing portrait of the first president in August 1814 as the British were advancing on Washington. Madison wrote her sister on August 23 that she had "ordered the frame to be broken, and the canvass taken out it is done, and the precious portrait placed in the hands of two gentlemen of New York, for safe keeping." Only then did she also leave the President's House for safety.[1]

After the purchase of Gilbert Stuart's portrait of George Washington, no other presidential portraits were acquired for the White House until 1857, when Congress commissioned George Peter Alexander Healy to paint portraits of John Quincy Adams, Martin Van Buren, John Tyler, James Knox Polk, Millard Fillmore, and Franklin Pierce. The commission also included a full-length portrait of then-President James Buchanan, which he sat for in 1859. After Buchanan left office in 1861, Congress informed Healy that it would not pay for the portrait. Since then, however, the White House has acquired portraits of all the presidents, including Buchanan.[2]

These and other portraits in Washington public collections were acquired for a variety of reasons. The unique mission of the National Portrait Gallery, for example, is to collect the portraits of men and women who have had a significant impact on American history and culture. Achievement at the national level is the driving force in the selection of works for the permanent collection. Among its notable works is the first version of Gilbert Stuart's full-length likeness of George Washington, known as the "Lansdowne" portrait.

Less familiar, perhaps because they are less accessible to the general public, are the portrait collections on Capitol Hill—in the Capitol itself, as well as in the United States Senate, the House of Representatives, and the Supreme Court. Large federal agencies also have extensive portrait collections, among them the Treasury Department and the Justice Department. Other national collections include those of the army and navy. Recently, the Federal Bureau of Investigation has begun to build a collection as well. The purpose of these federal agency collections is the same: the portraits are selected to represent the leaders of these institutions. The first to be formed was the collection at the Treasury Department. John Sherman, the secretary of the treasury from 1877 to 1881, initiated the Washington tradition of commissioning portraits of cabinet members. He acquired existing portraits of previous Treasury secretaries or arranged for them to be copied, beginning with Alexander Hamilton, the first secretary of the treasury. He wrote Hamilton's son on February 26, 1879, explaining that his budget was limited for this project: "I have no difficulty in making arrangements by which copies of portraits of other Secretaries (three quarter length, life size) will be obtained from competent artists for $500."[3] For this series Sherman used funds that had been appropriated for the purchase and care of furnishings at the Treasury Building. Sherman's own portrait by G. P. A. Healy, completed in 1881, conformed to the standard three-quarter pose (50 × 40 inches).[4]

Similar motivations have led historical societies and museums to collect portraits both central to their mission and to their institution's history. Mount Vernon owns portraits of George and Martha Washington and members of their family. Tudor Place, the home of Martha Washington's granddaughter, Martha Custis Peter, has portraits ranging from a miniature of George Washington (given to Martha Custis at the time of her marriage to Thomas Peter) to an early-twentieth-century portrait of Caroline Ogden-Jones Peter (one of the last private owners of the house) by Cecilia Beaux. Anderson House, the headquarters of the Society of the Cincinnati, has portraits of its original owners, Mr. and Mrs. Larz Anderson, as well as a number of paintings and miniatures of members of the society. Particularly notable in its collection is Beaux's full-length portrait of Mrs. Anderson. At Dumbarton House, now the headquarters of the National Society of the Colonial Dames of America, portraits relate to the history of the house and to Georgetown. These include a double portrait of Sarah and James Nourse, parents of Joseph Nourse, who lived in the house from 1804 to 1813, and a 1789 portrait by Charles Willson Peale of the three young children of Benjamin Stoddert, later the secretary of the navy under John Adams. The Stoddert portrait contains a remarkable view of Georgetown and the Potomac. The extensive collection of the Daughters of the American Revolution at its national headquarters includes portraits of members and their families, as well as other images that speak to the early days of this nation. Among the earliest of these is the mid-eighteenth-century portrait of Mary Lightfoot by John Wollaston, painted in nearby Virginia. The Diplomatic Reception Rooms at the State Department display portraits of the great diplomats of the past, among which are Thomas Sully's portrait of Thomas Jefferson and Charles Willson Peale's portrait of Joel Barlow. Private clubs—the Cosmos Club, the Metropolitan Club, and the University Club to name a few—all display portraits of distinguished members. Likewise, universities collect portraits of their presidents, faculty, and distinguished alumni. Two unusual repositories of portraits are the National Cathedral, where one can see several important American paintings (including one of Bishop William White by Thomas Sully), and the Georgetown Branch of the District of Columbia Public Library, which houses an 1822 portrait by James Alexander Simpson of Yarrow Mamout, an African American resident of Georgetown known for his remarkable longevity.

A different purpose motivated the founders of the fine arts museums in Washington—a desire to share their keen interest in art, including portraiture, with the public. For these institutions, among them the National Gallery of Art, the Smithsonian American Art Museum, the Hirshhorn Museum and Sculpture Garden, the Freer/Sackler Gallery of Art, the Corcoran Gallery of Art, and the Phillips Collection, artistic merit has taken precedence over the status of the sitter as the deciding factor for inclusion in their collections. Surprising, perhaps, is the fact that the idea of a national collection of American portraits was part of the initial planning of the Corcoran Gallery of Art and the National Gallery of Art.

William Wilson Corcoran intended to establish a national portrait gallery in Washington as part of his art museum. The Corcoran Gallery of Art opened to the public in 1874 in the building that now houses the Renwick Gallery. His idea that the gallery would collect portraits of individuals of national stature was in part to demonstrate that despite his southern sympathies during the Civil War, the Corcoran Gallery would be a national institution. His plans were made public by his curator, William MacLeod. He described the purpose of Corcoran's collection of portraits in 1879: "As our great men pass away, it is well not only to have authentic portraits but to gather them in such an abiding place as the Corcoran Gallery of Art, here in the metropolis of the nation, ever to remain on free exhibition to the public."[5] Corcoran had already acquired several important American portraits, including a full-length by Thomas Sully of Andrew Jackson. In 1875 he purchased the largest surviving set of engravings by Charles Balthazar Julien Févret de Saint-Mémin. The French émigré had created more than eight hundred profile drawings and duplicated them in engravings during his years in the United States, from 1793 to 1814. The collection of Saint-Mémin engravings included portraits of George Washington, Thomas Jefferson, Paul Revere, Mother Seton, and other notable figures. In 1879 Corcoran acquired fifteen portraits of American presidents for the gallery by George Peter Alexander Healy from Chicago collector Thomas B. Bryan. Many of these had been commissioned in 1842 by Louis-Philippe of France but had not been delivered because the French king was deposed during the Revolution of 1848. Corcoran planned to build an annex to the gallery to house the portrait collection, but he was unable to acquire the land.[6]

When the National Gallery opened to the public in 1941, its American collection included a number of eighteenth- and nineteenth-century portraits that had belonged to Thomas B. Clarke (1848–1931), a New York businessman and one of the foremost collectors of American art. Andrew Mellon acquired the collection after Clarke's death, intending that it form the core of a national portrait gallery, should one be established. When he wrote President Franklin Roosevelt on December 22, 1936, to offer his collection to the American public for a national gallery, he noted that "there is in addition, a large assemblage of American portraits from the Clarke and other collections, which would be suitable for a national portrait gallery."[7] In 1962, after the National Portrait Gallery was established by Congress, thirty-one paintings and sculptures were transferred to the new museum, including seven presidential portraits.[8]

Because so many public collections include portraits, it should not be surprising to find portraits in Washington private collections. Individuals in this city possess portraits for three reasons: they have inherited them from family; they have collected them for their historical or artistic merit; or they sat for the portraits themselves. Most of the portraits in this exhibition are not well known, in part because they have always remained in private hands. Many of the owners who have inherited portraits do not think of themselves as collectors, perhaps because they have not purchased the works they own. If owners do consider themselves collectors, it is usually because they possess portraits as part of a larger art collection. To our knowledge, only one Washingtonian in recent memory formed a collection devoted exclusively to portraiture, and this collection of artists' self-portraits was dispersed at auction in 1998.[9]

Family portraits in Washington collections conform to well-developed traditions. Usually they celebrate or commemorate important events in the individuals' lives. One long-held practice was to commission paired portraits of husband and wife. The portraits of Andrew Oliver Jr. and his wife Mary Lynde Oliver (cats. 2 and 3), the earliest pair of portraits in the exhibition, were painted by Joseph Blackburn in 1755, three years after their marriage. Among the earliest pendant portraits in America are those of Oliver's grandparents, Daniel and Elizabeth Belcher Oliver, completed by John Smibert in 1730 (figs. 1 and 2). A later pair of portraits of Latham Avery and his wife, Betsey Wood Lester Avery, of New London, Connecticut, which are attributed to Samuel F. B. Morse, were also painted within a few years of their marriage (cats. 13 and 14). The portraits of William and Rebecca Cone of Hartford (cats. 20 and 21), painted several years after their marriage, are unusual because they are accompanied by a portrait of their eldest son, James Brewster Cone (cat. 22).

Other portraits in the exhibition also represent family commissions, but the related portraits are no longer in the same collections. This includes John Singleton Copley's portrait of Peter Oliver (cat. 4), made when his brother Andrew Oliver (National Portrait Gallery) was also painted by this talented young colonial American artist. Gilbert Stuart's portrait of Elizabeth Bowdoin, Lady Temple (cat. 10), was painted in Boston for her daughter. At the same time, Stuart made two other versions as pendants to portraits of her husband, Sir John Temple, first British consul to the United States. The portrait of Catharine Peabody Gardner (cat. 18) was painted by Rembrandt Peale in Boston a year after her marriage to John Lowell Gardner. It was a commission by her parents, who were also painted by Peale. When Hiram Powers made the plaster model for the marble sculpture of Robert Wickliffe Jr. (cat. 25), he also made one of Wickliffe's new wife, Josephine Van Houtum. Powers later wrote

to Wickliffe's brother-in-law that because of a disagreement, he had destroyed the plaster model of her portrait rather than carve it in marble, the usual next step with his portraits. When Eastman Johnson painted his sister's portrait in 1856 (cat. 26) on a visit to her home in Superior, Wisconsin, he also painted one of her new husband William Newton. Delia Caton (later the second wife of Marshall Field), was painted by George Peter Alexander Healy (cat. 29) soon after her marriage to Arthur Caton, several months after Healy had painted Caton's parents and sister.

Double and group family portraits in the exhibition include the paintings of the Sergeant twins by Charles Willson Peale, the portrait by Charles Bird King of Sarah Weston Seaton and her two children, and Robert Street's double portrait of the two brothers James Bowdoin Sullivan and George Richard James Sullivan Bowdoin (cats. 7, 12, and 16, respectively). The most striking family group in the exhibition is the

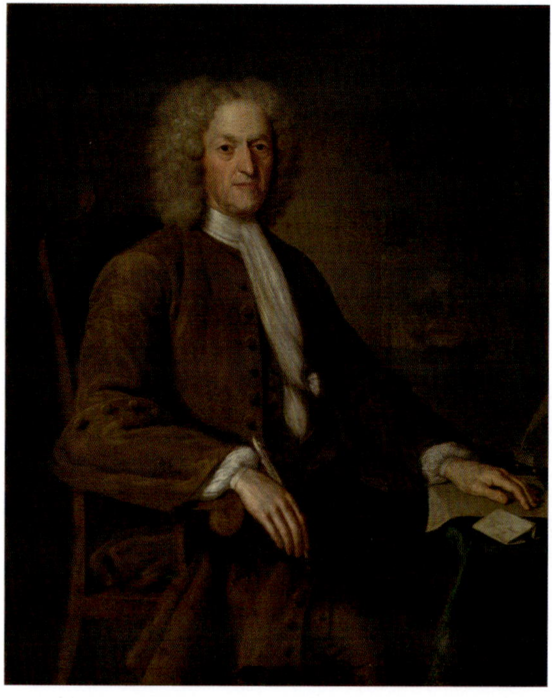

Fig. 1. *Daniel Oliver* by John Smibert (1688–1751), oil on canvas, 1729. Oliver Family

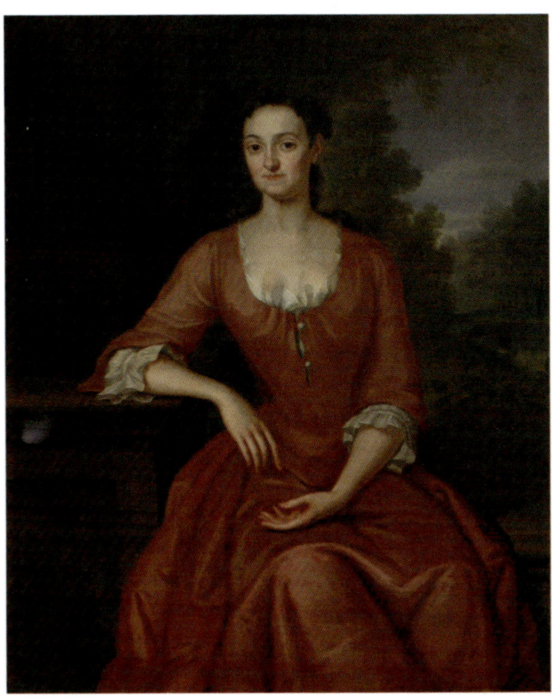

Fig. 2. *Elizabeth Belcher Oliver* by John Smibert (1688–1751), oil on canvas, 1730. Oliver Family

life-size painting of Hannah Skinner Church, her daughter Maria Church, and her daughter-in-law Elizabeth Bentley Church (cat. 11). Rather than celebrating the happy occasions of marriage or the pleasure of young children, it is believed instead to document a sad moment. The three women may have just learned that Elizabeth Bentley Church's husband, Edward Church Jr., was a bigamist, and that the elder Mrs. Church's husband, Edward Church Sr., had a mistress. Family portraits in this series include an equally large portrait by the same artist of Edward Church Jr. with his wife and their two children, as well as a slightly smaller painting of Edward Church Sr. (fig. 3).

Miniatures are among the most personal portraits made for family members. Dr. James Craik was painted during the American Revolution, when Charles Willson Peale and other artists made miniatures that could be finished quickly, with painting materials that were portable. So beloved was this image that his descendants had

it copied (cat. 5). The miniature of John Hite Morton (cat. 9) was painted by Benjamin Trott, a Boston artist who had settled in Philadelphia but went to Lexington, Kentucky, to paint portraits in 1805. One imagines that both of the originals were gifts to the sitters' wives or other family members. The desire for an intimate memento of a family member was not lost in the twentieth century, although the small, wearable keepsake of a loved one gave way to slightly larger images. Nevertheless the wax portrait of Dorette Fleischmann and the bronze relief of Warren Zimmermann (cats. 42 and 49) speak of a desire for a portrait that could be placed in a personal space—on a table beside a bed or chair, or, even more privately, held in one's hand—as a reminder, as was often the case in the nineteenth century, of a loved one who was absent.

Portraits of men often allude to their achievements. John Singleton Copley's portrait of Myles Cooper (cat. 6), painted after artist and sitter had both left colonial America for England, depicts Cooper in his Oxford academic robe. Copley had also represented him wearing these robes in an earlier portrait, completed in 1768 in Boston. The portrait of the Marquis de Lafayette (cat. 8) by Houdon is a second version of the one made in Paris in 1790 to celebrate his role in the formation of the French National Guard. John Clarke of Saratoga Springs (cat. 23) was painted at the end of his career, after his success in developing that resort city. The sculpture of British poet Alfred, Lord Tennyson (cat. 33), was part of a series of writers' and poets' busts made by American artist William Ordway Partridge. Rather than marking his success as a captain of industry, wealthy businessman Frederick Henry Prince commissioned his portrait from English painter Alfred Munnings (cat. 38) to signal his pride in his position as master of the hunt at Pau, France. This composition also captures Prince's immense pleasure in his championship horses and his hunting dogs, enthusiasms that he shared with his son. John Robinson's genre portrait of Alonzo Aden (cat. 47) commemorates his role in establishing the first private gallery in Washington

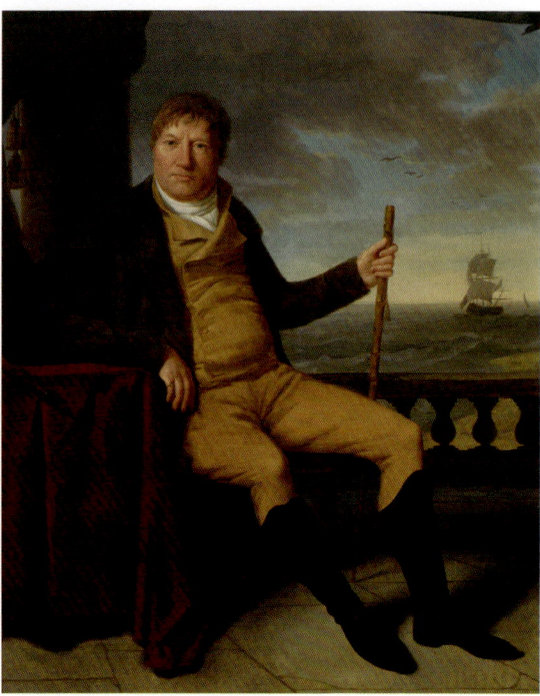

Fig. 3. *Edward Church Sr.* by Jacques-Antoine Vallin (c. 1760–1835?), oil on canvas, 1809. William Church Hagler, descendant of the sitter

devoted to African American art. Richmond Barthé's portrait of the Czech-born German dancer Harald Kreutzberg (cat. 44) honors his reputation as a major dancer and choreographer, as well as the triumphant reception he received during his American tours in the 1930s. Evelyn Nef commissioned a bronze portrait of her second husband to celebrate his eightieth birthday and to acknowledge his role as a major Arctic explorer and scholar (cat. 40).

This exhibition, which features mainly portraits of Americans, includes two portraits that were given as tokens of friendship. The portrait of Chinese merchant Howqua (cat. 19) is one of a group of identical images that were given to members of the firm of Russell and Company, prominent in the China trade in the 1830s. The portrait of Alexander II of Russia (cat. 28) was given as a gift in 1872 to Andrew Gregg Curtin, the American ambassador to Russia during President Ulysses S. Grant's administration. By request of the czar, this token of high regard was to remain always in the ambassador's family.

Women's portraits in the eighteenth and nineteenth centuries were often made to capture their singular beauty and sometimes record important personal events. Stuart's portrait of Elizabeth Bowdoin, Lady Temple (cat. 10), depicts a lively and lovely woman. The seated portraits of Phoebe Elliott Pinckney by Thomas Sully and Catharine Peabody Gardner by Rembrandt Peale (cats. 17 and 18) portray attractive young women in elegant white satin gowns and also reflect the introspective aspects of the Romantic era. Healy's portrait of Delia Spencer Caton Field (cat. 29) celebrates her charming demeanor, as well as her marriage to Arthur Caton in 1876. The desire to capture singular beauty or to record important events persists in the twentieth century. But portraits of women in this exhibition made during the last one hundred years are often of those who have also achieved success in the public arena, even if this is not readily apparent in the way they are depicted. Pauline Sabin (cat. 39), while elegant, beautiful, and wealthy, was a major player in contemporary politics, particularly in the movement to repeal Prohibition. Equally wealthy and attractive, Dorette Fleischmann (cat. 42) made her mark together with her husband as a major patron, especially of the ballet. Gwendolyn Cafritz (cat. 48) sought prominence as the premier hostess in Washington, creating a salon in which political and diplomatic figures could meet with ease. Ina Ginsburg (fig. 4 and cat. 56) was the liaison between hip artist Andy Warhol and the politically powerful in Washington, while Sally Quinn's reputation as a tart-tongued writer for *The Washington Post* defined her early years (fig. 5 and cat. 58 a–d). Kate Moss's fame as a major model is the reason Chuck Close made her portrait (cat. 61). Judith Martin, known universally as "Miss Manners," is remembered as a writer in her portrait by the presence of two of her books, *No Vulgar Hotel: The Desire and Pursuit of Venice* and *Miss Manners' Guide to Excruciatingly Correct Behavior* (cat. 62).

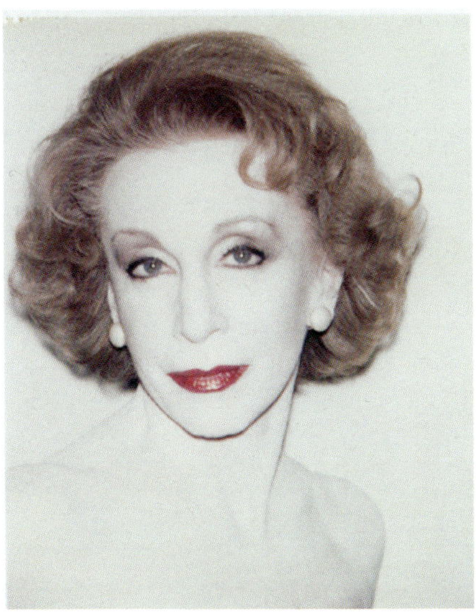

Fig. 4. Ina Ginsburg by Andy Warhol
(1928–1987), Polaroid, 1982. Ina Ginsburg

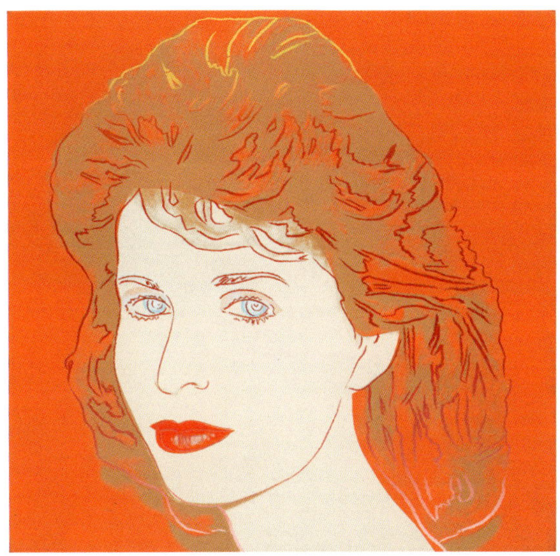

Fig. 5. Sally Quinn by Andy Warhol (1928–1987), synthetic polymer paint and silkscreen ink on canvas, 1986.
Sally Quinn

Among the children's portraits in the exhibition, the earliest represents young Ralph Izard
(cat. 1), who was painted in Charleston in 1754
by Jeremiah Theus before Izard's departure for
school in England. Izard was only twelve when
he was painted, but his pose and his clothes are
those of an adult. By contrast, Samuel Miller's
painting of a little girl with a basket of flowers
and a playful cat (cat. 24) clearly evokes childhood. For later artists, their own children were
frequent models. William Merritt Chase painted
his daughter Dorothy in a red dress (cat. 32),
possibly a costume for a "tableau vivant," the
popular late nineteenth-century family hobby of
re-creating "living paintings." Frederick Mac-
Monnies, best known as a sculptor, was living at
Giverny when he painted his charming eldest
daughter (fig. 6). Mary Cassatt and Lilla Cabot
Perry (fig. 7), artists known for their portraits
of children, often painted family members. On
occasion, however, they turned to others in their
extended circle to serve as models, as Cassatt did
in her portraits of Susan Valet (cat. 30) and Perry
did in her portraits of Hildegarde (cat. 35). The

evanescence of childhood as well as its charming innocence continued to motivate parents or
close relatives to commission portraits of children throughout the twentieth century. Robert
Henri's portraits of a five- and seven-year-old
brother and sister (cats. 36 and 37)—the only
paired portraits from this past century in this
exhibition—capture, in brilliant color and bravura
brushwork, the energy and intelligence of these
two youngsters. Paul Manship took a much more
classical approach to his interpretation of Frederick Prince III (cat. 41), but the smooth surface
of the face, the simple modeling of the hair, and
the costume of the sitter aptly describe the unsophisticated candor of a seven-year-old child. In her
profile medallion portrait of Warren Zimmermann
(cat. 49), Electra Waggoner used many of the same
techniques as Manship—the unlined face, the
minimally described hair—to portray this young
man on the cusp of adolescence.

Portraits can speak tellingly about centers
of wealth or artistic importance. The eighteenth-
century portraits in the exhibition were painted or
sculpted in some of the major American cities of

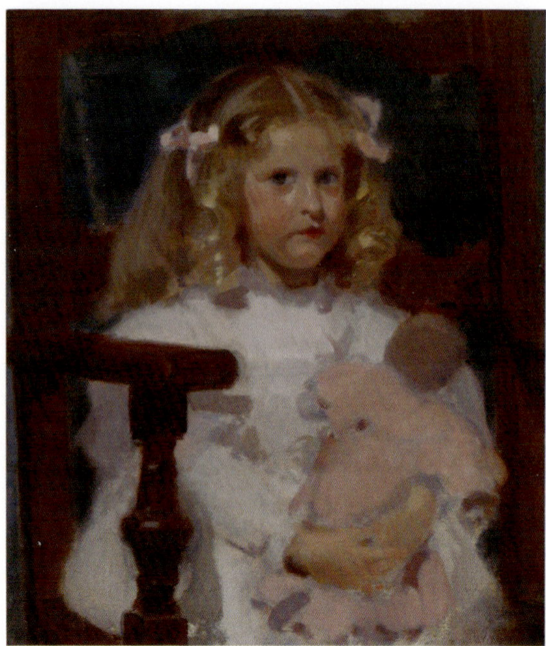

Fig. 6. *The Artist's Daughter, Berthe, with Her Doll, Amelia* by Frederick William MacMonnies (1863–1937), oil on canvas on Masonite, 1898. Private collection

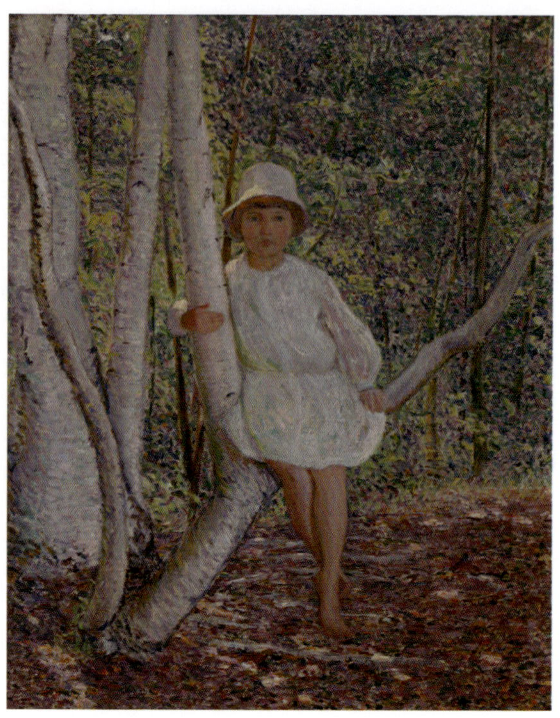

Fig. 7. *Anita Grew English* by Lilla Cabot Perry (1848–1933), oil on canvas, c. 1919. Mrs. Joseph G. English

the day—Boston, Philadelphia, and Charleston—as well as London and Paris. Before Washington became the nation's capital in 1800, portraits were made at the Virginia and Maryland homes of the sitters. These include Charles Willson Peale's portrait of Rebecca Lewis Innis (Mrs. Robert Innis) (fig. 8) of Gloucester County, Virginia, and British colonial artist John Wollaston's portrait of Ignatius Digges of Melwood (fig. 9) in Prince George's County, Maryland.

In the first half of the nineteenth century, portraits continued to be fashioned not only in the larger American cities and abroad but also in regional centers. After Washington became the national capital, artists such as Gilbert Stuart came to this city hoping for commissions. Surprisingly, because of the number of portraits that later came to reside in Washington, only three of the nineteenth-century portraits in this exhibition were painted here, all before the Civil War.

Robert Street's portrait of the Sullivan brothers of Boston (cat. 16) was painted in Washington while their father was in the city on government business. Also painted in the District of Columbia were Charles Bird King's family group of Sarah Weston Seaton, wife of William Seaton—co-publisher of the *National Intelligencer*—and their children (cat. 12) and Eastman Johnson's painting of the young woman known only by her first name, Hannah (cat. 27). The portraits of John Hite Morton (cat. 9), William and Rebecca Cone and their son (cats. 20–22), John Clarke (cat. 23), and Sarah Osgood Johnson Newton (cat. 26) were made in smaller cities like Lexington, Kentucky; New Haven and Hartford, Connecticut; Saratoga Springs, New York; and Superior, Wisconsin—evidence of the expansion of the United States and the growth of regional prosperity. Portraits made abroad during this era include the Church family women (cat. 11), made in Paris;

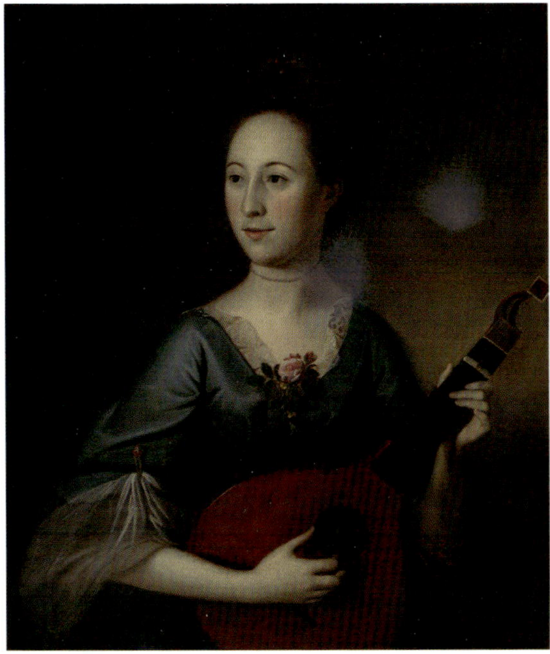

Fig. 8. *Rebecca Lewis Innis* by Charles Willson Peale (1741–1827), oil on canvas, 1775. Teresa Heinz Collection

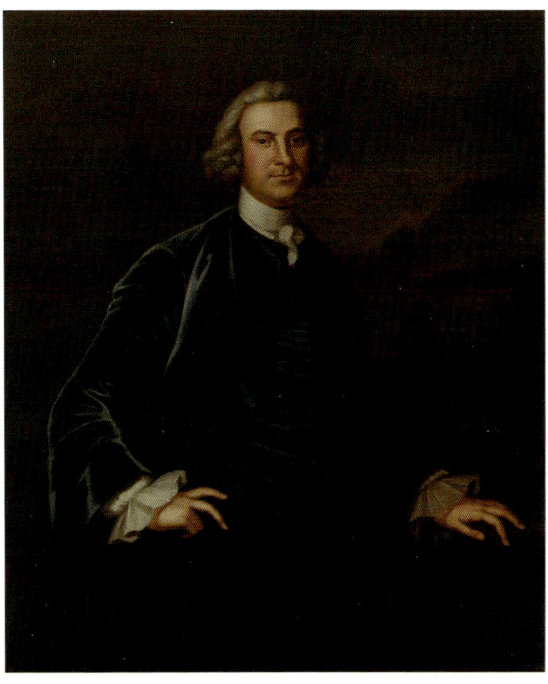

Fig. 9. *Ignatius Digges* by John Wollaston (c. 1710–c. 1767), oil on canvas, c. 1753. Private collection

Robert Wickliffe Jr. (cat. 25), sculpted in Florence; and Howqua (cat. 19), who was painted in Canton, China.

There is a long tradition in America of artists going abroad for training—in this exhibition are John Singleton Copley, Gilbert Stuart, Charles Willson Peale and his son Rembrandt Peale, and Thomas Sully, for example—and of Americans having their portraits made abroad. In the last half of the nineteenth century and into the early twentieth century, American artists and their patrons traveled and lived abroad with increasing frequency. Delia Caton (later the second wife of Marshall Field) was painted by George Peter Alexander Healy (cat. 29) in Paris on her honeymoon. Mary Cassatt, who had previously studied abroad, left the United States for France in 1874, returning only twice to America before her death in 1926. She was joined there by her parents and sister Lydia in 1877. There, as her

career began to blossom, she painted the informal portrait of her mother reading *Le Figaro* (fig. 10) and the charming portrait of Susan Valet (cat. 30), thought to be the cousin of her housekeeper. John Singer Sargent, born in Italy to American parents, received his artistic training in Paris, where in 1883 he painted fellow artist Albert de Belleroche (cat. 31). The Italian Giovanni Boldini was at the height of his powers as a painter of socially well-connected women when Mrs. William H. Crocker of San Francisco commissioned him in 1906 to paint her fifteen-year-old daughter Ethel Mary while Ethel was on holiday in France (cat. 34). When Mrs. Crocker went to Boldini's studio for her own sitting in 1910, she took Ethel Mary as a chaperone because of Boldini's reputation with the ladies. At the end of the sitting, Boldini gave Ethel a sketch (fig. 11).

While European artists have come to America to paint portraits since the colonial

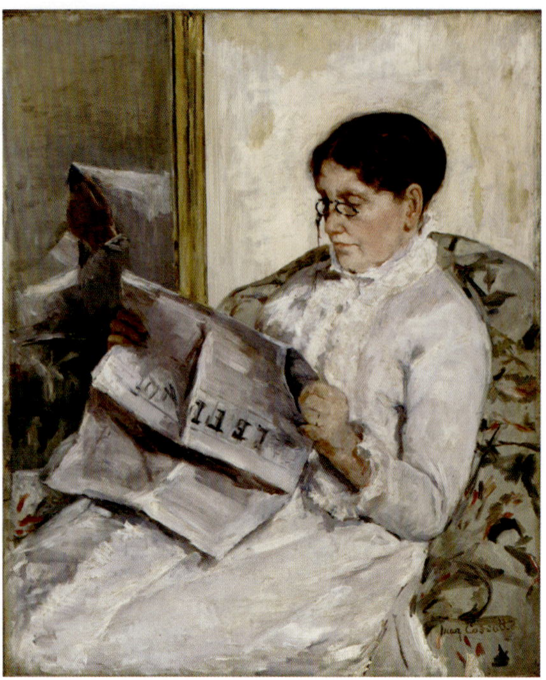

Fig. 10. *Reading Le Figaro* by Mary Cassatt (1844–1926), oil on canvas, 1878. Private collection

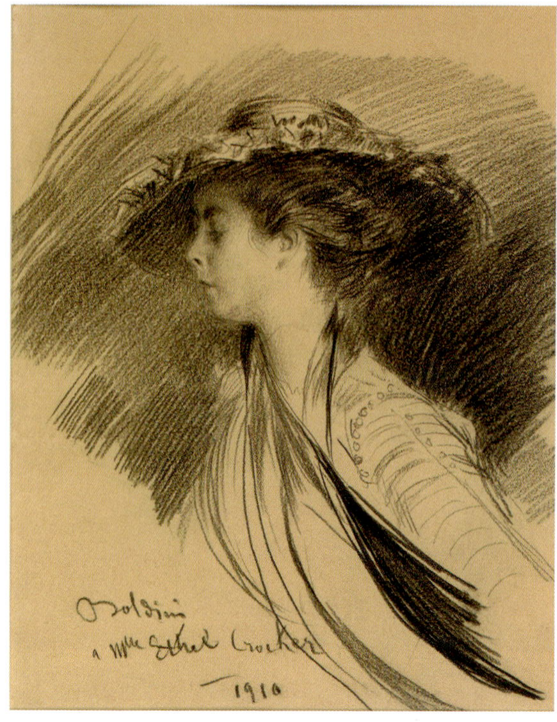

Fig. 11. *Ethel Mary Crocker (Countess de Limur)* by Giovanni Boldini (1842–1931), charcoal on paper, 1910. Private collection

era—eighteenth-century examples in Washington collections include John Smibert, Joseph Blackburn, and John Wollaston—this practice accelerated at the turn of the last century and continued for several decades, particularly in the years between the two world wars. Hungarian-born Philip Alexius de László, a naturalized British citizen, was on his third visit to America in 1925–1926 when he painted the social beauty and political dynamo Pauline Sabin (cat. 39). English artist Sir Alfred Munnings, who was known for his landscapes and equestrian portraits, painted the first of nearly a dozen portraits of banker and financier Frederick H. Prince and his family while in America. While Prince had known Munnings in England, the two met again in March 1924 as Munnings was traveling to Pittsburgh to serve as a judge for the International Exhibition at the Carnegie Institute. Prince approached

Munnings about a commission, and the portrait (cat. 38) was done at Prince's one-thousand-acre estate in Prides Crossing, Massachusetts. Most of the others, including a double portrait of Prince and his wife playing patience (fig. 12), were done in France, either in Paris or at Prince's estates in Biarritz or at Pau. Philanthropist, archaeologist, and collector Harris Dunscombe Colt and his wife Armida (fig. 13) were living in New York City when they commissioned a double portrait from English artist Claude Harrison in 1964, two years before they moved to Washington.

Artists who had spent time in America either before or during World War II often returned after the war. Washington *grande dame* Gwendolyn Cafritz (cat. 48) probably met Bernard Boutet de Monvel in Palm Beach, where he maintained a studio from the mid-1930s until the outbreak of World War II. Cafritz, however, was most likely

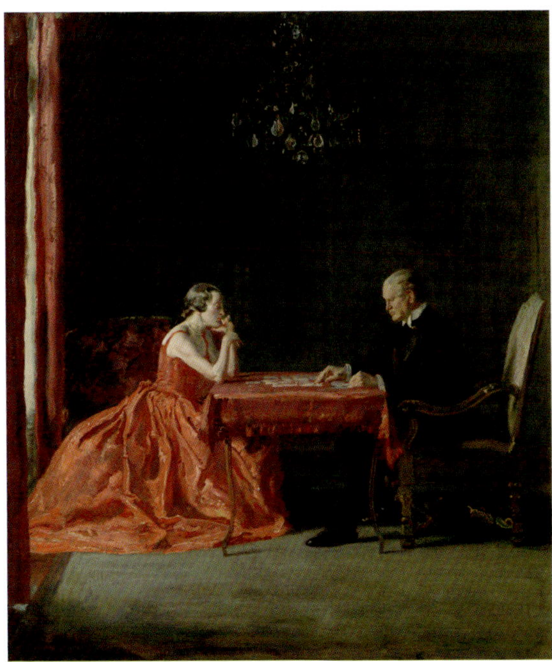

Fig. 12. *Patience* by Alfred Munnings (1878–1959), oil on canvas, 1933. Diana and Freddy Prince

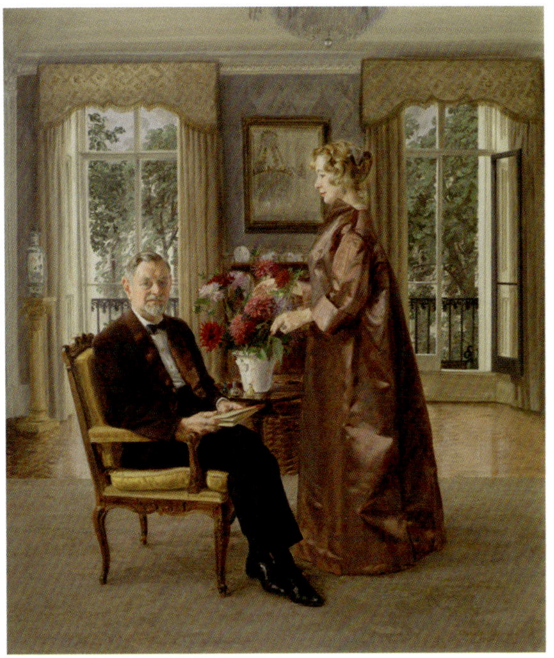

Fig. 13. *Mr. and Mrs. Harris Dunscombe Colt in Their Living Room* by Claude Harrison (1922–2009), oil on canvas, c. 1964. Mrs. Harris Dunscombe (Armida) Colt

painted in New York, where Boutet de Monvel maintained a suite at the Hampshire House when he returned to America in the brief period between the end of the war and his untimely death in an airplane crash in 1949. In 1940, with the outbreak of World War II, Salvador Dalí, like numerous other European artists, sought refuge in New York. Although he reestablished his primary residence in Spain in 1948, he returned yearly to New York City throughout the 1950s. There he met Dolores Suero (cat. 51), a woman from Cuba who was from a family that had a long-standing interest in art and architecture. Suero was part of the cosmopolitan and international circles in which Dalí flourished. Out of this milieu emerged a friendship and subsequently a portrait.

Given the close relationship between American sitters and European artists, it is perhaps fitting that the most recent work in this exhibition,

the 2008 portrait of Judith Martin (cat. 62), was done while Martin was living abroad. Martin and her husband spend several months a year in Venice. There they met her portraitist, Englishman Victor Edelstein, who, together with his Italian-born wife, also resided in Venice. Martin's portrait, like many in this exhibition, was commissioned to celebrate an occasion—in this case, a milestone birthday.

Most portraits from the late nineteenth and twentieth century in this exhibition, if not done by a European artist, were undertaken by artists based in New York City. New York's importance as a center of American artistic activity began in the early nineteenth century (although there are no examples in this exhibition) and grew during successive decades. After World War II, art produced, displayed, sold, and critiqued in New York affected art-making worldwide. William Merritt

Chase exemplifies the late-nineteenth-century artist who came from elsewhere, studied abroad, but found his fame—not in Boston, Philadelphia, Charleston, or any other regional center—but in New York. In 1913, the International Exhibition of Modern Art (known as the Armory Show) aided New York's reputation as a place where artists pushing stylistic boundaries could find a sympathetic home. When Delia Caton Field (cat. 29), who had a rather well-developed aesthetic sensibility, sought a bright young painter to undertake the portraits of her great-niece and nephew, she found Robert Henri, not in her hometown of Chicago and not in her newly adopted city of Washington, and not in Boston, so close to where she vacationed, but in New York. When Richmond Barthé (cat. 44), who had grown up in Louisiana but came of age studying at the Art Institute of Chicago, sought to locate his career where it would flourish, he, too, settled in New York. It was there that he met others interested in literature, theater, and dance and who would provide themselves as subject matter for his portraits. David Smith, who left the Midwest to study at the Art Students League of New York, found contact there with European artists like Czech-modernist painter Jan Matulka and Polish émigré John Graham, as well as emerging American painters such as Stuart Davis, Arshile Gorky, and Willem de Kooning, who each became important to the evolution of Smith's own work. His portrait of Lucille Corcos (cat. 43), made early in his career, is witness to the innovation in his sculpture that came about from the myriad influences and stimuli he found only in New York. Even Ethel Mundy and Electra Waggoner (cats. 42 and 49), each of whom had a rather peripatetic career, found New York to be a link between them and their subjects.

In the past forty years, when well-established Washingtonians sought to have their portrait made, they all went to New York. For a portrait that would celebrate their tenth wedding anniversary, Evelyn Nef and her husband selected Alex Katz (cat. 53), a New York artist who had developed a major reputation for his dramatic, larger-than-life portraits of friends and family. Rivaling Katz's reputation as an artist who challenged the abstract expressionists' hegemony and reintroduced figuration into art was Andy Warhol. Ina Ginsburg's portrait by Warhol (cat. 56), made in his New York "Factory," was a thank-you for both her role as cicerone during his numerous visits to Washington as well as for her interviews with notable political figures that he published in his magazine *Interview*. When *Washingtonian* magazine sought a hip artist for its cover story on Sally Quinn (see fig. 5 and cat. 58 a–d), it also turned to Warhol as a suitable match between subject and artist. William Haseltine's admiration for the expressive content of Eric Fischl's work led him to ask the artist, who was also a personal friend, if he would make his portrait (cat. 59). Fischl, recently returned from a fellowship at the American Academy in Rome, undertook the preliminary drawings and photographs for Haseltine's portrait in his New York studio.

In the same four decades, most collectors, too, have turned to New York for their acquisitions. William Beckman (cat. 54), Chuck Close (cat. 61), Gregory Gillespie (fig. 14 and cat. 57), and Kehinde Wiley (cat. 60) are all artists with a New York base. The power of New York as a magnet for ambitious artists is underscored by the fact that none of these artists came from New York. Gillespie grew up in New Jersey, Beckman spent his childhood in Minnesota, Close in the state of Washington, and Wiley in Los Angeles. New York's community of artists, dealers, major auction houses, and publications critiquing the making and selling of art is not matched elsewhere. This convergence also makes New York a mecca for collectors. Its draw as a rich and vibrant center for artistic activity of all kinds was why the self-portrait of West Coast artist Robert Arneson (fig. 15) was acquired there rather than in California.

As was true for the nineteenth-century loans in this exhibition, only three of the twentieth-century portraits were made in Washington. They provide an interesting window on the history of the artistic activity in this city. *First Gallery* (cat. 47), by the African American

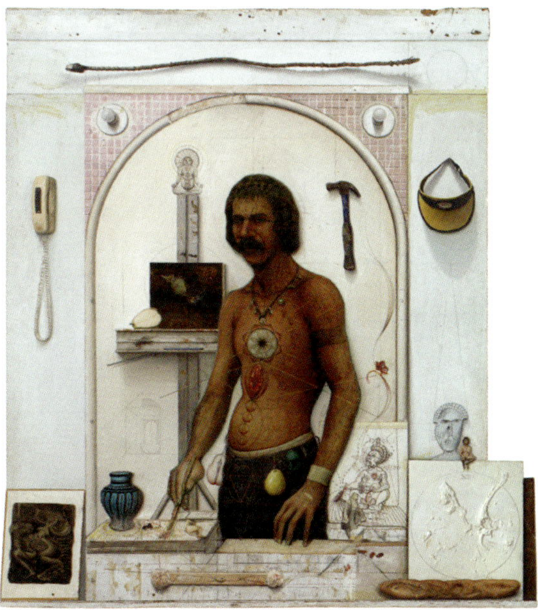

Fig. 14. *Self-portrait with Bread and Chakras* by Gregory Gillespie (1936–2000), oil on canvas, 1987–1988. Robert and Arlene Kogod

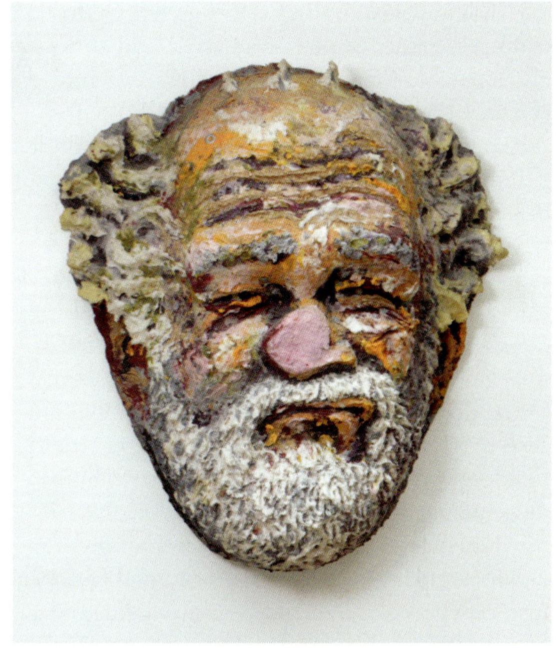

Fig. 15. *Up Against It* (self-portrait) by Robert Arneson (1930–1982), papier-mâché, 1981. Elizabeth and Jan Lodal

artist John Robinson, depicts the first private gallery in Washington established by African Americans. The Barnett Aden Gallery at 127 Randolph Place NW was founded in 1943 by James V. Herring and Alonzo J. Aden. Aden is shown sitting at his desk surrounded by the art that he had displayed in the gallery. In its first decade, the gallery showcased the art of African Americans, among them Robinson (cat. 45) and Frederick C. Flemister (cat. 46), an Atlanta-based painter. By the late 1940s, it became Washington's first integrated gallery, both in terms of the artists it represented, such as Jacob Kainen and Jack Perlmutter, and the clientele who came to openings and purchased works. Gene Davis (cat. 55), like Robinson, was born in the nation's capital and remained a life-long resident. However, Davis, unlike Robinson, was not content with representing the world around him. He was eager to be a player on the national scene. Indeed, as a central figure in the

Washington Color School, Davis participated in a broader American art movement that favored cool, unemotional abstraction.

This exhibition contains only one work by a known amateur painter—the portrait of Mamie Eisenhower (cat. 50) by her husband, Dwight David Eisenhower. President Eisenhower began painting in about 1948, inspired by the example of Winston Churchill, another amateur painter who put brush to palette as a form of relaxation, and encouraged by his own portraitist, Thomas E. Stephens. From then on, when he wasn't relaxing on the golf course he could be found in his small studio, in New York (while president of Columbia University), at the White House, or at Gettysburg (in retirement). He preferred to work from a photograph rather than directly from a model. Research for this exhibition led to the discovery that this portrait was painted in Versailles, France, his headquarters while he served as Supreme Allied Commander of NATO.

The portraits in this exhibition reflect the coming together of a sitter, an artist, and at times, also a patron. They provide, too, a window into the life of the sitter, the career of the artist, and the era in which they lived. The majority of these paintings and sculptures have not been exhibited or published previously. In many cases, little was known about the making of the image, its place in the history of the individual, or its role in the career of the artist. Information that explains the dynamics related to the creation of the portraits in the exhibition was gleaned from multiple sources. Often descendants could provide documentation such as a letter or an early photograph that identified the sitter or the date of the portrait. Some descendants also knew details about the lives of the individuals, but to separate fact from myth and to augment sparse details, we turned to family histories, genealogical data, census records, and newspaper accounts for additional information. Increasingly these records are online, which aided our research immensely. On occasion, we learned a great deal from an autobiography written by the sitter. But though Evelyn Nef's *Finding My Way: The Autobiography of an Optimist* was useful in giving us an overview of her life, it did not supply us with the facts about the making of her portrait by Alex Katz, or that of her second husband Vilhjalmur Stefansson by Antonio Salemme (cats. 53 and 40). This information came from an interview with Mrs. Nef, who also told us the story of how she acquired Katz's preliminary drawing (fig. 16). For details about the making of her husband's portrait, we relied on Stefansson's autobiography, but mostly on unpublished information given to us by the current director of the Antonio Salemme Foundation.

For research on the artists and the sitters, the resources in the Smithsonian Institution provided many answers. The Smithsonian American Art Museum/National Portrait Gallery Library furnished countless publications, including recent exhibition catalogues, which were notable for their new and wide-ranging research. The library's vertical files were a gold mine of information, and its online subscriptions were critical to

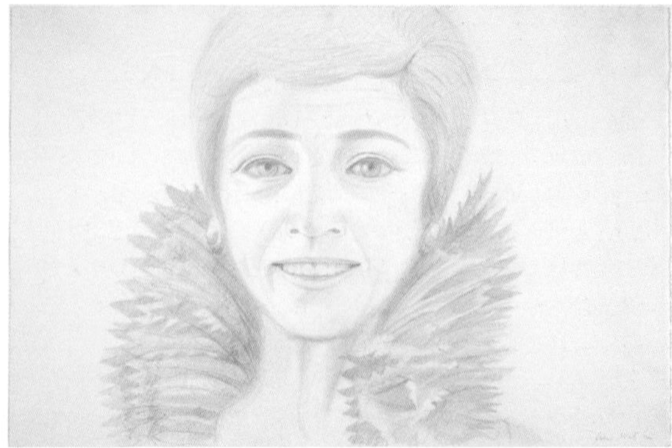

Fig. 16. *Evie* by Alex Katz (born 1927), graphite on paper, 1974. National Gallery of Art, Washington, D.C.; bequest of Evelyn Stefansson Nef

completing individual entries. The Portrait Gallery's own databases, the Smithsonian American Art Museum's Inventory of American Painting and Sculpture, and the holdings of the Archives of American Art all contributed essential information. Colleagues in many museums, historical societies, and universities responded willingly to our queries, generously sharing their files and unpublished research. Contemporary artists, their studio assistants, and their dealers provided specific details or personal perspectives on their work. Specialists including conservators, costume historians, and genealogists disclosed details that often solved puzzling problems. On one occasion, two landscape historians met with the owners of Joseph Blackburn's portrait of Andrew Oliver Jr. to identify the curious garden structure depicted in the background of the painting. As it turned out the portrait includes a rare image of a dovecote.

As with Evelyn Nef, living sitters told us how the portrait came about, why a particular artist was chosen, what it was like to sit for the artist, and their response to the final result—which in all cases was an enthusiastic one. Although fewer and fewer people sit for a painted portrait today, the pleasure in doing so is as great today as it was in the eighteenth and nineteenth centuries.

NOTES

1. On this portrait of Washington, see William Kloss et al., *Art in the White House: A Nation's Pride* (Washington, DC: White House Historical Association, 1992), 66–69; Dolley Madison to Lucy Payne Washington Todd, August 23, 1814, in David B. Mattern and Holly C. Shulman, eds., *The Selected Letters of Dolley Payne Madison* (Charlottesville: University of Virginia Press, 2003), 193–94; Carrie Rebora Barratt and Ellen G. Miles, *Gilbert Stuart* (New York: Metropolitan Museum of Art, 2004), 180–81, 260–62; and Thomas Fleming, "Dolley Madison Saves the Day," *Smithsonian* 40, no. 12 (March 2010): 50–56. While there has been some disagreement on whether the portrait is in fact by Stuart, the evidence is clear that it came from his Philadelphia studio and was sold in 1797 to Gardiner Baker, the manager of the Tammany Society's museum in New York. It was acquired after Baker's death by the United States government for the White House.

2. On these portraits, see Doreen Bolger and David Park Curry, "Art for the President's House: A Historical Perspective," in Kloss et al., *Art in the White House*, 17–49.

3. John Sherman to Alexander Hamilton, February 26, 1879, National Archives; copy courtesy of Richard Cote, curator, United States Department of the Treasury, Washington, DC.

4. On the portraits of the secretaries of the Treasury, see www.treas.gov/education/history/portraits .shtml for an online catalogue. Healy's letter to Sherman, dated March 27, 1880, arranging for a sitting the next day, is in the Papers of John Sherman, Library of Congress, vol. 209 (March 25–April 1, 1880), #46430 (copy courtesy of Richard Cote).

5. *Washington Evening Star*, May 3, 1879, quoted in *Corcoran* (Washington, DC: Corcoran Gallery of Art, 1976), 23.

6. The history of Corcoran as a collector is found in ibid, 22–24.

7. Andrew W. Mellon to Franklin D. Roosevelt, December 22, 1936, reproduced in David Finley, *A Standard of Excellence; Andrew Mellon Founds the National Gallery of Art in Washington* (Washington, DC: Smithsonian Institution Press, 1973), 47–48.

8. Finley, *Standard of Excellence*, 32.

9. See James M. Goode, *Contemporary Self-Portraits from the James Goode Collection* (Washington, DC: National Portrait Gallery, Smithsonian Institution, 1993). This collection was shown at the National Portrait Gallery, July 30–December 5, 1993, and was sold in Washington at Weschler's auction house, September 19, 1998.

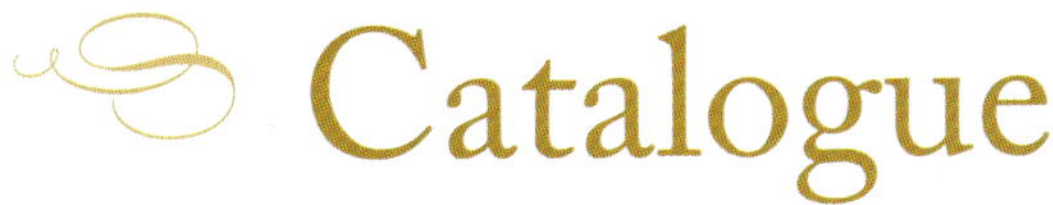# Catalogue

Authors' Note

Dimensions are given in height followed by width,
and do not include bases, supports, or frames unless
otherwise indicated.

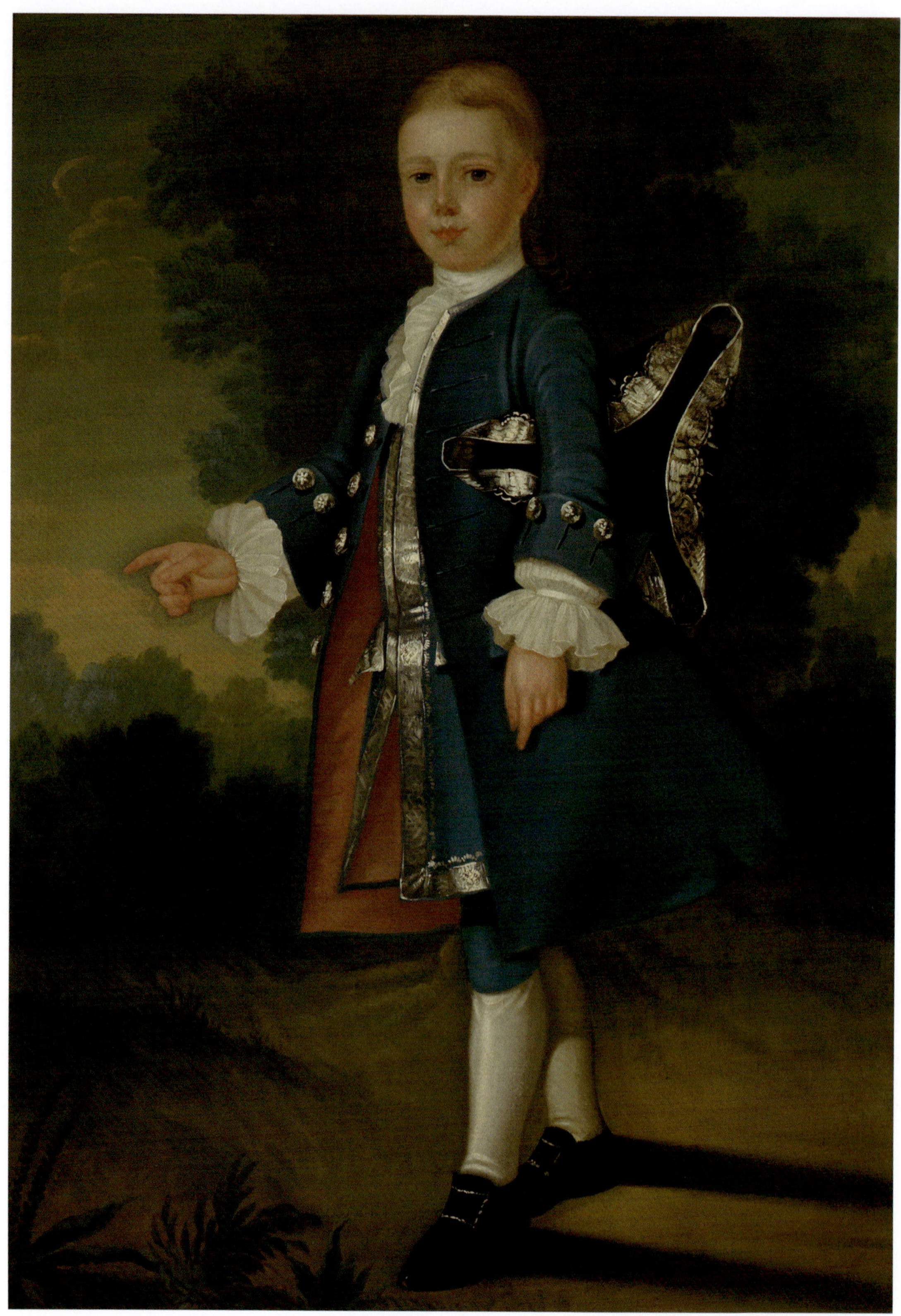

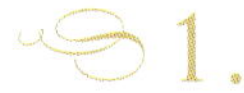 1.

RALPH IZARD

By Jeremiah Theus (1716–1774)

Oil on canvas, 110.5 × 76.2 cm (43½ × 30 in.), 1754
Private collection

AT THE AGE of twelve Ralph Izard (1742–1804) of Charleston, South Carolina, posed for Jeremiah Theus, marking the first of several occasions during Izard's lifetime when he sat for distinctive portraits.[1] By 1740 the Swiss-born painter, whose European training is undocumented, had settled in Charleston. This work, one of the artist's rare full-length portraits, shows how well Theus had mastered the poses and settings of English portraiture. The young Izard is dressed stylishly as an adult in a blue coat lined with pink silk and trimmed with silver buttons. His matching waistcoat is decorated with silver braid. Tucked under his left arm is a black tricornered hat, also trimmed in silver; silver buckles on his shoes complete the color scheme. Izard looks at the viewer with a grown-up gaze, but his chubby cheeks and unpowdered hair, pulled back in a queue, or ponytail, reveal his youth.

The occasion for the portrait was Izard's departure for school in England. Sending one's son to be educated in England was a tradition among upper-class Charlestonians of the mid-eighteenth century. The situation with the young Ralph Izard, however, was unusual. His mother, Margaret Johnson Izard, had died in 1743, and his father, Henry Izard, in 1748/1749. Ralph was their eldest child, and his broad gesture may be a reference to his newly inherited estate, the Elms.

Izard attended English schools for ten years, graduating in 1764 from Trinity Hall, Cambridge University. While abroad, he commissioned two new portraits. The first, by German artist Johann Zoffany (unlocated), shows him soon after graduation. The second, by Benjamin West and known as "The Cricketers," depicts him with a group of young friends; Izard, in a red uniform, holds a cricket bat.[2]

In 1767, Izard, who had returned to America in 1764, married Alice DeLancey of New York. The couple moved to London in 1771. Four years later, on a trip to Rome to enhance their knowledge of the classical world, they were the first Americans to be painted in Europe by Boston artist John Singleton Copley (1775; Museum of Fine Arts, Boston).[3] The Izards moved to Paris in 1776, during which time Ralph Izard became the unofficial representative—and defender—of the American cause. In 1780 he returned to Charleston without his family and tackled the repairs needed because of damage to his plantation when the British confiscated it. Izard served briefly as a delegate to the Continental Congress from South Carolina in 1782–83. His wife and children rejoined him at the Elms after the war. He later served as one of the state's first United States senators (1789–1795).

EGM

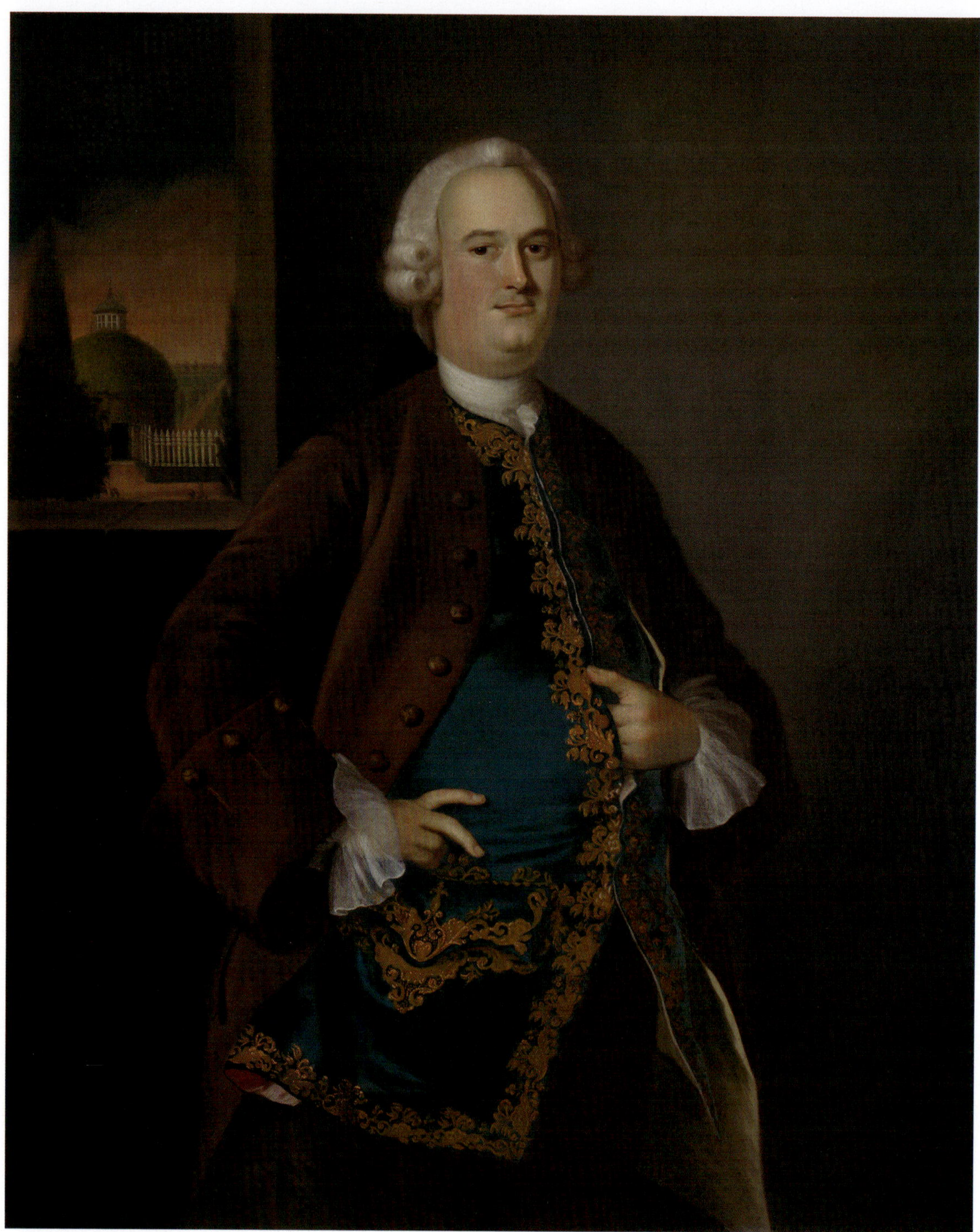

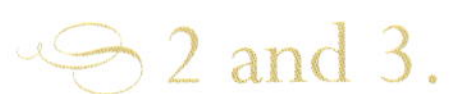

ANDREW OLIVER JR.
MARY LYNDE OLIVER

By Joseph Blackburn (fl. 1752–1777)

Each: Oil on canvas, 127 × 101.8 cm (50 × 40¹⁄₁₆ in.), 1755
Oliver Family

ANDREW OLIVER JR. (1731–1799) and his wife, Mary Lynde Oliver (1733–1807), were painted in 1755, three years after they were married.[1] The timing no doubt was due to the arrival that year in Boston of itinerant English portrait painter Joseph Blackburn. Oliver, the son of Massachusetts Lieutenant Governor Andrew Oliver and Mary Fitch Oliver, graduated from Harvard College in 1749 and received master's degrees from Yale College in 1751 and Harvard in 1752. The younger Oliver and his wife, the daughter of Benjamin and Mary (Bowles) Lynde Jr., lived in Boston on the Fitch family estate until 1760, when they lost their house to fire and moved to Salem. Oliver was appointed in 1761 as judge of the Court of Common Pleas for Essex County, Massachusetts. He also served as one of Salem's representatives to the Massachusetts General Court.

Oliver was a man of many interests, ranging from astronomy to music and poetry. John Adams described him in 1758 as "a very sagacious Trifler," and continued, "He can decipher, with surprising Penetration and Patience, any thing wrote in signs, whether English, Latin, or French. But to what Purpose? Tis like great skill and Dexterity in Gaming, used only for Amuzement. With all his Expertness he never wins any Thing. But this is his Way to fame. . . . He would be a famous Decypherer."[2] Oliver's serious pursuits included scientific observation; his *Essay on Comets* (1772) led to his election to the American Philosophical Society, America's first scientific association, in 1773. He, together with John Adams and John Winthrop, established the American Academy of Arts and Sciences in Boston in 1780.

Joseph Blackburn's birth and training in England are undocumented. He is first recorded in 1752 on Bermuda, where he painted portraits for two years before moving to Newport, Rhode Island. He was already a practiced and well-trained artist; his portraits reflect the qualities of contemporary English portraiture in the tradition of Thomas Hudson and Allan Ramsay. Blackburn left Newport late in 1754 with a letter of recommendation dated November 24 from merchant Thomas Vernon to James Boutineau of Boston describing the artist as a "Limner by profession . . . possess'd with the agreeable qualities of great modesty, good sence [*sic*] & genteel behaviour." Blackburn was popular in Boston, where he worked for four years before relocating to Portsmouth, New Hampshire. He had returned to England by January 1764.[3]

The Olivers' portraits are classic Blackburn images. Both sitters are seen in standing three-quarter-length poses, well dressed in blue and gold color schemes that echo each other. Pearls decorate Mary Oliver's hair and blue dress, and she holds a small bouquet in her left hand that appears to consist of a marigold and some sweet peas. The delicate treatment of the details of her lace bodice and sleeves exemplifies Blackburn's much-admired skill at representing fabrics.

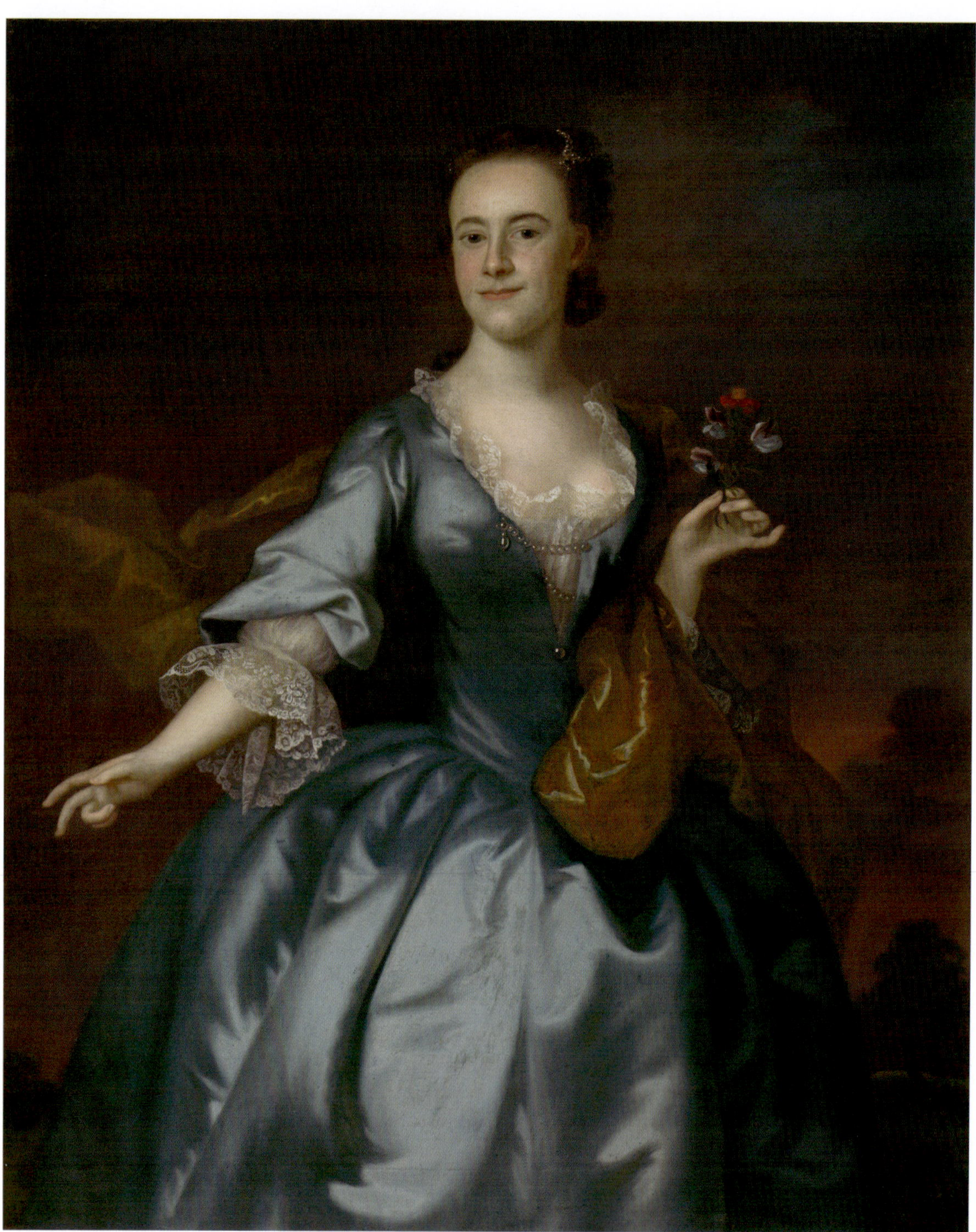

Andrew Oliver is posed in a manner common to men's portraits, often derived from contemporary manner books. His long blue vest is ornately trimmed in gold braid. He wears a wig and looks proudly out at us. In the background is a structure not seen in other American colonial portraits. It has recently been identified as a dovecote because of its masonry construction and cylindrical shape, the absence of windows, and the vegetation on the roof. Dovecotes, rare in American gardens but found frequently in England, were used to raise pigeons. The domesticated birds would fly in through the cupola, or glover, which had no windowpanes, and settle on nests built along the inside walls. Their eggs and the young squabs were harvested as food. A recent study of American garden structures in mid-Atlantic colonial America points to several surviving dovecotes, including one at Shirley plantation in Virginia, which this image resembles.[4] It seems highly likely that the younger Oliver built a dovecote on his inherited property in Boston, perhaps as a symbol of new wealth. Oliver's uncle, Peter Oliver (cat. 4), had a dovecote at his estate in Middleborough, Massachusetts, which he referred to in 1766 when writing to Governor Thomas Hutchinson, noting that during protests following the Stamp Act, he had protected the governor's "first Officers in my Pigeon House."[5]

EGM

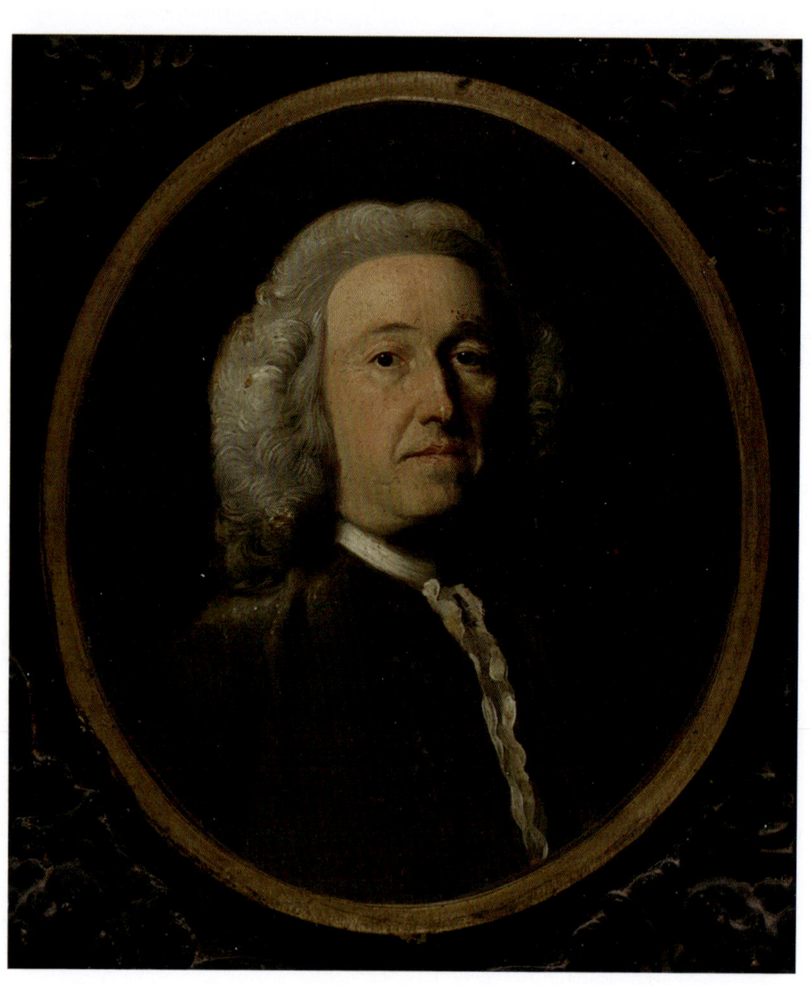

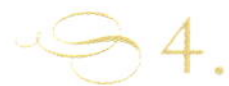 4.

PETER OLIVER

By John Singleton Copley (1738–1815)

Oil on copper, 12.7 × 10.2 cm (5 × 4 in.), c. 1758
Oliver Family

CHIEF JUSTICE PETER OLIVER (1713–1791), the son of Daniel Oliver and Elizabeth Belcher Oliver of Boston, graduated from Harvard College in 1730. He moved to Middleborough, Massachusetts, after he became co-owner of one of the largest iron-works in North America. His long judicial career began in 1744 with his appointment as a justice of the peace for Plymouth County. Named to the superior court in 1756, he became unpopular after he publicly supported the Stamp Act. In 1770 he presided at the Boston Massacre trials, in which John Adams was the lawyer for the British soldiers. Oliver delivered a summary to the jury stating that the soldiers had fired in self-defense. Governor Thomas Hutchinson, to whom he was related by marriage, then appointed Oliver chief justice of the superior court. However, juries refused to serve under Oliver when it was learned that he accepted part of his salary from the Crown, a critical issue in the rising tensions against England. He was impeached in 1774. After mobs prevented him from returning to his home in Middleborough, he spent more than a year in Boston before leaving for Halifax and then London when the British evacuated Boston in 1776. He died in Birmingham, England.[1]

Sometime between about 1758 and 1761 the young Boston-born artist John Singleton Copley was commissioned to paint several family portraits, including this large miniature of Peter Oliver in oil on copper. The Oliver family is well represented in colonial American portraits, beginning around 1730 with paintings of Oliver's parents (figs. 1 and 2) and siblings by John Smibert, and including a pair of portraits of Oliver and his wife, Mary, painted around 1733, the year they were married.[2] The format for this later oil is the same as the one that Copley painted of Oliver's brother Andrew at about the same time (National Portrait Gallery, Smithsonian Institution).[3] These extraordinarily vivid, small portraits are among a group of about thirty-five such miniatures that Copley painted in oil on metal beginning in 1755, some of which are on a gold ground. Many of the subjects are members of the Oliver family.[4] Copley, then near the beginning of what would be a highly successful career, first in Boston and later in London, also painted portraits in various formats of other members of the Oliver family, most of them in the late 1750s. They all reflect his stunning ability to capture likeness with directness and immediacy. They include portraits of Peter Oliver's children, Dr. Peter Oliver Jr. and Elizabeth Oliver (Mrs. George Watson); Andrew Oliver's son Andrew Oliver Jr.; Andrew junior's second wife, Mary Sanford Oliver; and their daughters, Griselda Oliver Waldo and Elizabeth Oliver Lyde.[5]

EGM

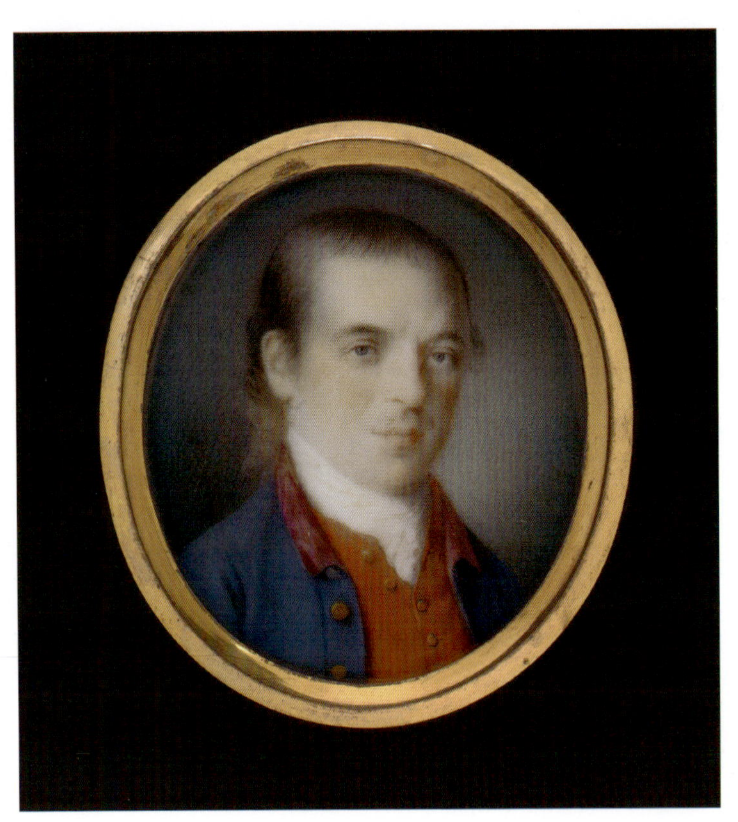

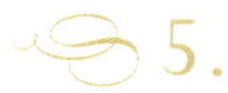 5.

JAMES CRAIK

Attributed to John Ramsier (1861–1936), after Charles Willson Peale

Watercolor on white glass, 6.4 × 5.4 cm (2½ × 2⅛ in.) oval, c. 1901, after a 1778 original
Alfred and Pie Friendly

JAMES CRAIK (1730–1814) was born near Dumfries, Scotland, and studied medicine at the University of Edinburgh. He served briefly in the British army before he came to America, settling in Winchester, Virginia, in 1751. As a surgeon in the Virginia militia during the French and Indian War, Craik formed a close friendship with George Washington. At Washington's request, Craik in 1777 joined the Continental army as assistant director general in the medical department. Although technically a civilian, he wore the colors of the Virginia militia uniform, a blue coat with a dark red collar and a scarlet waistcoat, as seen in this miniature. After the war Craik moved to Alexandria, Virginia, and became Washington's personal physician. He attended Washington at his death in 1799, and was a beneficiary of Washington's will, in which he is described as "My compatriot in arms, and old and intimate friend."[1]

Research for this exhibition has led to a surprising attribution for this miniature, long believed to be an undated copy of the portrait painted during the American Revolution by Charles Willson Peale (1741–1827).[2] He began the original miniature on April 26, 1778, when the American army was encamped at Valley Forge, Pennsylvania, and finished it on May 7.[3]

Conservator Carol Aiken recently suggested that the copy might be by Swiss artist John Ramsier, who immigrated to the United States in 1883. Ramsier settled in Louisville, Kentucky, where he created about three thousand miniatures between 1901 and 1934.[4] The Louisville provenance of the copy, as well as its size and technique and the glass support, are evidence that the copy is Ramsier's work, as is the ornate rosebud frame, which was recently removed during conservation.

While there is no record of the copy in Ramsier's daybooks, Craik's great-grandson, the Reverend Charles Ewell Craik, who lived in Louisville, was a patron of Ramsier's work. His payment for a portrait is among the earliest listed in the artist's daybook, on February 20, 1901: "Rev. Craik /515 W. Ormsby/1 miniature $ size $8." The payment was probably for the miniature of Craik's youngest son, Edward Whitney Craik.[5] If the copy of Peale's miniature was also painted in 1901, the occasion for the commissioning could have been the Louisville wedding of another of Craik's descendants, Eliza Morton Morris, to Charles Cotesworth Pinckney on May 23, 1901; the copy is now owned by their granddaughter and her husband.

EGM

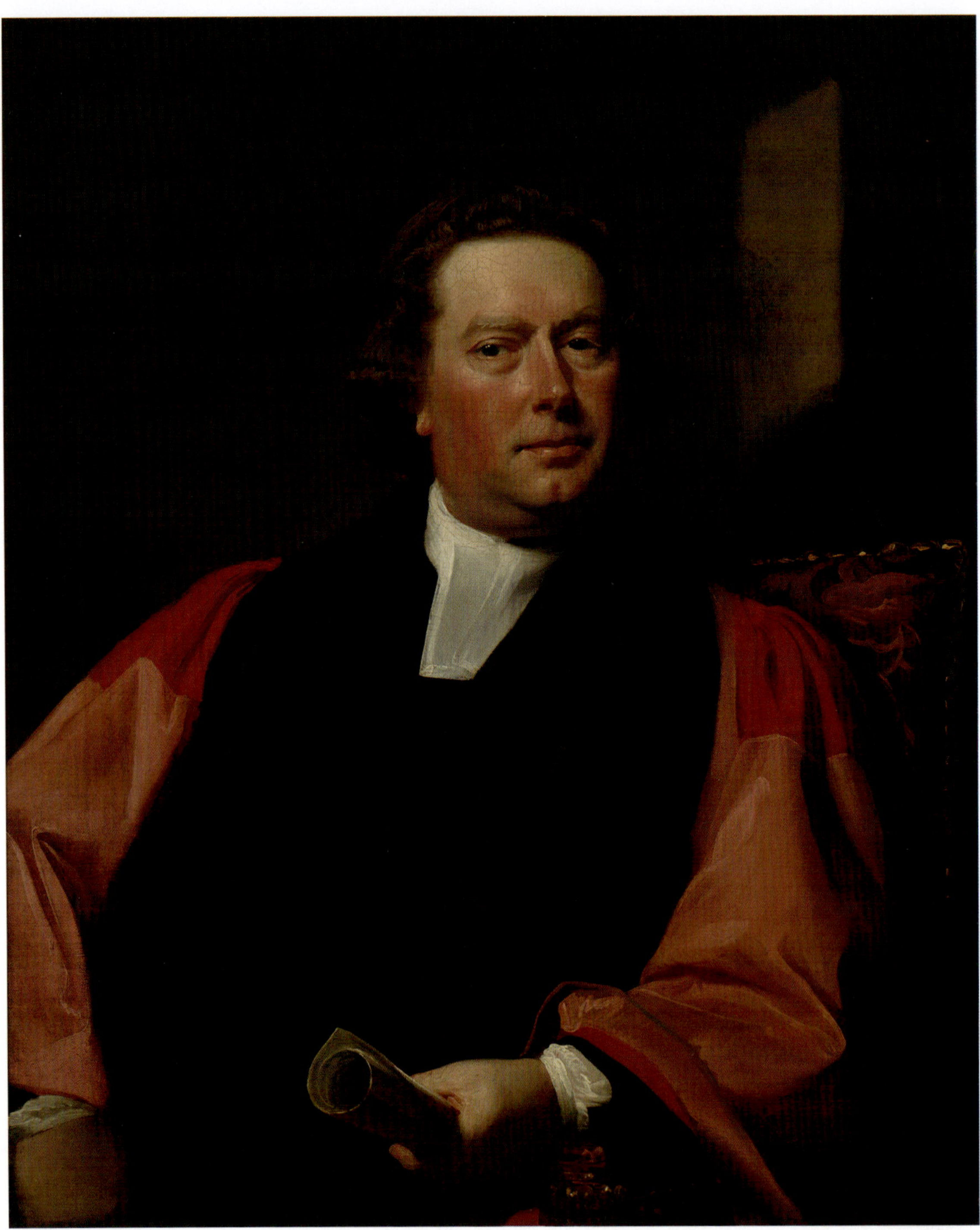

6

MYLES COOPER
By John Singleton Copley (1738–1815)

Oil on canvas, 91.4 × 71.1 cm (36 × 28 in.), c. 1780–1785
Teresa Heinz Collection

AMERICAN ARTIST John Singleton Copley painted this portrait sometime after he had moved to London in 1774. In a study of Copley's English work, Jules Prown described it as an "unidentified subject, a cleric [?]," wearing an "Oxford academic robe over clerical garb."[1] When the portrait's current owner found a likeness of Reverend Myles Cooper (1737–1785) wearing an identical Oxford robe among Copley's American paintings (cat. 6-1),

she proposed that Cooper was also the subject of the work done in England. Copley had painted Cooper in Boston in 1768, when the subject was the American president of King's College (now Columbia University), New York City.[2] The American and English versions are remarkably similar. The sitter's hair, eye color, and facial features are the same (allowing for the age difference), and the clothing is identical, except that the later, English portrait includes a black scarf or

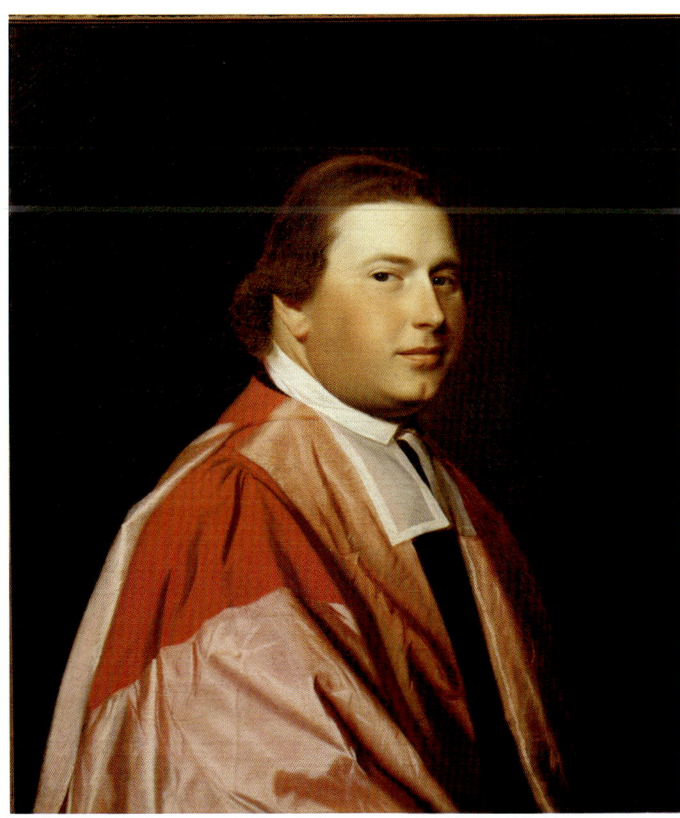

Cat. 6-1. *Myles Cooper* by John Singleton Copley, oil on canvas, 74.5 × 61.8 cm (29⅚ × 24⅚ in.), 1768. Columbia University in the City of New York; gift of the New-York Historical Society

stole over the Oxford academic robe. The English portrait is also slightly larger, in a format known as the "kit-cat," which permitted a broader composition, with space for Cooper's hands, one of which holds a document. The two works provide a telling comparison between Copley's American and English work. The artist's ability to capture likeness, personality, and color was consistent, but his brushwork became more fluid and bold in the paintings done abroad.

The Reverend Myles Cooper was born in England and educated at Queen's College, Oxford, before becoming an Anglican priest. In 1762 he was selected to be the next president of King's College. There, he instituted changes in the curriculum and aspects of college life that reflected his years at Oxford. In the late 1760s the university became the center of Anglican conservatism, and most of the faculty and half of the students became Loyalists. Cooper, an ardent Tory, fled New York in 1775 after a mob drove him out of his house, and he found safety on a British warship. Cooper returned to England and was appointed provost of Queen's College; in 1777 he became chaplain of St. Paul's Chapel in Edinburgh.[3]

Like Cooper, Copley left America before the start of the American Revolution. He settled in London, where his second career as a painter met with great success. He transformed his technique as a result of seeing paintings by earlier European and contemporary English artists. As in 1768, Copley in the later, English work represented Cooper in the robes that the subject had received when he was awarded the doctor of civil law degree by Oxford in 1767.[4] That event may have prompted his wish for his first portrait by Copley, when his academic robe became the subject of correspondence between artist and sitter.[5] When Cooper finally received the portrait in 1769, he was so pleased that he urged Copley to come from Boston to New York to paint portraits, a trip that Copley made in 1771.

EGM

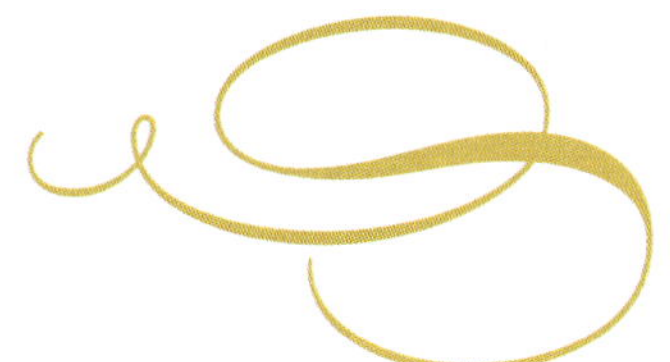

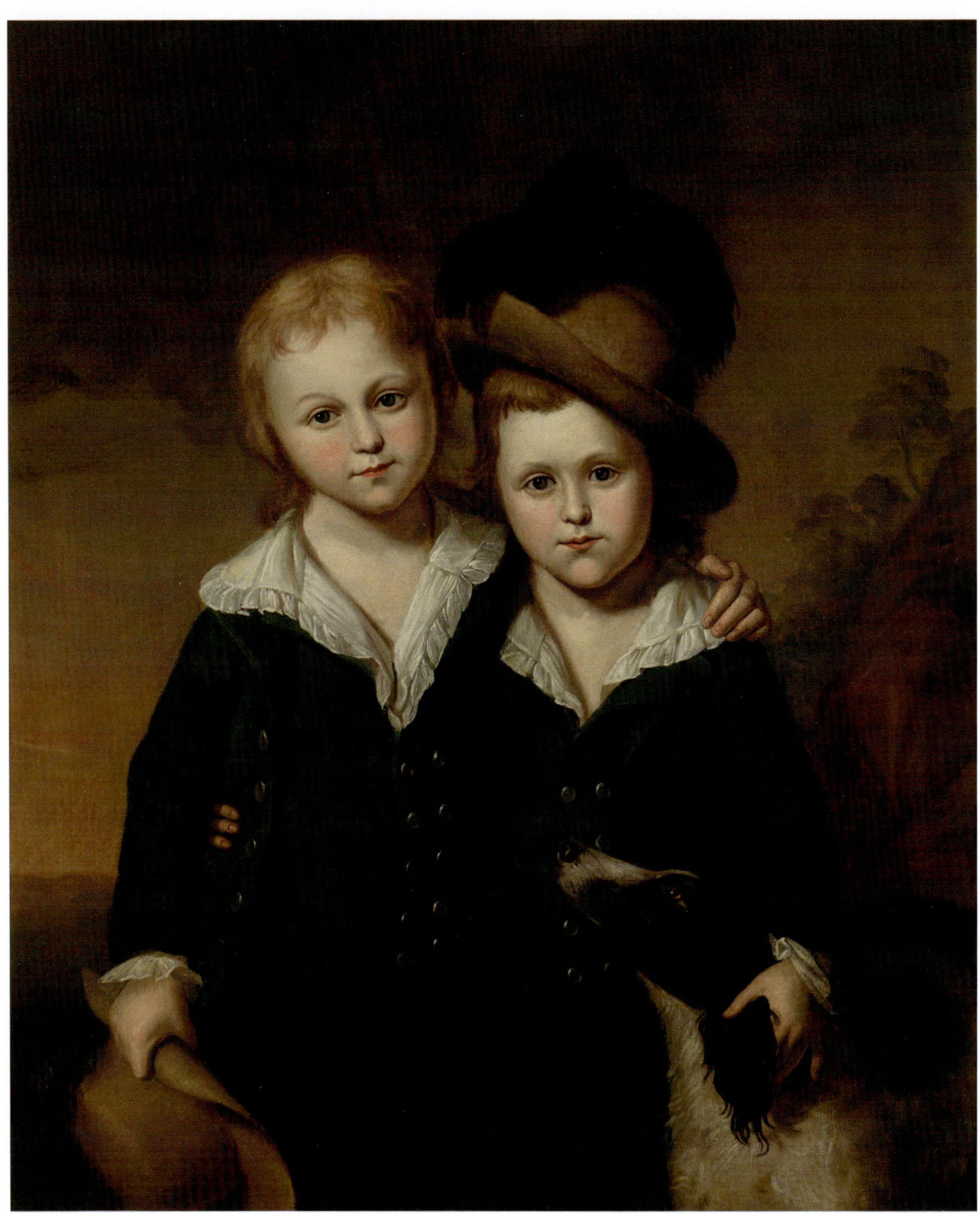

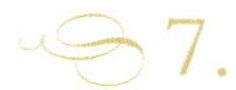

7.

THOMAS AND HENRY SERGEANT
By Charles Willson Peale (1741–1827)

Oil on canvas, 90.2 × 73.7 cm (35½ × 29 in.), c. 1786
Private collection

CHARLES WILLSON Peale's double portrait depicts Thomas (1782–1860) and Henry Sergeant (1782–1824), twin sons born January 14, 1782, in Philadelphia to Jonathan Dickinson Sergeant and Margaret Spencer Sergeant. Their heart-shaped faces are similar, but Thomas has blond hair and is taller than Henry, whose hair is brown. The boys wear identical dark green suits with white ruffled shirts. Henry wears a brown plumed hat and pats a black and white setter at his left, which looks up adoringly at the boys. Thomas holds his hat at his side, opposite the dog, and has his left arm around his brother's shoulder. The landscape setting includes a rocky outcrop to the right and a cloudy sky.[1]

Jonathan Dickinson Sergeant, a graduate of Princeton College, represented New Jersey in the Continental Congress in 1776 and 1777 and also served in the New Jersey Provincial Congress. The family relocated to Philadelphia after their Princeton home was burned by the Hessians on December 25, 1776, during the American Revolution. Sergeant was attorney general of Pennsylvania from 1777 to 1780.[2] Charles Willson Peale probably painted the double portrait in 1786, when he made portraits of the boys' parents. The three paintings are the same size, and one can imagine them displayed together.[3]

Margaret Sergeant's death in 1787 left her husband to care for their eight children. A year after her death, Peale was commissioned to paint two miniature copies of her portrait, for Jonathan Sergeant and "for her son."[4] Later that year Jonathan married Elizabeth Rittenhouse, the daughter of astronomer David Rittenhouse, and in 1789, Peale painted his bride's portrait in the same format as the others.[5] Thomas and Henry Sergeant attended the College of New Jersey, as Princeton University was then known, graduating with the class of 1798. Henry became a merchant in Philadelphia and served in the Philadelphia volunteers during the War of 1812. That year his brother Thomas, an attorney, married Sarah Bache, granddaughter of Benjamin Franklin.[6] Thomas died in 1860, thirty-six years after the death of his twin, who had died in 1824. Thomas and Sarah's grandson Thomas Sergeant Perry was the husband of American artist Lilla Cabot Perry, whose work is also represented in this exhibition (cat. 35).

EGM

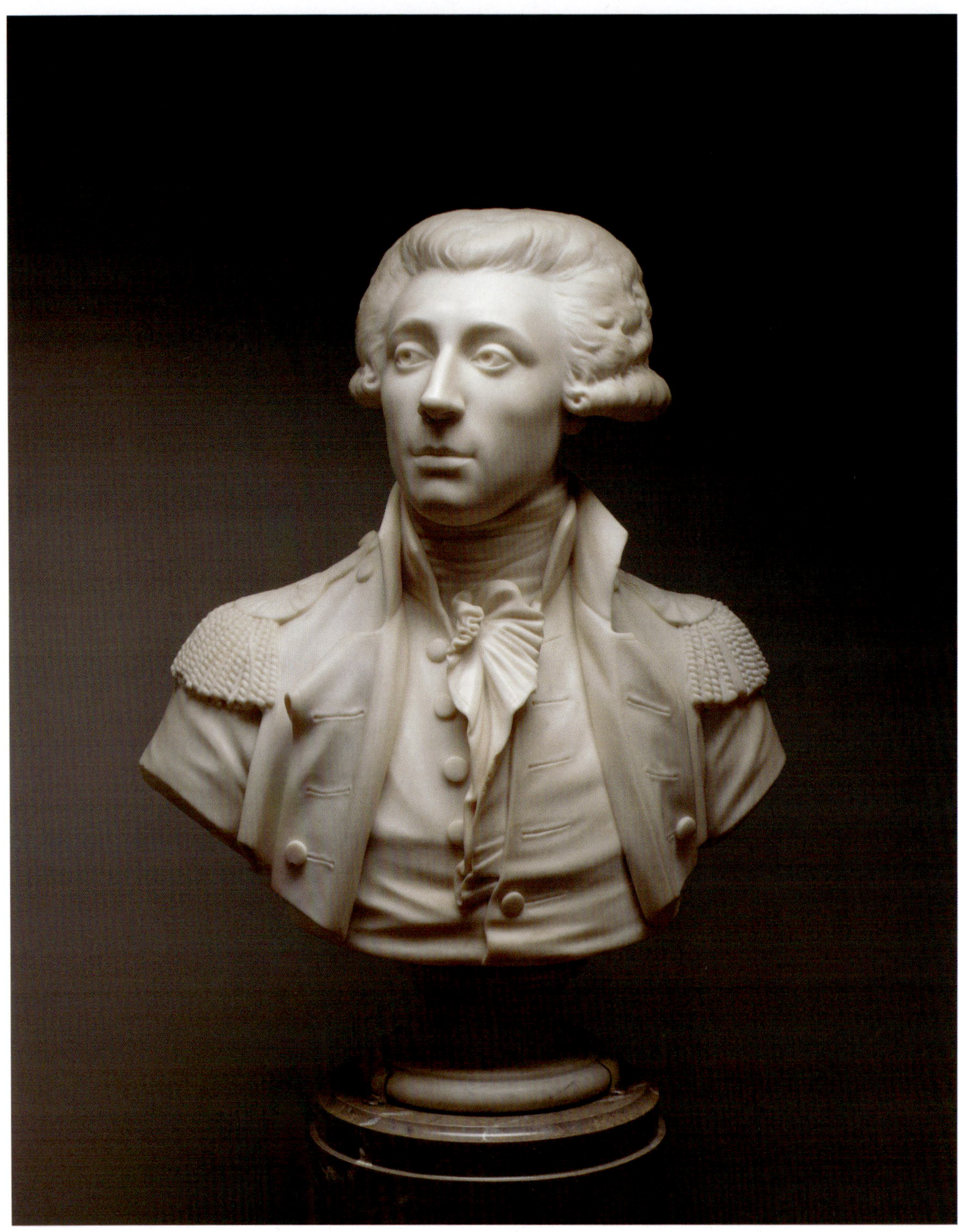

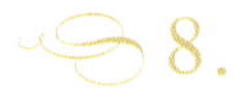

MARQUIS DE LAFAYETTE

By Jean-Antoine Houdon (1741–1828)

Marble, 61 cm (24 in.) height, 1790
D. Dodge Thompson

THE MARQUIS de Lafayette (1757–1834) came to America in 1777 to serve without pay on George Washington's staff during the American Revolution.[1] To celebrate Lafayette's role in the 1781 victory over the British general Charles Cornwallis at Yorktown, the Virginia legislature voted to commission Lafayette's portrait. Guided by Thomas Jefferson, the legislature in 1784 selected French sculptor Jean-Antoine Houdon to undertake the project. The following year, Houdon cast the life mask of the marquis in Paris (Herbert F. Johnson Museum of Art, Cornell University). From that cast, the artist carved two types of portraits, one showing Lafayette in his American army uniform and the second, seen here, in that of the French National Guard.[2]

Both image types were rendered in two marble examples. In 1786 Houdon presented a marble of the first type to the city of Paris on behalf of the Commonwealth of Virginia; it was placed in the Hôtel de Ville (unlocated). The second was exhibited at the Salon of 1787 and then sent to Richmond, where it is permanently on view in the Virginia Capitol. In 1789, Jefferson acquired a plaster version of the bust in Paris (Boston Athenaeum).

Houdon's second portrait type celebrates Lafayette's role in the French National Guard.[3] In 1789, Lafayette was elected to the French general assembly, or Estates-General, and drafted a Declaration of the Rights of Man, which was presented to the National Assembly. After the storming of the Bastille prison on July 14, he was chosen to form the National Guard, a citizens' militia, and serve as its commander. The guard commissioned the portrait in 1790 after Lafayette had organized a large celebration to commemorate the anniversary of the destruction of the Bastille. Two marble examples of this portrait exist, both showing Lafayette wearing a wig. The one at the Musée de Versailles has two signatures; the work here, the second, is also signed. Its provenance is unknown; it was first published in 1975 as in a private collection in Flushing, New York.[4]

Both portrait types exemplify Houdon's extraordinarily lifelike renditions of his contemporaries. The artist's careful study of physiognomy, anatomy, and character resulted in portrait sculptures that to this day typify the era of enlightenment. Houdon's likenesses have a quality of immediacy resulting not only from his use of life masks for accuracy but also his method of sculpting the iris of the eye and his tendency to show sitters' heads turned to one side, their mouths slightly opened.

Lafayette's popularity in France was short-lived. In 1792 he was impeached by the revolutionary government and captured in Flanders by Austrian forces while trying to flee to America. He was imprisoned for five years; when released in 1797, he returned to France. In 1824, Lafayette returned to America on a triumphal tour, visiting Jefferson at Monticello, where the plaster bust by Houdon that Jefferson owned was then on view.

EGM

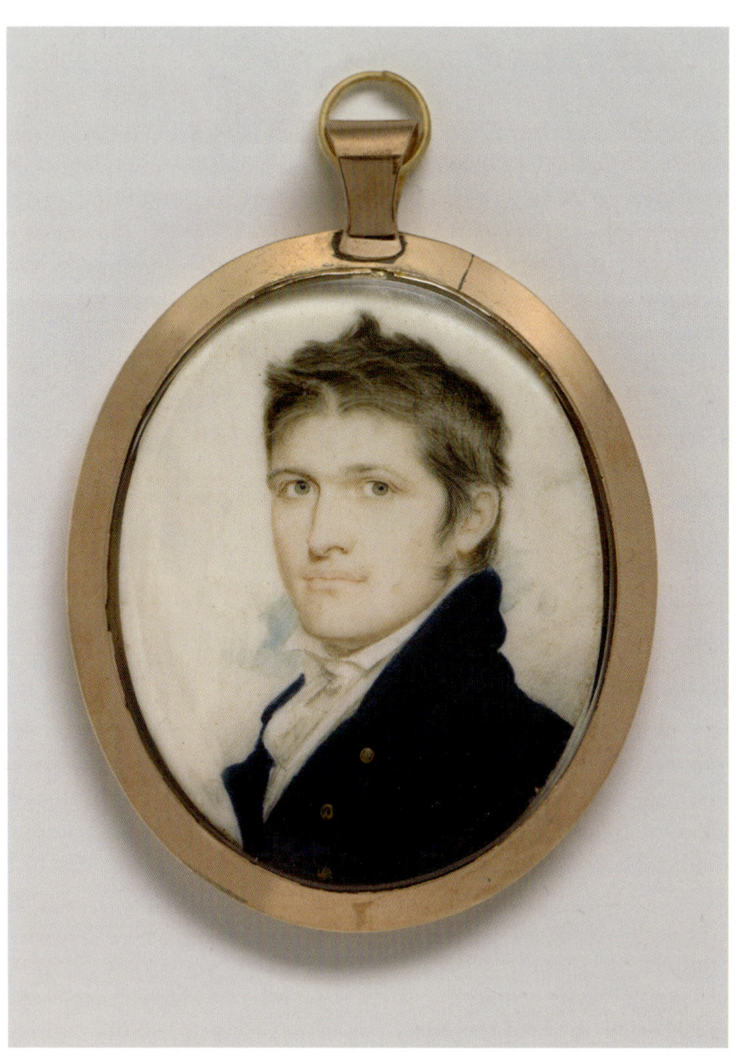

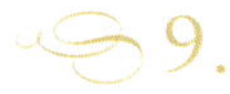

JOHN HITE MORTON
By Benjamin Trott (1769–1843)

Watercolor on ivory, 5 × 6.4 cm (2 × 2½ in.) oval, 1805
Alfred and Pie Friendly

JOHN HITE MORTON (1784–1830) of Lexington, Kentucky, a handsome young man with hazel eyes and windswept hair, looks out from this small portrait painted in 1805. Benjamin Trott, a resident of Philadelphia, painted the portrait on his only known trip to Lexington. As described by William Dunlap, Trott's first biographer and the first historian of American art, "[Trott] visited the western world beyond the mountains, travelling generally on horseback, with the implements of his art in his saddle-bags. This was a lucrative journey."[1] At least seven miniatures are known from his stay there, including this one of Morton and those of statesman Henry Clay and merchant Charles Wilkins.[2]

Morton married Sarah Price in 1802.[3] He was elected to the Kentucky State House of Representatives in 1810 with the support of Clay, his close political ally.[4] In 1817 he built Walnut Grove on the Harrodsburg Road outside Lexington. Morton was a founding director of the Lexington branch of the United States Bank. A Mason, he was a member of the welcoming committee for the arrival in Lexington of the Marquis de Lafayette (cat. 8) on May 16, 1825, when the Masons celebrated at their Greek Revival hall, then under construction.[5] He also served as treasurer of Transylvania University.[6]

Benjamin Trott was born in Boston and in 1793 advertised there as a miniaturist. He also painted briefly in Virginia with Boston artist William Lovett before moving to New York City in 1794. There he met Gilbert Stuart, who had just returned from an eighteen-year career in England and Ireland. Trott became a copyist of Stuart's oil portraits and followed Stuart to Philadelphia, where he was commissioned to paint several copies of Stuart's work. One was a portrait of Chief Justice Edward Shippen, copied so that Shippen could send the image to his daughter Margaret, the wife of Benedict Arnold; Margaret and her husband had fled America during the Revolution and were living in London. Trott traveled again to New York but seems to have moved to Philadelphia in 1804 before making his trip to Lexington the following year. He may have returned to Philadelphia by January 6, 1806, when Dunlap wrote to his wife that "Trot[t] finds sufficient employment here, & has raised his price from 30 to 40 dolls. [H]e is a man of genius, with excentricities [*sic*]."[7] Trott was successful in Philadelphia as a miniaturist through 1819, often in collaboration with portrait painter Thomas Sully, but after 1820 his work took him to other cities and is less well documented.

EGM

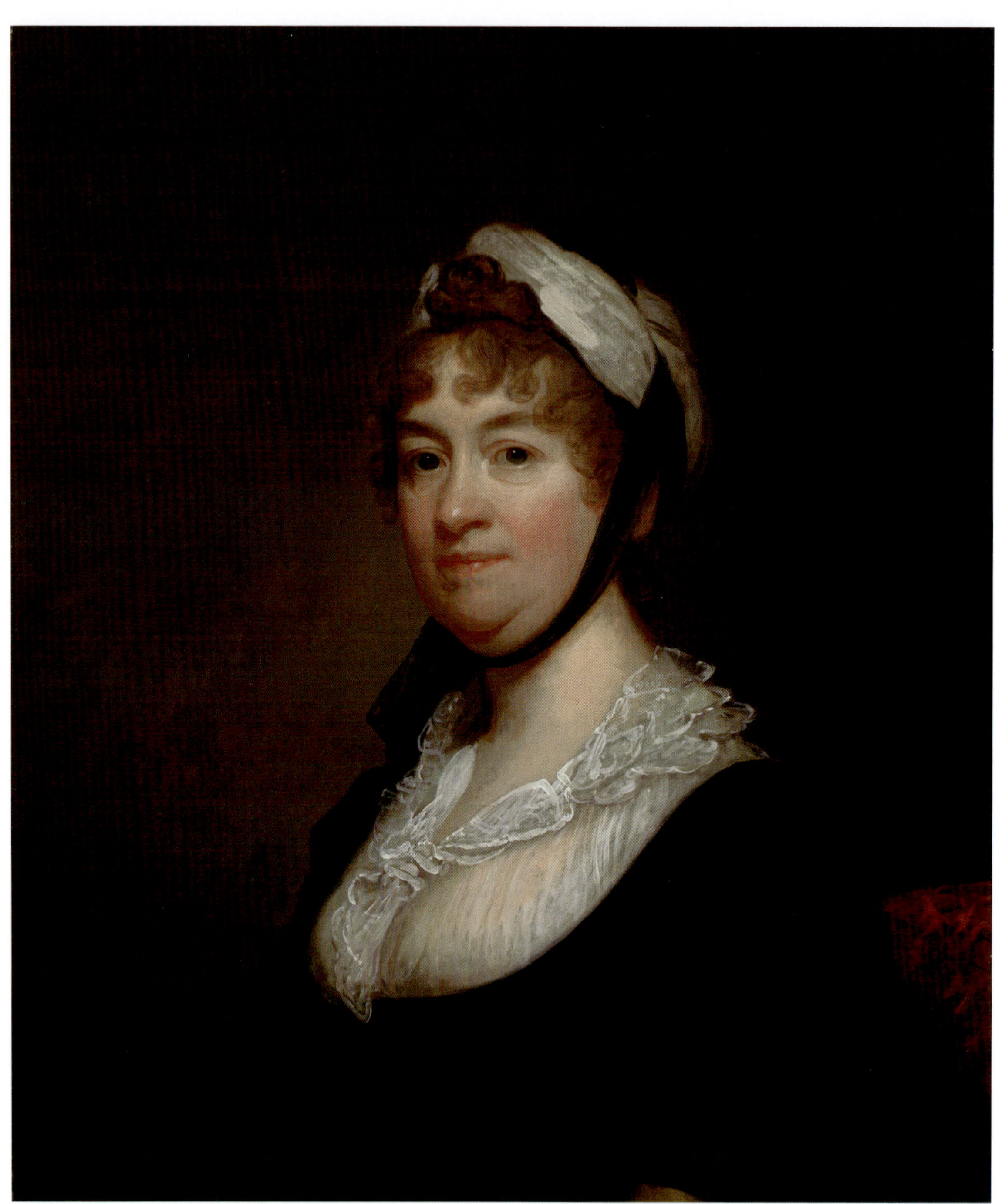

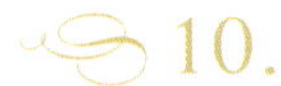

10.

ELIZABETH BOWDOIN, LADY TEMPLE

By Gilbert Stuart (1755–1828)

Oil on wood panel, 70.5 × 58.4 cm (27¾ × 23 in.) sight, 1806
The Honorable and Mrs. Russell E. Train

SOME AMERICAN families are known for their exceptional portraits. Among them is the Bowdoin family of Massachusetts. This portrait of Elizabeth Bowdoin, Lady Temple (1750–1809), the wife of Sir John Temple, is one of several that Gilbert Stuart painted of her and members of her family. Lady Temple and her brother, merchant and diplomat James Bowdoin III, were the children of James Bowdoin II, the post–Revolutionary War governor of Massachusetts. Robert Feke painted their parents' portraits in 1748, and around 1760, Joseph Blackburn depicted her and her brother in a double portrait (all Bowdoin College Museum of Art). John Trumbull portrayed Sir John Temple in 1784 (Canajoharie Library and Art Gallery, New York) and also painted a conversation piece of Sir John and Lady Temple with their two children, Augusta and Grenville, which was a gift for James Bowdoin III (private collection).[1] Sir John Temple, born in Boston in 1732, had served as surveyor general of customs in Boston from 1761 to 1767, the year that he and Elizabeth Bowdoin were married. A Loyalist, he and his family spent most of the years during the American Revolution in England. He was appointed the first British consul general to the United States in 1785, serving in New York until his death in 1798, and succeeded as eighth baronet in 1786.[2] This is one of three very similar paintings that Stuart painted of Lady Temple.[3] They depict her seated, turned to the left, looking straight at the viewer. Lady Temple wears an Empire-style black dress with a white transparent bodice designed to modestly cover the broad expanse of flesh that is revealed by the low cut of the dress. She wears a white turban whose black ribbon is tied under her chin. The red of the chair brings out the rosy color of her cheeks and lips. The portrait was her gift to her daughter, Eliza Bowdoin Winthrop (Mrs. Thomas Lindall Winthrop). Eliza mentioned the painting in a letter to her Aunt Sarah (wife of James Bowdoin III), dated Boston, November 26, 1806: "Stuart has just finished my mother's picture, which is an excellent likeness. He is also copying my father's, and my mother gives them to me."[4] After completing this portrait, Stuart painted an identical second one that is also on panel, as well as a larger one, on canvas, that depicts Lady Temple with her hands in her lap, in an elaborate setting including two columns and some drapery. As Eliza indicated in her letter, the paired portraits were intended for family members. Either this portrait or the other small one was to be paired with Stuart's copy of Trumbull's portrait of Sir John (both now owned by the Gibbes Museum of Art, Charleston, South Carolina), while the larger one was designed to match Trumbull's original portrait of him.[5] At this time Stuart also painted portraits of Eliza and her daughter, Elizabeth Temple Winthrop Tappan.[6]

EGM

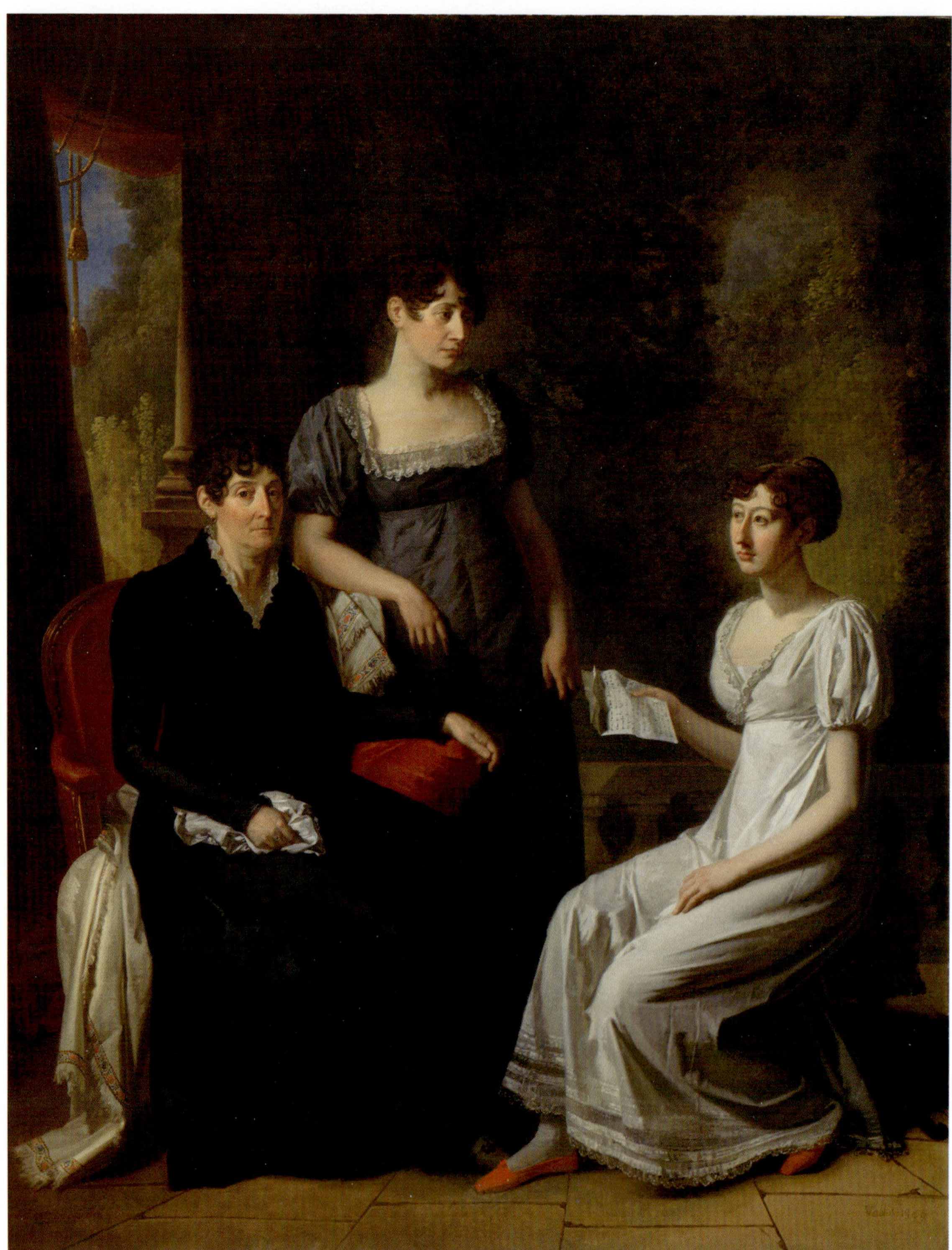

11

HANNAH SKINNER CHURCH, HER DAUGHTER MARIA CHURCH, AND HER DAUGHTER-IN-LAW ELIZABETH BENTLEY CHURCH

By Jacques-Antoine Vallin (c. 1760–1835?)

Oil on canvas, 206.4 × 157.5 cm (81¼ × 62 in.), 1809
Osborne Phinizy Mackie, descendant of the sitters

JACQUES-ANTOINE Vallin's monumental full-length painting of three women in the Church family depicts the varied reactions of Hannah Skinner Church (1753–?) and her daughter Elizabeth Maria Church (who was known as Maria; lifedates unknown) to the reading of a letter or document held by Elizabeth Bentley Church (1787–1850), Hannah Church's daughter-in-law.[1] While looking up at her sister-in-law, Elizabeth pauses as if waiting for their reactions.[2] Their glances and gestures, and even the colors of the dresses, carry the viewer's attention from the white dress on the right to the gray dress at center to the darker dress on the left, worn by the most discouraged-looking of the three women. What is the letter that Elizabeth holds? Family lore identifies it as the evidence that her husband, Edward Church Jr., was a bigamist and had married a woman named Marie Dubois in 1799. Although his three daughters from that marriage were born between 1800 and 1804, before his marriage on September 24, 1806, to Elizabeth Bentley in Derby, England, he had two sons with Marie Dubois—Edward and Daniel—who were born after that marriage.[3] To complicate the pictorial record, Vallin painted a

large group portrait, of the same dimensions as this painting, of Edward Church Jr. (1779–1845) with Elizabeth and their two children, Edward Bentley Church (1807–1847) and Elizabeth Hannah ("Eliza") Church (1809–1889/90).[4] In addition, Vallin also painted Edward Church Sr. (1740–1816) in a full-length portrait of slightly smaller dimensions (fig. 3).

The details of the commission of the portraits are not known. Edward Church Sr. was a Boston merchant who served as American consul in Lisbon, Portugal, from 1792 to 1797. Afterward he settled in Paris; he died in London in 1816, leaving most of his estate to his English mistress.[5] His son Edward Church Jr. was born in Boston in 1779, educated in England and France, and served as an officer in Napoleon's army. He left Paris for London with his second family in November 1809, and returned to the United States in June 1811, purchasing a farm near Lexington, Kentucky. In 1817, James Madison appointed him consul to L'Orient, France, so Church lived in Europe again until 1832, when he returned to Kentucky.[6] At that time he shipped the three portraits back to the United States. He proposed their future display on plans that he drew for an ideal small villa, which was never built.[7] His imagined placement of the paintings in the grand second-floor salon is indicated by the word "picture" in three places on the plan.

The artist Jacques-Antoine Vallin was a French painter of mythological and historical subjects as well as landscapes. He studied at the Académie Royale de Peinture in Paris and exhibited at the Paris Salon from 1791 to 1827. His paintings, neoclassical in style and subject matter, repeated well-known themes of the day. His other portraits include a similarly life-size full-length of French oculist Joseph Nicholas Blaise Forlenze (1807; National Gallery of Art, London), exhibited at the Salon in 1808.[8]

EGM

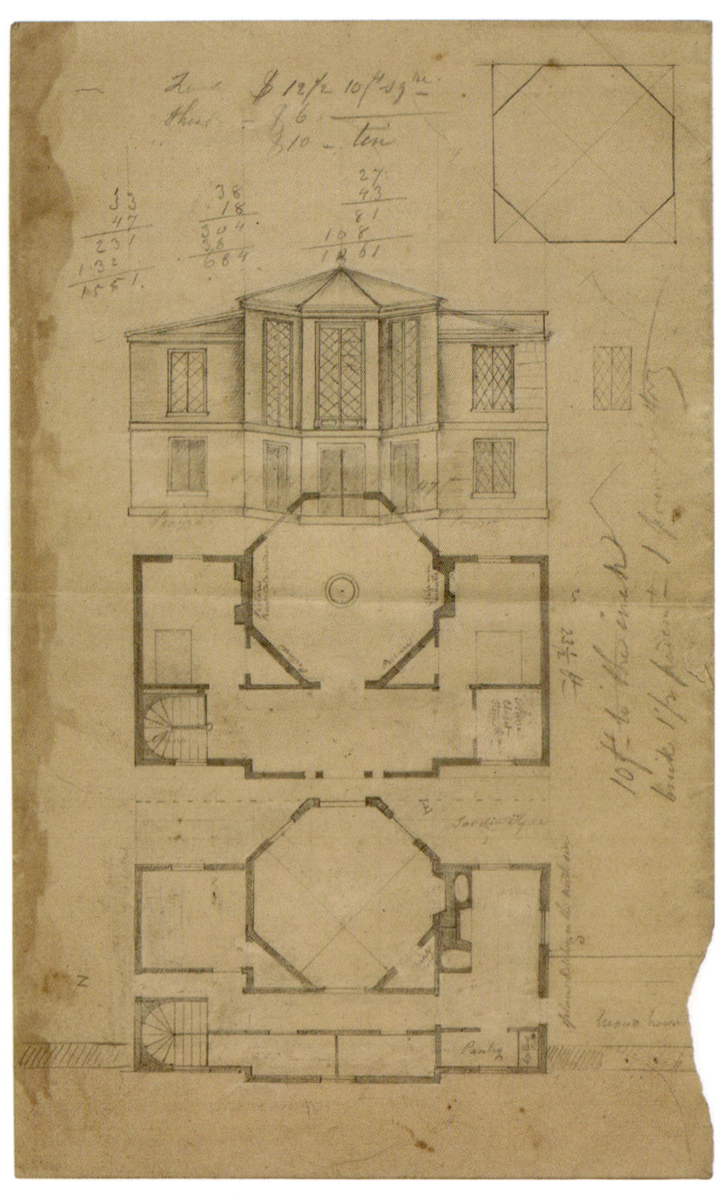

Cat. 11-1. *Plan for a Villa in Kentucky* by Edward Church Jr., pencil, pen, and ink on paper, c. 1832. Osborne Phinizy Mackie

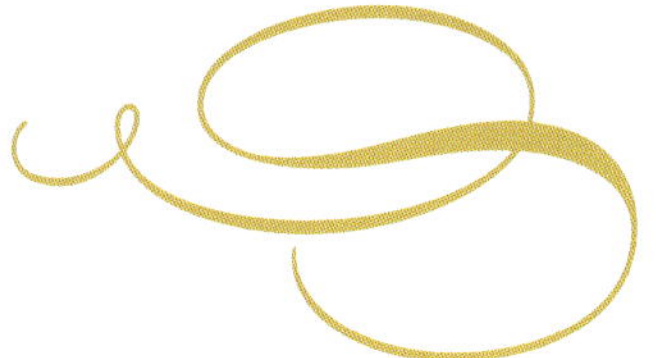

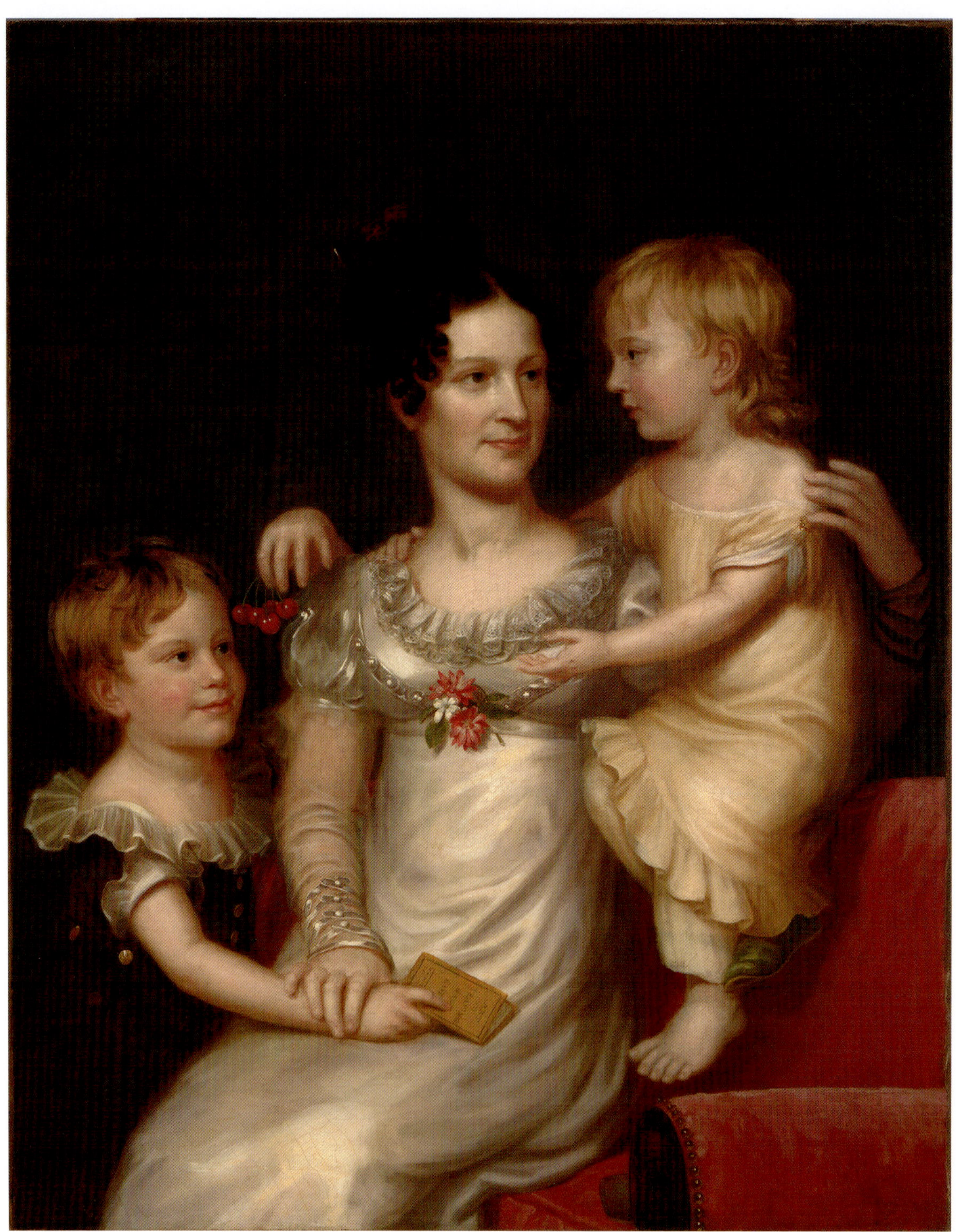

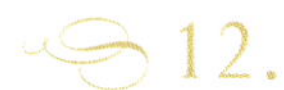

12

SARAH WESTON SEATON WITH HER CHILDREN AUGUSTINE AND JULIA

By Charles Bird King (1785–1862)

Oil on canvas, 112.4 × 87 cm (44¼ × 34½ in.), c. 1815
Private collection

CHARLES BIRD KING's portrait of Sarah Weston Seaton (1789–1863) and her children Augustine (1810–1835) and Julia (1812–1889) portrays the young family in a light and playful tone. Mrs. Seaton, seated on a red velvet sofa, wears a dress with an Empire waist, a style fashionable in about 1815. Her daughter Julia perches on the back of the sofa. Her son Augustine dangles an enticing bunch of cherries just beyond Julia's reach. Reflective of this mood of good-hearted mischief, Augustine holds in his right hand a small book, the title of which we can decipher as *The Art of Teasing Mad[e] Easy Washing[ton] 18 . . .*, a gentle indication of the role of this older brother.[1]

Sarah Weston (Gales) Seaton was the daughter of Joseph Gales, publisher of the *Raleigh (NC) Register*. In 1809 she married William Winston Seaton, a colleague of her father's. Three years later the couple moved to Washington, D.C., when Sarah's husband and brother, Joseph Gales Jr., became co-owners of the *National Intelligencer*. Sarah, fluent in French and Spanish, at times translated documents for the newspaper. The paper covered congressional proceedings during the years 1812–29 and was the official printer for Congress until after the election of 1828, when the paper opposed Andrew Jackson for president. The Seatons played leading roles in Washington's political and cultural affairs. One important event was the reception in 1824 for the Marquis de Lafayette (cat. 8) held at their new home on E Street, NW, between Seventh and Eighth Streets. William Seaton served as mayor of Washington from 1840 to 1850 and also as treasurer of the fledgling Smithsonian Institution.[2] Of their eleven children, several predeceased their parents; Augustine died at age twenty-six after a long illness contracted while serving with the army in Arkansas Territory. Julia married Columbus Munroe in 1839 and died in Washington in 1889.[3]

Charles Bird King was a newcomer to Washington when he painted this portrait, but he would soon become one of the capital's major resident portrait painters. Having studied painting in London with Benjamin West, King came to Washington in December 1814 after living briefly in Philadelphia. He left before the summer of 1815 but returned in the winter of 1816–17, finally settling in Washington in 1818. His studio was then at Twelfth and F Street, NW, a few blocks from the homes of the Seatons and the Galeses. King painted important political figures and distinguished Washingtonians, among them Joseph Gales Jr. and his wife, Sarah Lee; in 1830 he also designed the Gales's new Washington home, Eckington.[4] King is best known, however, for the portraits he painted of members of the tribal delegations that visited Washington in the 1820s and 1830s. The paintings, destroyed in 1865 in a fire at the Smithsonian Institution, are known through King's own copies and from lithographs.

EGM

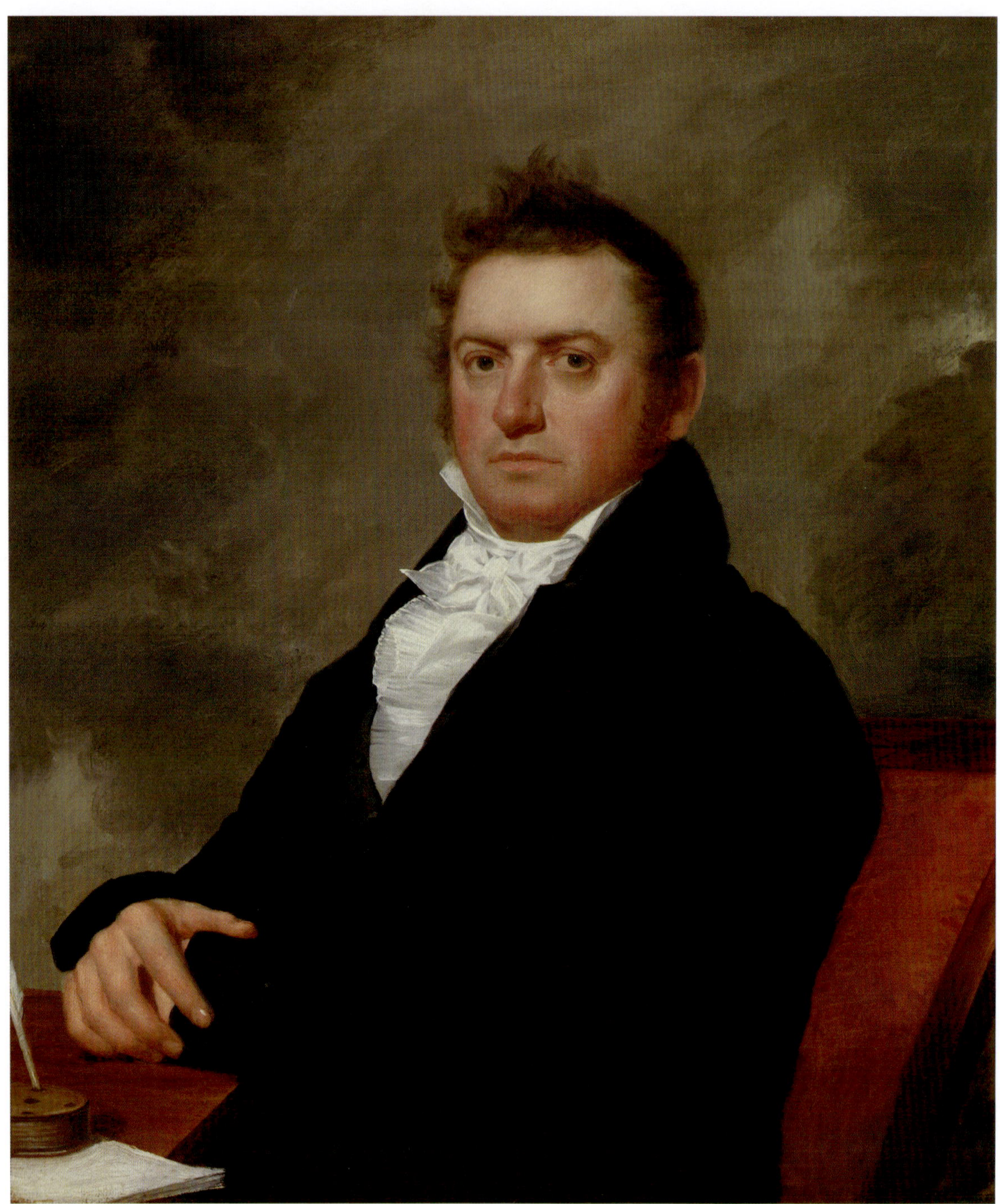

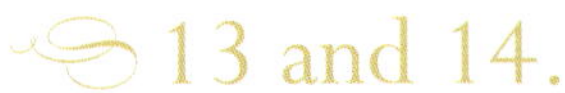
13 and 14.

LATHAM AVERY
BETSEY WOOD LESTER AVERY

Attributed to Samuel F. B. Morse (1791–1872)

Each: Oil on canvas, 76.2 × 63.5 cm (30 × 25 in.), c. 1820
Private collection

L ATHAM AVERY (1775–1845) was born in Groton, Connecticut. After his father, Daniel Avery, was killed in September 1781, when the British attacked Groton and neighboring New London at the Battle of Fort Griswold, his widowed mother moved with her eight children to Aurora, New York. Avery went to sea as a young man, making at least one voyage to China before focusing his trading interests on Guyana (Demerara). He spent about twenty years there before returning to Groton, where in 1816 he married Betsey Wood Lester (1787–1837), who was twelve years his junior. He purchased a house built by a cousin (now the Avery-Copp Museum), where he and Betsey raised their seven children.[1]

These very handsome portraits were probably painted within a few years of the Averys' marriage. Unsigned and undocumented, they are not mentioned in Latham Avery's will or his estate inventory, both of which are highly detailed. Because they have belonged to his collateral descendants, it is possible that they were painted for that branch of the family. Avery's nephew Daniel Dudley Avery attended Yale College and graduated in the class of 1830. Avery's many kindnesses to his nephew are legendary among Daniel Dudley Avery's descendants, who have been the owners of the portraits.

The paintings have many of the technical characteristics of portraits of the period by Samuel F. B. Morse (1791–1872), who lived in New Haven in the early 1820s. The handling of clothing details, the poses of the figures, and the treatment of faces and hands is similar to that in some of Morse's work from that era. The portrait of Avery is reminiscent of the painting technique of Morse's portraits of Alexander Calder of Charleston (c. 1820; Philip and Charlotte Hanes Collection, Winston-Salem, NC) and the Reverend Jeremiah Day, president of Yale. The portrait of Mrs. Avery, in her white dress with its lace ruffle and her decorative shawl, is notably reminiscent of Morse's portrait of his wife, Lucretia, painted in about 1820 (Mead Art Museum, Amherst College). Morse, who was born in Charlestown, Massachusetts, attended Yale from 1805 to 1810, when he painted his first portraits, in watercolor. From 1811 to 1815 he studied in London with Benjamin West, exhibited there at the Royal Academy, and developed an interest in history painting. After his return to Charlestown he supported himself with commissions for portraits. He was particularly successful on visits to an uncle in Charleston, South Carolina, where he spent the winters of 1818, 1819, and 1820. Among his numerous commissions was one for a full-length portrait of President James Monroe for the Common Council of Charleston (1820; Charleston City Hall). In 1819, Morse and his wife moved from Massachusetts to New Haven, where they were soon joined by his parents; the

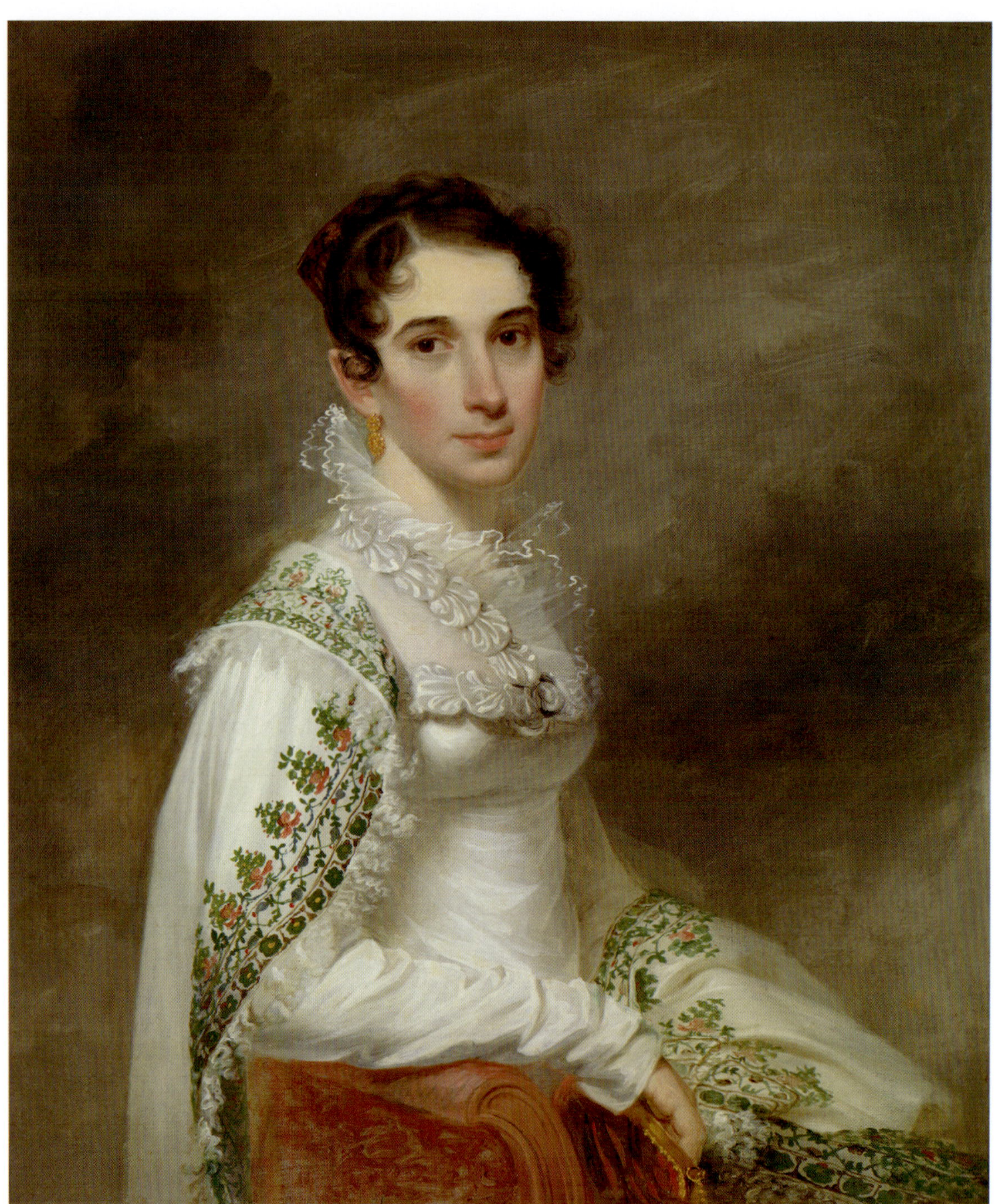

portraits he painted there include those of a number of Yale faculty, such as Jeremiah Day and Professor Benjamin Silliman (both 1823; Yale University Art Gallery). Morse often left the city to paint in Albany, Washington, D.C., and Charleston. Success gradually came his way through portraits and history paintings, among which is *The Old House of Representatives* (1822; Corcoran Gallery of Art); his career was interrupted by the sudden death of his young wife. Only later, in the 1830s, did Morse's early interests in electrical science, which he studied at Yale with Silliman, lead to his invention of the telegraph, for which he is best known today.[2]

EGM

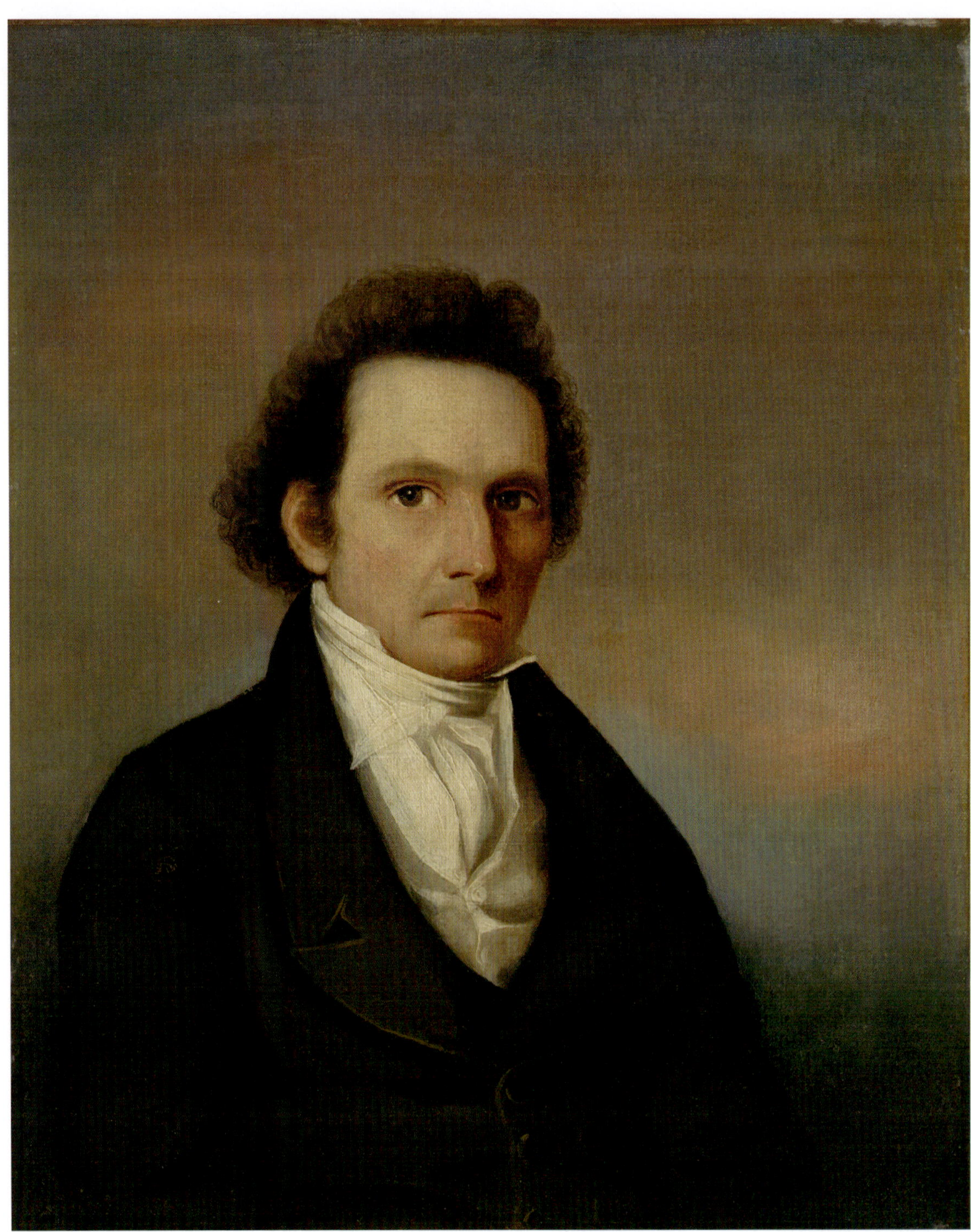

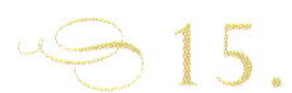

15.

SELF-PORTRAIT

By John James Audubon (1785–1851)

Oil on canvas, 31.8 × 25.4 cm (12½ × 10 in.), 1822–1823
Private collection

THIS SELF-PORTRAIT of naturalist John James Audubon, painted when he was thirty-seven, is one of his earliest attempts in oil. As a young man, he was already a keen observer of birds and their behavior and natural settings. Born on Saint-Domingue (modern-day Haiti) and raised near Nantes by his French father, Audubon came to the United States at age eighteen to avoid conscription into Napoleon's army. At Mill Grove, an estate near Philadelphia that his father had purchased, he soon met his future wife, a young English woman named Lucy Bakewell; they would marry in 1808. By 1805 he had already begun to draw birds in their natural positions, a practice not used by ornithologists of the day, whose images were made from birds that had been shot and stuffed. Audubon's considerable artistic talent was assisted by some formal art training in France, and he invented ways of arranging the dead birds in lifelike poses before sketching them with pencil and pastel. He carefully labeled the drawings with the identities of the birds, adding their scientific names and the places and dates where he saw them.[1]

Until the 1820s the drawings of birds were a passion and a hobby, while Audubon worked as an import merchant, partnering with Ferdinand Rozier, the son of a friend of his father's in Nantes, and then with his brother-in-law Tom Bakewell. Audubon had moved with his wife to Louisville, Kentucky, in 1808, and in 1810 settled in Henderson, where he later operated a mill. In 1819, after the mill failed, he began to make portrait drawings of family members and close friends in pencil and black chalk. The earliest examples were profiles in the neoclassical tradition popular in France at the turn of the century, which émigré Charles Balthazar Julien Févret de Saint-Mémin had introduced to Americans during the years 1796 to 1810. As Audubon gained experience, he began to make the bust-length portraits in three-quarter poses and worked on commissions. In 1820, after a brief period in Cincinnati, where he taught drawing and worked in the Western Museum, an institution similar to Peale's Museum in Philadelphia, Audubon left his wife and two sons in Cincinnati and began to follow his ornithological interest more seriously. As the idea for a publication called *The Birds of America* took form, he traveled south down the Ohio and the Mississippi Rivers, toward New Orleans, with a talented young artist, Joseph Mason, who became his assistant in completing the images of the birds. They worked in New Orleans and at river plantations and cities for the next two years, creating the first of the larger, more elaborate images of birds in their natural settings that are so well known today.

In the fall of 1822, in Natchez, Audubon met John Steen, a portrait painter from Washington, Pennsylvania, who agreed to give Audubon some lessons in oil painting in return for lessons in pastel. This self-portrait, one of Audubon's earliest paintings in oil, is the result. He painted it at Beech Woods, the plantation in Feliciana Parish, Louisiana, where his wife, Lucy, was employed by this time as a schoolteacher. As his first effort in oils, the portrait is striking in its similarity of approach to his portrait drawings, which are only slightly smaller. The work here has a linear quality in the treatment of the facial features—noticeable especially in the outlining of the eyelid and mouth. The resemblance to his pencil and black chalk portraits on paper can be seen by a comparison with a drawing of his brother-in-law Nicholas Augustus Berthoud (cat. 15-1), made in 1819. At the same time, the handling of the broad areas of coloring, not typical of his portrait drawings, resembles instead his use of watercolor, the new feature of the larger drawings of birds. The owner of the self-portrait in 1886, when it was first published, described it as a "portrait of himself in oil colors, taken by himself with the aid of a mirror."[2] Audubon painted similar portraits of his sons, following a time-honored artistic practice of using oneself and one's family as models for new techniques.

Audubon and Steen also collaborated as itinerant portrait painters, advertising in February 1823 that they charged fifty dollars for a life-size oil, thirty for a miniature. But their process was slowed by Audubon's continued focus on collecting birds, and the two parted company. Audubon returned to Louisville in October 1823 and in the following spring went on to Philadelphia, where artist Thomas Sully gave him additional lessons in oil painting. Unable to find an engraver and publisher for his watercolors in America, Audubon went to England in 1826. The first of the engravings for *The Birds of America* were completed that year. The full set of "elephant folio" volumes of the engravings was finally completed more than ten years later, in 1838. Although Audubon worked in oils again when finishing these images, the large watercolors of birds have remained his best-known work.

EGM

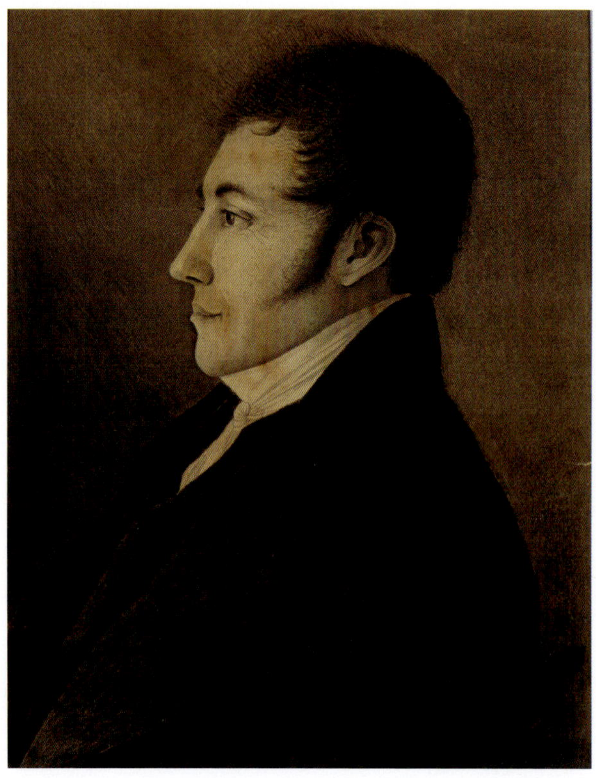

Cat. 15-1. *Nicholas Augustus Berthoud* by John James Audubon, black chalk on paper, c. 1819. Speed Art Museum, Louisville, Kentucky; gift of Mrs. Hattie Bishop Speed

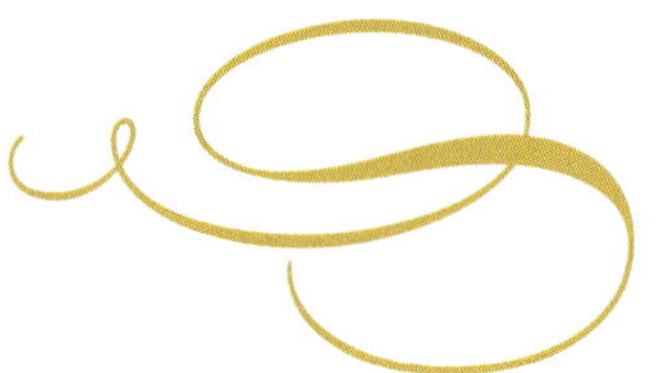

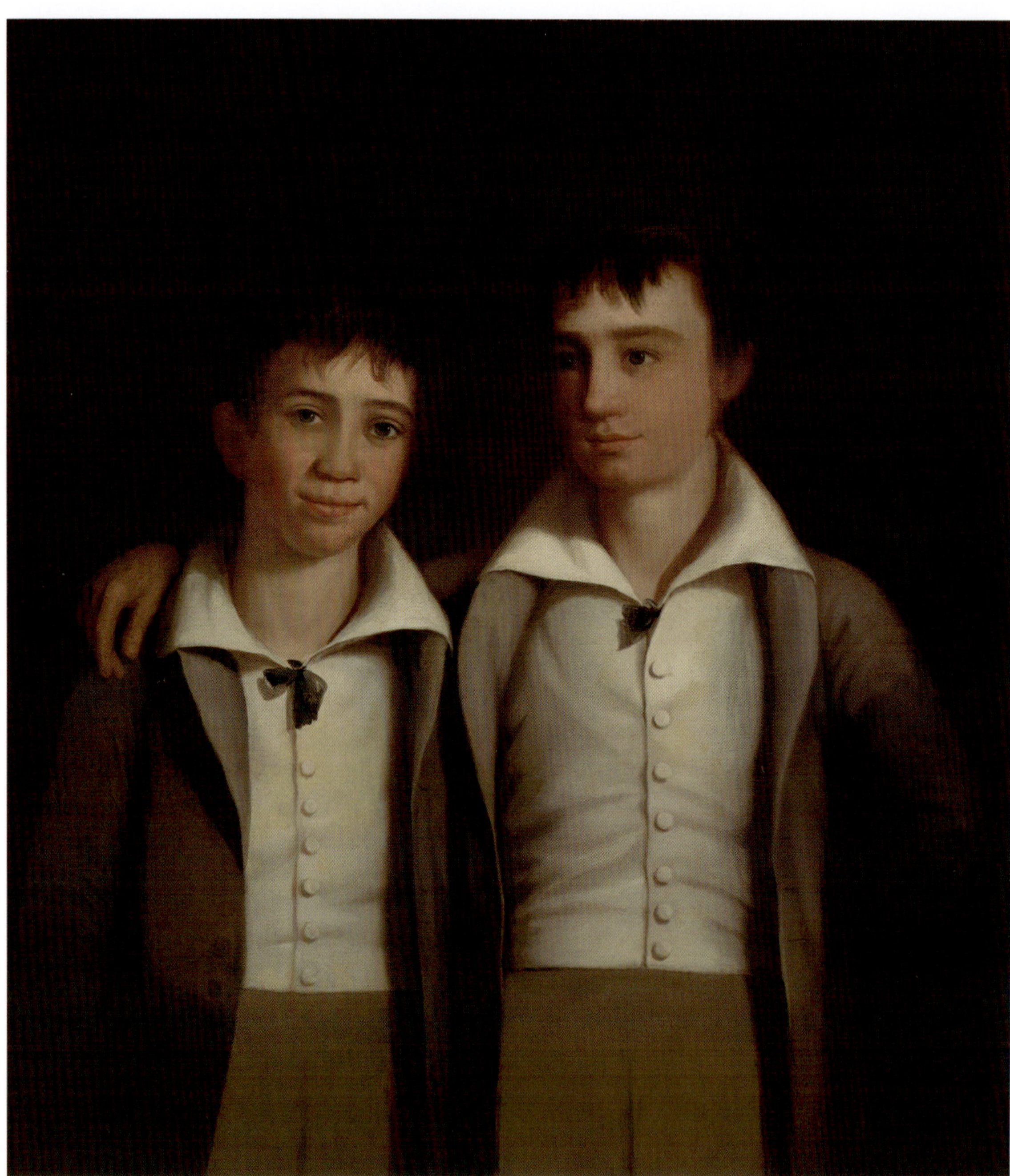

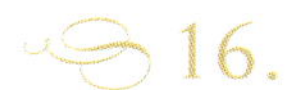

16

JAMES BOWDOIN SULLIVAN AND GEORGE RICHARD JAMES (SULLIVAN) BOWDOIN

By Robert Street (1796–1865)

Oil on canvas, 78.7 × 67.9 cm (31 × 26¾ in.) sight, 1824
The Honorable and Mrs. Russell E. Train

GEORGE RICHARD JAMES (Sullivan) Bowdoin (1809–1870) and his younger brother, James Bowdoin Sullivan (c. 1812–?), were the sons of George Sullivan and Sarah Bowdoin Winthrop Sullivan of Boston. Their mother, the granddaughter of Elizabeth Bowdoin, Lady Temple (cat. 10), inherited land from Lady Temple's sister-in-law, Sarah Bowdoin, the widow of James Bowdoin III, described by Sarah Bowdoin in her will, "all my real Estate in Milk Street in said Boston." To ensure an heir with the name "James Bowdoin" in the next generation, her will stipulated that upon Sarah Sullivan's death, the bequest would go to her "second son James Bowdoin Sullivan, he dropping the name of Sullivan, & taking, & retaining the name of Bowdoin." Should he die without legal heirs, the land would go instead to the older son, "now named George Richard Sullivan on condition of his . . . taking & retaining the name of George Richard James Bowdoin." A second bequest of $20,000 followed the same instructions.[1]

This double portrait of the young heirs was painted in Washington, D.C., in 1824 by Robert Street, an artist from Germantown, Pennsylvania.[2] Street first exhibited at the Pennsylvania Academy of the Fine Arts, Philadelphia, in 1815, and again in 1817, 1818, and 1822, and almost every year between 1834 and 1861. In 1824, however, he went to Washington, D.C., where he exhibited three large history paintings and painted

a portrait of Andrew Jackson (Sedalia Public Library, Missouri).[3] According to the artist's autobiographical statement, "At this period [I] painted a group for Col. Sullivan . . . who, on seeing the portrait of the General [Jackson], sent it to the President's mansion [the White House], where it remained some time, a credit to the artist."[4]

George Sullivan, the boys' father, was one of two commissioners from Massachusetts who presented the state's claim for reimbursement of expenses of the militia during the War of 1812. The two men arrived in Washington as early as July 1823 and remained at least through early November.[5] Sullivan was in the city again the following spring, and the boys apparently accompanied him, which led to the commission for the double portrait.[6] In July 1825 the older son, George, entered the United States Military Academy at West Point as George R. Sullivan, graduating under that name in 1829. After serving in the infantry for three years, he resigned from the army in August 1832.[7] It was probably about that time that he changed his name to George Richard James Bowdoin, an indication that he was the one who inherited the bequest, probably because his younger brother had died. George married Frances Hamilton, the granddaughter of Alexander Hamilton, and practiced law in New York as a partner in the firm of Bowdoin, Larocque and Barlow.[8]

EGM

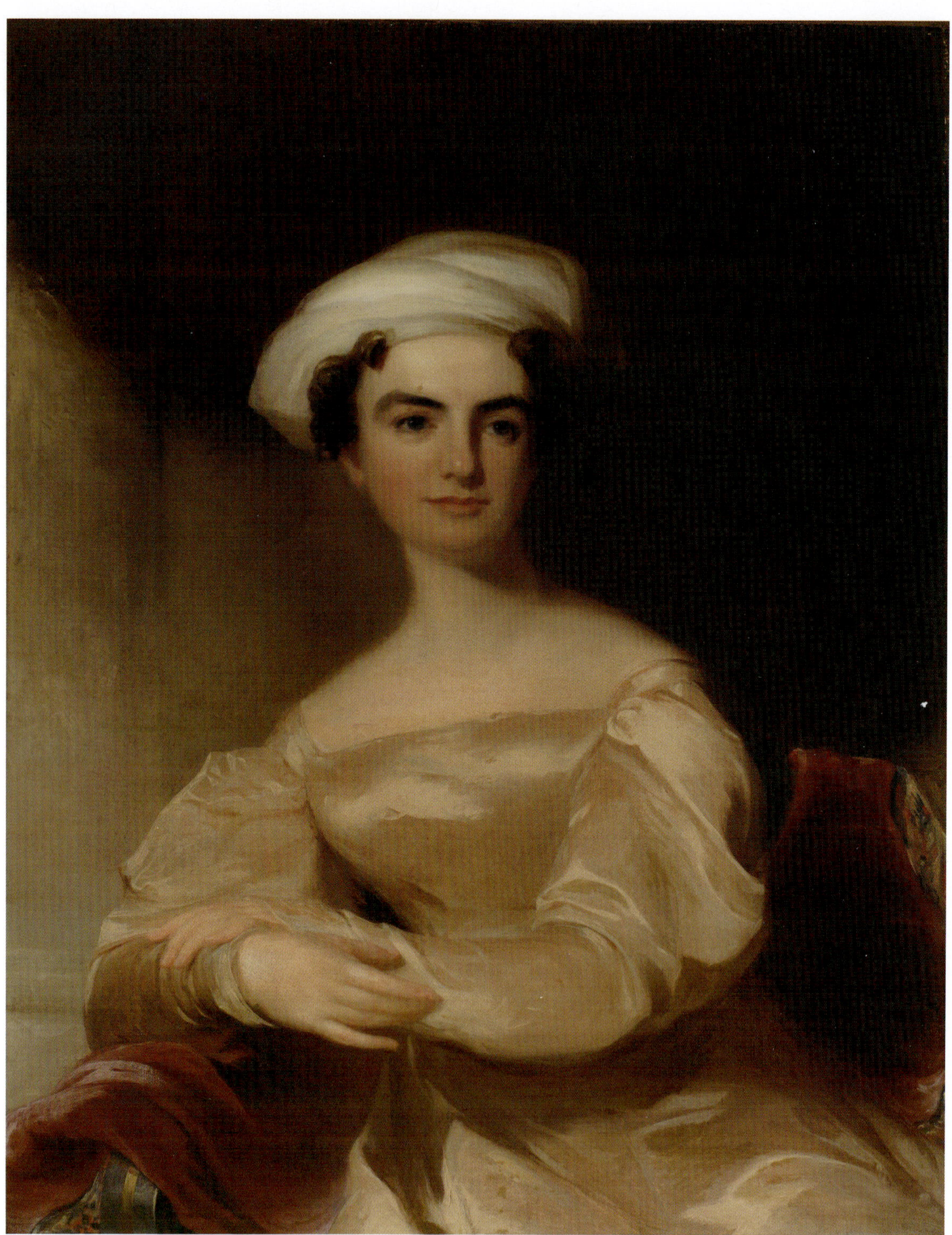

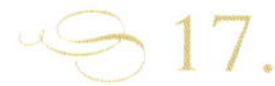 17.

PHOEBE CAROLINE ELLIOTT PINCKNEY

By Thomas Sully (1783–1872)

Oil on canvas, 91.4 × 71.1 cm (36 × 28 in.), 1827
Private collection

THOMAS SULLY has depicted Phoebe Caroline Elliott Pinckney (1791–1864) in a white silk gown and a matching turban that has allowed a few brown curls to escape. She is seated in a chair draped in red, her arms crossed, with her right elbow resting on the arm of the chair. The portrait is recorded in Sully's register as a portrait of "Mrs. Cotesworth Pinckney for Mrs. Elliott," for $120. Sully began the portrait on October 15, 1827, and finished it on November 23.[1] Its date is also inscribed in the upper left corner next to Sully's monogram: "TS 1827." The artist's careful records show that he had painted her sister, Mary ("Miss Elliott") in 1821 and her brother, William (1788–1863), in 1823, when William was serving in the South Carolina legislature (1814–32). In 1839 he painted Ann and Mary Elliott, William's daughters. All of the portraits are the same size.[2]

Phoebe Caroline Elliott, known as Caroline, was born in Beaufort, South Carolina, the daughter of the Sea Island, Georgia, cotton planter William Elliott II and Phoebe Waight.[3] In 1811, Caroline married Charles Cotesworth Pinckney (1789–1865), a Harvard-educated lawyer and rice planter who served briefly, from 1832 to 1834, as lieutenant governor of South Carolina. The Pinckneys raised their children with a strict religious upbringing, "swept up in the religious fervor of the Second Great Awakening."[4] The family's dedicated religiosity is reflected in the decision of Caroline and Charles's eldest son, Charles Cotesworth Pinckney (1812–1899), to become an Episcopal priest. Caroline Pinckney died at the Abbeville plantation to which the family had relocated during the Civil War.

Thomas Sully, the predominant portrait painter in America between 1810 and 1850, studied briefly with Gilbert Stuart in Boston and Benjamin West in London before settling in Philadelphia. Over his long career such prominent figures as Andrew Jackson, Thomas Jefferson, the young Queen Victoria, and the Marquis de Lafayette were among his portrait subjects. Like other successful northern painters, he often spent time in the warmer cities of the South, including Charleston. This portrait exemplifies his ability to capture the grace of the sitter and the shimmering quality of her silk gown.

EGM

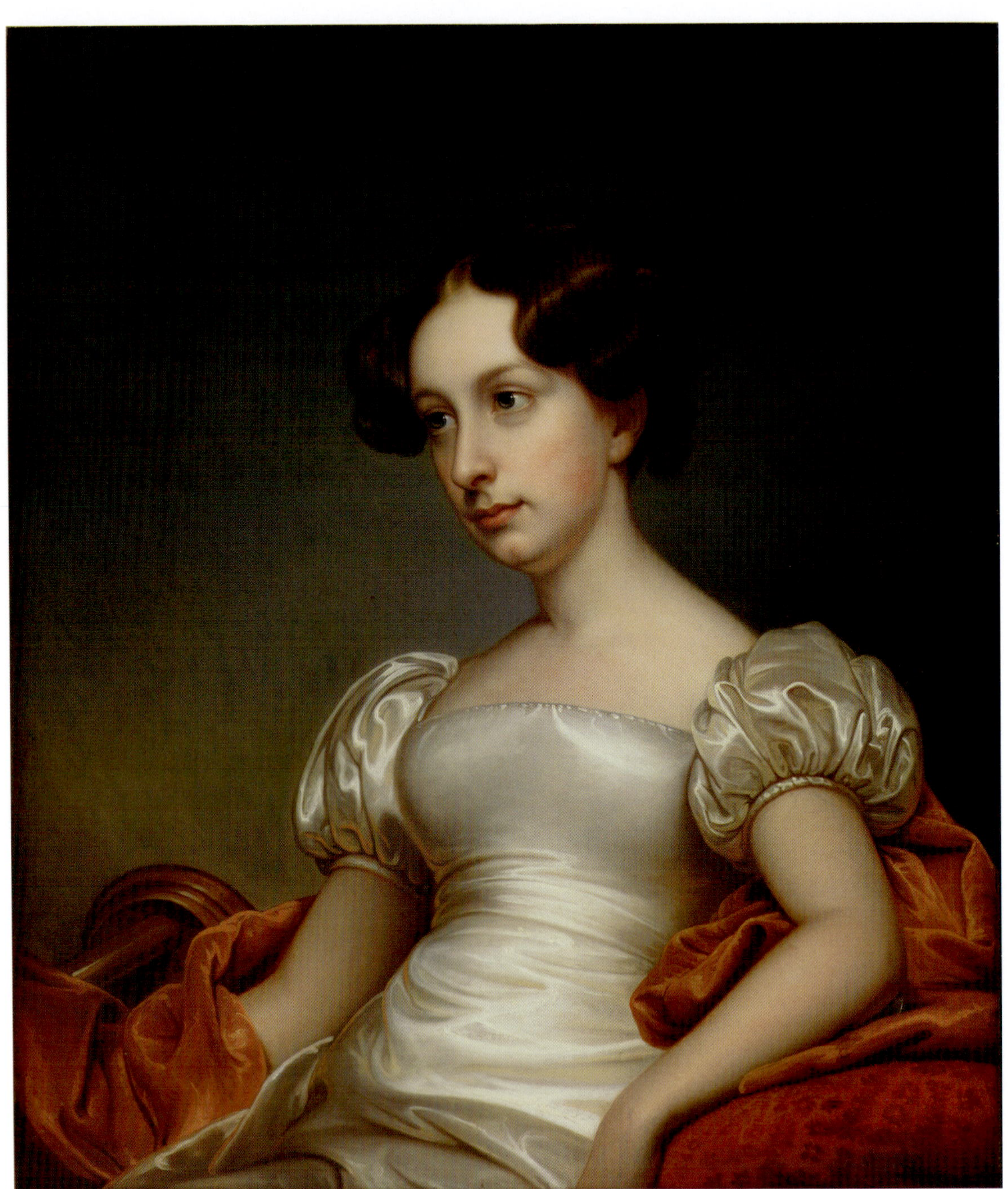

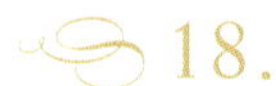 18.

CATHARINE PEABODY GARDNER

By Rembrandt Peale (1778–1860)

Oil on canvas, 77.5 × 64.8 cm (30½ × 25½ in.), 1827
Anita G. Herrick

REMBRANDT PEALE painted this richly colored image of Catharine Peabody Gardner (1808–1883), the daughter of wealthy Salem, Massachusetts, merchant Joseph Peabody (1757–1844) and his wife, Elizabeth (1767–1854), in 1827. Catharine wears an ivory-colored satin gown with short, gathered sleeves. Around her arms is a bright red shawl. Her glossy brown hair frames her face as she looks to the viewer's left, lost in thought. The portrait was painted the year after her marriage to Boston merchant John Lowell Gardner. Catharine described Gardner before her marriage as a "young gentleman whose merit far exceeds anything which I deserve or could have hoped for, however I shall endeavour to become more worthy of my good fortune, and trust that my attempts will not prove altogether fruitless."[1]

Catharine's portrait was in progress when Sophia Peabody, a distant cousin and amateur artist, saw it that October:

> Yesterday I went with Margaret Prescott to Harding's room; but found the noble man in the very act of moving, & we could not see a single picture. Nothing daunted, we tried to find Alexander but he had moved, & we could not. Then we went to Peale's, & saw Washington, Mr. Sparks, Charles Bonaparte, &cetera, & Mrs. Gardiner (Catharine Peabody) half finished. Peale was deeply engaged & did not stop to tell us who was who.[2]

Family tradition holds that Joseph Peabody commissioned his daughter's portrait; Peale had painted portraits of her parents a year earlier (private collection). When the portrait of Joseph Peabody was exhibited in 1828 at the Boston Athenaeum, however, the lender was John L. Gardner, which suggests that all three portraits were owned by the Gardners by that time.[3] Gardner served as director of several business organizations, including the Massachusetts Bank (1828–40) and the Boston Marine Insurance Co. (1826–38) and as manager of many properties, including those acquired through his marriage.[4] Among their five surviving children was John Lowell Gardner Jr., husband of Isabella Stewart Gardner, the art patron and collector who opened her Italianate villa in Boston as a museum in 1903, five years after his death.

Rembrandt Peale, the son and pupil of noted American painter Charles Willson Peale (1741–1827) of Philadelphia, developed a personal style that differed from his father's when he studied painting in France in 1808–10. After returning to the United States, Peale lived in Philadelphia, Baltimore, and New York, where he created and exhibited several large works, including his heroic portraits of George Washington, *Patriae Pater* (1824; United States Senate Collection), and *Washington Before Yorktown* (1824; private collection). In 1826 he went to Boston to learn the new technology of lithography, recently introduced from France. He remained there for two years, working on lithographs and painting portraits before traveling to Italy in 1828.[5]

EGM

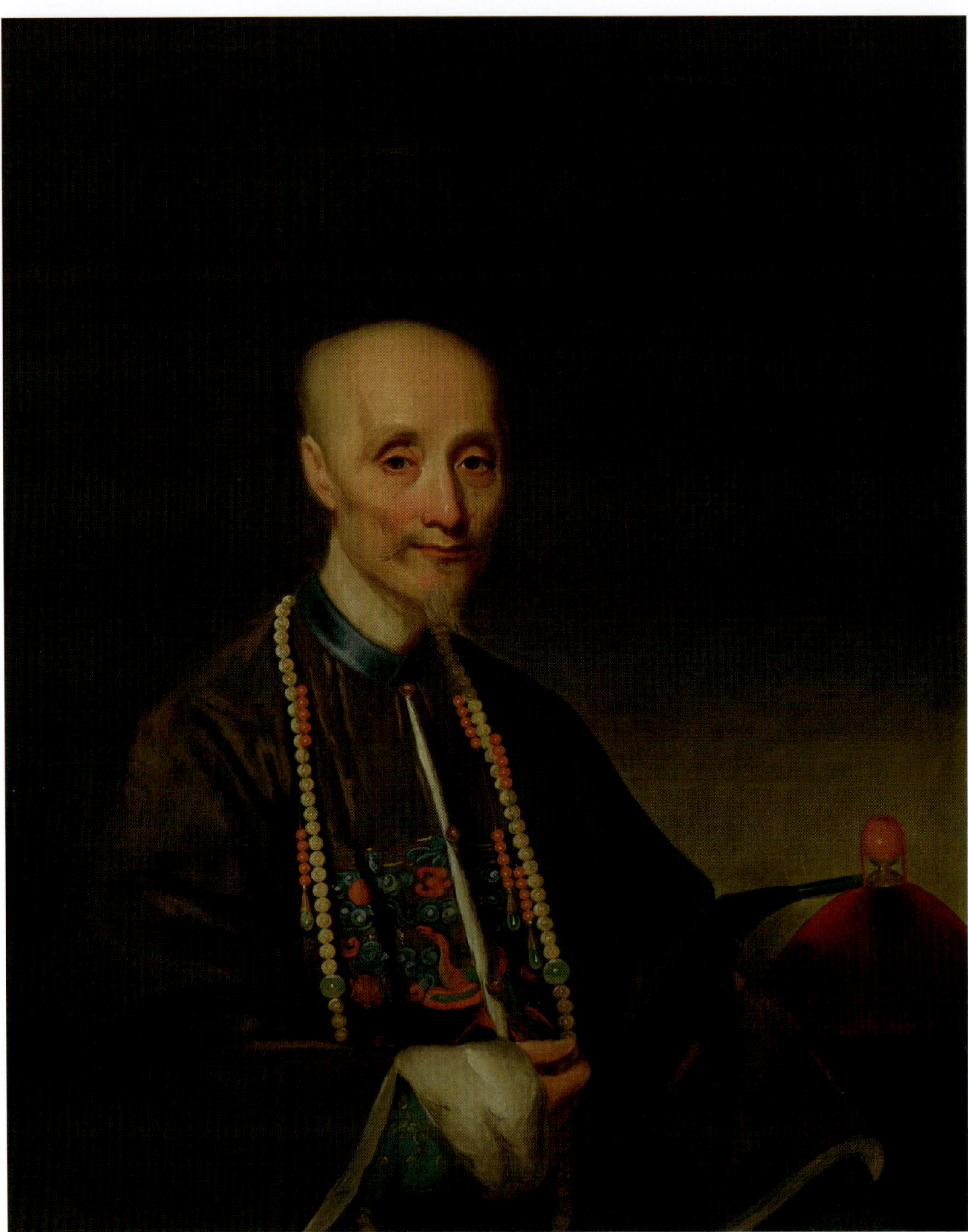

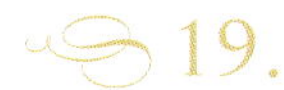 19.

HOWQUA (WU BINGJIAN)

Attributed to Lamqua (Guan Zuolin; Kwan Jok Lam) (1801–1860)

Oil on canvas, 76.2 × 63.5 cm (30 × 25 in.) sight, c. 1837
Oliver Family

CHINESE MERCHANT Wu Bingjian (1769–1843) was the leading member of the Cohong, the association of merchants in Canton, China, that traded with American and European companies in the early nineteenth century. The lucrative American trade in Chinese goods had begun with the departure of a ship named the *Empress of China* from New York for Canton in 1784. The trade ended in 1844 with the Cushing Treaty, which provided political recognition between the two countries.[1] During that period, Howqua, as he was known, had become legendary among the American traders for his wealth, business acumen, and interest in making secret international investments, handled in cash.[2] His prosperity was based in extensive tea plantations, as well as his property in Canton. "His methods, whether Chinese or Western, were so effective that the American merchants he employed found them useful in the conduct of their own business in later years."[3]

A number of the China Trade merchants returned home with portraits of Howqua. Six waist-length images of Howqua, including this one, are attributed to Chinese artist Guan Zuolin, or Kwan Jok Lam, known as Lamqua, or Lam Qua.[4] Lamqua, from Canton, has been called the "best documented of all the Chinese export artists who worked for the Western market."[5] The portraits depict Howqua wearing a brown silk robe decorated with elaborate blue and red embroidery, and long sets of beads. A cap at his side has a red stone that conveys the sitter's status.[6] Although the original owner of this version has not been identified, the first American owners of the other five portraits were all partners at one time in Russell & Company, the foremost American business in the China Trade.[7] The paintings that belonged to Robert Bennet Forbes and William Henry King are both described as gifts from Howqua upon their departure from Canton. The instigation for the gifts may have been Howqua's plan to sit for a portrait to give to Forbes's brother, John Murray Forbes. Howqua wrote Forbes in 1837, after he had left Canton: "I promised to sit for my portrait for you, but as yet I have had no leisure." John Murray Forbes became Howqua's most trusted business ally when he went to Canton in 1830 as an employee of Russell & Company. In 1834 he became a partner in the company, which he left in 1837 to establish his own trading company in Boston.[8]

Lamqua may have studied with English artist George Chinnery (1774–1852), who had settled in Macao in 1825 and often visited Canton. Lamqua certainly imitated his work. Lamqua's technique is a bit drier and shows less brushwork than Chinnery's, but he has clearly mastered the British tradition of portraiture. A fine small full-length portrait of Howqua by Chinnery (Hong Kong and Shanghai Banking Corporation, Hong Kong) was the first of many versions and copies of a different pose than that seen in the larger waist-length portraits. These have been attributed to both Chinnery and Lamqua, in a series of replicas that can be dated from about 1830.

Samuel Russell of Middletown, Connecticut, founder of Russell & Company, owned a portrait of this type.[9] Lamqua's work was included in exhibitions at the Royal Academy in London in 1835 and 1845 and at the Pennsylvania Academy of the Fine Arts, Philadelphia, in 1851 and 1860. Five portraits by him that belonged to Augustine Heard of Ipswich, including the one of Howqua, were exhibited at the Boston Athenaeum in 1850.[10] Lamqua is best known today, however, for a remarkable series of medical portraits of patients treated at a hospital in Canton founded by Dr. Peter Parker, an American medical missionary.[11]

EGM

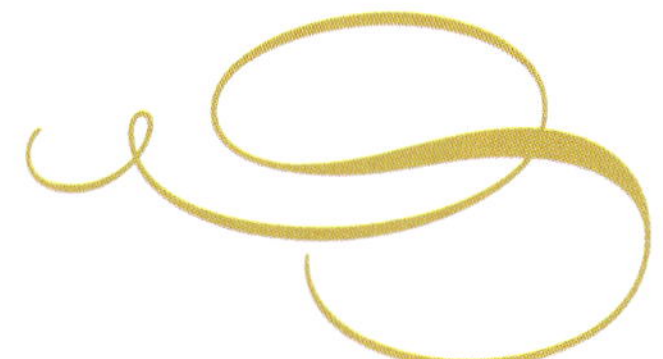

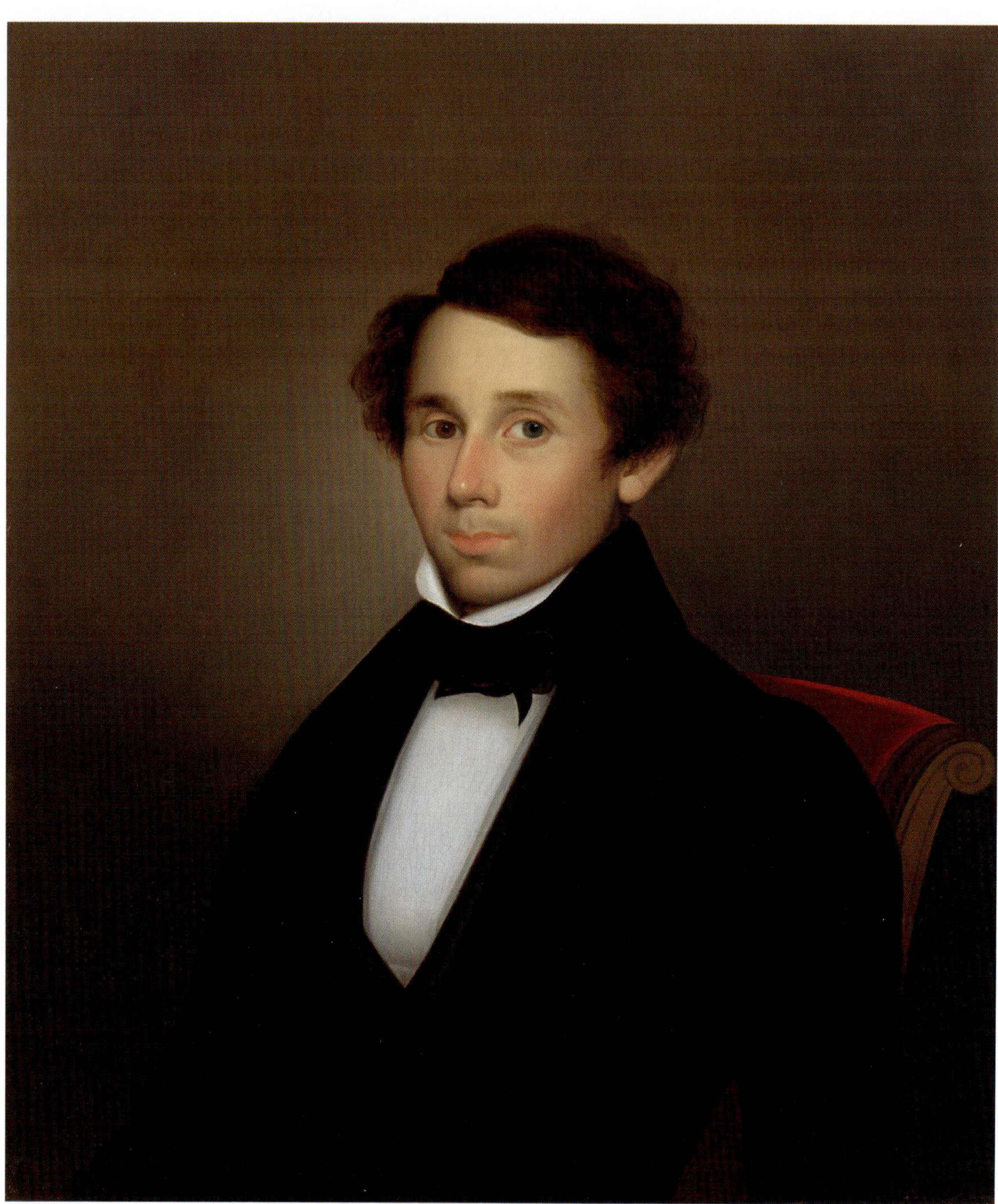

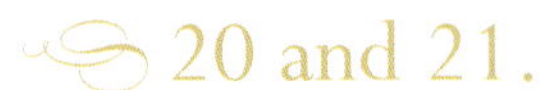 20 and 21.

WILLIAM RUSSELL CONE
REBECCA DAGGETT BREWSTER CONE

Attributed to Philip Hewins (1808–1849)

William Cone: Oil on canvas, 76.8 × 63.5 cm (30¼ × 25 in.), c. 1840
Rebecca Cone: Oil on canvas, 76.2 × 63.5 cm (30 × 25 in.), c. 1840
The Ellis Family Collection

WILLIAM RUSSELL CONE (1810–1890) of East Haddam, Connecticut, married Rebecca Daggett Brewster (1814–1890) of New Haven in 1833, and settled in Hartford, where Cone, a graduate of Yale College and Yale Law School, practiced law with William Hungerford. The Hungerford-Cone law firm was engaged in the "legal settlement of more important questions connected with insurance, railroads, and commercial business, than any other firm in the state."[1] Their most famous case, however, had international repercussions: Hungerford represented the Spanish Crown in the *Amistad* case in the U.S. Circuit Court trial of September 1839, which took place in Hartford. The Spanish sought to have the slaves from the schooner *Amistad* returned to Cuba to be tried for the murder of the ship's captain. The court, however, found in favor of freedom for the Africans, which led to appeals that went all the way to the Supreme Court.[2] (At that point, the Hartford law firm was no longer involved.) After his retirement in 1860, Cone served as director of several firms, including the Aetna Bank, the Aetna Fire Insurance Company, and the Hartford and New Haven Railroad Company. He was also president of the Wadsworth Athenaeum (1884–1890).[3]

The artist Philip Hewins, from Sharon, Massachusetts, worked for a time in the dry-goods business in the Boston area in the 1820s prior to taking up painting. He studied with Reuben Rowley, an artist who worked in New York State before moving to Boston. In June 1833, after witnessing a procession escorting President Andrew Jackson through Hartford, Hewins painted a portrait of Jackson (Connecticut Historical Society).[4] He remained in Hartford as a portrait painter for the rest of his short life. The portraits here were attributed to Hewins after their current owner brought them to the attention of the National Portrait Gallery. Ellen Miles, the author of this entry, thought they might be by Hewins, who had been recently identified as the artist of two Hartford portraits owned by Miles's family.[5] The careful modeling of the faces and the treatment of clothing details are virtually the same, as is the positioning of each figure, as if turned slightly to the side, and the depiction of a chair with a bright spot of red upholstery. The attribution also helped validate the identity of the Cones as the sitters, which had been uncertain. As further confirmation, the portrait of Mrs. Cone can be seen in a photograph of 1875 of the interior of the Cones' house in Hartford. A date for the portraits is suggested by the clothing styles and corroborated by

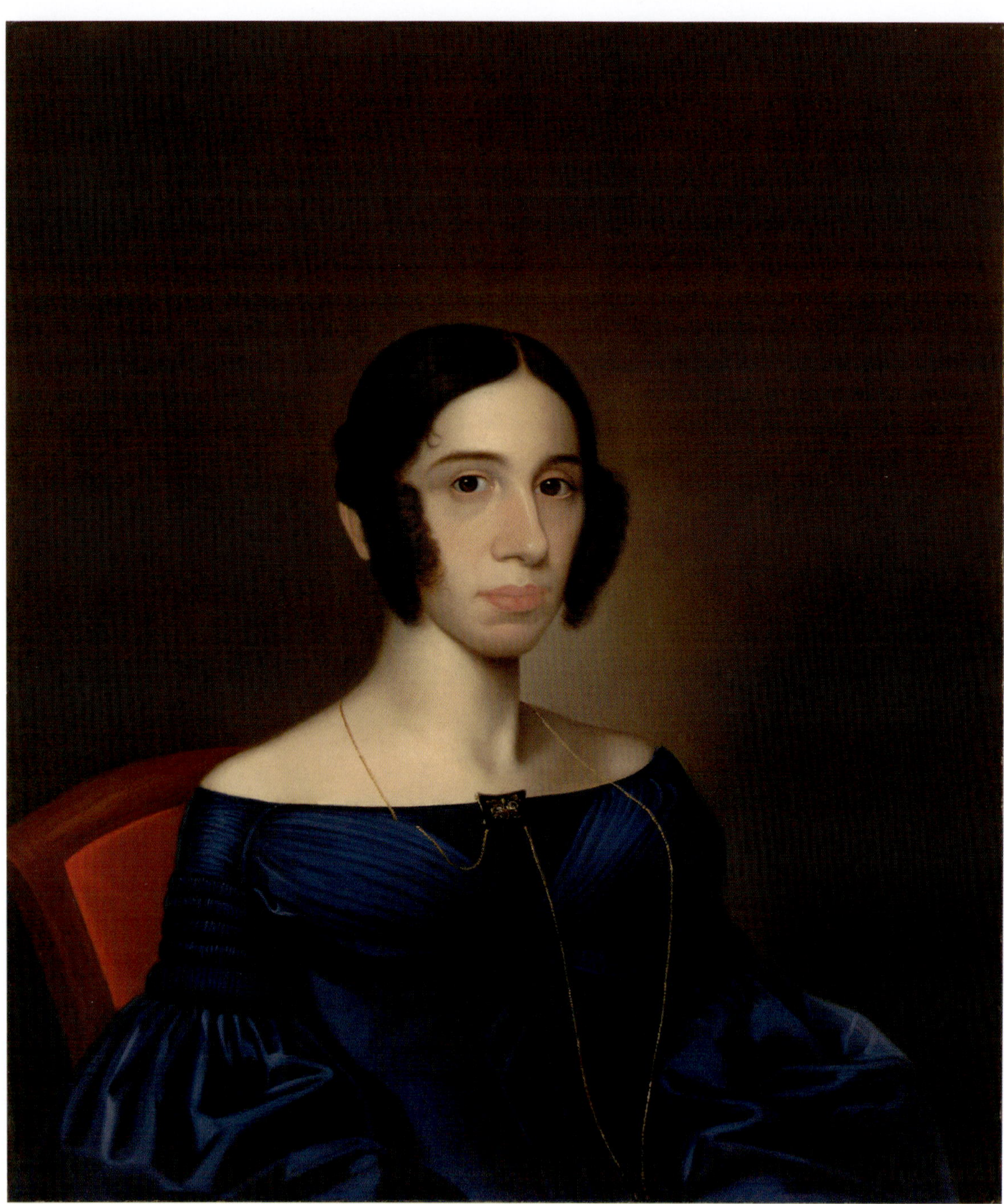

Cat. 20-1. Canvas stamp of Edward Dechaux on verso of painting, before 1840. The Ellis Family Collection

the canvas stamp on the reverse of each painting (cat. 20-1). Described as the "most common New York City stencil mark," it is the commercial marking of Edward Dechaux, who was a dealer of artists' supplies in New York City from the early 1830s until the 1850s. This particular form of the name "Edward Dechaux" indicates that the canvases were manufactured before 1840.[6]

EGM

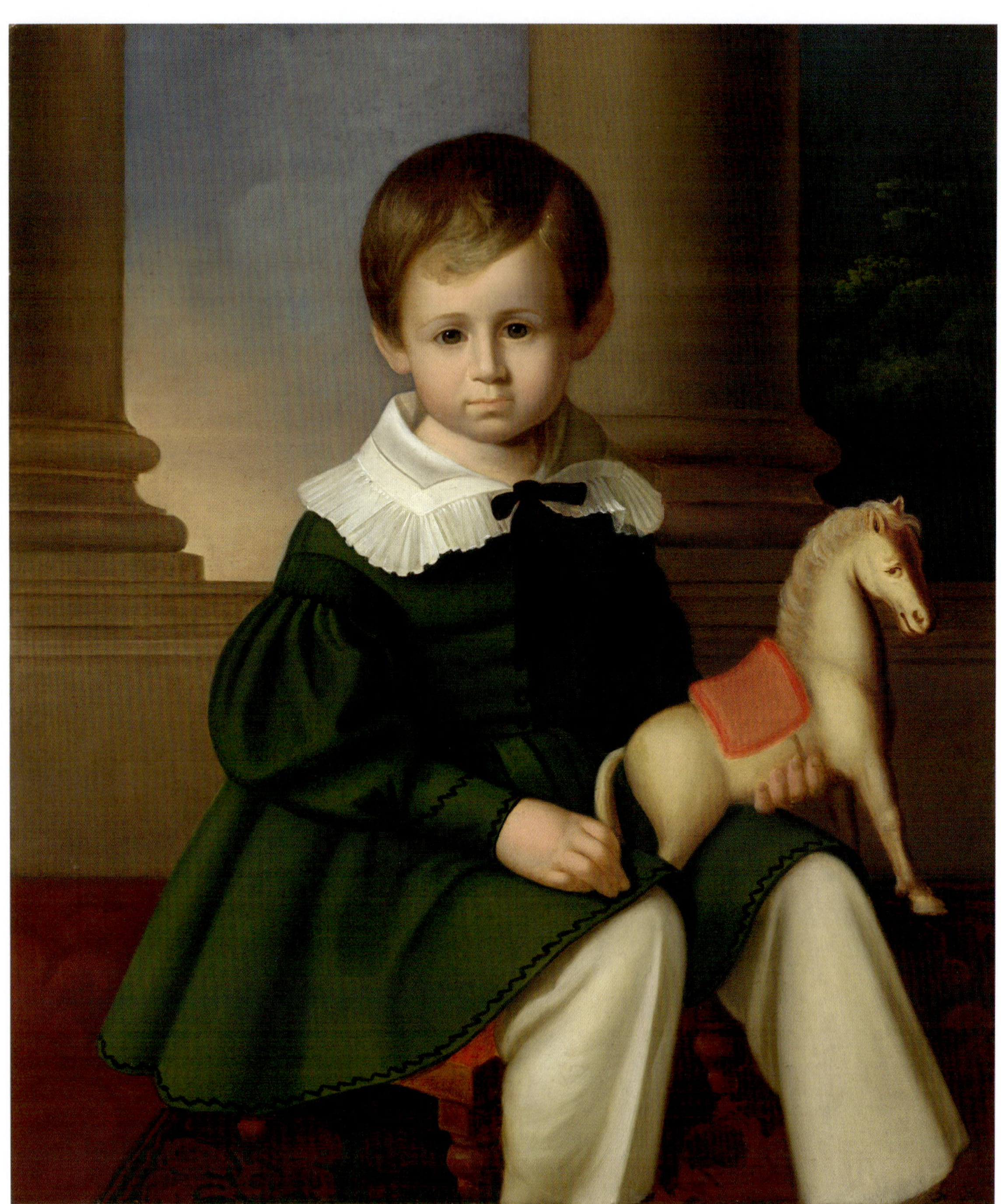

 22.

JAMES BREWSTER CONE

By an unidentified artist (possibly Philip Hewins, 1808–1849)

Oil on canvas, 76.2 × 63.2 cm (30 × 24⅞ in.), c. 1840
The Ellis Family Collection

THE ELDEST son of William and Rebecca Cone of Hartford, Connecticut (cats. 20 and 21), James Brewster Cone (1836–1918) graduated from Yale College in 1857. After travel and study in Europe, and appointment for a year as American vice consul in Lyons, France, he returned to Hartford to work for the Hartford Carpet Company. He married in 1863; two sons died in infancy. From 1864 to 1883 he manufactured coaches and carriages in New York City. He then returned to Hartford to manage the family estate.[1] Although family tradition held that this portrait represented his younger brother, William Allen Cone (1840–1853), the child's apparent age of about four years, in combination with the style of clothing, suggest that the boy is instead the Cones' oldest son, James. His long pants and jacket, and the white shirt with a wide frill, were the fashion in the late 1830s, as seen in portraits by Robert Peckham (1785–1877), including *The Hobby Horse* of about 1840 (National Gallery of Art, Washington) and *The Raymond Children* of about 1838 (Metropolitan Museum of Art). The same type of knee-length smock worn with a ruffled shirt and the ankle-length pantaloons are also seen in the portrait of another Connecticut child, Marcus Dwight Filley of Bloomfield, Connecticut

(private collection), painted in 1839. In addition, as happens very rarely, the smock that Marcus wears in the portrait has been preserved at the Connecticut Historical Society, Hartford.[2]

It is quite likely that Philip Hewins, the artist who painted the portraits of James Brewster Cone's parents, was the painter of this portrait. Hewins painted Marcus Filley's portrait (the artist's name is inscribed on the reverse), as well as the pair of portraits of Filley's parents (Connecticut Historical Society). The composition here, of James Cone, is more complex than the others, showing most of the child's figure as well as the toy horse that he holds. The technique is similar, however, to the other portraits by Hewins. In addition, James Cone's portrait is the same size as the pair of his parents and has the same canvas stamp on the reverse: "PREPARED BY EDWARD DECHAUX NEW YORK." The stamp is the commercial mark of Edward Dechaux, who was a dealer of artists' supplies in New York City from the early 1830s until the 1850s. The particular form of the first name on the stamp indicates that the canvas was manufactured before 1840.[3] All of this strongly suggests that the three portraits were painted at the same time.

EGM

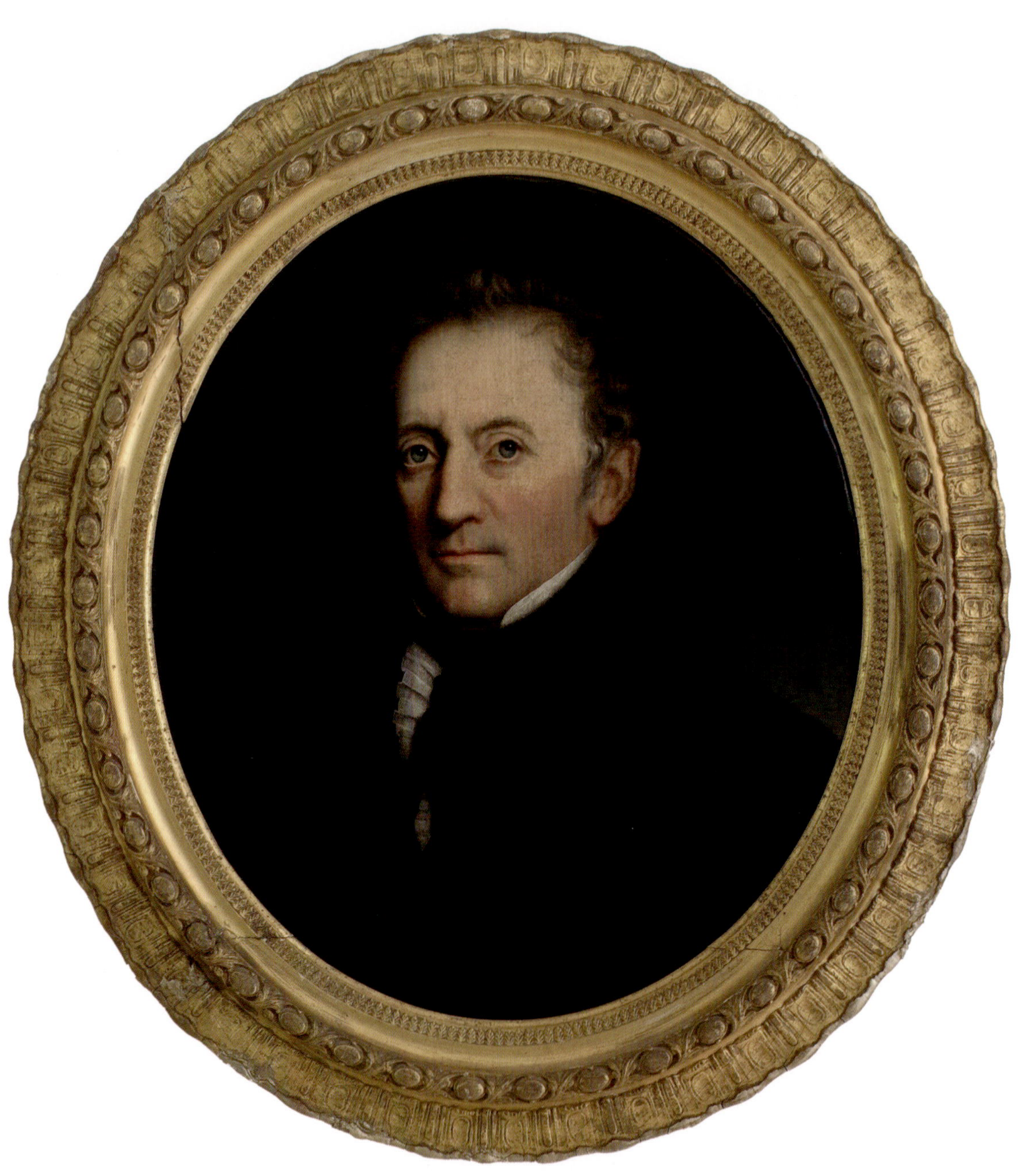

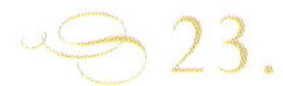

23.

JOHN CLARKE
By Nelson Cook (1808–1892)

Oil on canvas, 58.4 × 49.5 cm (23 × 19½ in.) sight, 1845
Mr. and Mrs. B. Francis Saul II

T HIS PORTRAIT brings together John Clarke (1773–1846), the well-known developer of Saratoga Springs, New York, with Nelson Cook, a local portrait painter. Clarke emigrated from Yorkshire, England, to New York City sometime after the Revolutionary War. A chemist, he opened the first soda fountain in New York City in 1819, selling carbonated mineral water mixed with syrups. In 1823 he and a business partner, Thomas Lynch, bought Congress Spring, the largest of several mineral springs in Saratoga Springs. Clarke married Eliza Bryar White, widow of New York attorney Charles White, and moved to Saratoga Springs. He soon built a water-bottling factory adjacent to Congress Spring. Clark was the first businessman to put spring water in distinctive bottles and market it on a large scale. The earliest surviving bottles with his name were made during the partnership with Thomas Lynch (died 1833) and are marked "LYNCH & CLARKE/NEW YORK." From 1833 until Clarke's death in 1846, the bottles were marked "JOHN CLARK/NEW YORK."[1] Clarke's original design for the short, stocky bottle became the standard used by other spring owners in the area, and the bottles became known as "saratogas."

The springs became a popular destination for visitors who wanted to drink the beneficial mineral water, which was free except for the slight fee paid to "dipper boys." Hotels were built near Congress Spring, and the two villages, at Congress Spring and High Rock Spring, became the

Village of Saratoga Springs in 1826. That same year, Clarke landscaped the area near the spring as Congress Park. In 1832 he and other businessmen opened a railway line from Schenectady to Saratoga Springs. In about 1840 he built a rectangular Greek Revival–style pavilion over Congress Spring and added a circular pavilion over nearby Columbian Spring, both for the comfort and shelter of visitors to the springs. He also hired a band to play in the summer. His own Greek Revival–style house, built in 1832, stood nearby on Circular Street.[2]

This portrait, the later of two known portraits of Clarke, depicts the septuagenarian in a surprisingly literal, almost photographic, style. Inscribed on the reverse "Painted by Nelson Cook 1845," the portrait was done in Saratoga Springs the year before Clarke died.[3] Nelson Cook was born in nearby Malta. His father Joseph and his older brother Ransom were both furniture makers. After his marriage, Nelson traveled through Canada with his wife, serving as agent for his brother, who also manufactured hardware. He settled in Toronto in 1837 and took up portrait painting, working at first from prints. Owing to ill health and chronic debt, he returned to Saratoga, where in 1840 his advertisement read: "Nelson Cook Portrait Painter. Nearly opposite the Collumbian [*sic*] Hotel, Saratoga Springs. Specimens seen at his rooms."[4] Cook later worked also in Rochester, Buffalo, Rome, and New York City. The portrait agrees as a likeness with the profile face in the full-length image (cat. 23-1) that was cut in black

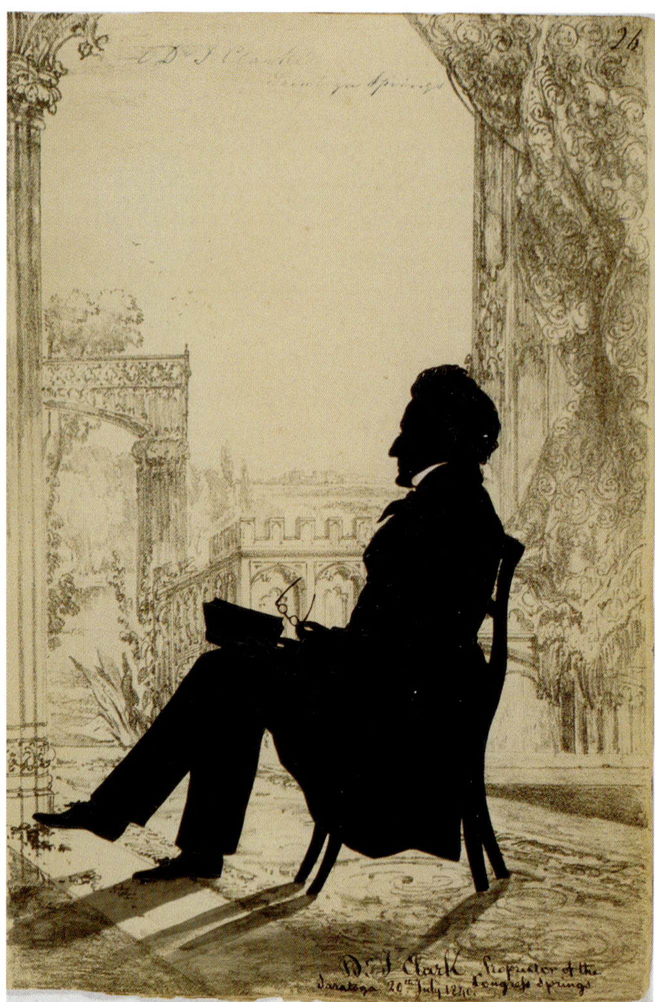

Cat. 23-1. *John Clarke* by Auguste Edouart
(1788–1861), lithograph, chalk, and cut paper,
1840. National Portrait Gallery, Smithsonian
Institution; gift of Robert L. McNeil Jr.

paper by Auguste Edouart in July 1840, on his
first visit to the resort. The French silhouettist
inscribed and dated the duplicate, which he kept
for himself: "Dr. J Clark, Proprietor of the Congress Springs, Saratoga, 20th July 1840." The title
"Doctor" was a courtesy accorded the sitter for
his profession as a chemist. The background view
is not unique to Clarke's portrait or descriptive
of the buildings he owned. Edouart used the

same lithographic scene of a Gothic-style porch
for several other portraits, including some that
he made that summer in Saratoga of other sitters. Edouart returned to Saratoga Springs every
summer for the next four years, finding new
clients for his hand-cut images among the city's
visitors.[5]

EGM

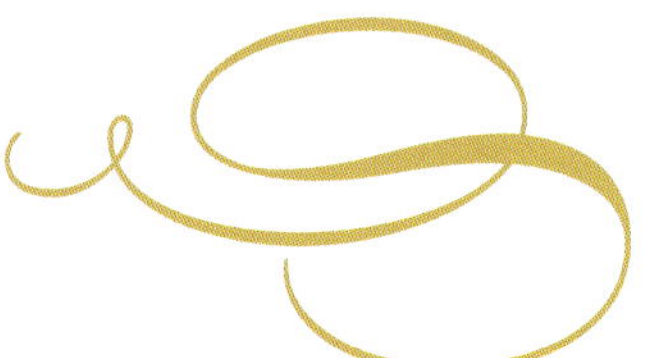

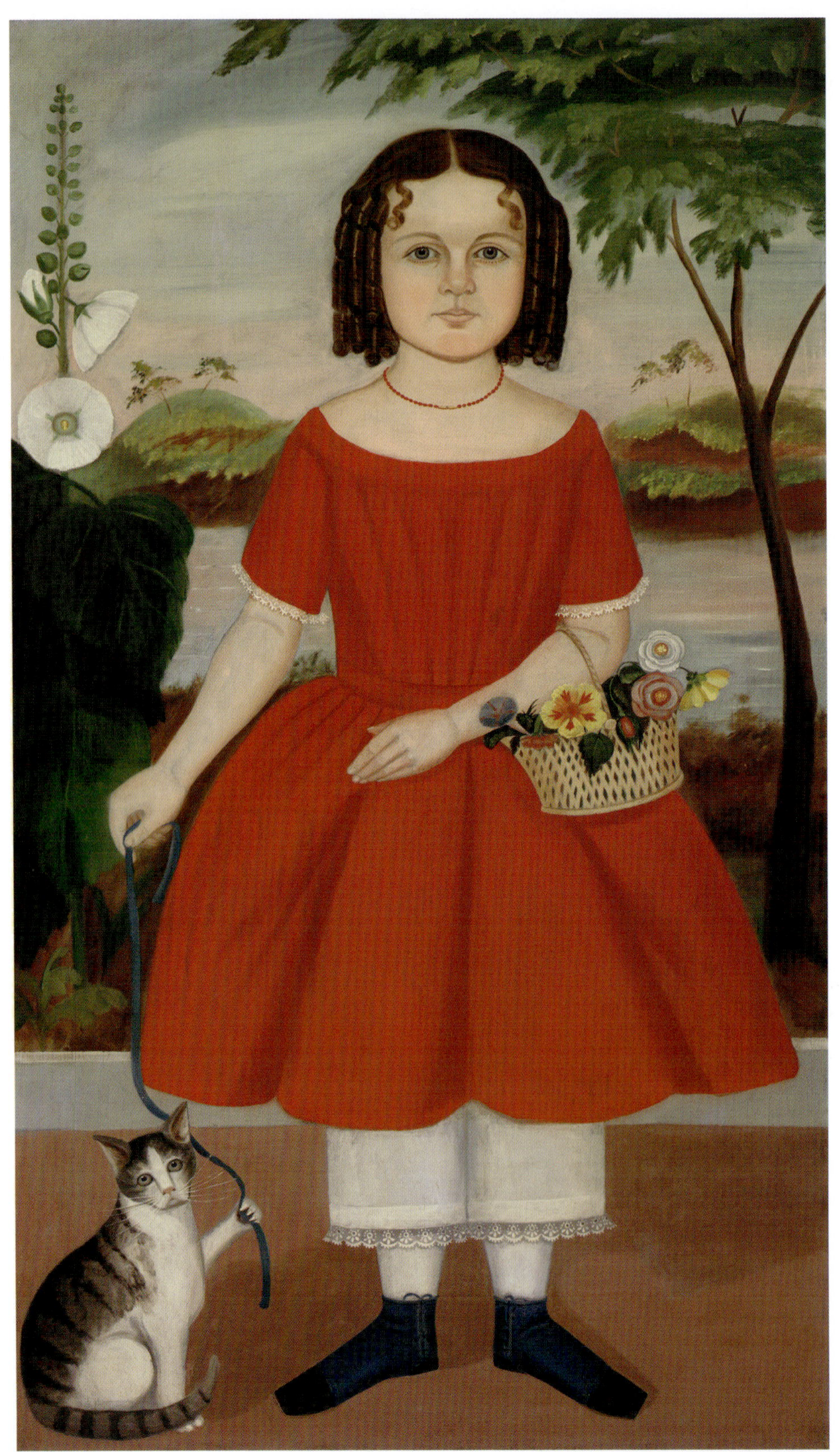

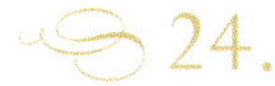 24.

PORTRAIT OF A YOUNG GIRL

By Samuel Miller (c. 1807–1853)

Oil on canvas, 101.6 × 68.6 cm (40 × 27 in.), c. 1845
Teresa Heinz Collection

THE UNIDENTIFIED young girl in this charming portrait faces straight ahead, her hair, dress, pantaloons, and feet symmetrically balanced in the composition. Her right arm is stretched out to our left, and she holds one end of a blue ribbon. A small cat plays with the other end of the ribbon, at her feet. Over her left arm is a basket of flowers. She is set against a brightly colored landscape of hollyhocks, a small tree, a body of water, and a sunset beyond some mountains. *Portrait of a Young Girl* is attributed to a little-known Massachusetts artist named Samuel Miller because of its similarity to his only signed portrait, *Emily Moulton* (Currier Museum of Art). The inscription on the reverse of that portrait reads: "Painted in 1852 by Mr. Miller who lived on the South Corner of Pearl and Bartlett Streets, Charlestown, Mass., U.S.A."[1] The city directory of Charlestown for 1852 lists a "Samuel Miller, portrait painter" at 70 Bartlett Street.[2] At that time an independent city, Charlestown became part of Boston in 1874.

Portrait of a Young Girl is strikingly similar to another portrait of a little girl that has been attributed to Miller, *Picking Flowers* (New York State Historical Association). In that portrait the little girl reaches with her right hand to pick a rose from a rosebush; a cat plays at her feet. As is true of this portrait, the sitter's identity is unknown. Miller is recognized today for his full-length portraits of children shown with a pet or an elaborate, detailed flower arrangement.[3] His figures are stiff and frontally posed, "generally with full-cheeked, squarish faces and prominent ears," as described by Carol Troyen. She continues, "The blue-green tinge to the flesh tones in these portraits, probably coming from the underpaint with which Miller prepared his canvases, is also typical."[4] Although a total of seventeen paintings have been attributed to Miller, no other documented works have been identified. Miller, the son of Robert and Ann Miller of Boston, died on October 18, 1853, at the age of forty-six, of heart disease.[5]

EGM

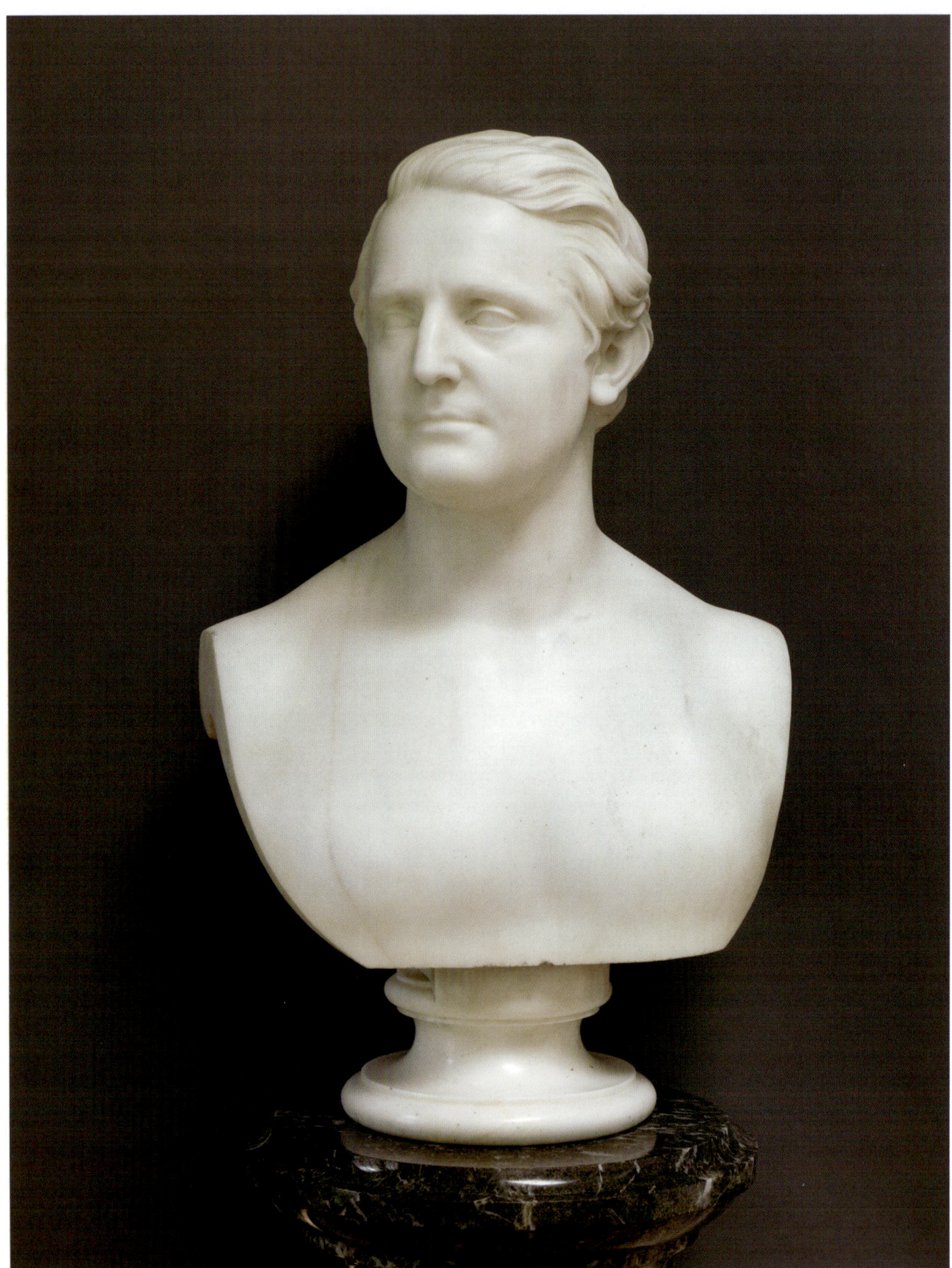

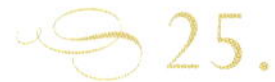

25.

ROBERT WICKLIFFE JR.

By Hiram Powers (1805–1873)

Marble, 69.2 cm (27¼ in.) height, with socle, c. 1846
Caroline Scott Despard

ROBERT WICKLIFFE Jr. (1816–1850) of Lexington, Kentucky, was a graduate of that city's Transylvania University. He served in the Kentucky legislature before going to Italy in 1843 as United States chargé d'affaires to the dukes of Savoy in Turin. He commissioned this portrait from American sculptor Hiram Powers, a Cincinnati artist who had settled in Florence in 1837, where he became one of the best-known American artists for his neoclassical sculptures, including *The Greek Slave* (1844). Powers also made a portrait of Wickliffe's wife, Josephine Van Houtum, whom Wickliffe met in Italy and married there in 1846.[1] The date of the original plaster models for the portraits is not known, but he probably made them around 1846.

Wickliffe's first documented contact with Powers occurred in 1844, when he recommended Powers to his brother-in-law, William Preston (1816–1887) of Louisville, as the sculptor for a statue for the city, explaining that "one of [Powers's] busts is worth fifty of Harding's portraits. . . . Since Thorwaldsen's death Powers has no rival as a sculptor." Wickliffe added that he had written a "critique on his statues," but was uncertain whether it had been published.[2] After Charles Edwards Lester, United States consul at Genoa, published a biography of Powers that caused Powers much embarrassment, Wickliffe encouraged Powers to write his own account of his contacts with Lester.[3] Powers, Wickliffe, and others also accused Lester of shipping Italian artwork to America without going through the proper customs channels.[4]

Wickliffe paid two hundred dollars as a down payment for the marble portrait, but the balance was left unpaid when he returned to Lexington in 1849. He died there the following year. The portrait was carved in 1857 in Seravezza marble.[5] In 1861, William Preston wrote Powers asking the sculptor to send the finished marble to him in Lexington. Powers wrote:

> I took great pains with it—for I regarded Mr. Wickliffe as one of my best friends. An unfortunate misunderstanding (in which I was drawn—not so much by any act of his own, but by the misconceptions of his Lady) broke off all communication between us—and I destroyed the model of Mrs. Wickliffe's bust which had also been ordered. The model of his own bust I preserved, for it is a noble head, and it gave me always a melancholy pleasure to contemplate it.[6]

Preston agreed to pay the three-hundred-dollar balance due on the commission but did not finally acquire the marble until 1866, after the Civil War.

EGM

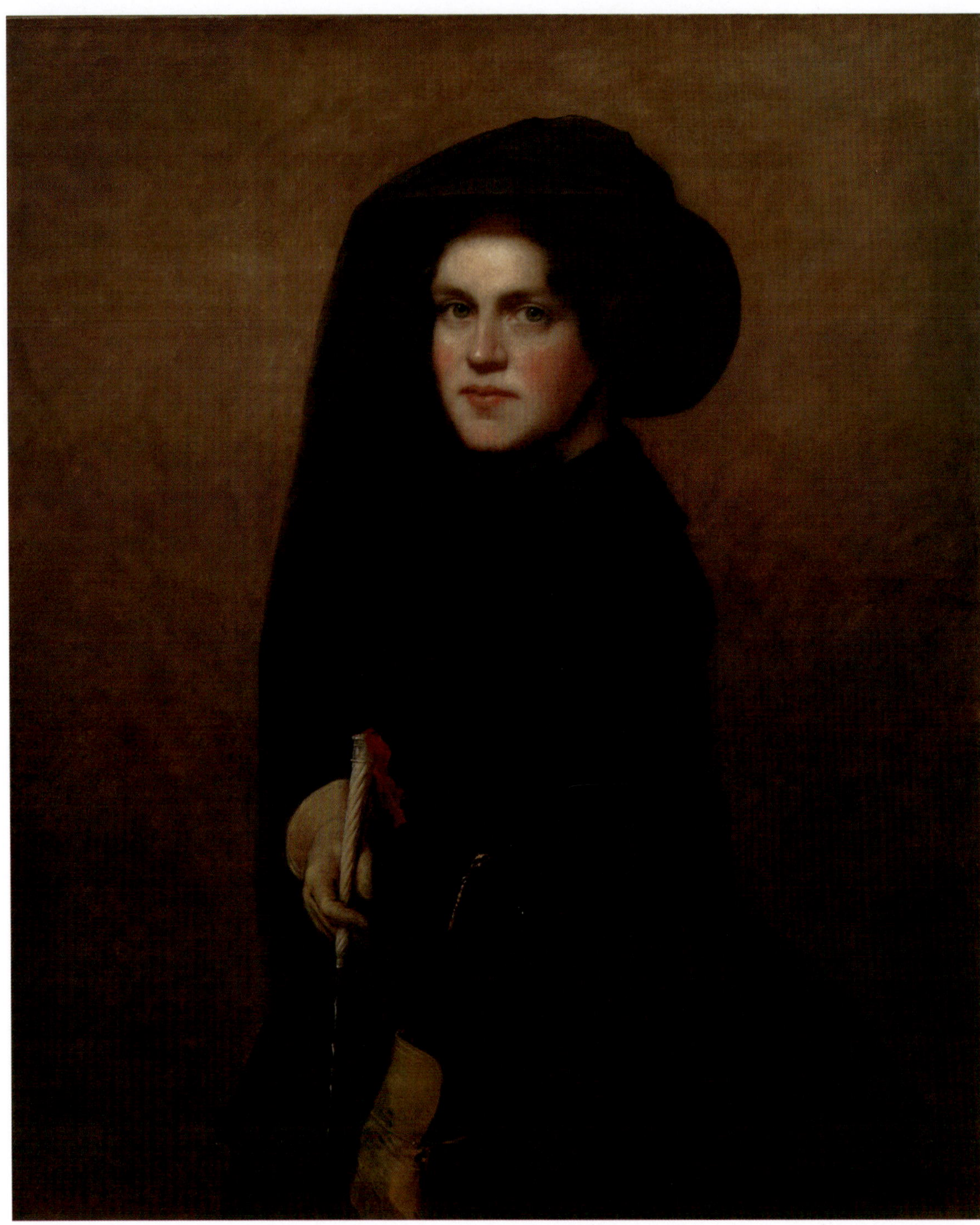

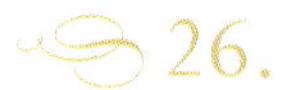 26.

SARAH OSGOOD JOHNSON NEWTON

By Eastman Johnson (1824–1906)

Oil on canvas, 89.5 × 72.4 cm (35¼ × 28½ in.), 1856
Sarah May Edmonds Broley

T HIS PORTRAIT of Sarah Osgood John-son Newton (1831–?) was painted by her brother Eastman Johnson in 1856, at the beginning of his long, successful career. Johnson was then living in Washington, D.C., where his parents had moved in 1846 from Maine.[1] After returning in 1855 from studying painting in Germany and Holland, he made a trip the following summer to Superior, Wisconsin, to visit his brother Reuben; Sarah; and her husband, William H. Newton, who had all recently settled there. That October he painted his sister's portrait. Sarah is seen turned to the viewer's left, dressed in a riding habit, with a black hat and veil and tan leather gloves. She holds an ivory-handled crop; its red ribbon adds a bright, decorative touch amid the predominately black and browns of the painting. A trace of red on her lips and cheeks offers additional luster, as does a small gold chain at her waist.[2] Her determined appearance seems characteristic. She was described a few months later as stalwart and ready for frontier life when she arrived in St. Paul in below-zero weather:

> The estimable lady of one of our first citizens came through last evening from Superior, and during the entire drive of three hundred miles, the thermometer ranged from 10 to 45 deg. below zero. Her external dress was a pair of buffalo boots, a buffalo over coat, a large otter cap and a pair of fur pantaloons into which she introduced herself, and enjoyed, we are assured,

a pleasant and comfortable trip. Let our territorial stage drivers be cautious, lest, among a barbarous load of genus homo, they may entertain some *Angels* unawares![3]

Johnson painted William Newton's portrait on the same visit (1856; St. Louis County Historical Society, Duluth), which curator Teresa Carbone has described as revealing a "man experiencing success."[4] He also made a charcoal study of Newton's sister, Mary Newton Hayes (1856; Museum of Fine Arts, Boston).

On his visit to Superior, the artist explored the area and invested in real estate in the growing frontier community, which had developed on land ceded by the Anishinabe (Ojibwa) to the United States government in 1854. He returned to Washington the following spring, but went back to Superior that summer to paint and sketch the Ojibwa, who had settled at nearby Grand Portage. After property values collapsed in Superior and his investments failed, he turned again to portraiture, spending part of the winter of 1857–58 in Cincinnati. In 1858 he settled in New York City. Among the works he had painted in Washington was *Negro Life at the South* (1859; New-York Historical Society), which brought him fame when it was exhibited in 1859 at the National Academy of Design. The rest of his long and very successful career as one of America's most creative post–Civil War artists was based in New York City.

EGM

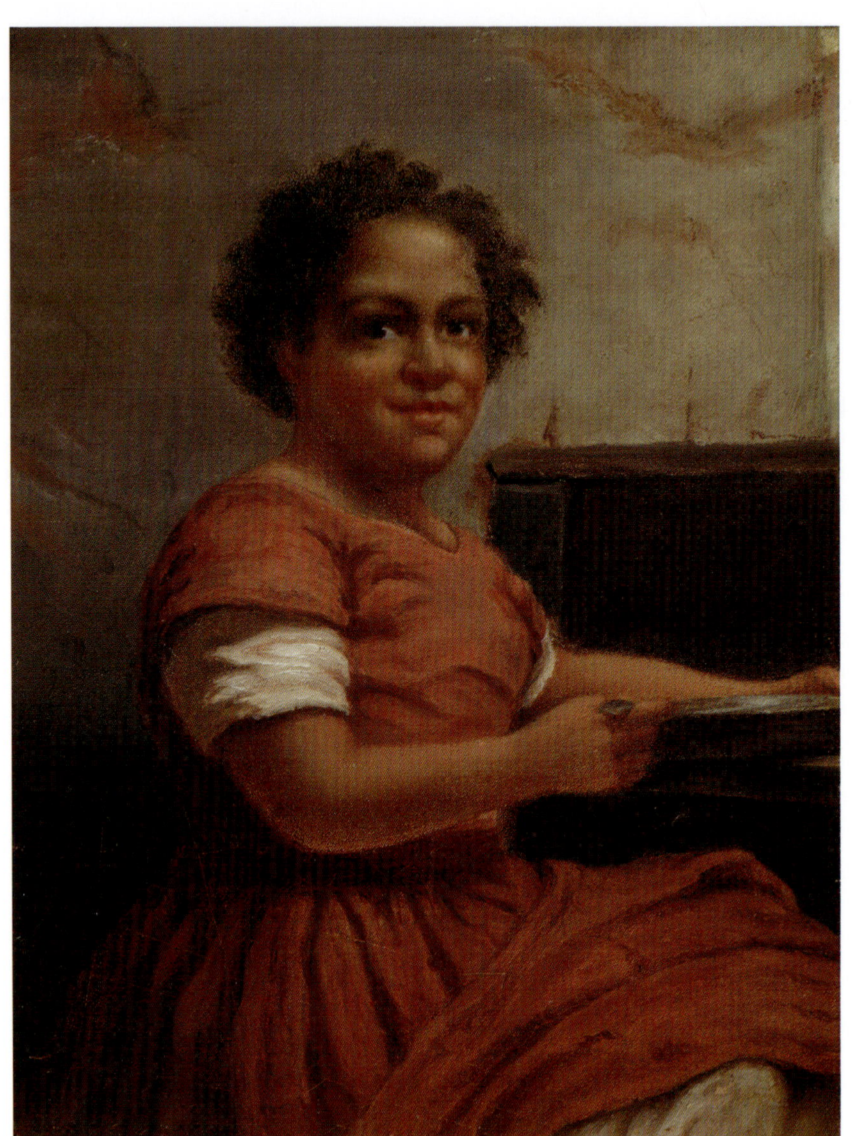

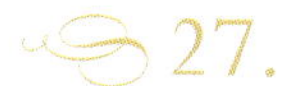

27.

HANNAH

By Eastman Johnson (1824–1906)

Oil on millboard, 21 × 15.9 cm (8¼ × 6¼ in.), c. 1859
Private collection

WHEN THIS small, sensitive portrayal of a young African American woman was discovered recently in North Carolina, it had no attribution, sitter identification, or known history.[1] The owners were able to identify the subject as "Hannah" from her similarity to the likeness of a young African American woman in a slightly larger painting, *Hannah Amidst the Vines* (cat. 27–1). That painting is signed "E. Johnson/ 1859." This portrait is clearly by the same artist, Eastman Johnson, and represents the same person, in the same red dress. In turn, the identity of Hannah in *Hannah Amidst the Vines* is confirmed by the listing of the painting in the catalogue of the artist's estate sale:

> Hannah Amidst the Vines. This is the study of a chubby-faced little negro child standing on a wooden balcony or piazza which is partly overgrown by a large grape vine. She rests her left arm on the rail of the balcony and shyly gazes out of her deep-set eyes towards the spectator.[2]

Patricia Hills and Teresa Carbone, who together recognized *Hannah Amidst the Vines* as the painting listed in the estate sale, included it in their exhibition of Johnson's work. To date Hannah has not been further identified.

Johnson depicted Hannah in the same year that he painted the twelve African Americans who are the subject of his important work, *Negro Life at the South* (1859; New-York Historical Society), exhibited to great acclaim in 1859 at the spring exhibition at the National Academy of Design in New York City. The painting, which became known as "Old Kentucky Home" almost as soon as it was exhibited, in fact depicts a scene in Washington, D.C., as Professor John Davis of Smith College recently documented. The view is of the backyard of a house, where African American adults and children are seen in everyday activities. Hannah is very similar to the figure on the right, dressed in blue, who looks directly at a white woman, one of the artist's sisters, as she enters the yard. The house that is depicted was located on F Street, in Northwest Washington, near the corner of Thirteenth Street. Johnson's parents and siblings lived next door at 266 F Street, which is the house visible on the right, through the trees. The two buildings, identified by John Davis, can be seen on a detailed city map of 1857.[3]

These paintings and others result from Johnson's focused interest on African American themes, a subject that occupied him after he rejoined his parents and sisters in Washington in 1855 on his return from studies in Germany and Holland. They express Johnson's sympathetic views of abolition and his awareness of the burdens of slavery. Another of Johnson's paintings of an African American, *The Freedom Ring* (1860; Hallmark Fine Art Collection, Kansas City, Missouri), depicts Rose Ward, a young girl who is seated on the floor, looking intently at the ring on her index finger. That painting memorializes an actual event: the

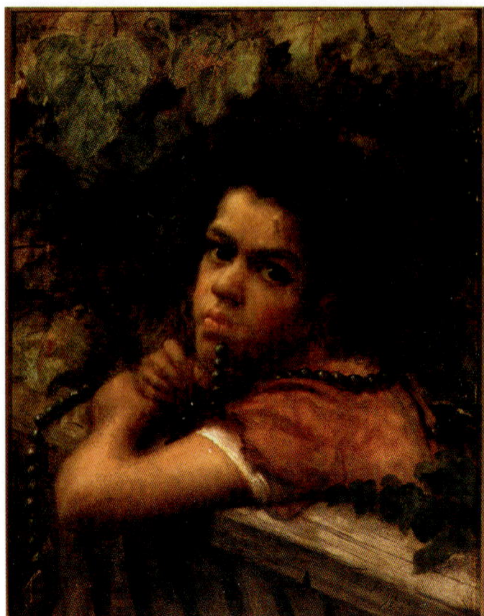

Cat. 27–1. *Hannah Amidst the Vines* by Eastman Johnson, oil on canvas, 1859. Georgetown University Library Special Collections Research Center, Washington, D.C.

purchase of the young girl's freedom by the congregation of the Plymouth Church in Brooklyn, led by the minister, Henry Ward Beecher, the brother of Harriet Beecher Stowe. During the collection of cash contributions, one member of the congregation, Rose Terry, offered a ring to help pay the cost. When it was discovered that sufficient money had been raised for the purchase, the ring was no longer needed and was given to the girl. She was then christened with the name Rose Ward, after Rose Terry and Henry Ward Beecher, and she became known as "Little Pinky."[4]

The Freedom Ring was exhibited in 1860 at the National Academy of Design with four other paintings by Johnson. One, *Kitchen at Mount Vernon* (1857; private collection) shows an African American woman with three small children in the brick kitchen of George Washington's Virginia home. Johnson also painted an outside view of Mount Vernon. Although the artist moved from Washington to New York in 1858, he continued to paint images in this vein through the Civil War years and into the late 1860s.

EGM

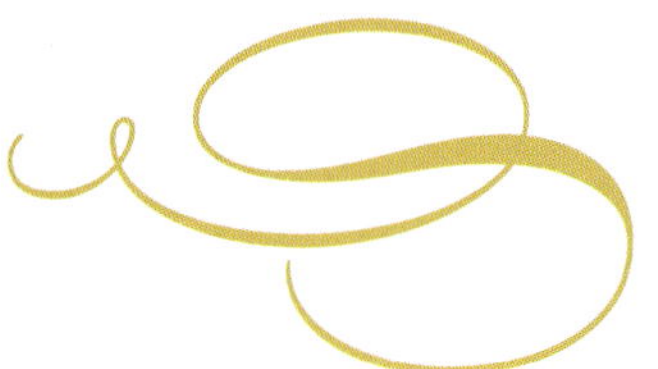

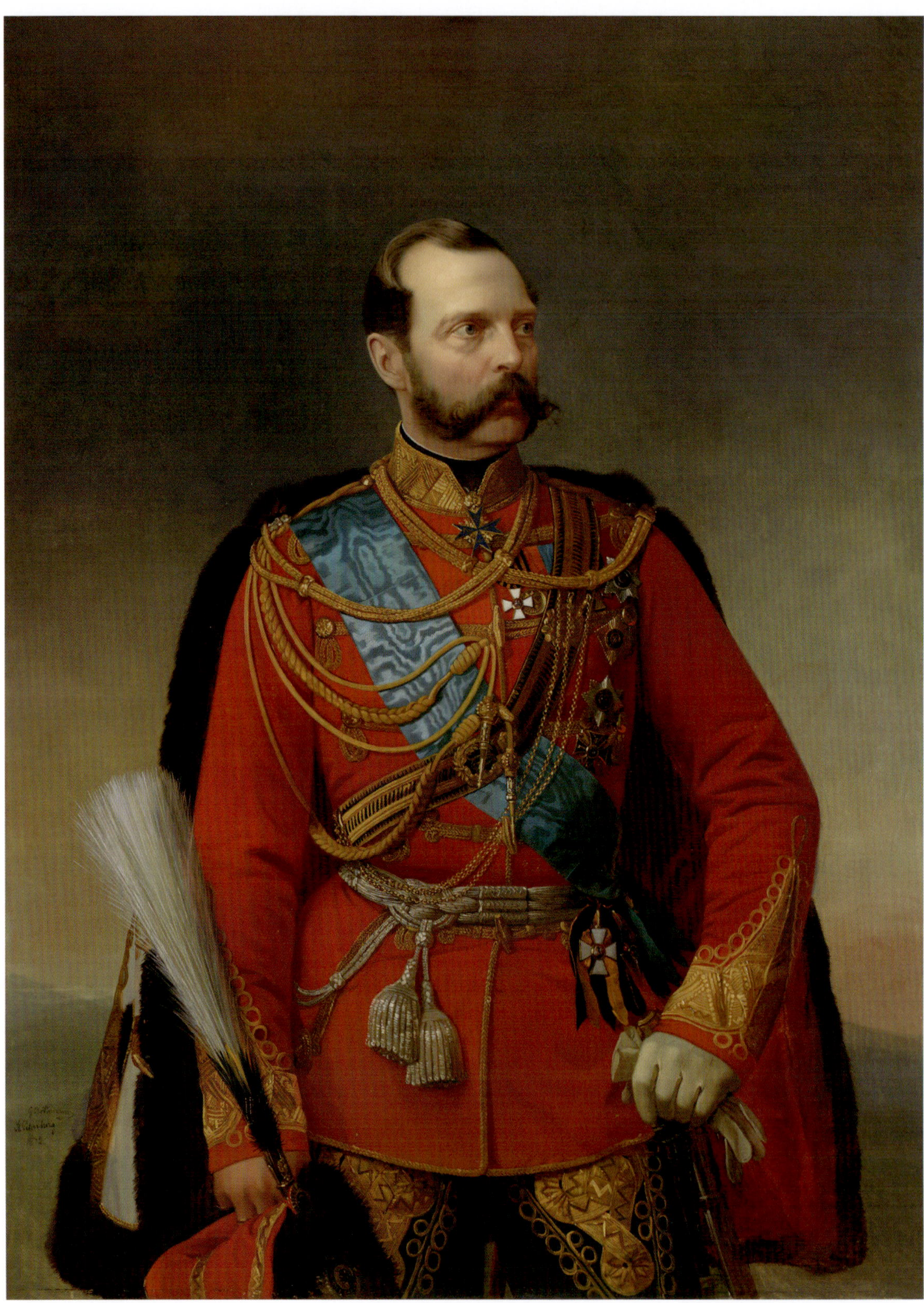

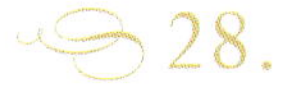 28.

CZAR ALEXANDER II OF RUSSIA

By Gregor Ivanovich Bothmann (d. 1891)

Oil on canvas, 182.9 × 137.2 cm (72 × 54 in.), 1872
Ambassador Curtin Winsor Jr.

ALEXANDER II (1818–1881) succeeded his father, Nicholas I, as czar of Russia in 1855, at the end of the Crimean War, and soon embarked on a series of reforms to modernize the country. The American ambassador to his court from 1869 to 1872 was Andrew Gregg Curtin (1815–1894), a political ally of Abraham Lincoln's. Elected governor of Pennsylvania in 1860 on the new Republican Party ticket, Curtin served until 1867. He then sought selection as the vice-presidential candidate to run with Ulysses S. Grant, but he was blocked by political opponents.[1] President Grant appointed Curtin as United States minister to Russia in 1869. No doubt he was popular with the czar, who was also an admirer of Lincoln's. Parallels in the careers of Lincoln and the czar are remarkable. Both men sought to free formerly enslaved peoples in and expand the territories of their respective countries. Both men faced violent opposition, Lincoln during the Civil War and Alexander through the actions of radical students, beginning in 1866 with the first attempt on the czar's life. Like Lincoln, the czar was assassinated, killed in 1881 by a terrorist bomb.[2]

This portrait was a gift to Curtin soon after he resigned his position as the United States minister in 1872 because of poor health. A letter from Russia's foreign minister, Prince Alexander Mikhailovich Gorchakov (1798–1883), to the ambassador, dated June 6, 1872, explains the origin of the portrait:

His Majesty the Emperor desiring to favor you with a special token of his high regard wished that on leaving Russia you would take his portrait.

It has been made per order of Her Imperial Majesty. She charged me to send it to you with the express desire that it stay forever in your family in honor of the consideration that you have always manifested toward Russia and of the legacies of respect and affection that you leave here.[3]

In 1905, upon the settlement of Curtin's estate, his son, W. W. Curtin of Philadelphia, proposed to the other heirs "that if they would give him the picture of the Czar he would renounce all claims to any further part of the estate" of his father. The portrait and the accompanying letter are now owned by his descendants.[4]

Gregor Ivanovich Bothmann, a painter from Lübeck, Germany, worked in St. Petersburg, Russia, from 1846 until at least 1879.[5] He is best known for his portraits of members of the Russian royal family. These portraits include the full-length likeness of Alexander II (1850; Helsinki University Museum),[6] a portrait of Alexander II's eldest son, Grand Duke Nicholas Alexandrovich (State Museum of Tsarskoye Selo, St. Petersburg),[7] and a full-length posthumous portrait of Alexander II's father, Emperor Nicholas I, in the uniform of a Cossack general, which was commissioned by Alexander II out of respect for the deceased czar.[8] Biographical information about Bothmann is scarce, but it is known that he was awarded the title of academician by the Russian Academy of Arts (then known as the Imperial Academy of Arts) in St. Petersburg in 1853 for his portrait of Nicholas I.[9]

EGM

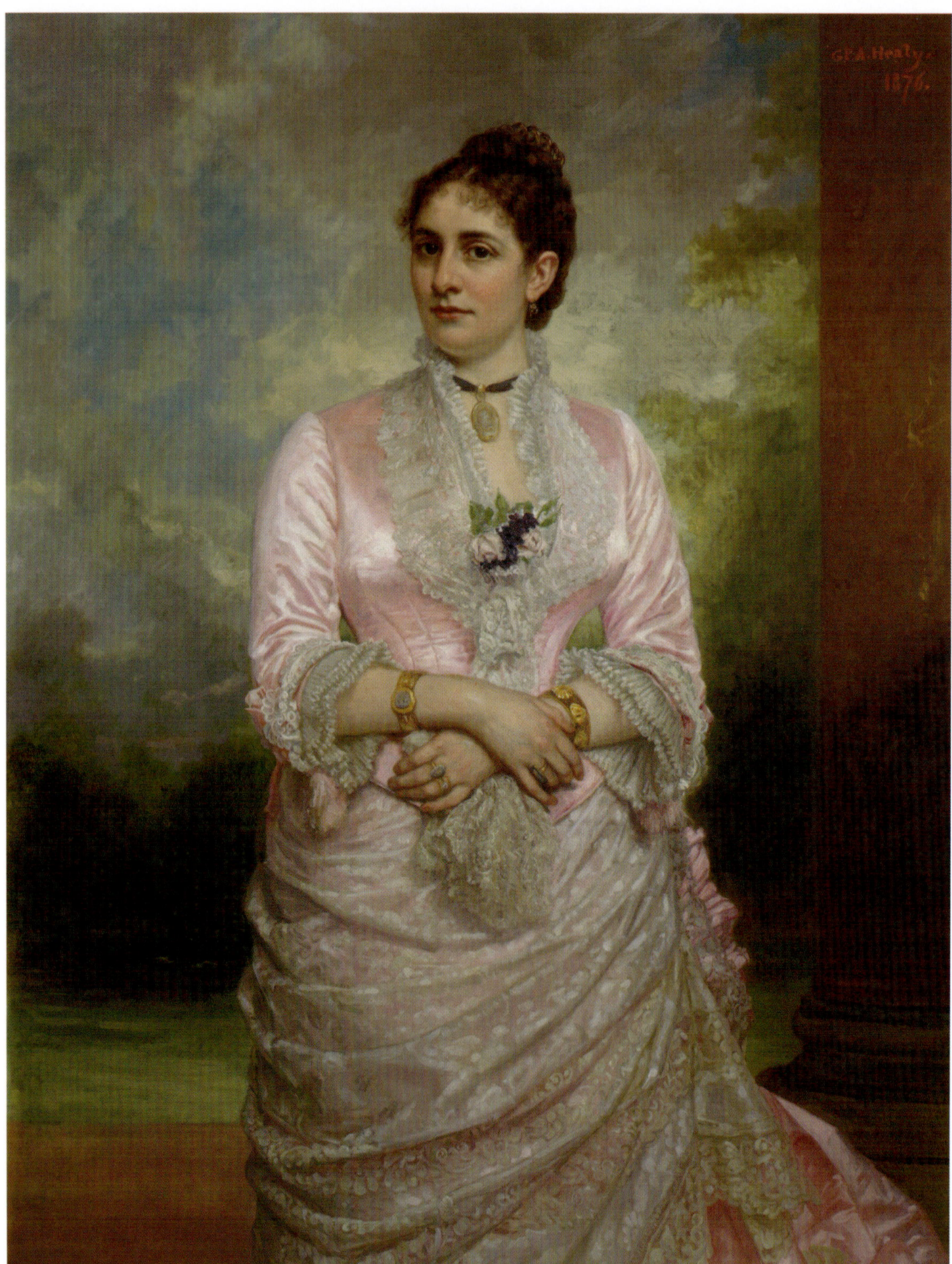
G.P.A.Healy.
1876.

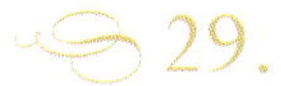

DELIA SPENCER CATON FIELD

By George Peter Alexander Healy (1813–1894)

Oil on canvas, 121.9 × 91.4 cm (48 × 36 in.) sight, 1876
Private collection

DELIA SPENCER (1853–1937),[1] the daughter of Chicago hardware tycoon Franklin F. Spencer, married Arthur J. Caton (1851–1904) on May 10, 1876. He was the son of state supreme court justice John Dean Caton, whose own wealth was a result of successful investments in the telegraph. After a lavish society wedding, the young Caton couple sailed for Europe on May 21, 1876, arriving back in New York on October 17.[2] On their return to Chicago they became the center of the city's social elite. Arthur Caton, a lawyer, was a well-known sportsman with a strong and lasting interest in horse racing. Delia, witty and outgoing, embraced her new life with energy and charm, entertaining friends at their home on Calumet Avenue, which became "one of the most fashionable in the city."[3] Her personal wealth soon merited her a positive report by the credit rating firm of R. G. Dun and Company.

Delia's husband commissioned her portrait from American artist George Peter Alexander Healy while the couple was in Paris on their honeymoon. Healy had painted portraits of Caton's parents and sister the previous spring in Chicago. Those of "Miss and Mrs. Caton" were exhibited at his gallery that May. One reviewer noted, "They are both works of art that possess a high degree of excellence."[4] One of the best-known and most admired American portrait painters of the era and himself a Chicago resident, Healy also maintained a studio in the French capital. The portrait exemplifies Healy's French training as well as Delia Caton's

sophistication. She stands in an outdoor setting, her head turned slightly to the side, as she looks flirtatiously at the viewer. Her pose, with her arms crossed, and her pink silk dress, which is elegantly draped with white lace, call attention to her curvaceous figure. A small bouquet of flowers is tucked in the bodice of the dress, its bright colors a contrast to her dark eyes and hair. She wears fine gold jewelry: two bracelets, a necklace, rings, and earrings.

As Healy noted in a letter he wrote to Mr. Caton in November, the portrait was delivered to their Chicago home that fall. "We were all happy to learn that you and Mrs. Caton arrived home safely," he wrote, "and also that Mrs Caton's portrait was so promptly in place. I trust by the time I have the good fortune to be settled in Chicago that none of your friends may wish for any change in the work that gave me so much pleasure to paint." He enclosed a receipt for Caton's payment: "[T]welve hundred and fifty dollars in gold for a Bishop's half length portrait of his wife Mrs. Arthur J. Caton; painted in Paris."[5] He closed by stating, "Present me warmly to your family on both sides." Healy thought so well of the painting of Delia Caton that he painted a copy for himself, which can be seen in a photograph of Healy's Paris studio (Archives of American Art) taken in the 1880s.[6]

A Bostonian by birth, Healy had gone to Paris initially in 1834; he studied briefly with French artist Antoine-Jean Gros and became friends with Thomas Couture. As his fame grew, King Louis-Philippe commissioned him to return to America to copy existing portraits of all of the American presidents, among them one of the versions of Gilbert Stuart's "Lansdowne" portrait of George Washington. Healy's ability to create successful images of statesmen, military figures, society ladies, and their families would make him one of the most popular portraitists of the mid-nineteenth century. In 1856, Healy moved to Chicago, where he maintained a busy portrait studio during the Civil War. He returned to Europe in 1867, settling in Paris in 1872. Having become a painter of international fame, he worked in Europe and America until 1892, when he returned permanently to Chicago.[7]

Delia Caton's marriage to Arthur Caton was apparently not a happy one. Within a year of her husband's death in 1904, she married Marshall Field (1834–1906), one of Chicago's wealthiest businessmen, in London. A multimillionaire, Field had established himself by the mid-1860s as one of America's foremost retailers.[8] The Caton couple had socialized frequently with Field,

who lived in a house designed by Richard Morris Hunt on Prairie Avenue, directly behind the home of Arthur and Delia, and had often traveled with him to Europe. An article of 1905 that described Delia as "second to none in Chicago society" noted that she had inherited her first husband's estate as well as property from her father. Field's worth at the time was estimated at more than $100 million.[9] It has more recently been acknowledged that she and Field became lovers after the death of Field's first wife in 1896. The jewelry she wears in the portrait was painted out after she married Field.[10] Their marriage was tragically short-lived, however, as Field died less than a year after the wedding. Delia Field, who inherited nothing of Field's fortune, moved to Washington, D.C., and spent the remaining years of her life as a well-known hostess to ambassadors, senators, and cabinet members in her large house on Sixteenth Street, known as the Pink Palace.[11]

EGM

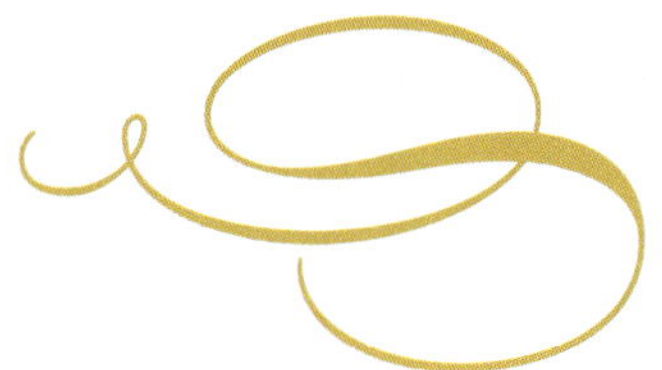

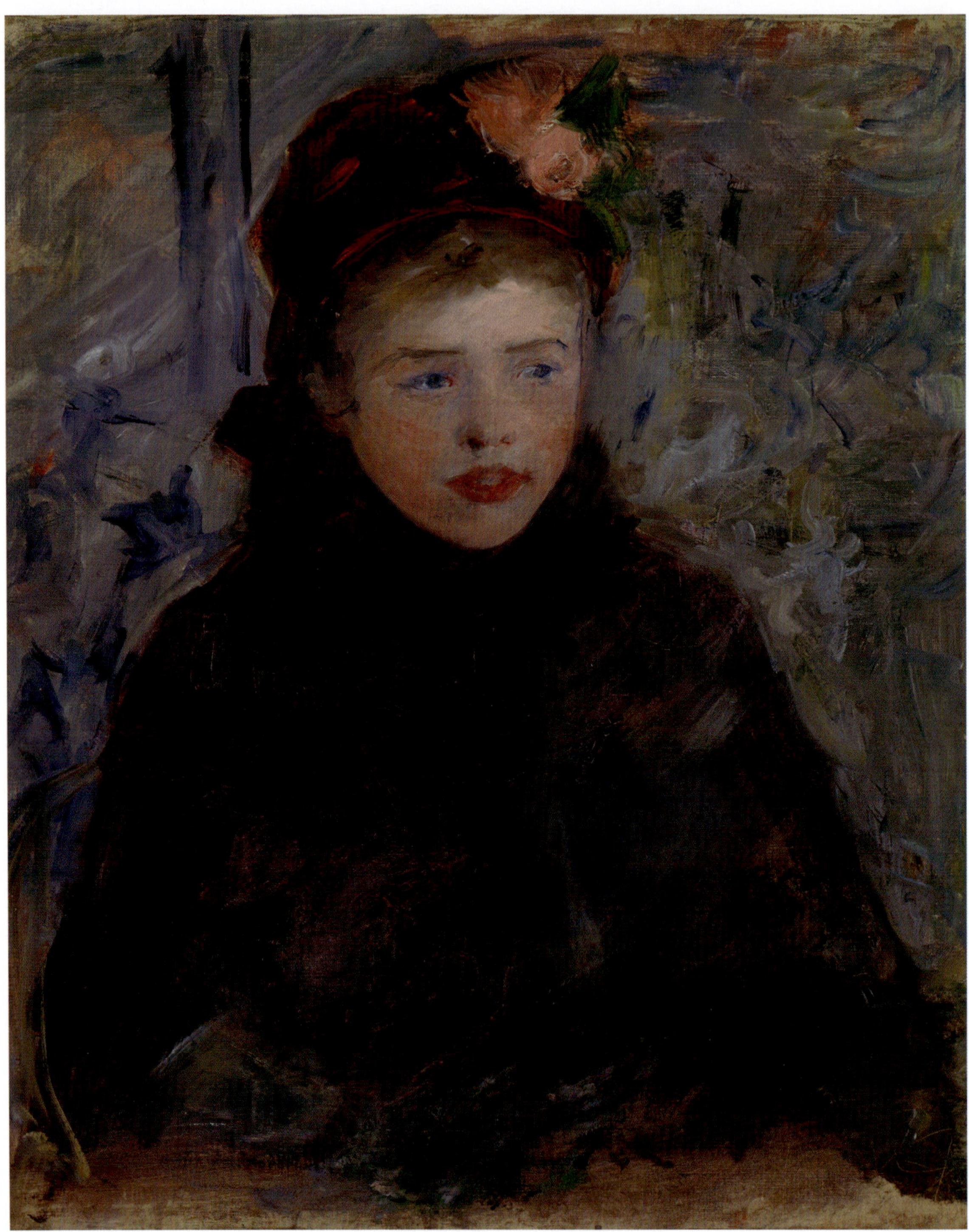

SUSAN IN TOQUE WITH ROSES
By Mary Cassatt (1844–1926)

Oil on canvas, 63.5 × 53.3 cm (25 × 21 in.), c. 1881
Joan and Bernard Carl Collection

MARY CASSATT, known for her evocative portraits of children that depict their youthful innocence and zest for life, vividly captures these qualities in her portrait of Susan Valet, thought to be the cousin of her Alsatian-born housekeeper Mathilde Valet.[1] The brilliant touches of color and the animated brushstrokes of the background that Cassatt employs in this painting speak to the artist's evolving style. Her work was influenced by her familiarity with the work of various impressionist painters, among them Claude Monet, Camille Pissarro, Pierre-Auguste Renoir, and Edgar Degas.

Mary Stevenson Cassatt was born near Pittsburgh, in Allegheny City, Pennsylvania, but grew up in the Philadelphia area. At age fifteen she entered the Pennsylvania Academy of the Fine Arts. Ambition, as well as travels with her wealthy family at a young age, led her to seek further training in Paris, then considered the capital of the international art world. In 1866, she began her studies with Jean-Léon Gérôme, an academic artist known for his religious and history paintings who taught many aspiring American artists, including Thomas Eakins. In the summer of 1870, at the beginning of the Franco-Prussian War, Cassatt returned to America. In the fall of 1872, shortly after the war ended, she went back to Europe, deciding in 1874 to live permanently in France. Although she undertook a major mural for the Women's Building at the 1893 World's Columbian Exposition in Chicago, had

solo shows in New York, and exhibited in various group exhibitions in the United States, she returned to America only twice before her death, in 1898 and in 1908.[2]

Edgar Degas, who befriended Cassatt in the late 1870s, had a major impact on her work and was crucial to her acceptance among the avant-garde artists in Paris known as the impressionists. In 1879, Degas invited her to exhibit in the fourth exhibition of the impressionists; she again showed with them in 1880, 1881, and 1886. Degas described her as having "infinite talent." She said of him, "The first sight of Degas['s] pictures was the turning point in my life."[3] As her mentor, he taught her printmaking and introduced her to Japanese prints and their unique spatial perspective. He also imparted to her his attitude toward subject matter. Eschewing the academic approach of the posed portrait, Degas sought instead to render the figure in both ordinary and transient moments, as if caught by the lens of a camera. He encouraged Cassatt to compose her canvases in a like manner and abandon the last vestiges of her academic training by applying paint more freely. Cassatt immediately gravitated toward the new approach. In the portrait of Susan Valet, a sense of immediacy and spontaneity shows in the young teenager's pose and in the painterly treatment of the background and costume of the sitter.

CKC

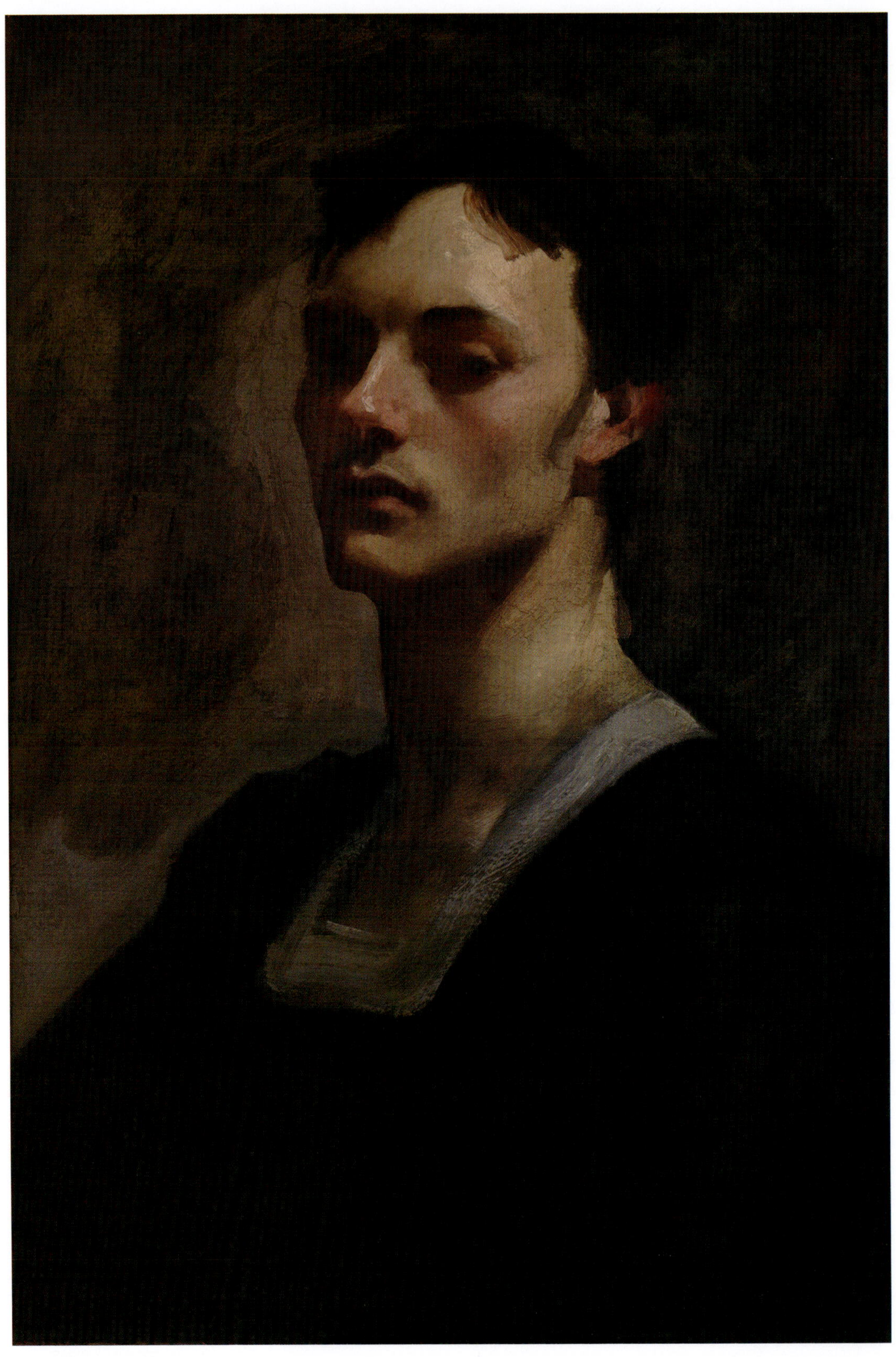

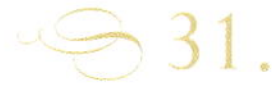

31

ALBERT DE BELLEROCHE

By John Singer Sargent (1856–1925)

Oil on canvas, 63.5 × 41.9 cm (25 × 16½ in.), 1883
Private collection

JOHN SINGER SARGENT painted this stunning image of his friend, artist Albert de Belleroche (1864–1944), in Paris during the early years of his long, successful career. Sargent had recently received acclaim for *El Jaleo* (1882; Isabella Stewart Gardner Museum), a large painting of Spanish musicians and dancers, when it was exhibited at the Salon of 1882. He was now at work on a portrait of Virginie Avegno, Mme. Gautreau, which would obtain notoriety at the Salon of 1884 for its hauteur and risqué dress and pose; it is now known by its Salon title, *Madame X* (The Metropolitan Museum of Art).[1] Belleroche, the son of Edmund Charles, Marquess de Belleroche, and Alice Sidonie Vandenburg Baruch, was a student of French artist Charles-Emile-Auguste Durand (1838–1917; known as Carolus-Duran). He met Sargent in 1882 at an annual dinner given for Carolus-Duran, who had been Sargent's teacher in the 1870s when he was at the École des Beaux-Arts. Sargent's nickname for him was "Baby Milbank," because Belleroche was then using the last name of his stepfather, Harry Vane Milbank, who had married Belleroche's mother in 1871.

Sargent made four paintings and four drawings of Belleroche, all head-and-shoulder images (one is a caricature) in 1882 and 1883.[2] He painted this portrait during the summer of 1883, at the same time he was at work on the portrait of Mme. Gautreau. The challenges of painting at Les Chênes, her estate at Paramé, were considerable, and Sargent occasionally returned to his new studio in Paris at 41 boulevard Berthier. There he painted this work, which was initially planned as a larger image. Belleroche later described its initial appearance:

> Amongst the other pictures which Sargent painted in this new studio, I will mention a three-quarter life-size portrait of a young man in Florentine costume. This picture which was originally intended to represent an Italian gentleman holding a large double-handed sword, was finally cut down to the bust and the theatrical accoutrements removed. Sargent considered this portrait one of his best studies. . . . With the exception of the portrait of Madame Gautreau, I do not believe that Sargent ever had so many sittings as for this portrait.[3]

In the only known sketch for the large composition (Yale University Art Gallery), the figure of Belleroche is turned to the viewer's right, and his right arm is raised. The painting retains the pose, in reverse, together with the square-necked shirt, but the resulting image focuses on the sitter's strong face and bone structure, dramatically lit from the side and outlined against the dark background. Sargent's extraordinary talent for observing and capturing a telling moment produced this decidedly personal image.

Sargent's images of Belleroche have recently received close study. The artist's great-nephew, Richard Ormond, in his catalogue raisonné of Sargent's paintings, was the first to suggest that Belleroche might have been the subject of a profile drawing long thought to represent Mme. Gautreau (c. 1883; Yale University Art Gallery). The drawing shows a head in profile, and agrees in pose with a painting of Mme. Gautreau that depicts her seated at a table. But the drawing also shows details suggesting that it instead represents Belleroche. Art historian Dorothy Moss has elaborated on this proposal: "The apparent gender-blurring that scholars have noticed in the Yale sketch is indicative of the intense level of desire that went into his portrait of Gautreau through Belleroche."[4] The similarity between images of a man and a woman as drawn by Sargent brings up unresolved questions about Sargent's sexual orientation; he never married, but there is no sign that his attraction to Belleroche was sexual rather than sensual. The two remained friends after Sargent moved to London following the *Madame X* scandal. Belleroche became a skilled lithographer and, on a trip to London,

showed Sargent some of his work, leading to Sargent's experimentation with the medium. Among Sargent's rare lithographs are two portraits of Belleroche. About Sargent, Belleroche wrote: "Sargent's boldness and his masterly brush strokes were only the outcome of a great gift—I may say unique to him—of a wonderful rapidity of vision by which he could throw his work on the canvas in a very short time, which enabled him to finish his work quickly without losing the freshness of his first impression."[5] The painting of Belleroche remained one of Sargent's favorite images; he hung it in his Tite Street (London) dining room. Belleroche's son, Count William de Belleroche, wrote the owner of the portrait in 1948 that Sargent had told him, "when I was taken to meet him at Tite Street that he considered your picture the best portrait of a man he had painted."[6]

EGM

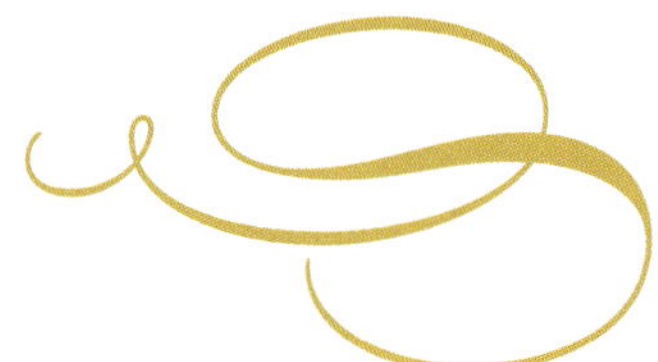

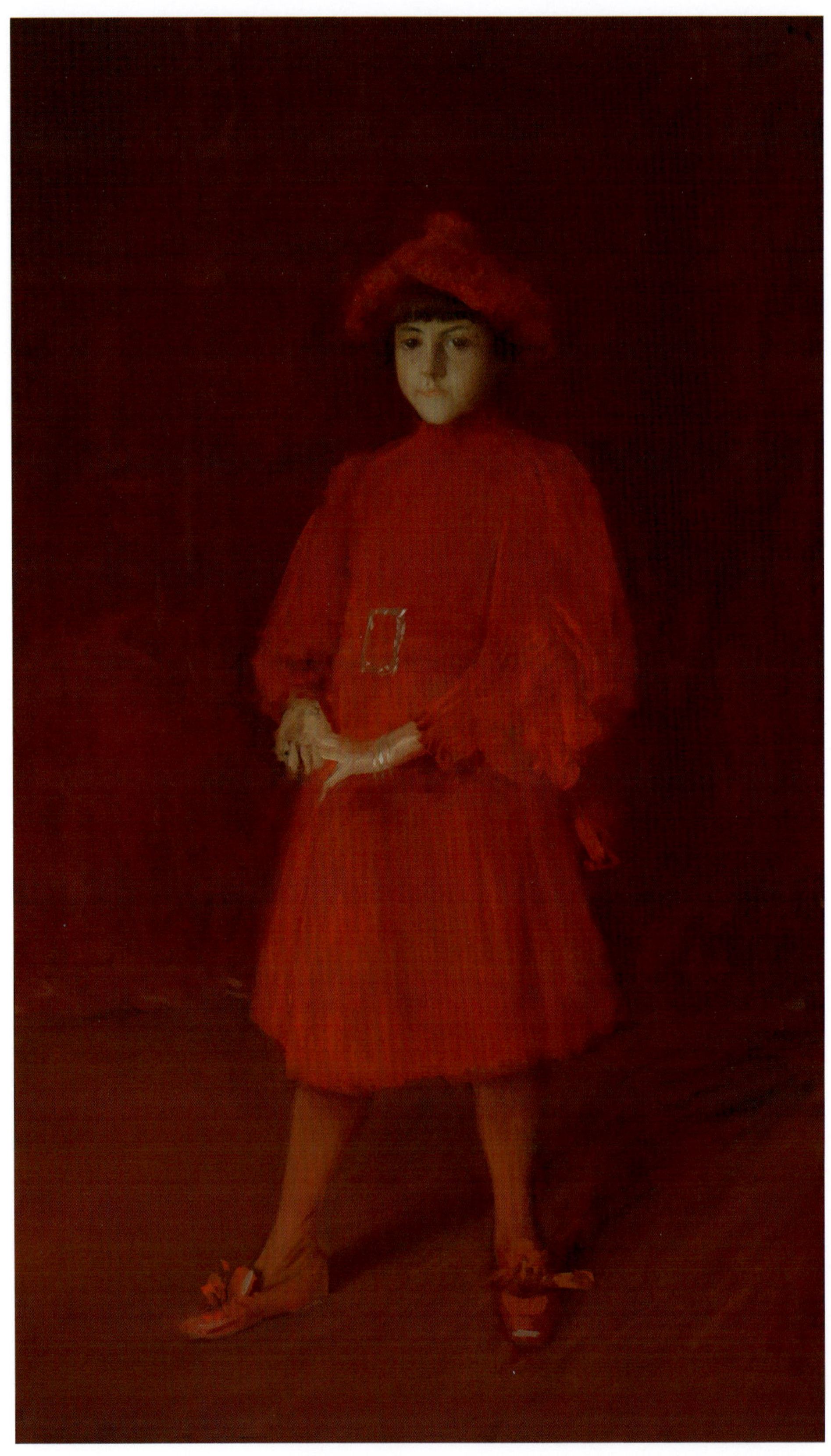

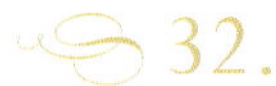

32

PORTRAIT OF MY DAUGHTER (DOROTHY BRÉMOND CHASE)

By William Merritt Chase (1849–1916)

Oil on canvas, 147.2 × 86.4 cm (58 × 34 in.), 1899
Teresa Heinz Collection

WILLIAM MERRITT Chase, one of America's leading late-nineteenth-century artists, was born in Indiana and grew up in Indianapolis, where his interest in drawing led to an apprenticeship with local painter Barton S. Hays. After training at the National Academy of Design, New York, in 1869–71, Chase studied in Germany at the Munich Royal Academy from 1872 to 1878. He then returned to the United States and taught at the Art Students League in New York City for eighteen years. His Tenth Street studio became a popular meeting place for artists and patrons. Beginning in the summer of 1891, Chase also conducted classes at the art colony of Shinnecock Hills, near Southampton, Long Island. He and his wife, Alice Gerson, whom he had married in 1886, moved there the following summer, into a house and studio designed by Stanford White. For the next decade, Chase and his family would spend the summers there.[1]

While most of the paintings that Chase made at Shinnecock are landscapes, he also painted canvases showing interiors of the house and studio, many of which include his wife and their young daughters. This portrait represents their daughter Dorothy Brémond Chase (1891–1953) at about age eight. She is entirely in red, wearing a dress with a pleated neckline and pleated sleeves, a red belt and red stockings, red shoes with bows, and a conical hat. The styling of the clothes and hat are dramatic in shape as well as color, and the shoes are reminiscent of the slippers worn by men in seventeenth-century Dutch or Spanish portraits. Her dark hair and eyes, and her silver belt buckle and silver bracelets, are the only contrast.[2] Chase had earlier experimented with a daring use of red in the painting variously titled *Study of a Young Girl, An Idle Moment,* or *At Her Ease* (1884; National Academy of Design), submitted to the National Academy of Design in 1890 as his diploma presentation piece.[3] In his use of single colors, Chase was no doubt influenced by the monochromatic works of his friend, the painter James McNeill Whistler.

Dorothy may be depicted dressed for a "tableau vivant" or "living picture," a popular form of home entertainment at which family and friends enacted famous paintings or historical scenes. Betty Fisher, daughter of the Chases' family physician and a family friend, created costumes for elaborate productions of this type at Shinnecock.[4] In the portrait, the subdued reddish background has touches of black that suggest the folds of a curtain, and the shadows cast by her legs hint at a stage with footlights. Also, her gesture—resting the fingers of her left hand against her open right palm, as if counting or narrating—points to a dramatic context. That this is a theatrical piece is further indicated by several photographs of Dorothy that show her alternately wearing an Arabic robe, a kimono, an eighteenth-century flowered silk dress, and a Turkish dress with a gauze shawl and a jeweled tiara. One photograph shows her peeking out between the folds of a theatrical curtain.[5] Chase often painted his daughters in these costumes.[6] One of Chase's best-known portraits, *My Little Daughter Helen as an Infanta* (1899; Joel R. and Mary Ellen Strote), imitates the work of the seventeenth-century Spanish artist Diego Velázquez, whom he much admired. The painting represents his four-year-old daughter (whose middle name was Velázquez) in a dress that imitates the one worn by the Spanish Infanta Margarita of Austria in a portrait of her once attributed to Velázquez (c. 1665; Museo del Prado).[7] Chase's patron, Mrs. Henry Kirke Porter, commissioned the portrait "after seeing the artist's daughter posed in a tableau in this costume, which Mr. Chase brought from Spain."[8] Chase painted the portrait of Helen in 1899, probably the year he made this one of Dorothy.

Portrait of My Daughter (Dorothy Brémond Chase) was included in the exhibition "Paintings by William Merritt Chase" held at the Mahoning Institute of Art, the forerunner of the Butler Institute of American Art, in Youngstown, Ohio, in 1916. A letter from J. G. Butler Jr. to the artist discusses the exhibition and a lecture.[9] The portrait was sold as "Artist's Daughter" in the sale of Chase's estate in 1917.[10] Acquired by the Butler Institute, it was shown in the museum's inaugural exhibition in October 1919. In December 1967 the Butler Institute deaccessioned the portrait, perhaps because the museum had a second painting by Chase of one of his daughters (probably Alice), titled *Did You Speak to Me?*, which he had painted at Shinnecock in about 1897.[11] The Heinz family acquired *Portrait of My Daughter* from the Kennedy Galleries in New York in May 1968.

EGM

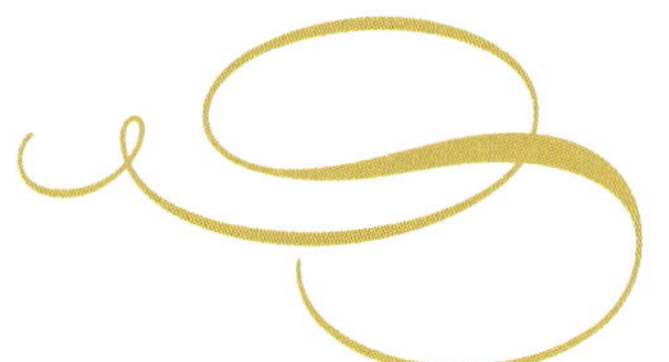

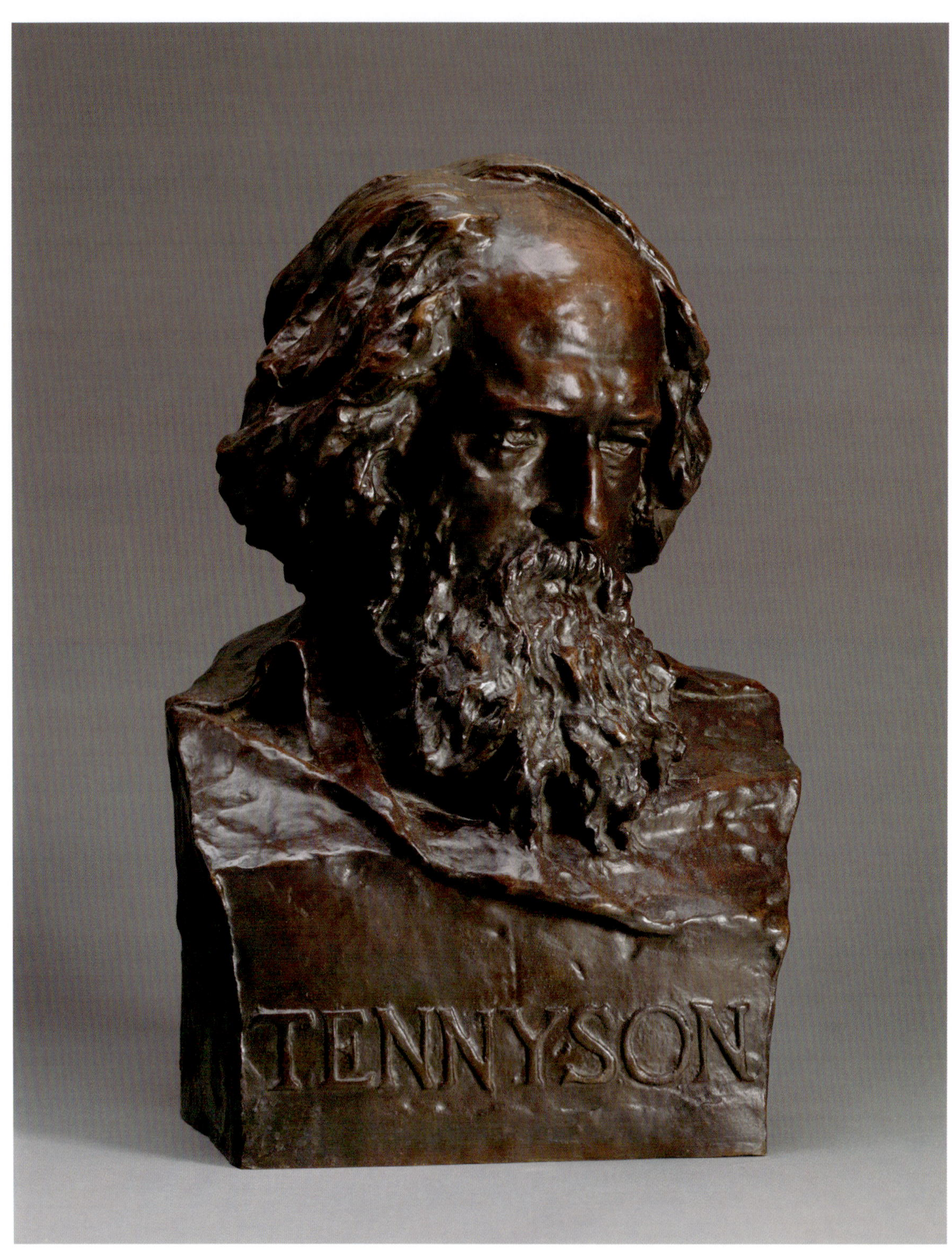

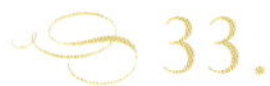

33.

ALFRED, LORD TENNYSON
By William Ordway Partridge (1861–1930)

Bronze, 53.3 cm (21 in.), copyright 1899
D. Dodge Thompson

BORN IN PARIS, France, to American parents, William Ordway Partridge became a sculptor after considering a literary profession. When he exhibited ten sculptures at the World's Columbian Exposition in Chicago in 1893, critics praised his work, particularly the study for a statue of Alexander Hamilton. That success led to commissions for the public sculptures for which he is best known today, among them an equestrian statue of Ulysses S. Grant (Grant Square, Brooklyn) and full-length bronze figures of Alexander Hamilton (Hamilton Grange, New York, and Columbia University, New York City). He also created a portrait relief of James Smithson (bronze, Pembroke College, Oxford University) commissioned by the Regents of the Smithsonian. In his writings and lectures Partridge promoted the concept of an American school of sculpture. He also wrote two novels, poetry, and a character study, *Nathan Hale: The Ideal Patriot . . .* (1902).[1]

This portrait of Alfred, Lord Tennyson (1809–1892) was one of a number of busts that Partridge made of writers and poets. The portrait was based on a life sitting: "[T]he sculptor was extremely fortunate in the advantage he enjoyed in preparing Tennyson's bust, as he passed a day with the poet and was thus able to work from life."[2] Copyrighted in 1899, seven years after Tennyson's death, the bronze casts are inscribed with the poet's name in capital letters on the front. They are variously signed and dated, and some signatures include the copyright date. This example is signed "W. Ordway Partridge S[c]" below his left shoulder, and "AUBRY BRO'S FOUNDERS, N.Y." is inscribed below his right shoulder. Seven bronzes (including this example), three plasters, and two versions in marble are known.[3] Partridge made one bronze for the library of Patrick Anderson Valentine of New York, together with bronze busts of Robert Burns and Percy Bysshe Shelley. Valentine—a partner of Philip Armour, founder of the Chicago meatpacking firm of Armour & Company—married Armour's widow in 1902, and the couple moved to New York City. That year, he commissioned from Partridge a group in marble and bronze that represented Homer reciting from the *Iliad*. In 1912, Valentine commissioned Patridge to make bronze busts of composers Richard Wagner and Ludwig van Beethoven for his music room.[4]

Tennyson is considered the leading poet of the Victorian age in England. Elegies written on the death of his college friend Arthur Hallam in 1833, published anonymously in 1850 with the title *In Memoriam*, and his friendships with Queen Victoria, William Gladstone, and Thomas Carlyle led to his appointment as poet laureate. He was elevated to the peerage in 1884. Tennyson wrote "Crossing the Bar," which became his most famous single poem, during a voyage across the English Channel to his home on the Isle of Wight in 1889. Henry Van Dyck of Princeton, New Jersey, who owned one of the marble versions of the portrait, stated: "This is essentially the head of the music-master of any age. The spirit's impatient, patient battle with the eternal drag of material things is written on these features. That Tennyson fought the battle well is known in his long life, his great work. The record of the fight is written in this face."[5]

EGM

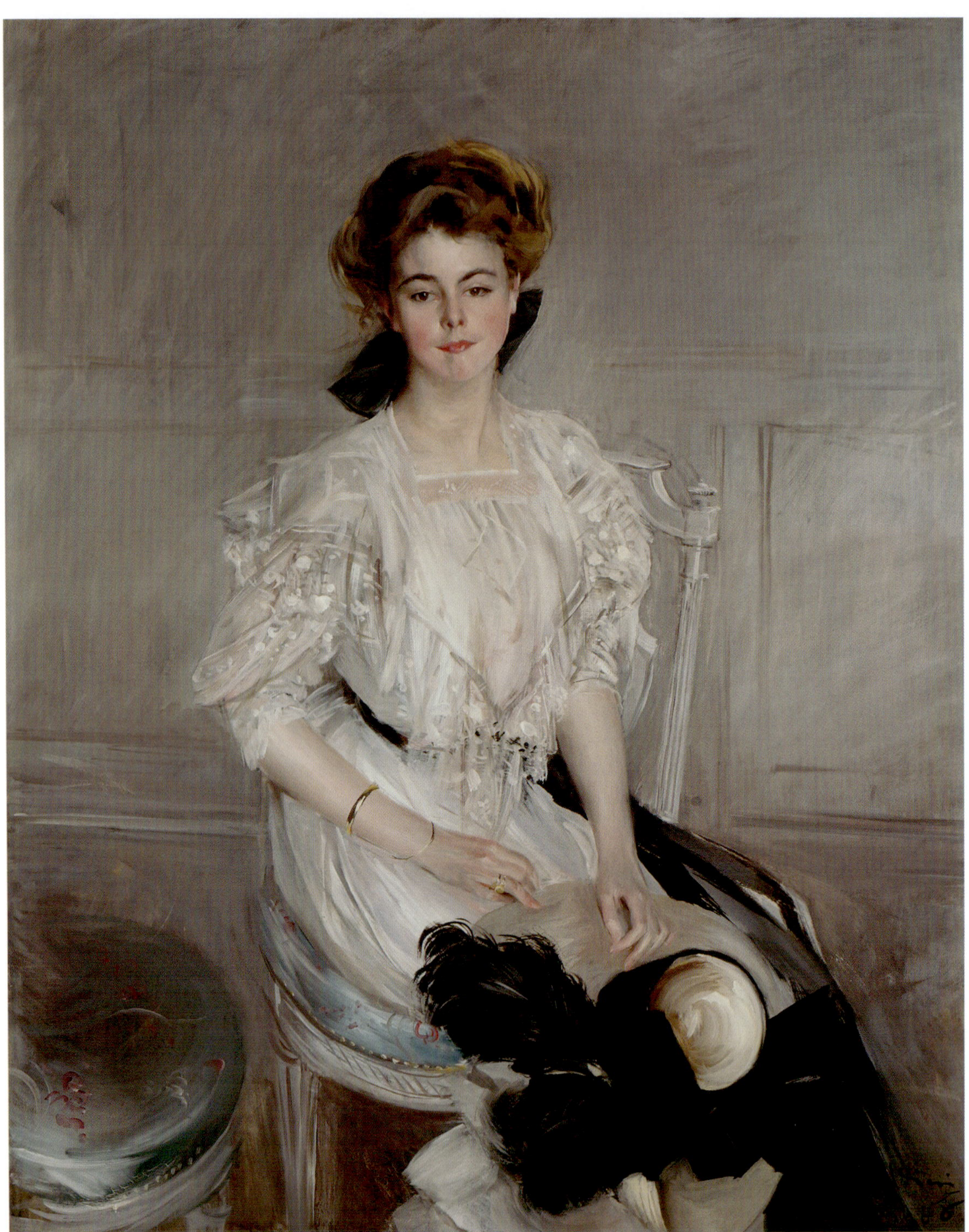

34

ETHEL MARY CROCKER (COUNTESS DE LIMUR)

By Giovanni Boldini (1842–1931)

Oil on canvas, 145.7 × 116.8 cm (57⅜ × 46 in.), 1906
Private collection

ITALIAN-BORN Giovanni Boldini was living in Paris and was at the height of his artistic powers and reputation when Mrs. William H. Crocker (1863–1934), who was then living in San Francisco, commissioned him to paint her oldest daughter and namesake, Ethel Mary (1891–1964).[1] Mrs. Crocker's choice of Boldini for her daughter's portrait was probably not a random one, as she was clearly a knowledgeable connoisseur of art of the period. The Crockers had a substantial collection of contemporary French paintings, including works by Jean-Baptiste-Camille Corot, Edgar Degas, Jean-François Millet, Camille Pissarro, Pierre Puvis de Chavannes, and Pierre-Auguste Renoir, and she is given credit for introducing impressionism into California in the early 1890s.[2]

Boldini, the son of a painter, moved to Paris in 1871, after first visiting that major artistic center at the time of the 1867 Exposition Universelle. An affable as well as talented individual, Boldini almost immediately became part of the avant-garde in Paris. He befriended important artists such as Degas and Édouard Manet and fellow portrait-painters Paul César Helleu, John Singer Sargent, and James McNeill Whistler. As early as 1874, he won critical acclaim with his first entry into the Salon de Champs du Mars. His clients, among them the Duchess of Marlborough, came from the most fashionable ranks of international society. Boldini's portraits were noted for their carefully executed faces bathed in a gentle light and their fluid and swift brushwork, which he used to render the costume of the sitter. As here, his subjects were usually depicted as if the artist were working from a slightly lower vantage point, lending the subject an inherent elegance and stature. The subject's pose was frequently animated by a slight twist of the body. As one critic of the era noted, his figures give the impression "of just having sat down, of just being about to rise."[3]

Ethel was the granddaughter of Charles Crocker (1822–1888), one of the four major investors in the Central Pacific Railroad—the final link in the transcontinental railroad—and founder of what became the Crocker National Bank. Like many young girls from wealthy families, she was a frequent traveler to Europe, making her first trip as a three-year-old.[4] In 1906 she and her younger sister, Helen Victoria (1896–1966), left with their governess for Europe aboard the *Deutschland* on April 28, ten days after the devastating San Francisco earthquake. Her portrait was completed before their return on the *Caronia*, which arrived in New York on October 31.[5] Mrs. Crocker must have liked the portrait, as she commissioned one of herself and her younger daughter in 1910.[6]

After her graduation in 1909 from St. Timothy's School in Maryland, Ethel continued to make numerous trips to Europe.[7] In January 1916 she was part of a group of young women who joined Mrs. Whitelaw Reid, wife of the former ambassador to France (1889–92) and Great Britain (1905–12), to drive ambulances during World War I and aid in the reconstruction of the village of Vitrimont. It was during this time that she met her future husband, André Marie Adrian, Count de Limur, a pilot in the French Flying Corps. They were engaged in November 1917 and married on March 17, 1918, in New York, where her family maintained an apartment at the St. Regis.[8] In 1939 he served as the French attaché in Washington, resigning his post in October 1941 in protest against the Vichy government. The de Limurs and their three children remained in Washington, where Ethel became an integral part of Washington life and a supporter of numerous charitable causes in the nation's capital.[9]

CKC

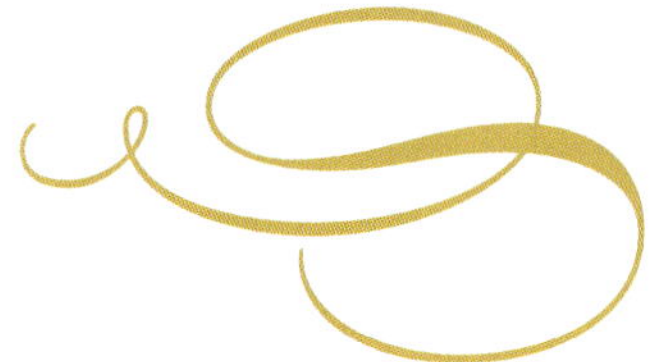

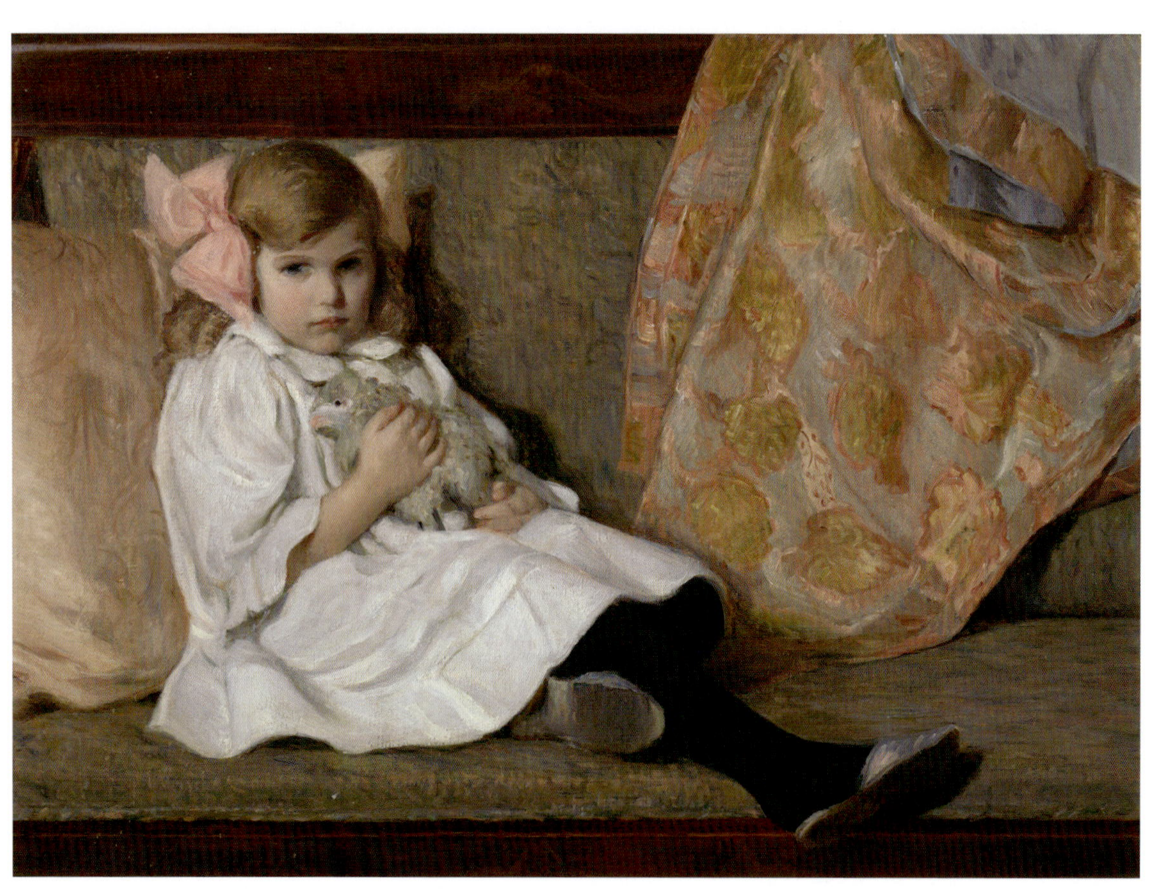

35

HILDEGARDE

By Lilla Cabot Perry (1848–1933)

Oil on canvas, 81.3 × 101.6 cm (32 × 40 in.), c. 1912
Joan and Bernard Carl Collection

CHILDREN WERE frequently featured in Lilla Cabot Perry's work. She reveled in their innocence and unsophisticated and unspoiled beauty. In the early years of her career, Perry's three daughters—Margaret (born 1876), Edith (born 1880), and Alice (born 1884)—served as her primary models, but as they grew older they no longer embodied all that she held dear about youth. She continued to paint them as adults, but she still wanted to paint children because of their "unspoiled" nature. Perry turned to Hildegarde, the daughter of a friend, to be her model. Starting around 1911 and continuing for at least a year, Hildegarde posed for the artist on numerous occasions.[1]

Lilla Cabot, the oldest of eight children, was born into a distinguished Boston family. When she wed Thomas Sergeant Perry in 1874, she married into a family that was equally notable.[2] In 1884, shortly after the birth of her last child, Perry, who had expressed an interest in art from the time she was a teenager, began taking painting lessons, first from Alfred Quentin Collins and then from Robert Vonnoh and Robert Bunker. While the ambitions of most women can be limited when their husbands take new positions, the opposite proved true for Perry when she and her family moved to Paris in 1887. There, she was soon expanding her artistic horizons by visiting museums in that city as well as in Madrid and London. She also continued to study art, first at the Académie Colarossi, then at the Académie Julian, and briefly in Munich with Fritz von Uhde. The year 1889 was a banner one for Perry: she entered the classes of Alfred Stephens, had two portraits accepted at the prestigious Salon de la Société des Artistes Français, and became enchanted with the work of Claude Monet after seeing an exhibition of his paintings at the Georges Petit Gallery. Monet's paintings inspired Perry to live in Giverny, his home outside Paris. Although she returned to Boston that November, Perry would spend nine summers in Giverny between 1889 and 1909. During that time she became close friends with Monet as well as the American artists living there who admired his approach to painting. Monet's impact was immediate; Perry's palette became more colorful and her treatment of the paint surface more fluid.

In 1909, Perry moved permanently to Boston after a decade of multiple relocations (Japan 1898–1901; Boston 1901–5; Paris 1905–9). With Hildegarde as her willing model, it was as if she were returning to the heady days of the 1890s, when her portraits of her own children were integral to her success as an artist. Although those portraits set the subjects both indoors and out, all the images of Hildegarde were placed in an interior, giving Perry less chance to exhibit her enthusiasm for light-filled, plein-air painting. Instead, she exercised her color sensibility by creating a composition of subtly modulated tones, in this case a "symphony" of color built around the theme of pink. Just as she had won resounding recognition at the 1893 Columbian Exposition in Chicago when seven portraits were exhibited in the Palace of Fine Arts—the most by any woman in the fine arts pavilion—her paintings of Hildegarde, shown at the 1915 Panama Pacific Exposition in San Francisco, garnered the artist a bronze medal.

CKC

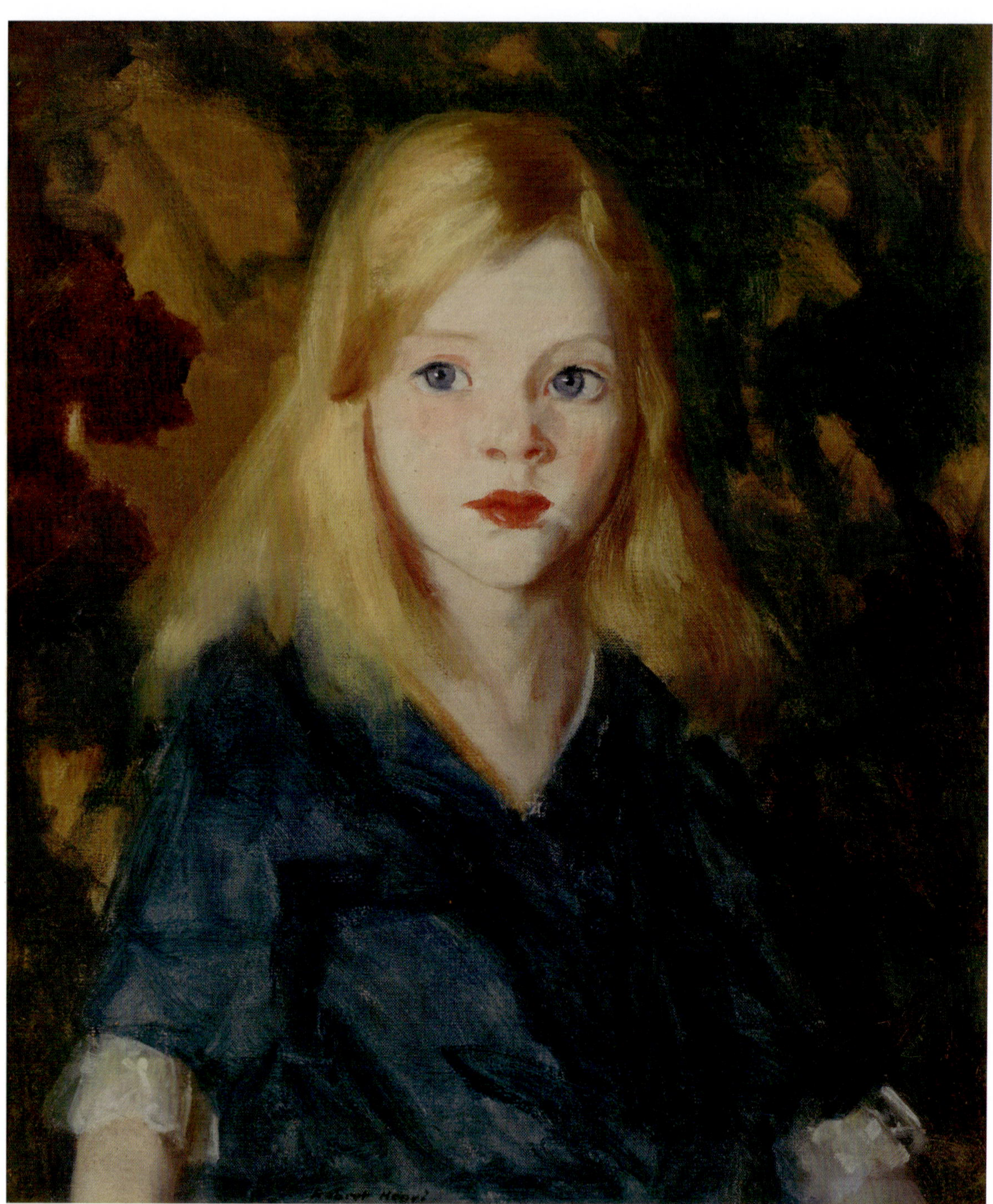

SISTER
BROTHER

By Robert Henri (1865–1929)

Each: Oil on canvas, 61 × 50.8 cm (24 × 20 in.), 1915
Private collection

ROBERT HENRI's artistic reputation was at its height when Delia Spencer Caton Field (cat. 29), the widow of department store magnate Marshall Field, asked him to come to the summer home of her niece in Beverly Farms, on Massachusetts's North Shore, to paint the portraits of her great-niece and nephew, then ages five and seven. Delia Field had been close to her sister's daughter since the younger woman's childhood. After she married in 1907, Field continued to see her niece and her niece's family frequently.[1] As Field had no children, she was particularly devoted to her niece's. Henri's record books show that he painted two portraits each of his small subjects when he visited Beverly Farms in October 1915 on his return from Maine, where he had spent the summer with artist George Bellows and his wife, Emma.[2]

What led Field to commission Henri to make these portraits is a matter of speculation, as no correspondence between Field and Henri exists. But Field came from a family that valued portraiture, and she was clearly sympathetic to modern art. She had her own portrait painted in Paris in 1876 by eminent American artist George Peter Alexander Healy, and in 1921 she sat in Washington, D.C., for the esteemed Hungarian painter Philip Alexius de László (Newberry Library, Chicago).[3] Her contemporary collection included Mary Cassatt's *On a Balcony* (1878/79; Art Institute of Chicago), and J. Alden Weir's *Two Sisters* (c. 1890–99; Spanierman Gallery, New York City).[4] It is entirely possible that Field came to know Henri's work from his exhibitions in Chicago, but she was a frequent traveler who often maintained an apartment in New York, so she could easily have seen Henri's work in exhibitions there.[5] When she and friends motored west in the summer of 1915, she visited the Panama-Pacific Exposition in San Francisco, where Henri was among the exhibitors in the American pavilion.[6] Field probably shared the opinion of the critic who wrote, "Henri has six delightful examples, the most charming of them being 'Pat,' a delicious roguish boy with Irish blue eyes. He is full of energy and mischief and his brilliant color shows well against a deep rose ground."[7] Field's enthusiasm for Henri's work led her to purchase in 1915 at least two (*Laughing Gypsy Girl* [unlocated], *Imaginative Boy* [New Britain Museum of American Art]), if not three, other paintings by the artist.[8]

As for Henri, who also had no children, he must have derived much pleasure from the commission. While in Holland in the summer of 1907, he had begun a series of portraits of youth painted for his own enjoyment, and on a trip to Ireland in 1913 children loomed large as subjects

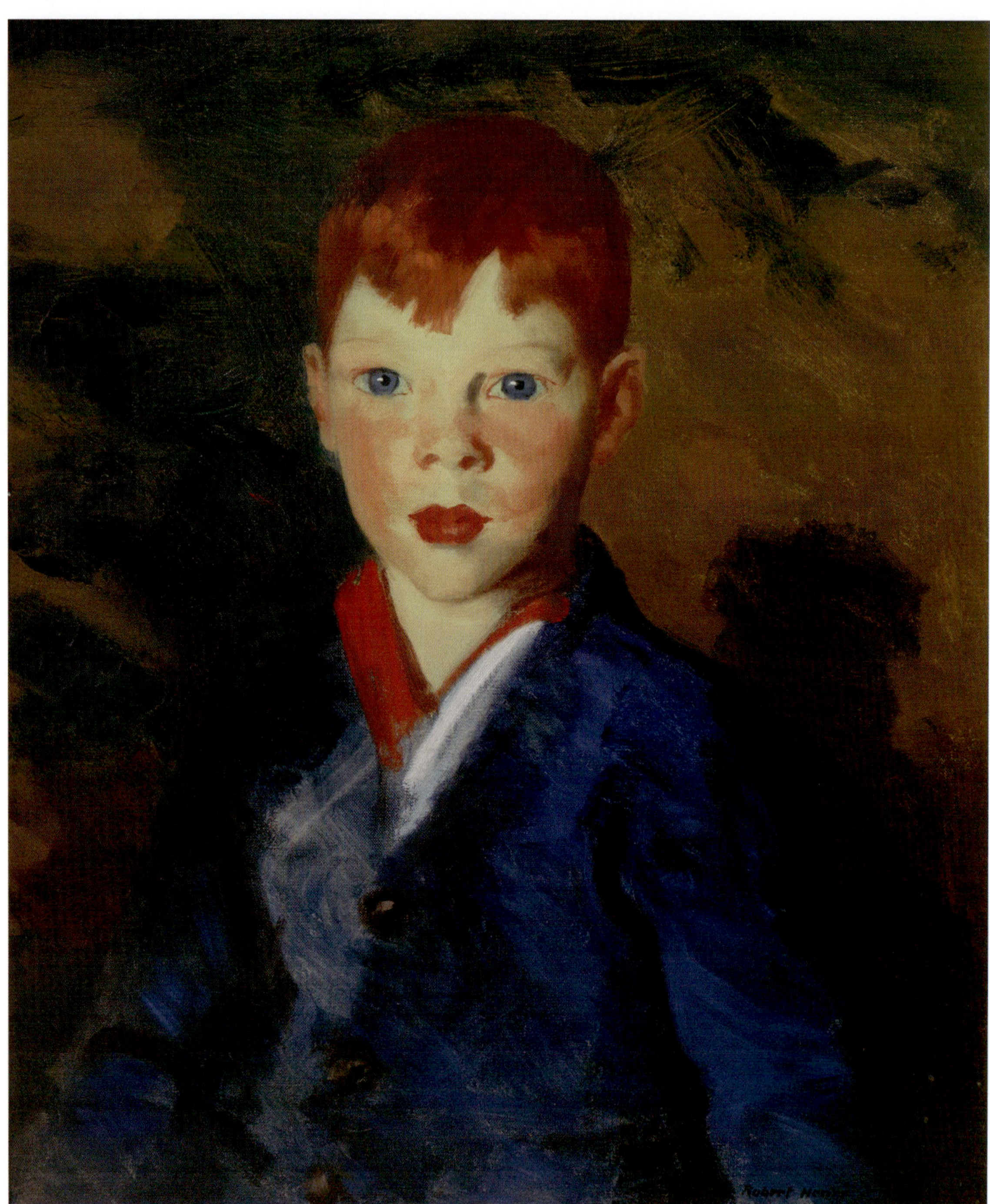

of his work. For Henri, children were "vital creatures . . . healthy, optimistic types, rich in human
dignity and thoroughly natural and unaffected"
and an "antidote to the evils of oversophistication
that stifled man when he reached adulthood."[9]
Like his work in Ireland, these two portraits
reflect the artist's new emphasis on bravura brushwork and brilliant touches of colors, as well as his
desire to capture the vibrant personalities of his
young subjects.

CKC

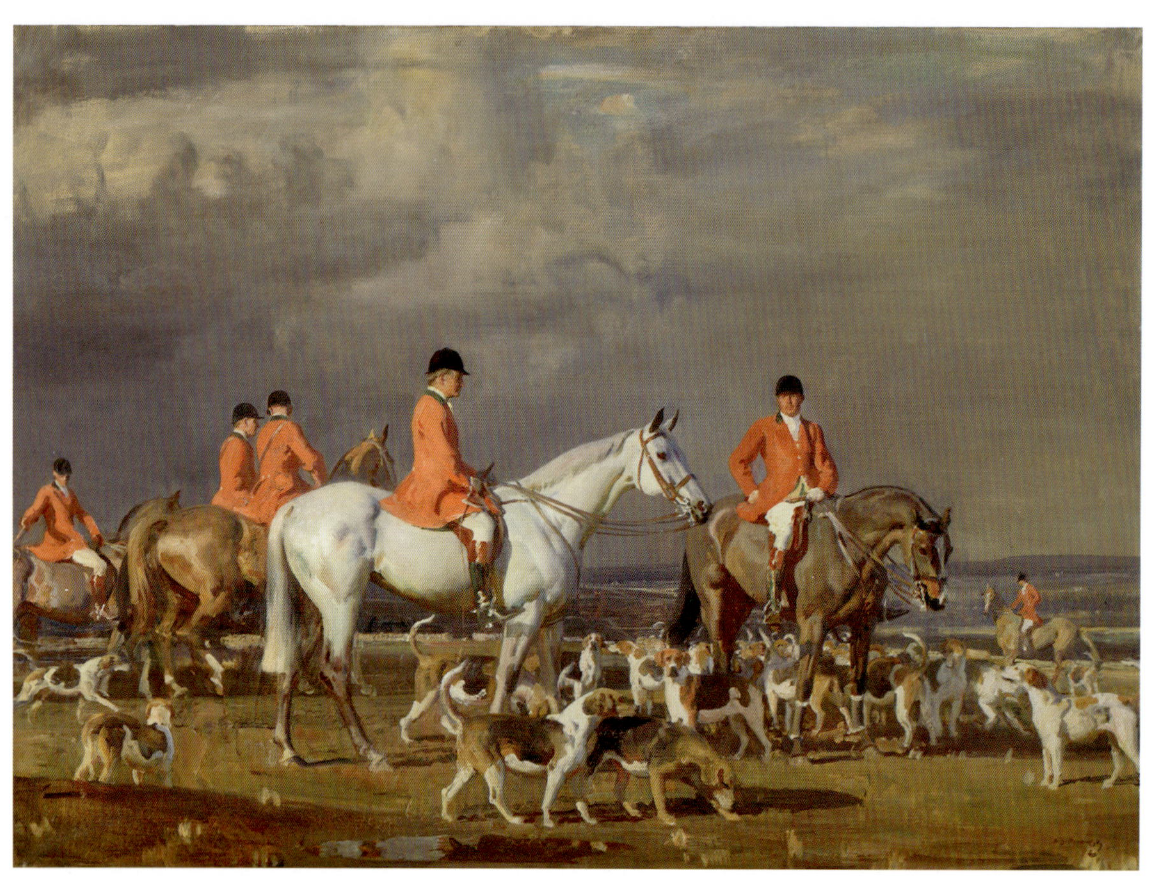

THE PAU HUNT (FREDERICK HENRY PRINCE AND FREDERICK HENRY PRINCE JR.)

By Sir Alfred James Munnings (1878–1959)

Oil on canvas, 85.7 × 113.7 cm (33¾ × 44¾ in.), 1924
Diana and Freddy Prince

IN MARCH 1924 the English painter Alfred Munnings, who was known for his equestrian portraits, boarded the *Berengaria* in South-ampton to come to Pittsburgh, Pennsylvania, to serve as a judge for the highly regarded International Exhibition at the Carnegie Institute, now the Carnegie Museum of Art. On board was Frederick Henry Prince (1859–1953), whom the artist had known from previous encounters at the English Club in London. As the two chatted, Prince insisted that Munnings come to his Prides Crossing, Massachusetts, home to paint him, presumably with his hounds and horses. As a condition of the portrait, the artist insisted that Prince be shown on a gray, or at least have one in the picture. Distressed, Prince replied that all his grays were currently with the stud in France. The resourceful Munnings, when taken by museum director Homer Saint-Gaudens to visit the young Paul Mellon (1907–1999), discovered, however, that Mellon had an impressive gray that he did not want to keep, as his team consisted of all browns. Presumably, the gray that the family patriarch rides in this portrait is the one he had recently purchased from Mellon. Prince's son and name-sake (1885–1962) is portrayed on the right, facing the viewer.[1]

Frederick Henry Prince, who completed less than two years at Harvard University, began his career as a stockbroker and investment banker. His fiscal talents led him to create one of the era's most successful conglomerates as he merged numerous small companies and railroads into the Union Stock Yard and Transit Company and added to those holdings the large meatpacking entity of Armour and Company. Not shy about indulging in creature comforts commensurate with his wealth, Prince maintained a seventy-room home, Princemere, on one thousand acres at Prides Crossing until 1933. He purchased Marble House in Newport, Rhode Island, from Mrs. Oliver Hazard Perry Belmont in 1932, all the while keeping an elegant residence in Biarritz—Villa Ardour—and a country estate—Villa St. Helénè—in Pau, France. He was equally at home in London clubs and historic Parisian hotels.[2]

In the 1920s, with the tragedy and disruption of World War I behind him, Prince, like other wealthy Americans, resumed intercontinental travel with renewed vigor. As his portrait-ist noted, "Mr. and Mrs. Prince . . . thought no more of crossing the Atlantic than we would of [*sic*] crossing a street."[3] A keen participant in fox hunts (as was his son), Prince achieved notable leadership within this sporting community at Pau, which had been established by the English in the 1840s as the site of major continental hunts. Beginning in 1910, he served as master of the hunt at Pau for about thirty years.[4]

Prince was clearly pleased with this portrait as during the next several years, Munnings painted numerous portraits of him, his wife, and his son.[5]

CKC

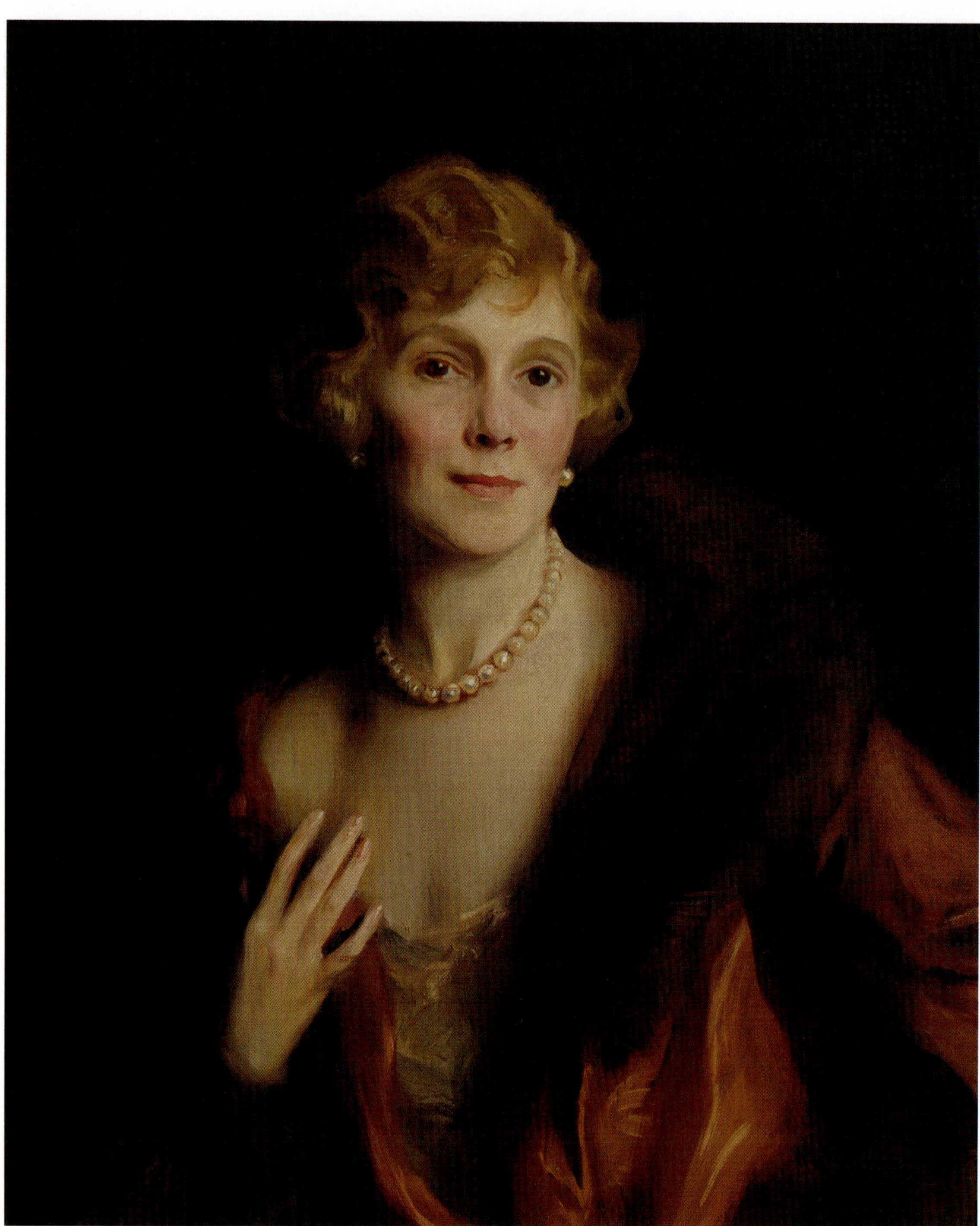

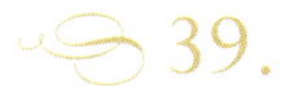

39.

PAULINE MORTON SMITH SABIN DAVIS

By Philip Alexius de László (1869–1937)

Oil on canvas, 73.7 × 59.7 cm (29 × 23½ in.), 1926[1]
Sheila Smith Cochran

IN 1929, Pauline Morton Smith Sabin (later Davis) (1887–1955) founded the Women's Organization for National Prohibition Reform (WONPR). She was the powerhouse behind this energetic and effective organization and a significant force in the passage of the Twenty-First Amendment (December 5, 1933), which abolished prohibition. Her efforts on behalf of the repeal of the Eighteenth Amendment merited a cover portrait on *Time* magazine (July 18, 1932), accompanied by an extensive essay detailing her background and political savvy.

Political genes ran in Sabin's family: Her grandfather, Julius Sterling Morton (1832–1902), who moved from Detroit to Nebraska in 1854, served in the territorial legislature from 1855 to 1858, was appointed by President James Buchanan as secretary of the Nebraska Territory (1858–61), and was secretary of agriculture under Grover Cleveland (1893–97). Her father, Paul Morton (1857–1911), was appointed to Theodore Roosevelt's cabinet as secretary of the navy (1904–5). Money and social status—highly desirable political assets—were also hers. In 1907 the Chicago–born Morton married James Hopkins Smith Jr. (1881–1967), a banker and world-class sailor. Divorced in 1914, she married Charles Hamilton Sabin (1868–1933), president of the J. P. Morgan–affiliated Guaranty Trust Company, two years later.[2] Sabin's own political career began in 1919, when she was elected to the Suffolk County Republican Committee.[3] A heavy social schedule was no deterrent, and in 1920 she joined the New York State Republican Committee; in 1921 she founded the New York–based Woman's National Republican Club, serving as its president

from 1921 to 1926. She also made national news as the first female member of the Republican National Committee (1924–28). In 1933, she served as co-chair of Fiorello LaGuardia's mayoral campaign. During World War II she was the national director of the volunteer forces for the American Red Cross.

Philip Alexius de László painted Pauline Sabin's portrait on his third visit to the United States. When he arrived, the Hungarian-born naturalized British citizen was no stranger to the highest level of society, either in his adopted country or in America. During his first visit in 1908, he painted the portrait of President Theodore Roosevelt, and on his second, in 1921, those of President and Mrs. Warren G. Harding. He began this third sojourn in October 1925 with the goal of painting the portrait of President Calvin Coolidge. While here, he painted approximately thirty portraits, including those of Mrs. Coolidge; George Eastman, founder of the Eastman Kodak Company; Andrew Mellon, financier, who at the time was secretary of the treasury, and his daughter Ailsa; Ambassador Frank Billings Kellogg, secretary of state for the Coolidge administration; Adolph S. Ochs, owner and publisher of the *New York Times*; and a double portrait of Ambassador and Mrs. Larz Anderson III, whose grand Washington residence now houses the Society of the Cincinnati. Known for his elegant style and lyrical handling of paint, de László completed his portrait of the charismatic and vivacious Sabin shortly before he returned to Europe. She signed the artist's sitter's book on April 2, 1926.[4]

CKC

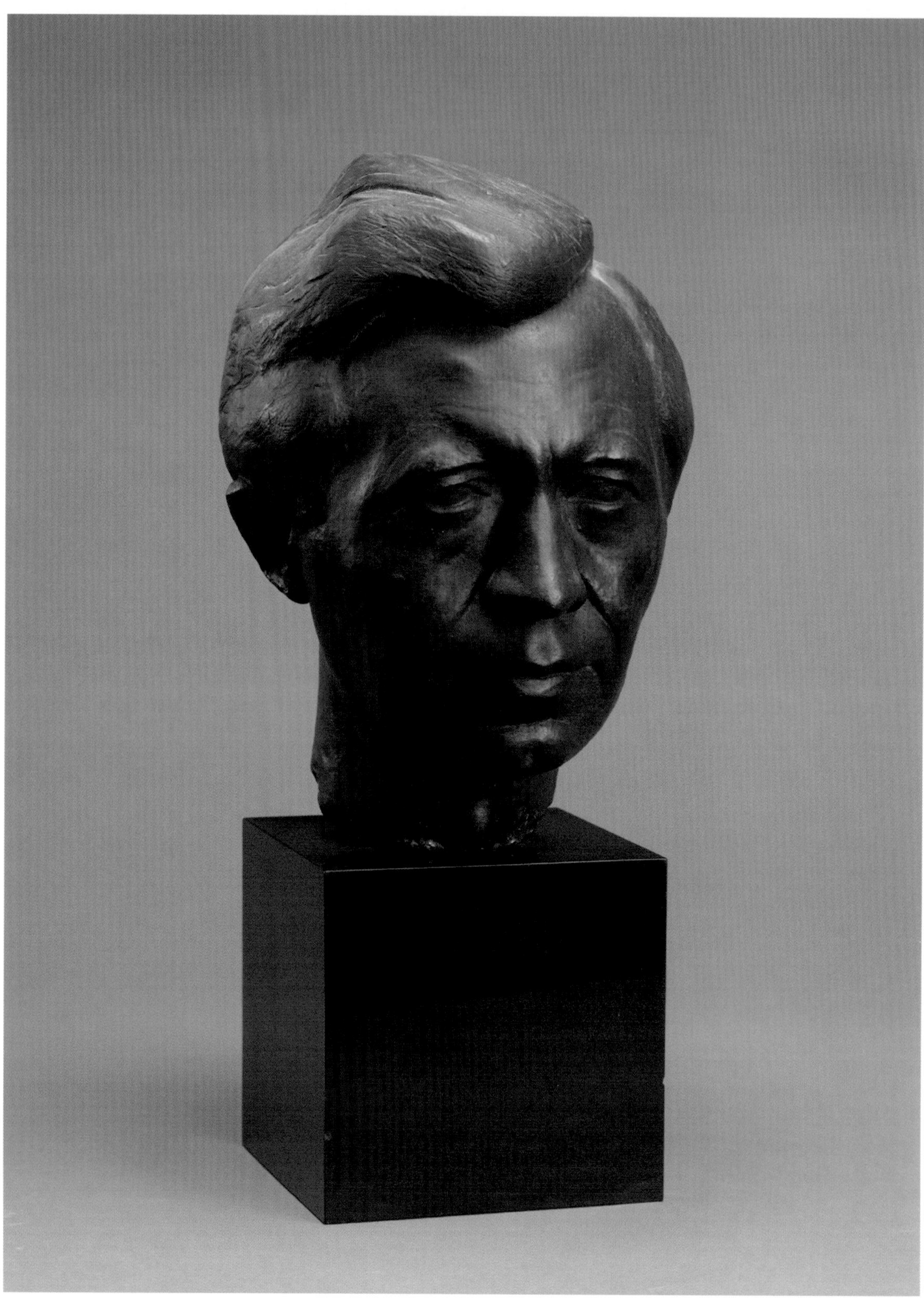

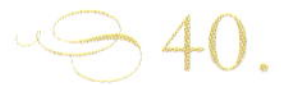

40

VILHJALMUR STEFANSSON

By Antonio Salemme (1892–1995)

Bronze, 31.8 cm (12½ in.), c. 1926 (cast 1965)
The Dickey Center Institute of Arctic Studies, Dartmouth College, Hanover, New Hampshire; bequest of Evelyn Stefansson Nef[1]

VILHJALMUR STEFANSSON (1879–1962), one of America's premier Arctic explorers of the early twentieth century, was born in Canada, but moved with his parents to the Dakota Territory when he was less than a year old. A 1903 graduate of the University of Iowa, he was awarded a Phoebe Hearst Fellowship in anthropology in 1904 at Harvard University, where he worked primarily at that institution's Peabody Museum of Natural History. In 1905 he joined other students from the museum on a trip to Iceland. Noting that the Icelandic people, who ate only meat, experienced no tooth decay, Stefansson began the first of his lifelong studies on the relationship between health and diet. His seminal Arctic voyage was a 1906 trip to the Mackenzie River Delta. A series of mishaps led Stefansson to stay with the Inuits for the following year. His knowledge of their language and customs, gleaned from the experience, initiated his decades-long study of the culture, much of it supported by the American Museum of Natural History in New York City. His last Arctic expedition took place between 1913 and 1918.[2]

While living in New York, Stefansson became an integral part of the Greenwich Village community. There he befriended Antonio Salemme and his wife. The Italian-born sculptor had immigrated with his family to the United States in 1904; after serving in the Italian army in World War I, he settled in New York in 1919.[3] Shortly after he completed a full-length figure of actor Paul Robeson (destroyed), he undertook the head of Stefansson. During the modeling phase, Stefansson sat for Salemme about two hours each morning.[4] Habitués of Romany Marie's, the Salammes introduced the explorer to this Village restaurant that served as a social club for numerous writers and artists, among them Stuart Davis, Arshile Gorky, Gaston Lachaise, Edna St. Vincent Millay, and Eugene O'Neill. It was there that he met his future wife, Evelyn Schwartz (fig. 16 and cat. 53), who as a seventeen-year-old was known for her performance of folk songs, often in French. Their friendship began in earnest after her divorce from puppeteer Bil Baird in 1936. Hired in 1939 as a research assistant for Stefansson's ever-growing collection of scientific literature related to polar exploration, Schwartz married Stefansson in 1941. During the next two decades they lived primarily near Hanover, New Hampshire. In 1947 he was appointed Arctic consultant at Dartmouth College and curator of his world-renowned Stefansson Collection of polar literature, which the college had acquired. His wife absorbed his enthusiasm for this cold world. During their time in Hanover she managed his extensive library, taught a course on Arctic studies at the college, and published several popular books on the subject.[5] To celebrate Stefansson's eightieth birthday, Evelyn asked Salemme if he would cast a bronze of her husband's 1926 portrait. "Since you did yours," she wrote, "many painters and a few sculptors have done portraits of him, but all have tried to make him look intrepid. You are the only one who caught his gentleness, and a poetic quality."[6]

CKC

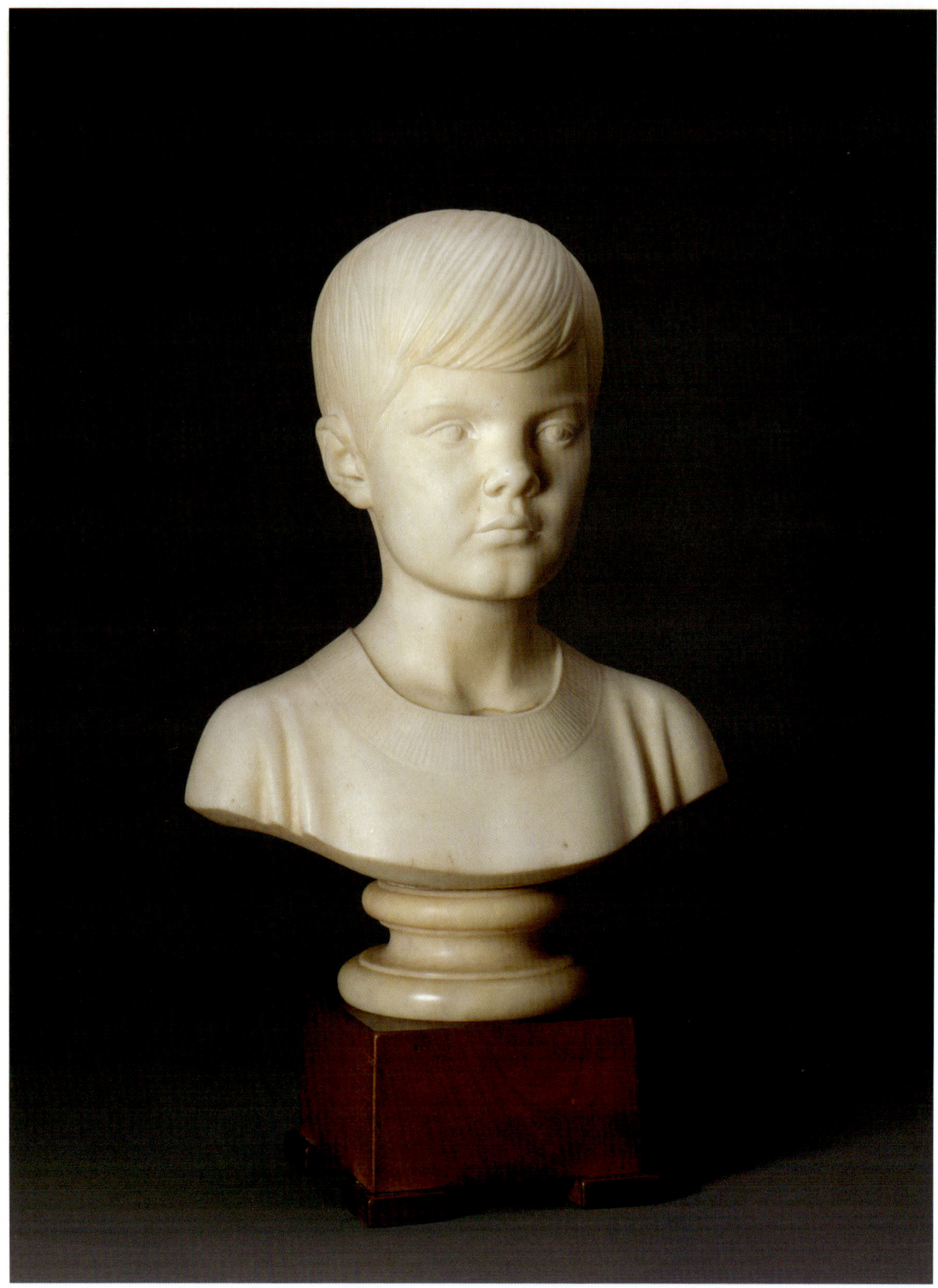

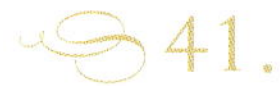

41.

FREDERICK HENRY PRINCE III

By Paul Manship (1885–1966)

Marble, 43.2 cm (17 in.) height, 1928
Diana and Freddy Prince

PAUL MANSHIP was among America's foremost sculptors when he carved this portrait of seven-year-old Frederick Henry Prince III (1921–1964). Talented and personable, the sculptor had a career distinguished by important apprenticeships and prizes. After moving from St. Paul, Minnesota, where he was born, to New York City in 1905, he studied briefly at the Art Students League before initiating a two-year apprenticeship with noted sculptor Solon Borglum and completing his training at the Pennsylvania Academy of the Fine Arts in Philadelphia with Charles Grafly. In 1909 he won a Prix de Rome that enabled him to work from the American Academy in Rome for the next three years. The award forever shaped his fascination with historical art, particularly archaic Greek, Assyrian, and Egyptian sculpture, and was the foundation for his enthusiasm for contemporary European culture. In 1921, Manship, now married, left with his wife for an extended stay abroad. In his Paris studio at 6 rue du Val de Grâce, he fulfilled numerous commissions from both Americans and Europeans. At the request of his wife to have her fourth child in the United States, they returned to New York. By 1927 his primary base of operation was a large studio at 319 East Seventy-second Street.[1] His diaries reveal, however, that he frequently visited and worked in France until the beginning of World War II.[2]

Along with his monumental works, Manship from time to time undertook commissions for children's portraits.[3] Of these, his interpretation of the classically handsome Frederick Prince is among his most naturalistic and charming. A letter in recently discovered papers of Manship suggests that the boy's portrait was commissioned by his mother and stepfather. On May 28, 1928, the latter wrote, "Rest assured that Mrs. Thayer and all of us who have seen the bust of little Peter are delighted with it." In closing, he noted, "I am only too glad to send you check as requested for $5,000, same being one-half of the total amount."[4]

"Peter," as the child was called by his mother, the former Elizabeth Harding (1897–1961), was the son of Frederick Henry Prince Jr. (1885–1962). His parents met in Washington, where her father, William P. G. Harding (1864–1930) was serving as the second chairman of the Federal Reserve Board. The two married in 1917, just before Prince, who had flown in World War I as part of the French Flying Corps and the Lafayette Escadrille, returned to France to join the American Aviation Service. The couple divorced in 1923. Shortly thereafter, Elizabeth married New York banker Eugene Van Rensselaer Thayer (1881–1937).[5] In later life, Frederick Prince III emulated his father and deceased uncle, Norman Prince (1887–1916), a founder of the Lafayette Escadrille, by serving in the air force in World War II.[6]

CKC

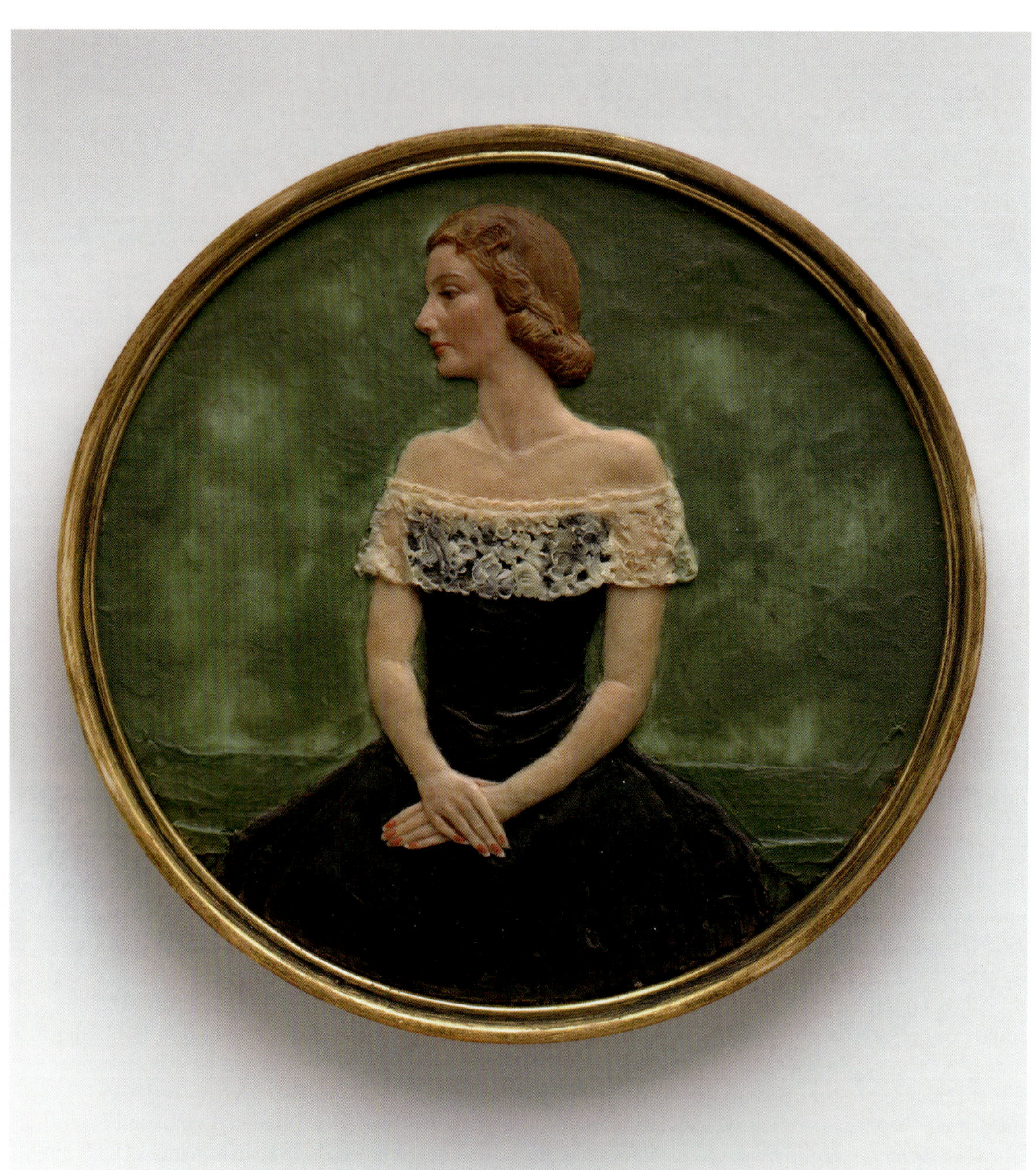

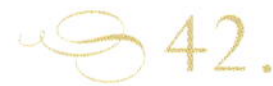

DORETTE KRUSE FLEISCHMANN

By Ethel Frances Mundy (1876–1964)

Beeswax and powdered pigments, 21.9 × 18.7 cm (8⅝ × 7⅜ in.) framed, c. 1934–1935
Joan Fleischmann Tobin

DORETTE BOUFFLEUR KRUSE (1906–1994), a Cincinnati, Ohio, debutant, was a junior at Smith College when she became engaged to fellow Cincinnatian Julius ("Junkie") Fleischmann (1900–1968), a graduate of Hotchkiss and Yale University. With her marriage on January 7, 1928, she inherited more than access to the fortune established by Julius's grandfather, Charles, who invented and patented a method for preserving yeast; she inherited the lifestyle of a man whose energy and enthusiasms knew no bounds.

Together with her husband, she was part of a circle that included wealthy New Yorkers such as Lincoln Kirstein, Nelson A. Rockefeller, and Edward M. Warburg, who were major patrons of American ballet. So strong was the Fleischmanns' commitment to the Ballet Russe de Monte Carlo—a company founded abroad but which performed mainly in America—that it was known as the Fleishmann Monte Carlo Ballet. The couple's support of cultural enterprises was not, however, limited to dance. The Metropolitan Opera, the New York Public Library, the School of Drama at Yale, and the Cincinnati Art Museum benefited from their largesse, as did the National Arboretum, to which Mrs. Fleischmann donated a column made by Benjamin Latrobe for the old U.S. Capitol. In the commercial world, Julius was a successful producer of Broadway plays, chairman of the board of a company that distributed foreign films, and a director of the publishing house Farrar, Straus and Cudahy, interests that she shared. Together they amassed a major collection of art and antiques. Their trip around the world in 1928 on their 225-foot yacht, *Carmago 1*,

led to the creation of Pacific Island maps used in World War II, as well as numerous donations to the Smithsonian Institution. In the 1950s, the Fleischmanns were also the impetus behind Third Street South, the elegant shopping section of Naples, Florida.[1]

Dorette Fleischmann's portraitist, Syracuse-born artist Ethel Frances Mundy, created a name for herself when she revived the art of medallion portraiture in wax. The technique, which dates to the time of the Egyptians and was fashionable in the Victorian era, captured the American imagination in the 1920s and 1930s. Mundy, who studied at the Art Students League in New York with American impressionist John Twachtman and later held a position designing stained glass in the Pittsburgh studio of Deske and Greene, perfected her technique in about 1910 after much experimentation. She began each of her medallion portraits by making a foundation of wax for the medallions, which she called a "cookie." On this she drew the figure's outline before she began building up the form with dry ground colors embedded in the wax. Her delicate tools were those designed for dentistry. Mundy exhibited frequently and was often the subject of articles in art and lifestyle magazines. Her long list of prominent clients included Henry Clay Frick, Andrew Mellon, J. Pierpont Morgan, John D. Rockefeller, and Gertrude Vanderbilt Whitney, among others. An exhibition of Mundy's miniatures and sculptures at the Syracuse Museum of Fine Arts in 1938 featured this portrait of Dorette and four members of the extended Fleishmann family.[2]

CKC

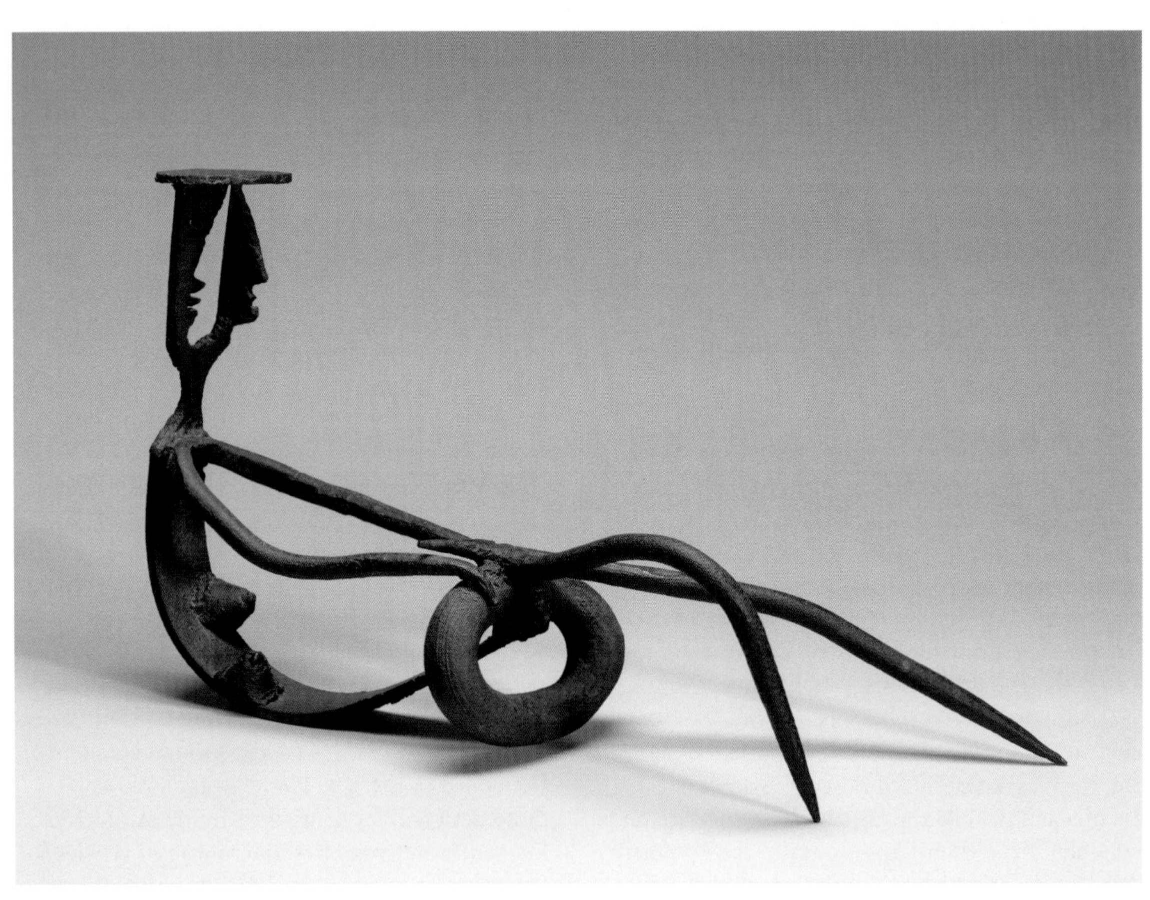

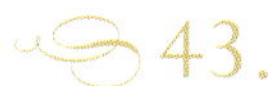

SEATED FIGURE (LUCILLE CORCOS)
By David Smith (1906–1965)

Iron painted black, 40.6 cm (16 in.) height, 1936
David C. Levy

LUCILLE CORCOS (1908–1973) and David Smith and their respective spouses—painter Edgar Levy (1907–1975) and sculptor Dorothy Dehner (1901–1994)—were close friends. The four first met at the Art Students League in New York in the late 1920s. During the 1930s, Dehner and Smith often visited the Levys in their Brooklyn Heights home, and Lucille and her husband were frequent visitors to the farm that Smith and his wife purchased in 1929 at Bolton Landing, New York, near Lake George.[1]

Smith, who was born in Decatur, Indiana, exhibited an initial interest in art as a teenager when he took a correspondence course in cartooning from the Cleveland Institute of Art. His fascination with metal and welding probably grew out of a job he had in South Bend as a riveter for the Studebaker automobile factory. But not until he moved to New York City in 1926, where he met and married Dehner, did he take his artistic inclinations seriously. Encouraged by Dehner to take classes at the Art Students League (1927–1932), there the Czech-born modernist painter Jan Matulka introduced him to the work of major European artists. Of equal importance was Smith's friendship with Polish émigré John Graham, who acquainted him with contemporary American painters Stuart Davis, Arshile Gorky, and Willem de Kooning, among others.

Smith began making small metal sculptures in the summer of 1932 at the Bolton Landing farm. In 1934 he established a studio, which he used until 1940, in a shed on the property of the Terminal Iron Works, a commercial welding company on the Brooklyn waterfront.

Smith's welded iron portrait of Corcos, like much of his work in the mid-1930s, pays homage to the cubism of Pablo Picasso and Julio González, the surrealist-inspired work of Alberto Giacometti, and the constructivism of Naum Gabo.[2] At the time, this portrait, which takes advantage of negative space enclosed by linear metalwork to suggest body mass, was one of Smith's most clearly defined pieces relating to the human figure. Addressing one of the issues of central concern to sculptors of the twentieth century—that of the base—Smith shaped the work to allow the curve of the spine to serve as the object's resting place.

As artists, Smith and Corcos could not be more dissimilar in aesthetic approach. Although she, too, trained under Matulka, Corcos was known for her witty, complex, genrelike portrayals of the urban landscape. Her first magazine cover was the January 1931 issue of *Vanity Fair.* In subsequent years, she became a regular contributor to *Life, Fortune, Collier's, Mademoiselle,* and the *Saturday Evening Post.*[3] Her most famous painting, *Children's Games,* was reproduced in *Life* magazine on August 20, 1951.[4] Corcos was also a noted illustrator of books for both children and adults.[5] She rounded out her artistic career by participating in numerous exhibitions, including those at the Whitney Museum of American Art and the National Academy of Design in New York, the Carnegie Museum of Art in Pittsburgh, the Art Institute of Chicago, and the Pennsylvania Academy of the Fine Arts in Philadelphia.[6]

CKC

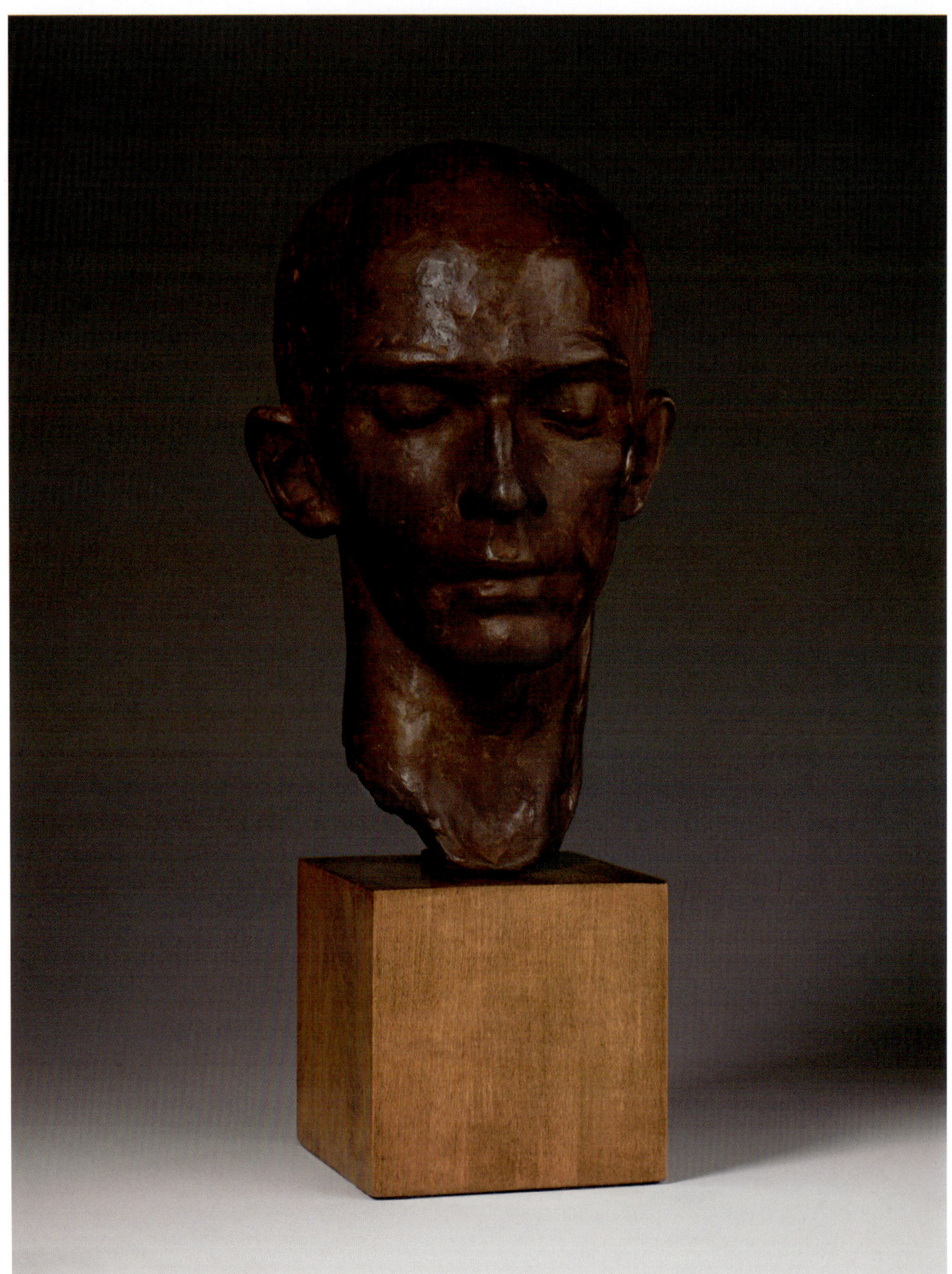

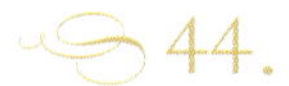

HEAD OF A DANCER (HARALD KREUTZBERG)

By Richmond Barthé (1901–1989)

Bronze, 31.1 cm (12¼ in.), c. 1937
Robert L. Johnson/The Barnett Aden Collection

RICHMOND BARTHÉ was the nation's most noted African American sculptor when he was invited to show in 1944 at Washington's Barnett Aden Gallery in the group exhibition "The Negro in Art."[1] In all likelihood, the gallery's director, Alonzo Aden (cat. 47), knew Barthé personally. The sculptor had shown at Howard University Art Gallery in 1930 and 1940, and in two exhibitions that Aden had curated, one for the 1936 Texas Centennial Exposition, the other for the 1940 American Negro Exposition in Chicago.[2]

Born in Bay St. Louis, Mississippi, Barthé was a month old when his father died. His mother fostered his artistic talents, and at age eighteen, with no formal artistic training and no education beyond the seventh grade, he won a drawing prize at the New Orleans County Fair. The art critic for the *New Orleans Times-Picayune*, impressed by his talent, attempted to get him admitted to an art school in New Orleans. Segregation was in full force, however, and Barthé was denied admission. Subsequently, one of his works attracted the attention of a Jesuit priest, who encouraged Barthé to apply to the Art Institute of Chicago, where Barthé would study (1924 to 1928). In 1930, Barthé moved to New York City. Over the course of the decade, he participated in numerous solo and group exhibitions that gained him increasing critical attention, as did his monumental *Mother and Son* (1935; destroyed), which was shown at the 1939 World's Fair.[3] Beginning about 1949, Barthé made Jamaica his home base, but following five years in Europe, he went in 1975 to Pasadena, California, where he remained until his death.[4]

By the early 1920s, Harald Kreutzberg (1902–1968), who was born in Czechoslovakia, had become one of Germany's most important dancers, known for his roles in traditional ballets and expressive dance dramas.[5] In 1926 he shaved his head for his part in *Don Morte* (based on a story by Edgar Allan Poe), a look that he retained as his trademark. Kreutzberg, also a noted choreographer, first performed in New York in 1927. He returned to the city periodically during the 1930s, and his sold-out performances received rave reviews.[6] Barthé, who took classes from Mary Radin, a member of the Martha Graham dance company, undoubtedly met Kreutzberg in the context of his own intense interest in this medium.[7] His fascination with the movement of dancers also led him to create six dance figures for the 1937 exhibition "Dance International, 1900–1937" at Rockefeller Center. Barthé probably executed the full-length figure of Kreutzberg (c. 1937; unlocated) and a plaster head of him (c. 1937; Barnett Aden Collection)—both of which closely relate to the bronze illustrated here—after the Rockefeller Center show, as neither were included in that exhibition. Given Kreutzberg's popularity, either or both would have been had the works existed at the time. In 1939 the critic for the *New York Times* raved about the bronze when it was shown at the Arden Gallery on Park Avenue, calling it the "magnificent head of Harald Kreutzberg."[8] The *Washington Post* critic also singled it out for attention when it appeared in the nation's capital in 1944.[9]

CKC

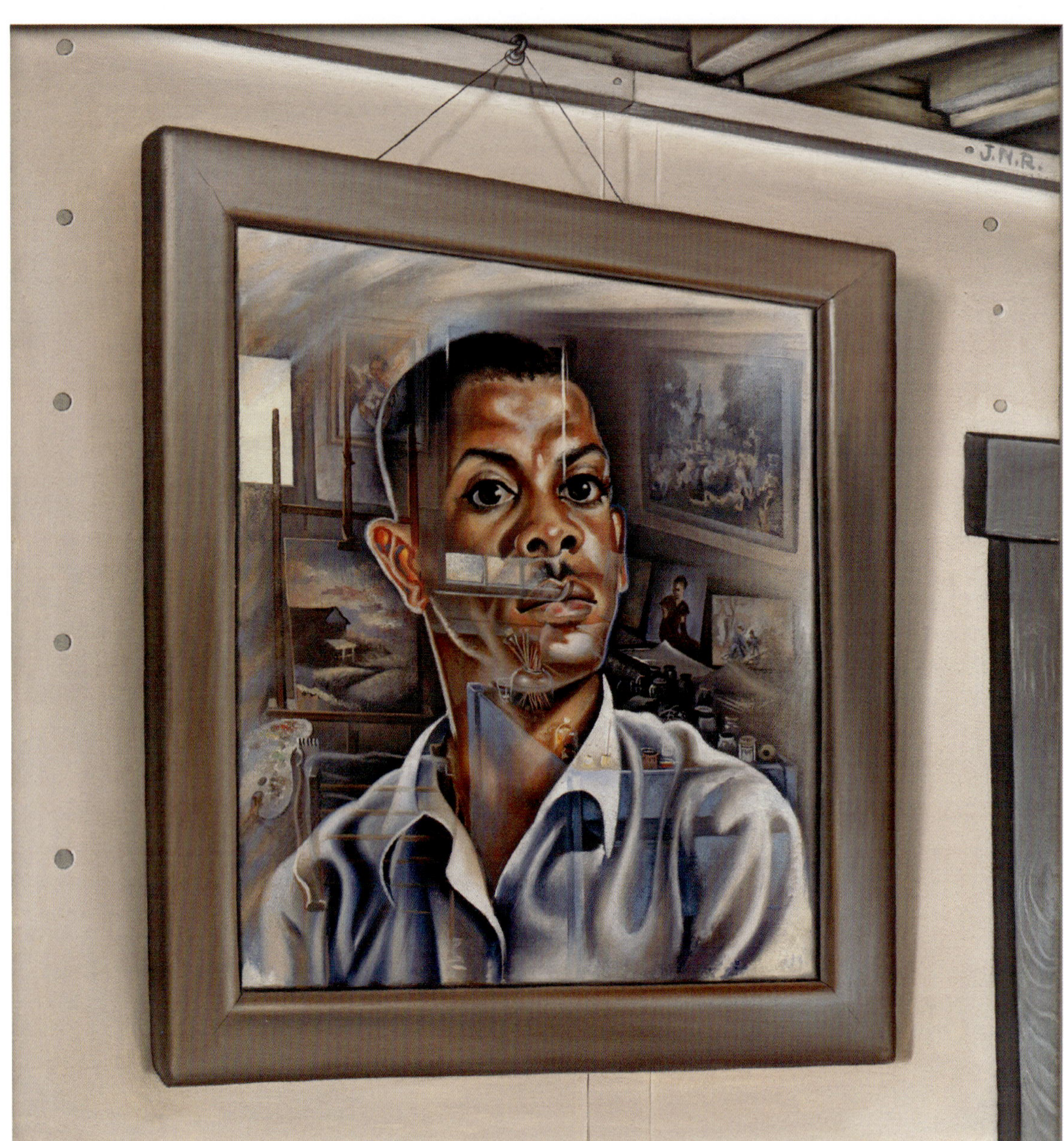

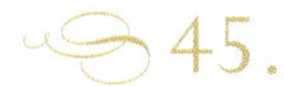

SELF-PORTRAIT AS A YOUNG MAN WITH MIRROR

By John N. Robinson (1912–1994)

Oil on canvas, 56.2 × 51.1 cm (22⅛ × 20⅛ in.), c. 1940
Robert L. Johnson/The Barnett Aden Collection

JOHN ROBINSON was born in segregated Washington, D.C., near Thirty-seventh and Prospect Street, in a section of Georgetown then known as Holy Hill. One of five children, he was raised by his grandparents, Anna and Ignatius Barton, after his mother died when he was eight and his father disappeared. With only a junior-high-school education, he left school to help support his family. One of his jobs was dusting cars at the Key Bridge Garage, where his grandfather was the night watchman. In his spare time, Robinson drew. A chauffeur, impressed, showed the work to his sister, Elizabeth Thompson, who in turn presented it to her friend James Herring, head of the Howard University Art Department. Herring arranged for Robinson to study with James A. Porter, a painter and fellow Howard faculty member. In exchange for custodial work, Robinson gained tuition-free admission to Porter's class, in which he remained for only a semester; it would be his sole formal training in art. Robinson did not have the luxury of a full-time career as an artist. In 1934 he married Gladys Washington, and together they had seven children. Beginning that same year, he worked with the Civilian Conservation Corps in Lynchburg, Virginia. He then had a brief tenure at the Washington Navy Yard before becoming, in about 1936, a cook at St. Elizabeths Hospital, where he remained until he retired in 1970. Robinson lived in the Anacostia neighborhood of Washington from the time his grandparents moved there in 1929 until his death.[1]

Although Robinson continued to paint into the early 1990s, his most prolific period was probably the 1930s and 1940s. Both his self-portrait and the portrait of the director of the Barnett Aden Gallery, Alonzo Aden (cat. 47), date to the latter decade. Robinson first showed at the Barnett Aden Gallery in February–March 1945 in a group show that included William H. Johnson, Lois Mailou Jones, Celine Tabary, Prentiss Taylor, Hale Woodruff, and Porter. He showed there again in January 1946, twice in 1947, in August–September 1948, and in October–November 1952, when his work was featured in an exhibition of work from private collections.[2] His first major solo exhibition was at the Corcoran Gallery of Art in 1976; his last, at the Washington Project for the Arts, was in 1993. Robinson's art depicts his immediate world—his family and Washington neighborhoods. As Paul Richard, art critic for the *Washington Post*, noted, Robinson's paintings are "hymns to the ordinary."[3]

Like many young artists, Robinson used himself as a model. What is notable about this image is the complexity of its space. Robinson depicts not only his facial features reflected in the mirror but also the paintings in his studio, as if to say "I am my art."

CKC

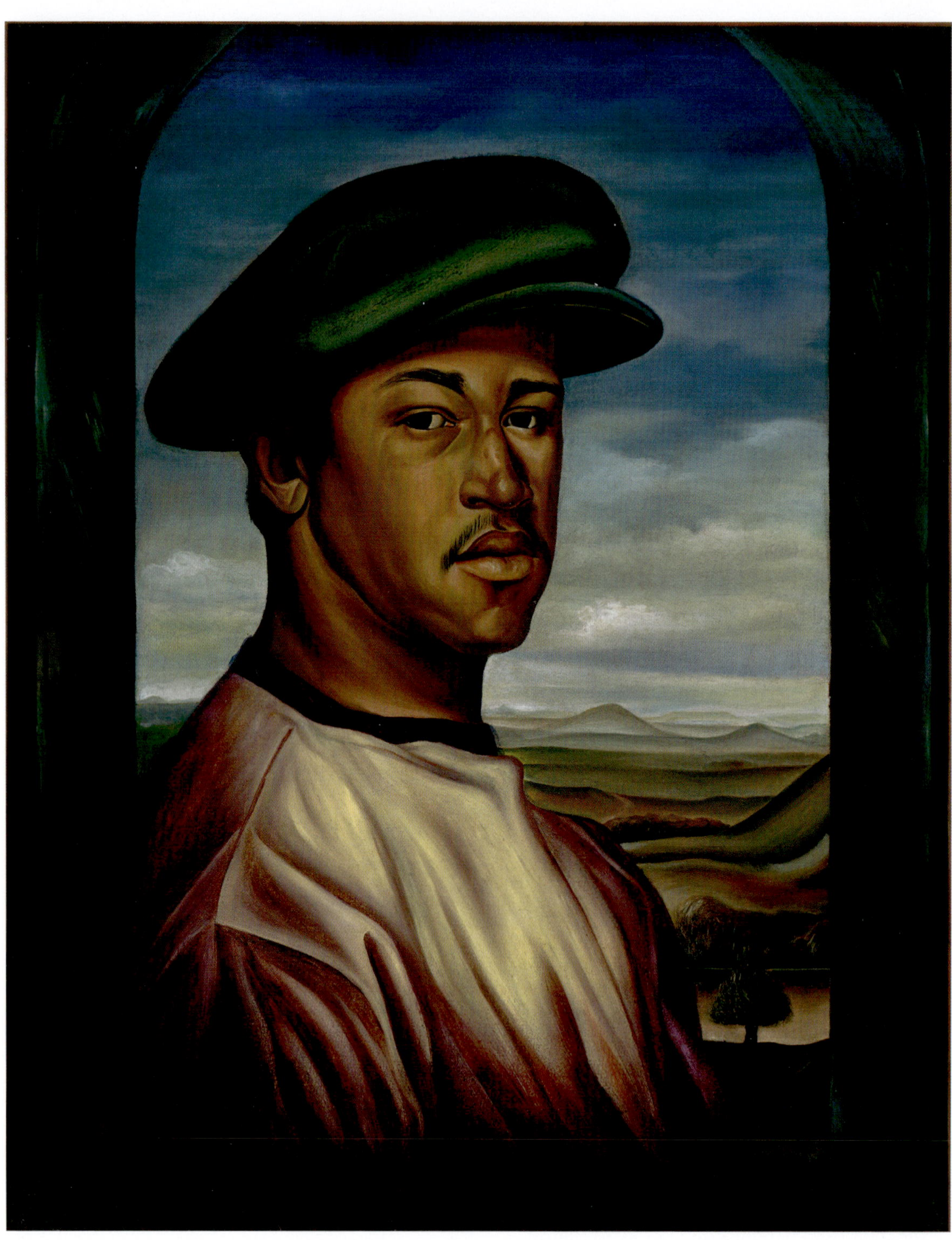

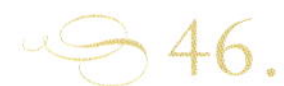 46.

SELF-PORTRAIT
By Frederick C. Flemister (1917–1976)

Oil on canvas, 76.8 × 61.3 cm (30¼ × 24⅛ in.), 1941
Robert L. Johnson/The Barnett Aden Collection

FREDERICK FLEMISTER's 1941 self-portrait is one of two known self-portraits by this talented African American painter. Both show Flemister in contemporary dress, but the pose he has selected and the landscape background reveal his desire to associate himself with the great artistic traditions of the late-fifteenth-century Italian Renaissance.

Born in Atlanta, Georgia, Flemister entered Morehouse College—the private, all-male, historically black college located in his hometown—in 1935. During his four years at Morehouse, he studied with the eminent African American artist Hale A. Woodruff. Upon graduation, Flemister spent a year (1940–41) at the John Herron Institute of Art in Indianapolis, where Woodruff, a graduate of the noted school, secured a scholarship for him. In 1941, Flemister returned to teach at Atlanta University, but his career there was interrupted in 1942 by military service.[1]

In February 1944, Flemister participated in an exhibition at the Barnett Aden Gallery in Washington, D.C., called "The Negro in Art."[2] The gallery director, Alonzo Aden (cat. 47), must have known either Flemister or his work since at least 1940, as the artist had won first prize for his self-portrait *Man with a Brush* (cat. 46-1) in an exhibition, also called "The Negro in Art," that Aden had organized for the Tanner Hall Art Galleries at the American Negro Exposition in Chicago that same year.[3] For the 1944 Washington exhibition, Aden also included the work of Woodruff, and that of several of his other students.[4] His action suggests that Aden was familiar with the 1942 exhibition that Woodruff had organized

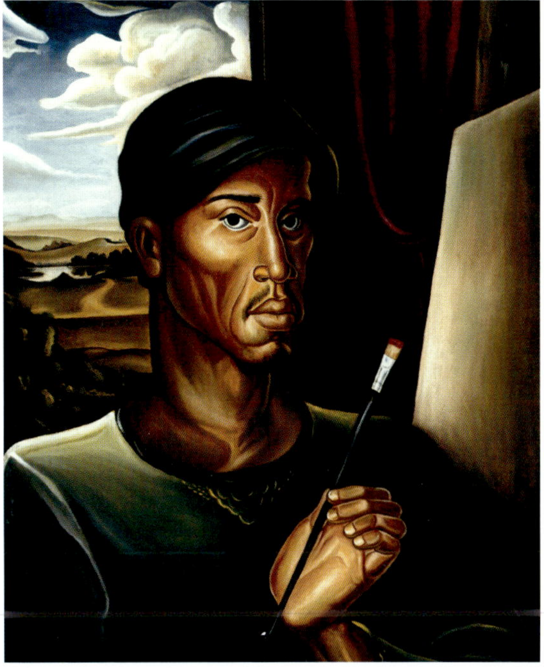

Cat. 46-1. *Man with Brush* by Frederick Flemister, oil on canvas, 1940. Clark Atlanta University Art Collection, Atlanta, Georgia

at Atlanta University, in which Flemister won first prize for his painting *The Mourners* (1942; Clark Atlanta University Art Gallery).[5] Although Flemister never again participated in a show at the Barnett Aden Gallery, and little is known about his artistic output after World War II, his early work continues to be included in major exhibitions surveying African American art.[6]

CKC

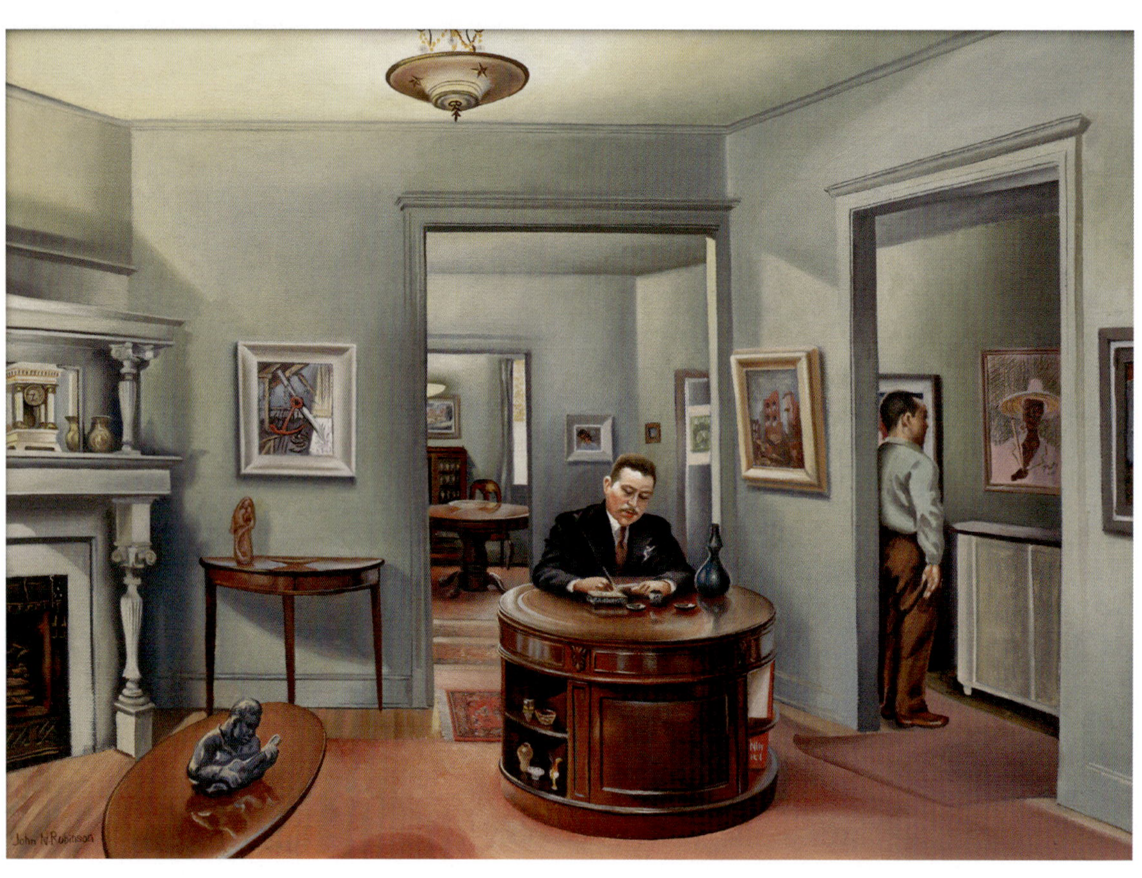

John N. Robinson

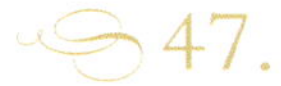

47.

FIRST GALLERY (ALONZO J. ADEN)

By John N. Robinson (1912–1994)

Oil on canvas board, 45.7 × 61 cm (18 × 24 in.), 1947
Robert L. Johnson/The Barnett Aden Collection

ALONZO J. ADEN (1906–1961) is shown here sitting at his desk in the Barnett Aden Gallery, which he co-founded in 1943 with James Vernon Herring (1887–1969). Located at 127 Randolph Place, Northwest, in Washington, D.C., it opened on October 16, 1943. The gallery, named in honor of Aden's mother, Naomi Barnett Aden, played a major role in promoting the work of both local and national artists for the next quarter-century. As director of the gallery and its driving force, Aden initially displayed mainly the work of African American artists, but from the early 1950s on, he assembled exhibitions that were noted for being racially integrated.[1]

Aden, who grew up in Spartanburg, South Carolina, and first came to Washington as a teenager to attend school, enrolled at Howard University in 1927. His early mentor, Herring, was a native of Clio, South Carolina, and a graduate of Syracuse University, with a bachelor's degree in art. Herring came to Howard in 1921, initially to teach drawing in the architecture department. But shortly after his arrival, he took the initiative to establish an art department, which he headed until his retirement in 1952. In 1928, after considerable effort, he was able to establish an art gallery at the university. Herring, a keen judge of talent—he recruited such subsequently well-known painters as Lois Mailou Jones, James A. Porter, and Alma Thomas to the art department—hired Aden, a former student, as the first curator of the Howard Gallery of Art in 1930. The two began living together about 1929. Aden, who graduated from Howard in 1933, continued

to work as a curator at the university gallery until 1935, when a Rockefeller Foundation Scholarship enabled him to complete a museum course and apprenticeship at the Buffalo Museum of Science. Clearly talented, he was asked in 1936 to curate an exhibition on African American life for the Texas Centennial Exhibition. Two years later he received a travel grant to study in Europe. Upon his return he was asked to organize an exhibition, "The Negro in Art," for the Tanner Hall Galleries at the 1940 American Negro Exposition in Chicago. After becoming director of the Barnett Aden Gallery, Aden continued to work with other African American institutions, and in 1945 he helped Tuskegee Normal and Industrial Institute (now Tuskegee University) establish its art gallery.[2] After Aden's death, Herring continued to run the gallery on Randolph Place; when Herring died, the gallery was sold to pay his debts.[3]

Washington native John Robinson (cat. 45) first showed at the Barnett Aden Gallery in 1945, exhibiting this painting there in May 1947. It is entirely possible that the artist has portrayed himself looking at the paintings on the wall. Robinson was a careful observer of reality: the desk at which Aden sits exists today, and the sculpture on the left, *Guitar Player*, is the work of Cuban artist Theodoro Ramos-Blanco. The domestic nature of the gallery's interior was consistent with the goals of the founders, as they sought to encourage individuals to purchase art for their home.[4]

CKC

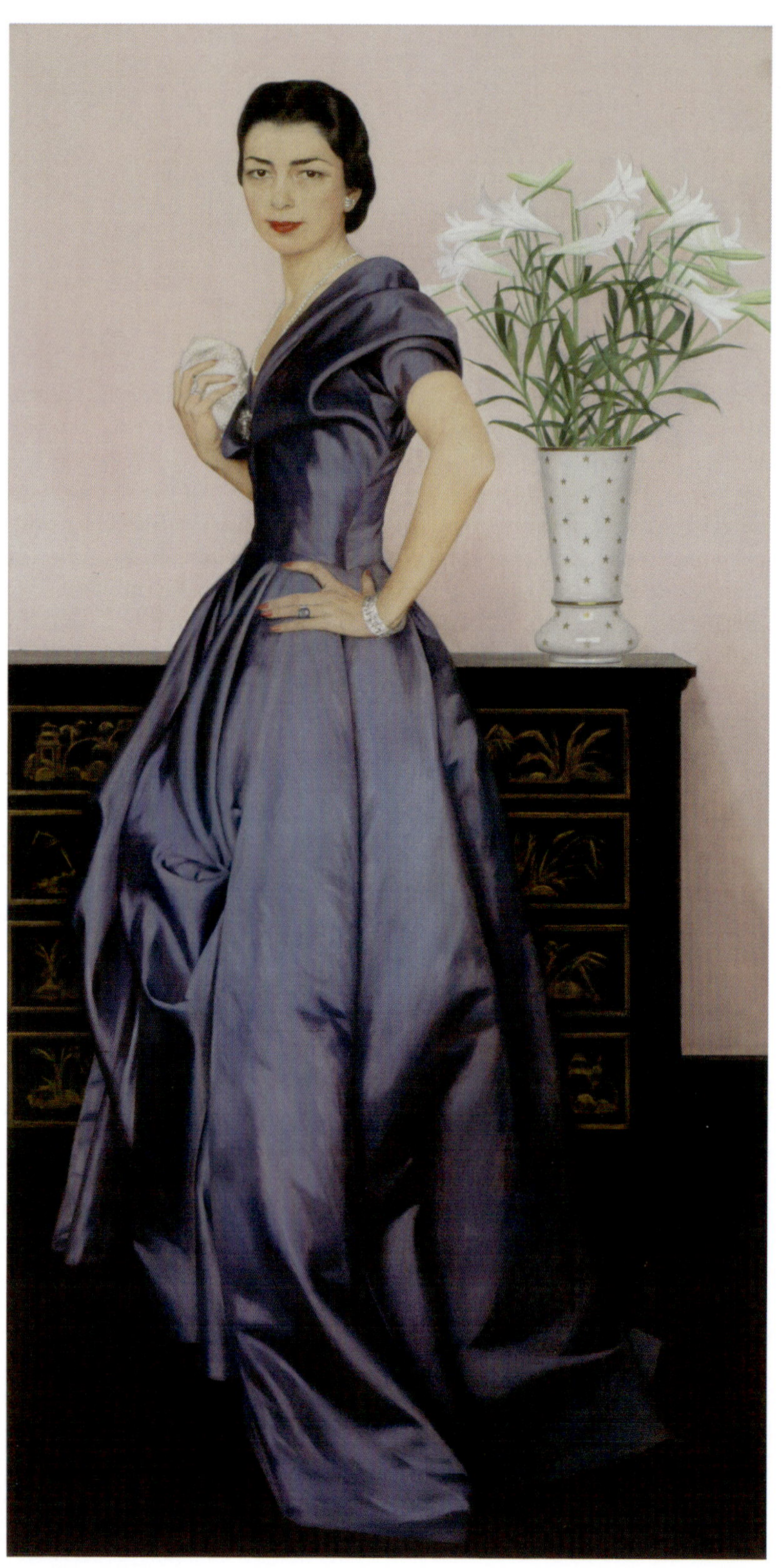

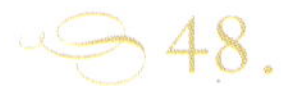

48.

GWENDOLYN DETRE CAFRITZ

By Bernard Boutet de Monvel (1884–1949)

Oil on canvas, 137.8 × 80.6 cm (54¼ × 31¾ in.) framed, 1948
Private collection

"**I**THINK IT has the clean linear design of a Botticelli, and the elegance of an English portrait … and that's the way I would like my children to remember me," said Gwendolyn Cafritz (1910–1988), speaking of her portrait by Bernard Boutet de Monvel in a 1956 interview with Edward R. Murrow.[1] At the time, Cafritz's reputation as one of Washington's premier hostesses was at its apogee. Born in Budapest, Hungary, the energetic and ambitious Gwendolyn Detre immigrated to the United States with her family in the 1920s. She married Morris Cafritz (1887–1964) in 1929.[2] A Washington native who became one of the city's most successful real estate developers, Morris supported her social ambitions, taste for designer clothes, and interest in avant-garde architecture. Their large, art deco–style house on Foxhall Road, NW, completed in 1938, served as the venue for her increasingly elaborate and visible parties.[3] Attention to those events reached a national audience in 1949 when *Time* magazine published a brief piece on Washington titled "Life Among the Party Givers," and asked rhetorically, "Now that wealthy Perle Mesta was moving to Luxembourg to be the U.S. minister … who would take her place as the No. 1 party giver?" The answer was the "lynx-eyed Cafritz." Cementing that nomination was the August 1 issue of *Life*. Its five-page story quoted her as saying, "The kind of dinner I like is to have an ambassador, a Supreme Court Justice, one Republican, one Democrat, and one person in the limelight."[4]

Slowed by the death of her husband in 1964 and her own ill health, Cafritz gave her last large party, described as a "trip back into Washington social history," in June 1986.[5]

Cafritz had studied art history in Budapest, and her interest in art may have been one of several impulses that led her to commission her portrait from Bernard Boutet de Monvel, a French artist who first came to America in 1926 and returned frequently to paint the portraits of the social elite.[6] Presumably, Cafritz first met him in Palm Beach, Florida, where she had a home and he maintained a studio before World War II.[7] His name may also have resonated with Cafritz, as his father, Maurice, was responsible for the well-liked paintings on the theme of Joan of Arc owned by the Corcoran Gallery of Art in Washington.[8] The sitter and artist were well matched, as he liked designer clothes, high-fashion furniture, and an elegant lifestyle as much as she. Her portrait, typical of the artist's crisp, elegant technique, shows Cafritz in a designer dress with her favorite jewels. It was probably painted in New York sometime after the artist returned to America in November 1947 to attend the opening of his new show, "Profiles," at the Knoedler Gallery and before his departure for France in March 1948.[9] By April 4, 1948, the portrait had attracted the attention of a *Washington Post* reporter.[10] Boutet de Monvel died in a plane crash the following November.[11]

CKC

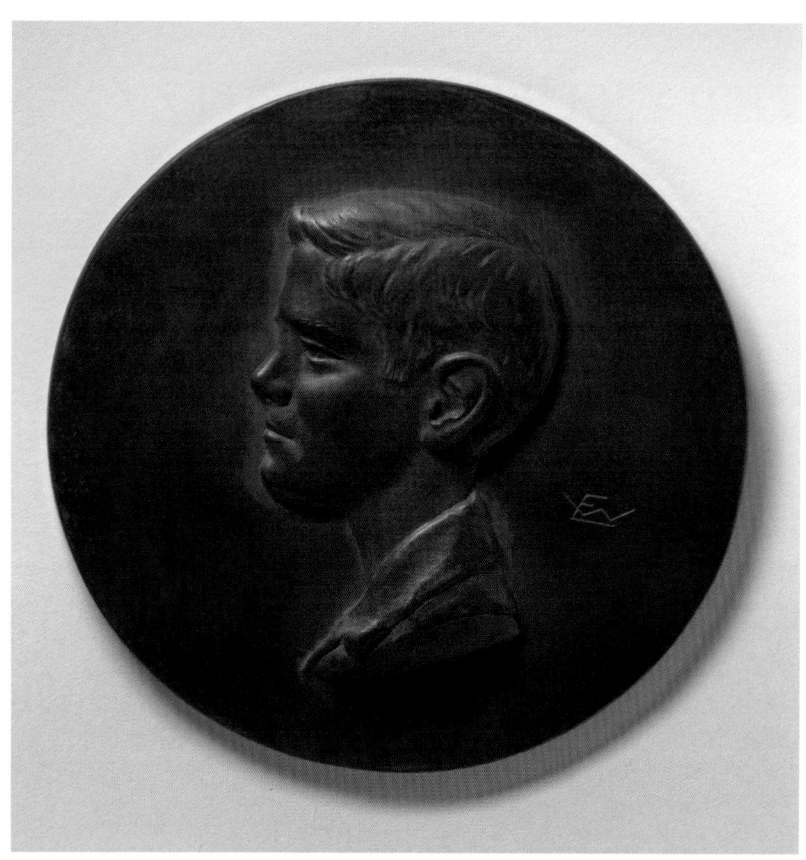

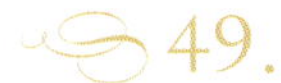

49.

WARREN ZIMMERMANN

By Electra Waggoner (Biggs) (1912–2001)

Bronze, 26 cm (10¼ in.) diameter, c. 1948
Mrs. Warren Zimmermann

ELECTRA WAGGONER made this portrait of Warren Zimmermann (1934–2004) when he was thirteen. It may have been a thank-you from the artist, who rented the Zimmermann family's summer home in Southampton in 1948, or possibly Barbara Zimmermann, the boy's mother, who was a friend of the artist's, asked for a portrait of her son before he left for his freshman year at Deerfield Academy.[1] Waggoner, who used her maiden name as her professional one, was well known for having "a way with children."[2]

Electra Waggoner was the granddaughter of William Thomas (W. T.) Waggoner (1852–1934), who made a substantial fortune in the cattle and oil businesses. As a young woman she did not let wealth stand in the way of her pursuit of a career in the arts.[3] Indeed, her status as heir to a fortune that included a ranch of more than 500,000 acres in northern Texas doubtless gave her the freedom to explore her talent in a vocation notorious for its lack of financial reward. Sent east as a teenager, Waggoner graduated from Miss Wright's School in Bryn Mawr, Pennsylvania, and took classes at Columbia University in New York. She studied briefly in that city with sculptor Katherine Breese and in Boston with Arnold Geissbuhler, then completed her apprenticeship in Paris.[4] She was married for a short time in 1933.[5] She spent most of the decade in New York, but came to the nation's capital in 1936 to sculpt a portrait of John Nance Garner.[6] In 1937 she received an honorable mention for a black marble bust in the Paris Salon, and in 1938 she had a major show at Jacques Seligmann & Company in New

York.[7] In 1942 she married Lieutenant Colonel John Biggs. His assignment brought her back to Washington. While here, she had an exhibition of her work at the Corcoran Gallery of Art (October 28–November 18, 1945), and she completed a bust of President Harry Truman intended for the Missouri State Capitol.[8] Around 1946, Waggoner and her husband returned to Texas. The Red River Valley Museum in Vernon, Texas, has the largest collection of Waggoner's work.[9]

In selecting a circular design for her portrait of the young Zimmermann, Waggoner chose a form that had its antecedents in Roman sculpture. It was popular during the Italian Renaissance and reinvigorated as a major motif in late-nineteenth- and early twentieth-century American art by such eminent sculptors as Augustus Saint-Gaudens, Daniel Chester French, and Paul Manship (cat. 41). Waggoner herself employed it on previous occasions, including a medallion portrait of her daughter.[10]

Zimmermann, who grew up in Haverford, Pennsylvania, graduated from Yale University in 1956 and received a master's degree from Cambridge University in 1958. He became a distinguished career diplomat, serving as ambassador to Yugoslavia (1989–92) at the end of his thirty-year service with the State Department. He later wrote *Origins of a Catastrophe: Yugoslavia and Its Destroyers—America's Last Ambassador Tells What Happened and Why* (1996) and *First Great Triumph: How Five Americans Made Their Country a World Power* (2002).[11]

CKC

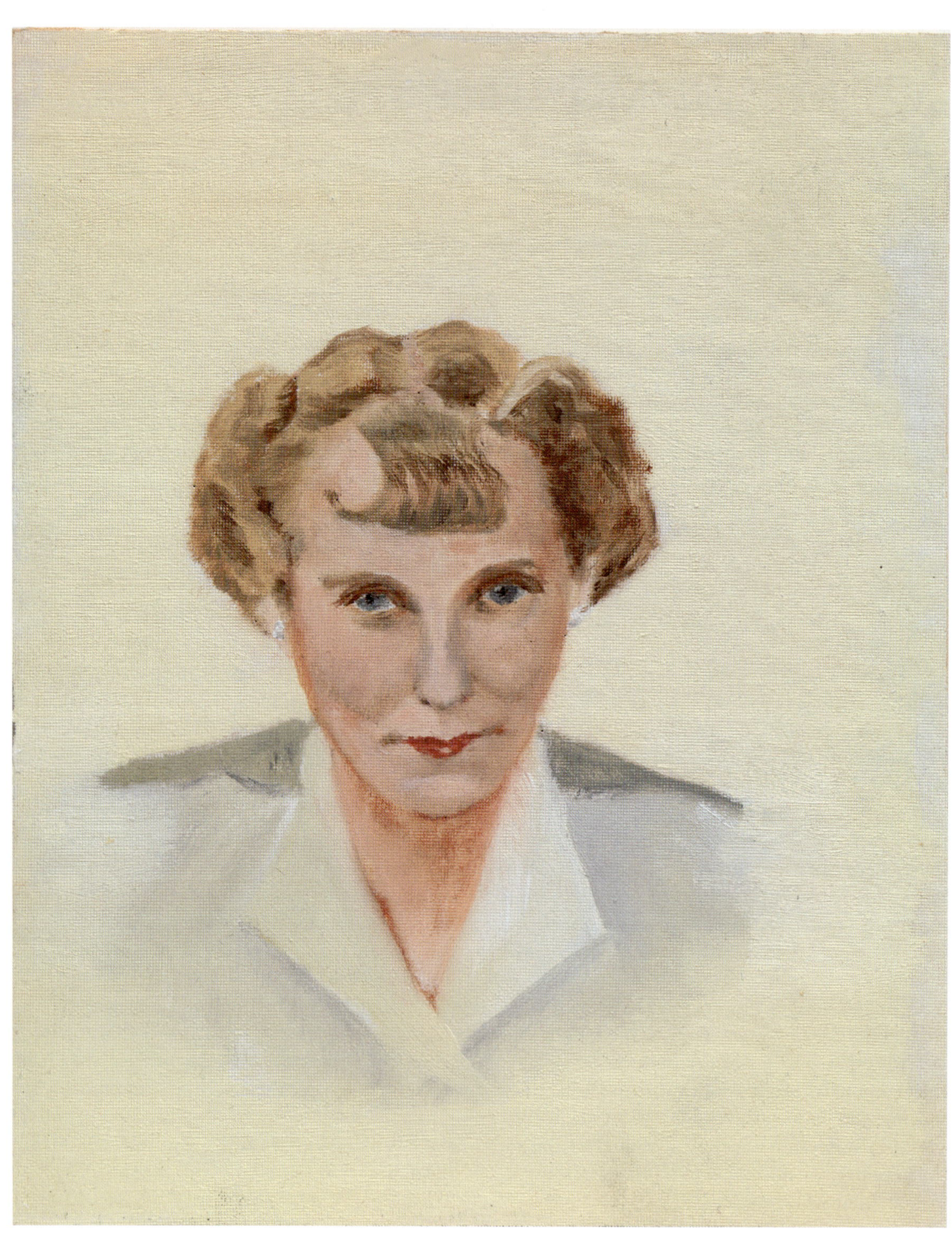

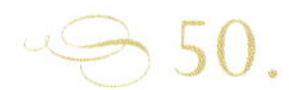

50.

MAMIE GENEVA DOUD EISENHOWER
By Dwight David Eisenhower (1890–1969)

Oil on artist's board, 17.8 × 14 cm (7 × 5½ in.), c. 1952, after 1941 photograph
Susan Eisenhower

IN EARLY 1947, as General Dwight D. Eisenhower—then chief of staff of the U.S. Army—sat at his residence at Fort Myer, Virginia, for the second of more than twenty portraits of him by the Welsh-born, New York–based artist Thomas E. Stephens (1886–1966), the two talked about the art of painting. Eisenhower noted that painting had been a major form of relaxation for Winston Churchill during the war years. When Stephens encouraged him to try his hand, Eisenhower responded by saying that he "couldn't draw a straight line or a round circle," belying the training he had received in mapmaking as a student at West Point.[1] According to Eisenhower, who was soon to become president of Columbia University (1948–52) in New York, the two next discussed painting in his Morningside Heights residence as Mamie Eisenhower (1896–1979) sat for a portrait by Stephens.[2] Inspired by Stephens's work and support, Eisenhower seized the opportunity to use the paints remaining on Stephens's palette to begin his own image of his wife. Stephens, delighted at the turn of events, subsequently sent Eisenhower a set of colors.[3] By the summer of 1948, Eisenhower was fully engaged in the new hobby and that fall sent a painting to a New York charity auction in support of the Urban League.[4] At Columbia, Eisenhower used a penthouse retreat in which to work; at the White House he maintained a small second-floor room near the elevator for keeping his supplies readily available. When he retired to Gettysburg, Eisenhower, who also liked to paint landscapes and still lifes, noted, "I have tried more portraits than anything else. I have also burned more portraits than anything else."[5]

Eisenhower's small but charming portrait of his wife aptly captures her cheerful demeanor and signature hairstyle—close-cropped with perfectly trimmed bangs. It speaks to the compelling nature of a portrait, even when done by an amateur. The painting, which is on artist's board purchased in Versailles, France, was made when Eisenhower was on leave of absence from Columbia serving as Supreme Allied Commander of NATO.[6] Eisenhower usually painted from photographs rather than from life, and the inscription on the back, "Mamie [19]41," suggests that he used a favorite image taken of her during the year they celebrated their twenty-fifth wedding anniversary.[7] Although this portrait was not done from life, the phrase "model wife," with its multiple meanings, seems apt. Mamie Eisenhower was indeed an exemplary spouse, supporting Dwight as he rose from a West Point graduate to Supreme Commander of the Allied Expeditionary Forces during World War II to an equally exalted position in civilian life—president of the United States. The two had married in July 1916. During the next thirty-seven years of Dwight's military career, Mamie moved thirty-five times. When she entered the White House in 1953, Washington was a familiar city: not only had they spent the years 1946 to 1948 just across the river at Fort Myer, but they had also lived at the Wyoming Apartments on Columbia Road twice—first in 1927–28 and again in 1929–36; and during World War II she maintained an apartment at the Wardman Park Hotel.[8]

CKC

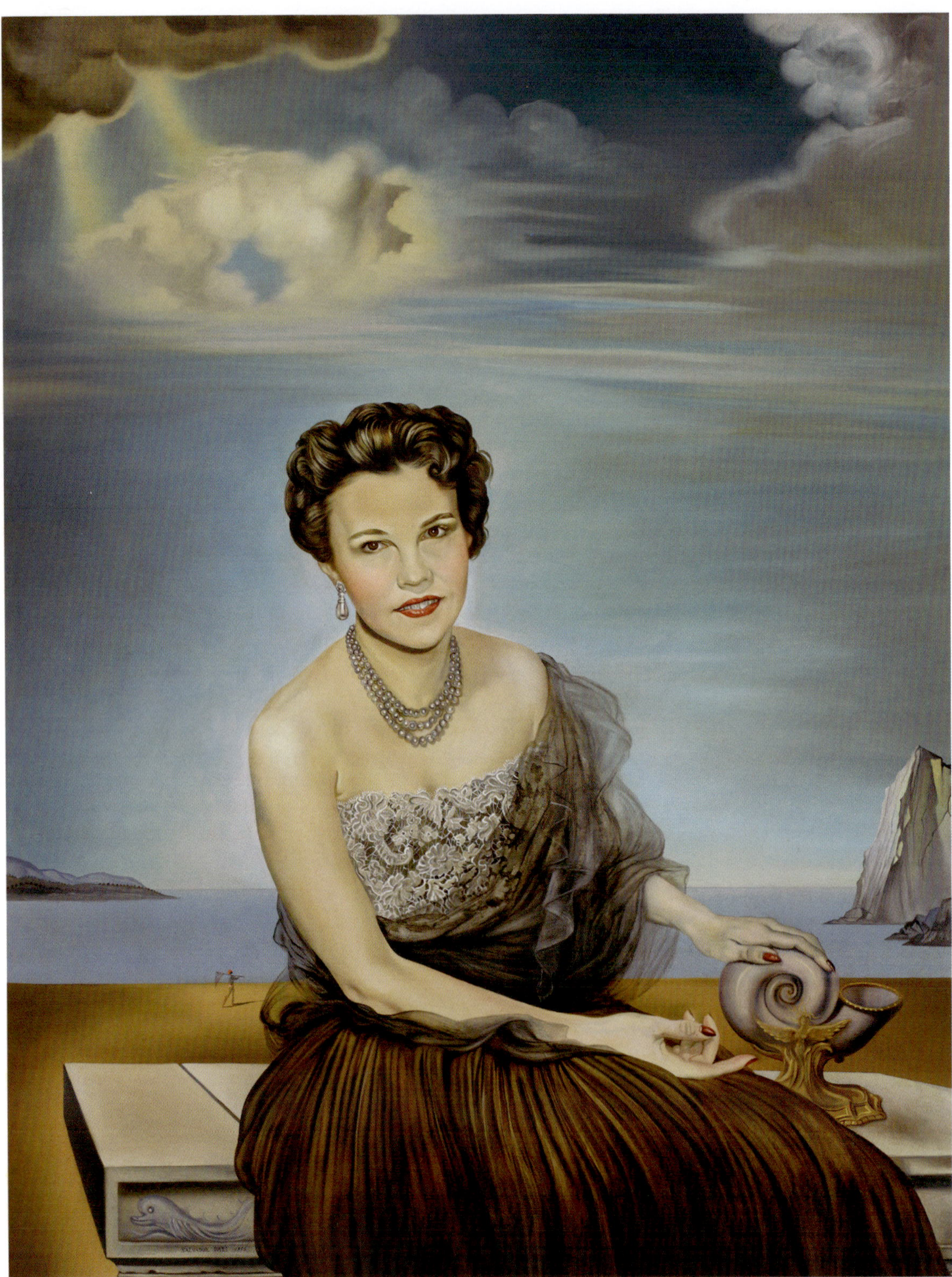

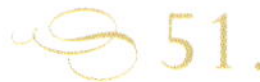

51.

DOLORES SUERO
By Salvador Dalí (1904–1989)

Oil on canvas, 99.7 × 74.9 cm (39¼ × 29½ in.), 1955
Carlos and Rosa de la Cruz, courtesy of Isabel de la Cruz Ernst

WHEN ONE thinks of the work of Catalonian-born Salvador Dalí (1904–1989), whose full name— Salvador Domingo Felipe Jacinto Dalí i Domènch, first marquis of Púbol—is as complex as his imagination, his fantasy landscapes, such as the *Persistence of Memory* (1931; Museum of Modern Art, New York) rather than his portraits first come to mind. Yet from his earliest days, when he used his family as subjects, portraiture has been an important part of his oeuvre.[1] Moreover, when Dalí, who first came to America in 1934, returned with his wife at the outbreak of World War II to spend eight years in the United States, portraiture was a crucial means of support. He was a favorite of wealthy women, particularly those with international credentials, such as Helena Rubinstein and Lady Mountbatten. In a review of his 1943 exhibition of recently completed portraits at New York's Knoedler Gallery, the critic for *ARTnews* gave credit to Dalí's "meticulous technique" that greatly improved "modern standards of craftsmanship." The writer also noted that the portraits on display were reputed to have cost "five figures."[2] As one biographer perceptively observed years later, the portraits brought the artist "three most desirable rewards: wealth, publicity, and a permanent place in The Set."[3]

Although Dalí returned to Spain in 1948, he and his wife, Gala, came to the United States for about five months each year for the next decade. While in New York, they usually lived at the St. Regis Hotel on East Fifty-fifth Street. Their bedroom served as his studio.[4] The mid-1950s were a particularly busy time for Dalí in America. He had exhibitions at the Carstairs Gallery (1955, 1956), and in 1955 Chester Dale gave Dalí's recently completed *Crucifixion* to New York's Metropolitan Museum of Art. The following year Dalí loaned *Sacrament of the Last Supper* (1955) to the National Gallery of Art in Washington.[5]

The Cuban-born Dolores Suero (1918–1992), whose parents' home in Havana was designed by the well-known architectural firm Carrère & Hastings, maintained an apartment at the Carlyle in New York from 1949 until 1962.[6] While in the United States, the recently divorced Suero became part of the community of cosmopolitan women intimately involved in charitable causes.[7] Either her knowledge of the art world or her social contacts could have led her to Dalí. The commonality of their native tongue would have provided an additional bond. Dalí, who became a friend, began the portrait with sketches made in Suero's apartment. He completed it with only one formal sitting.[8] The carefully crafted image reveals Dalí's delight in rendering the textures of the subject's dress and jewelry. She is placed in an imaginary landscape, which draws its inspiration from the seacoast near Dalí's Catalonian home in Port Lligat (Cadaqués), in a region of the Costa Brava that was also a favorite of the sitter.[9] When Suero left New York to join her family, who had moved to Madrid at the time of the Cuban Revolution, the portrait remained in New York. Dalí saw it again in 1965 when Suero's son and his wife gave a cocktail party in his honor in their Park Avenue apartment.[10]

CKC

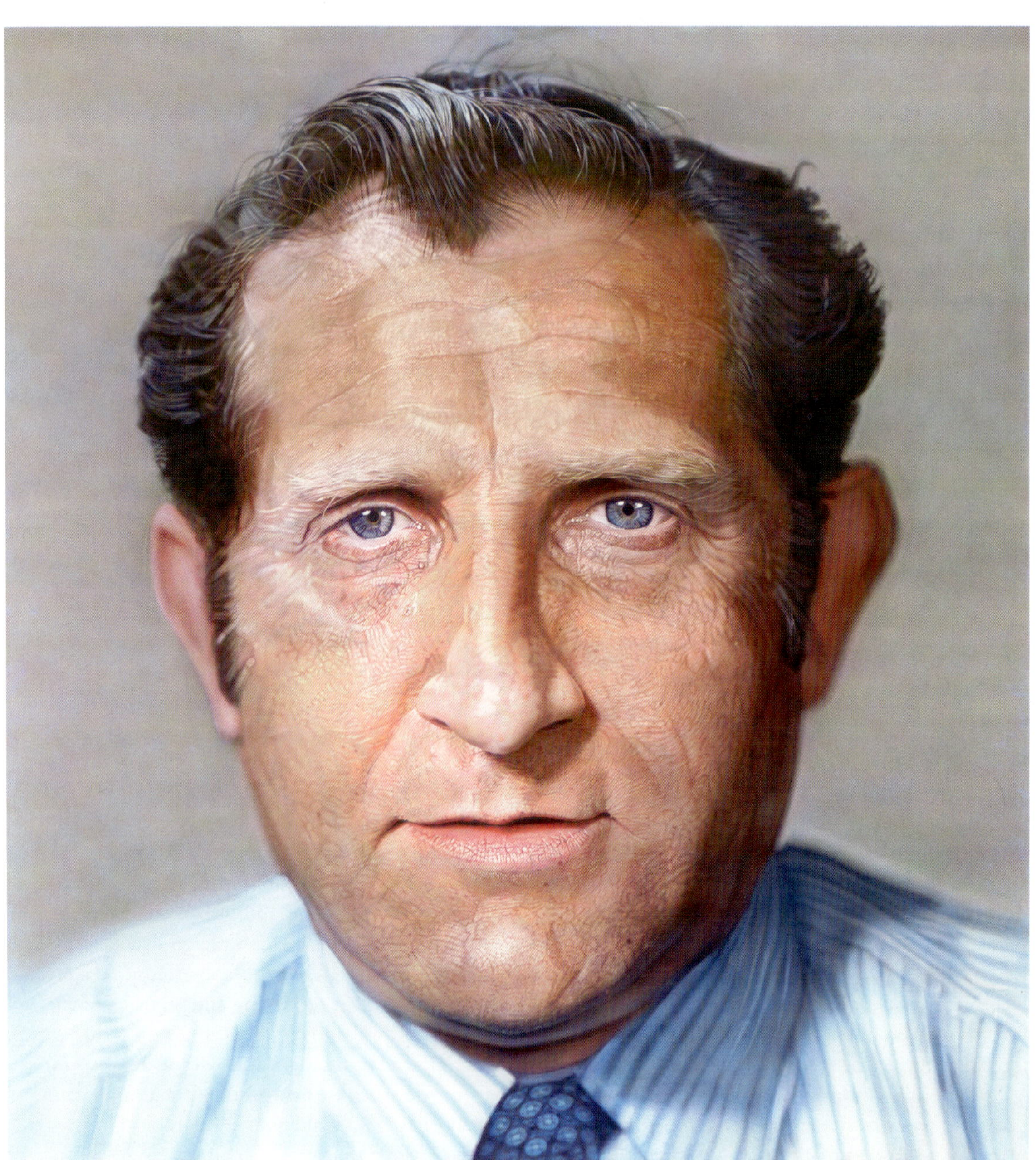

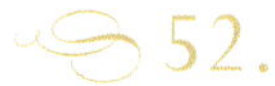

NAT (NAT ROSE)

By Chuck Close (b. 1940)

Acrylic on canvas, 254 × 228.6 cm (100 × 90 in.), 1971
National Gallery of Art, Washington, D.C.; partial and promised gift of Anita and
Burton Reiner, 2005.108.1

WHEN CONTEMPORARY collector Anita Reiner and her husband bought Chuck Close's portrait of the artist's father-in-law, Nat Rose (born 1924), their aesthetic intuition would serve them well. The artist's reputation continued to grow during the 1970s, and today he reigns as one of America's preeminent artists. "We buy on impulse," Mrs. Reiner admitted. "In 1970, we had seen his black and white paintings in the exhibition '22 Realists' at the Whitney Museum. On December 23, the following year, we were at the Bykert Gallery—Close's dealer at the time—and we fell in love with his new paintings using color. Ironically, as we left the gallery . . . I saw a man approaching that looked familiar. 'Did you,' I said to him, 'ever have your portrait painted?' 'Yes,' he replied. 'Well [I said], we just bought it.'"[1]

As a young artist, Close, a native of Monroe, Washington, who had received his MFA with highest honors from Yale University in 1964, faced the dilemma of all serious artists who seek to become seminal figures within the art-historical canon: how to create work that would be irrevocably stamped with a unique stylistic signature. After a Fulbright grant to study in Vienna, a teaching appointment at the University of Massachusetts, and a move to New York City, Close began to focus in his SoHo studio on a series of large black-and-white painted heads, including his own *Big Self-Portrait* (1967–68; Walker Art Center, Minneapolis). He began that painting by taking a photograph of himself and creating a grid on both it and his large canvas. Close liked using a photograph as a source rather than an actual model because the photographic process automatically reduced a three-dimensional image to a two-dimensional one. It also eliminated any emotional interaction with the subject during the painting process—traditionally an essential aspect of portraiture. In Close's early portraits such as *Nat*, he used an airbrush to replicate on his canvas the pictorial information contained in the photograph, grid by grid. By focusing on abstract details rather than the whole image, Close sought to escape any preconceived notions about the rendering of an image.[2] With these early paintings, Close established a process that would be fundamental to his work, despite modifications in technique or the outward appearance of subsequent works.

Nat represents one of four early examples of Close's transition from black and white to paintings with color. Close, who observed that only three colors were needed to construct the full chromatic range of a color photograph—red (magenta), blue (cyan), and yellow—employed the same principle in *Nat*. Using an airbrush, he applied the colors in three separate layers. Every area of the painting has some of all three colors in varying densities. The relative percentage of each color controls the hue and its intensity, and the relative density of the combined colors determines value. To avoid traditional approaches, Close wore tinted filters on his glasses so he would see only the colors he was spraying at any given moment.[3]

CKC

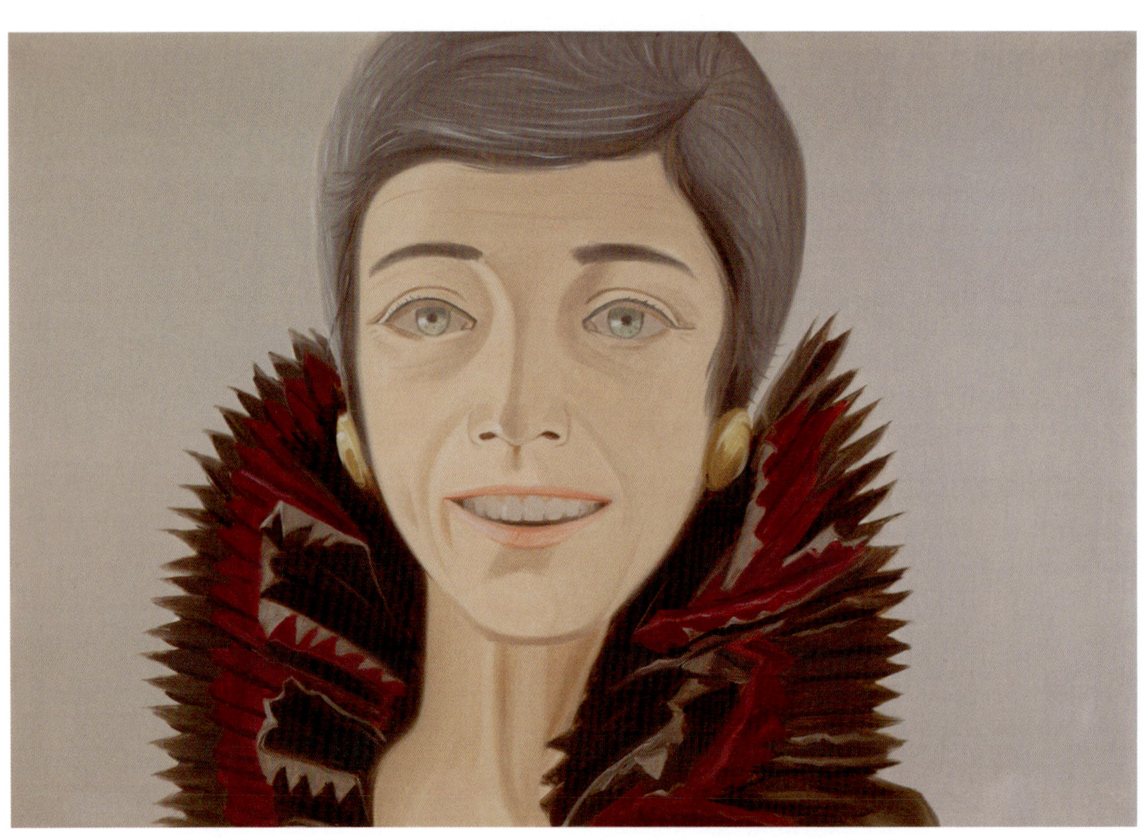

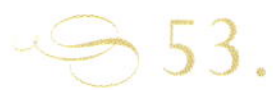 53.

EVIE (EVELYN STEFANSSON NEF)

By Alex Katz (b. 1927)

Acrylic on canvas, 86.4 × 121.9 cm (34 × 48 in.), 1974
Corcoran Gallery of Art, Washington, D.C.; gift of Evelyn Stefansson Nef
(2010.008.020)

THE TITLE, *Finding My Way: The Autobiography of an Optimist,* of a book published shortly before the author's ninetieth birthday conveys the essence of Evelyn Stefansson Nef's personality and her fundamental approach to life, but it gives no hint of her charisma or her extraordinary ability to reinvent herself, qualities that become apparent in her elegant narrative.[1] Nef (1913–2009), who became an Arctic scholar in her thirties, a psychotherapist in her fifties, and later an arts patron and philanthropist, was born Evelyn Schwartz in New York City. One of four sisters, her secure family life was shattered by the death of her father in 1927, which exacerbated her mother's mental and emotional decline. Adventuresome and outgoing, Nef became part of the social and artistic scene in Greenwich Village in her late teens. It was there that she met Buckminster Fuller, with whom she had a short but intense affair, and where she met her first husband, puppeteer Bil Baird. When their four-year marriage disintegrated in 1936, she returned to the Village to live, subsequently finding work at the famous Gotham Book Mart on Forty-seventh Street. She reconnected with the noted Arctic explorer Vilhjalmur Stefansson (cat. 40), who was impressed with her keen intelligence. He subsequently hired her as a research assistant. The two were married in 1941. For the next two decades they lived primarily in the Hanover, New Hampshire area, where she gained such deep knowledge of the Arctic that, in addition to serving as the librarian of her husband's polar collection, she taught an Arctic seminar for two years in the Polar Studies Department at nearby Dartmouth College. She also published the best-selling book *Here Is Alaska* (1943) and, with her husband, served as a consultant to the army and navy on the Arctic during World War II. Stefansson died in 1962, and she moved to Washington, D.C., the following year. Through mutual friends, she met the man who in 1964 would become her third husband, John Ulrich Nef (1899–1988). A historian of economics, John Nef had joined the faculty of the University of Chicago in 1929 and founded the university's well-known Committee on Social Thought in 1941.[2] His passion for art was an interest that Evelyn quickly absorbed.[3] Trips to Europe were frequent, and John's friendship with artist Marc Chagall and his wife quickly became hers as well. In 1971 the French artist presented the couple with a 10 × 17-foot mosaic mural in the garden of the Nefs' N Street home in Georgetown.[4] A man known for generous gifts, John Nef suggested celebrating the couple's tenth anniversary by commissioning a portrait of his wife from New York art star Alex Katz, a man who had defied the abstract expressionists' mantra that a good painting could not represent a visible subject.[5] Katz, known for his portraits of friends and well-known personalities in New York's arts world, created a dramatic head-and-shoulder portrait of Evelyn, which shows her face framed by the elaborate collar of a dress designed by noted French couturier Mme. Grès.[6] The simple, bold, flat forms, characteristic of Katz's style, capture her inherent energy, intelligence, and zest for life. Subsequently, the Nefs were in Paris and discovered the preliminary study for this portrait in a show featuring work by Katz. Naturally, they acquired it (see fig. 16).[7]

CKC

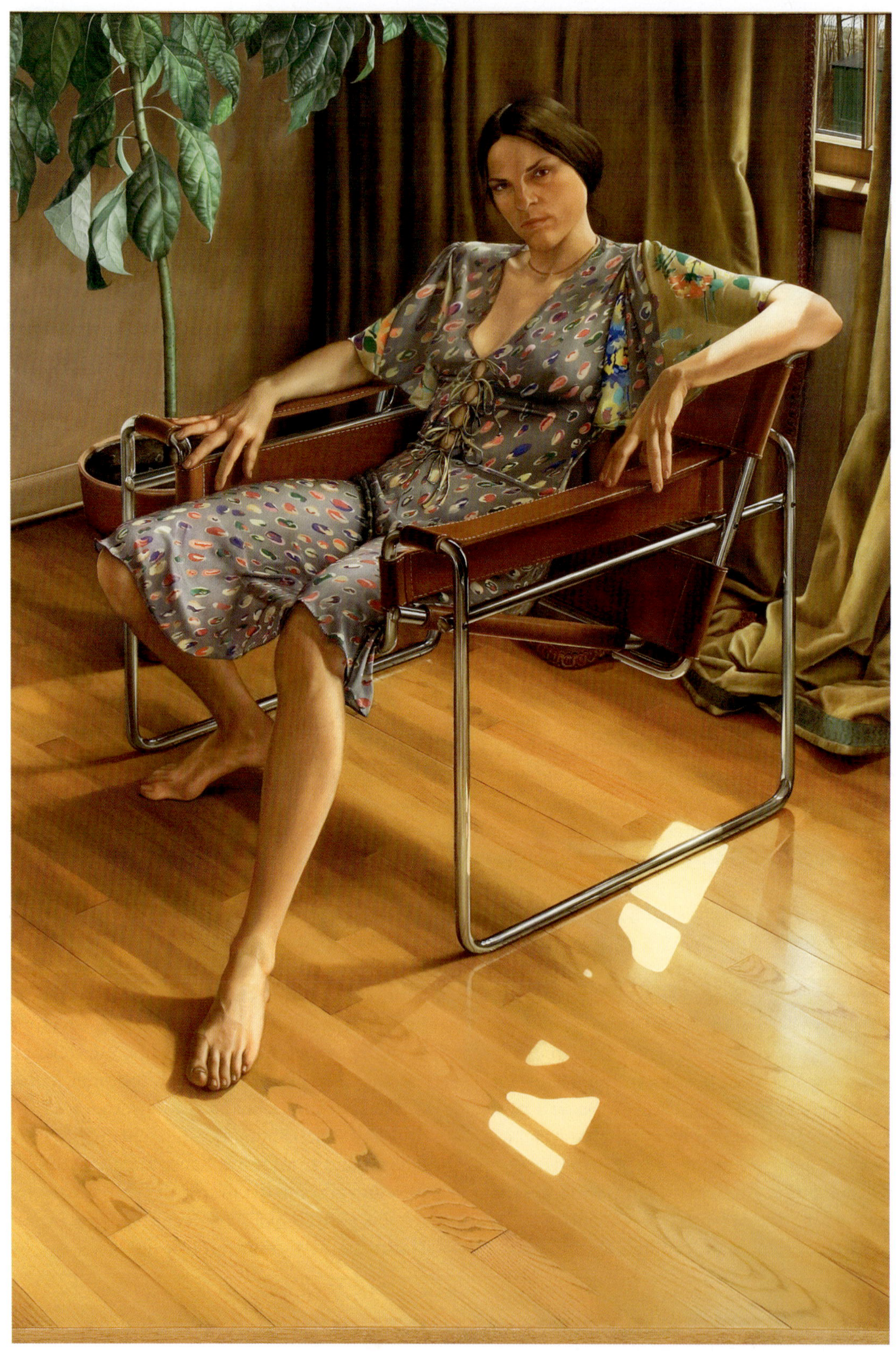

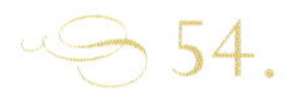

54

DIANA #3 (DIANA MOORE BECKMAN)

By William Beckman (b. 1942)

Oil on panel, 182.9 × 127 cm (72 × 50 in.), 1976
Private collection

I am not a traditional portrait painter. I am not interested in achieving a likeness that suits my sitters. I am more interested in what feels right to me. I only paint people I know really well—wives, girlfriends, my parents, close friends. My way of being with someone I like is by painting that person. It gives me company. Although story-telling is not a part of my painting, I do include things in paintings that have very personal meaning.[1]

IN 1971, William Beckman began a series of paintings in which his then-wife, Diana Moore (born 1946), a sculptor, served as the model. Over the next two decades, she was the subject of a variety of works, ranging from small head-and-shoulder portraits to large full-length studies. *Diana #3* is among the more complex compositions in which she figures, and one of the rare works in which she is not posed frontally.[2]

Beckman and his wife had met at the University of Iowa in the mid-1960s, where they were both studying art, she for her BA and he for his MA and MFA. In 1969, the year their daughter, Deidra, was born, they moved to New York City. Their East Broadway home was the loft previously occupied by another figurative painter, Alfred Leslie.[3] Beckman's use of a highly detailed interior space for *Diana #3* relates to the small, spatially complex trompe l'oeil boxes—several of which featured his wife—that he had painted between 1968 and 1971.[4] Here, however, he expanded the scale, challenging himself by literally taking his art to another level. One can only speculate whether, having left the Midwest, he was influenced by direct contact with the large portraits by artists such as Chuck Close (cats. 52 and 61) and Leslie.[5] The careful articulation of the figure and objects, and their highly tactile quality, speaks to Beckman's love of Northern Renaissance painting, with its precise rendering of reality. Everything in *Diana #3* is meticulously observed, whether the front and back of the plant leaves, the voluptuous mass of the velvet curtain, or the variegation of the wood floor. Beckman delights in juxtaposing elements: the hardness of the varnished floor opposed to the soft curtains; the highly patterned and richly colored, supple dress around the monochromatic, hard, sculpture-like limbs of the figure; even the chair's matte leather surface contrasts with its reflective steel frame. The play of light repeatedly captures Beckman's imagination. Most notable is the light from the window that is reflected on the floor, which calls to mind the use of light in Jan van Eyck's *Madonna in the Church* (1437–39; Gemäldegalerie, Berlin).[6] But unlike the ethereal attitude of the Madonna in the fifteenth-century painting, the questioning gaze of the sitter—directed as it is toward the artist and the viewer—and the sensuality of her pose underscore the earthy actuality of this late-twentieth-century work.

CKC

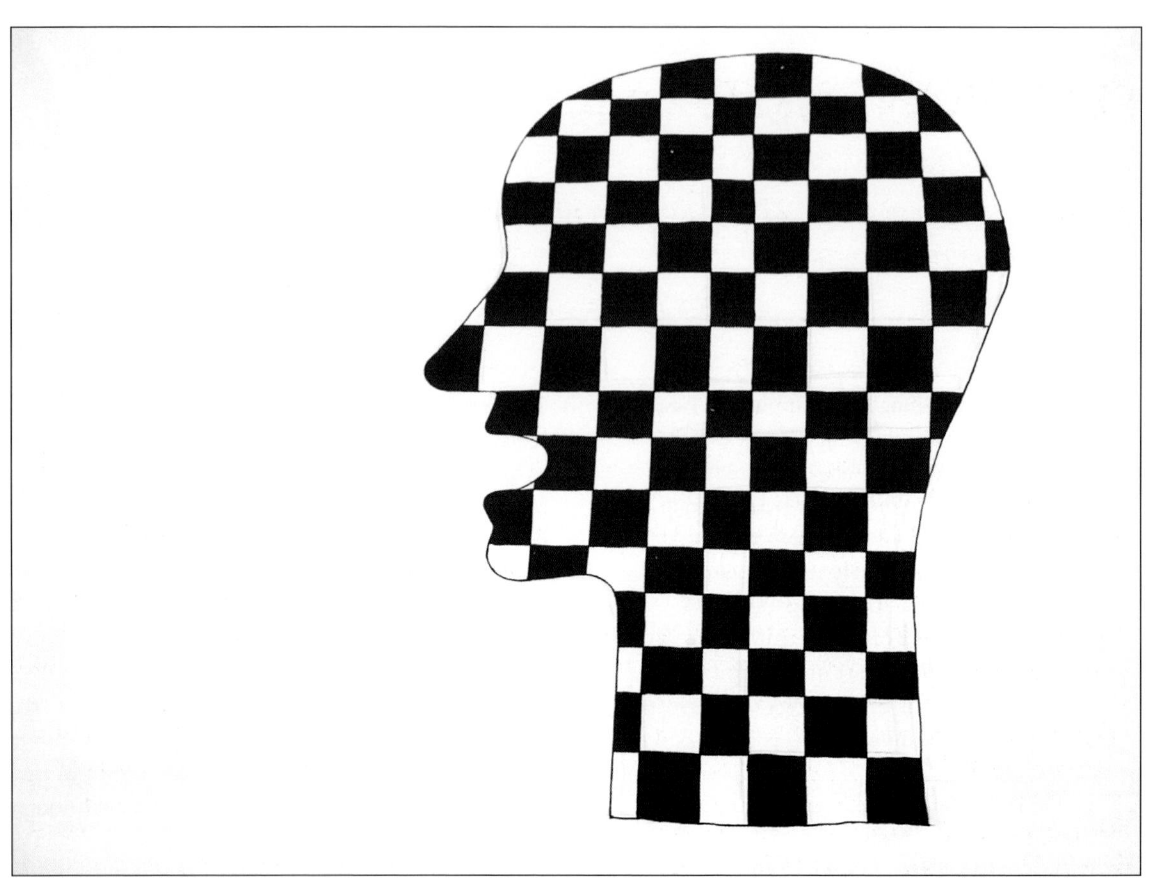

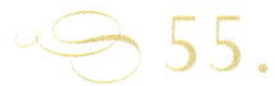 55.

SELF-PORTRAIT
By Gene Davis (1920–1985)

Acrylic on canvas, 228.6 × 279.4 cm (90 × 110 in.), 1982
Xavier Equihua

GENE DAVIS was one of the few painters from Washington to achieve a national reputation. His preoccupation with painting began in 1949; before that, he worked primarily as a journalist, first as a sportswriter and then as a political reporter. His first solo show at the Dupont Theatre Gallery in 1952 featured figurative black-and-white drawings and revealed the influence of Arshile Gorky and Paul Klee. Although fellow painter Kenneth Noland arranged for a one-person exhibition at Catholic University the following year, Davis gathered only limited recognition until the early 1960s, when he began to exhibit his signature stripe paintings. These works garnered a major profile in the *Washington Post* and continuing favorable reviews; they also attracted the attention of major art historians, curators, and critics, among them Clement Greenberg. He arranged for a New York gallery (Poindexter) to handle Davis's work and included the artist in the seminal exhibition "Post-Painterly Abstraction" (1964). Equally important to Davis's reputation was the 1965 traveling exhibition, "Washington Color Painters," which also included work by Morris Louis, Howard Mehring, Kenneth Noland, and Tom Downing.[1]

Davis was so closely identified with the variations of stripe paintings that when he first exhibited his profile self-portraits in Washington in early 1983, no one quite knew what to make of them. *Washington Post* critic Paul Richard called them both "imposing and preposterous."[2] Today these paintings can be seen as an extension of the aesthetic explorations that Davis undertook throughout his career. As in this self-portrait, he continued to use unprimed canvas, liking the way the paint and support merged as one. He had always favored large paintings for their "instantaneous impact," liking a "one-shot impression on the eye."[3] Images appeared in his earliest drawings, which were also black and white. Although he eschewed the theatricality of abstract expressionist painting, Davis admired the work of Franz Kline, and between 1969 and 1975 created a series of black-and-white striped paintings.[4] In making striped paintings, Davis loved the optical "push/pull effect" that occurred when colors were juxtaposed; here one gets the same visually energetic result from the contrast of black and white. The rhythmic pattern also alludes to Davis's appreciation of music of all kinds.[5] Knowledgeable about the history of art, Davis might also have made the painting as an homage to the great artist and chess player Marcel Duchamp, who also made a profile self-portrait.[6] Here the open mouth—as if the subject is speaking—is fitting for a man who reveled in thinking and talking about art.[7] One can almost hear Davis saying, "When you are struggling to achieve recognition, there is a greater tendency to take chances and to shoot from the hip. A hungry fighter is often more daring and bold. Once you achieve some success and recognition, there can be a tendency to rest on your laurels. I would like to think I have avoided that."[8]

CKC

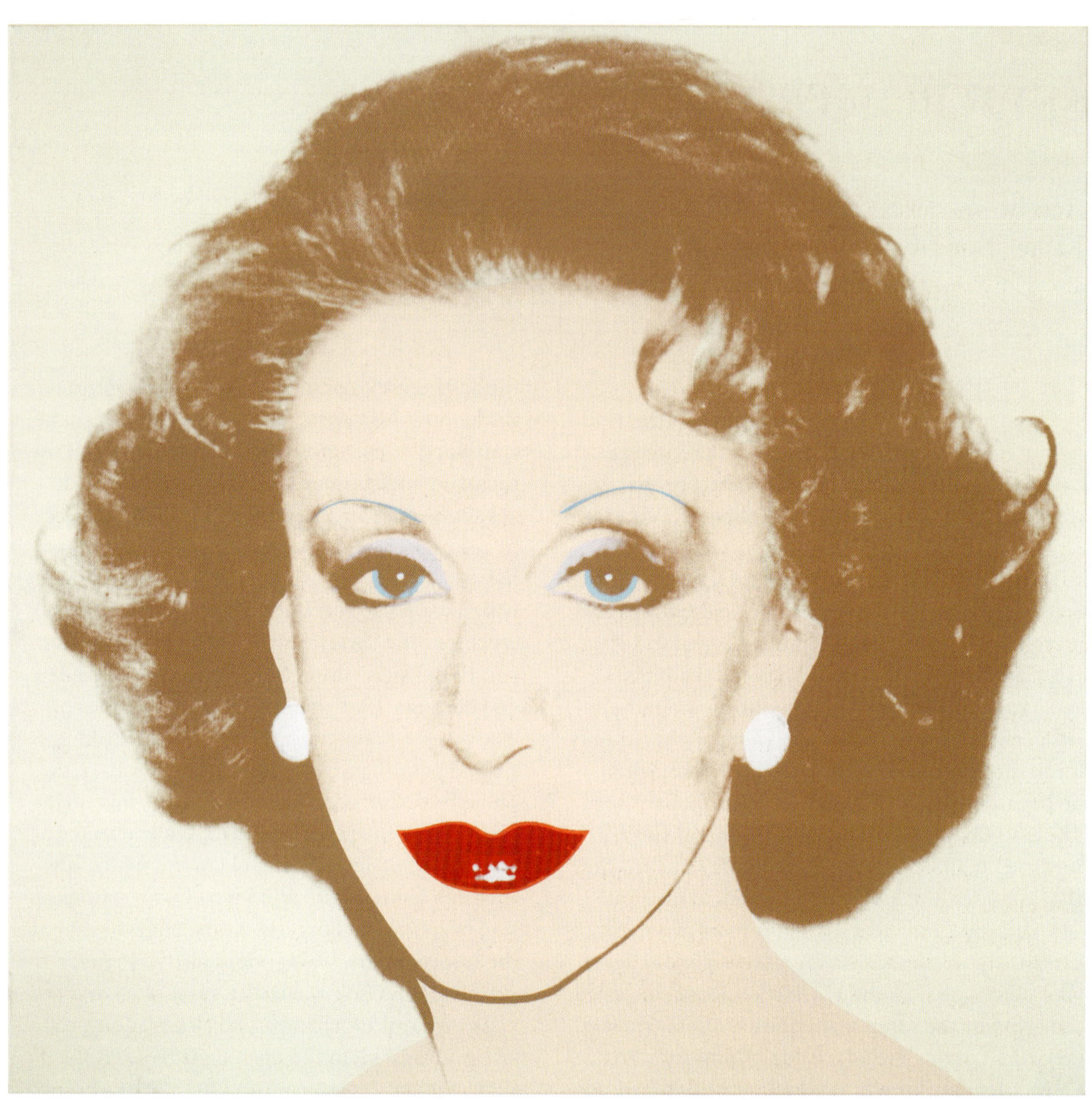

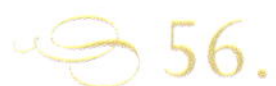

INA GINSBURG

By Andy Warhol (1928–1987)

Synthetic polymer paint and silkscreen ink on canvas, 101.6 × 101.6 cm (40 × 40 in.),
1982
Ina Ginsburg

ANDY WARHOL, one of the most significant artists of the late twentieth century, was an inveterate entrepreneur. Best-known today for his paintings and prints of celebrities, Warhol was also a serious filmmaker beginning about 1963 and a publisher from 1969 until his death. The initial impetus behind *Inter/ VIEW*—after 1977 just *Interview*—was the desire to create a magazine that would promote the artist's underground films. But by about 1974, the publication had become a monthly, "catering to and defining the culturally hip."[1] Its celebrity interviews were an unqualified success. The perceptive Warhol quickly realized the synergy between the printed word and portraiture, with one often leading to the other. Fascinated by the mysteries of political power, the artist saw Washington, which he called "Hollywood on the Potomac," as a potentially unlimited source of portraits, both visual and verbal.[2]

One spider drawing the powerful into Warhol's web was Ina Ginsburg. Elegant and charming, the Austrian-born Ginsburg traveled with ease among Washington's social and political elite.[3] She originally met Warhol in 1975, when Firooz Zahedi, nephew of the Iranian ambassador Ardeshir Zahedi, asked her to give a dinner party for Warhol. The two became instant friends, and when Warhol came to Washington he often stayed with her. On each occasion she made certain that he met those whom he might want to know.[4] Ginsburg's first piece for *Interview*—a request

from editor Bob Colacello—was an updated reprint with new photography of an article she had done on Nuha al-Hegelan, the Syrian-born wife of the Saudi ambassador.[5] Her subsequent pieces included interviews with luminaries such as German filmmaker Werner Fassbinder, entrepreneur and collector Baron Thyssen-Bornemisza, actor Donald Sutherland, Philippine president Ferdinand Marcos, Federal Reserve chairman Paul Volker, and Secretary of State Warren Christopher.[6] "*Interview*," said Colacello, recalling the glory days of the magazine, "was about high and low. Ina, 'our Woman in Washington,' interviewed top-level people—people who weren't necessarily seeking publicity. She gave us a gravitas we hadn't had. Moreover, Andy loved her parties. She always managed to have at least a half-dozen senators and an equal number of ambassadors at dinner."[7]

Warhol, who made his silkscreen-on-canvas portraits from Polaroids (see fig. 4), photographed Ginsburg in 1982 at his "Factory" at 860 Broadway.[8] For the sitting, she was seated in a large chair, and her face was covered with white makeup. Her kabuki-like appearance was necessary to get a good image on the acetate that was used in the next step of the process. "It was actually very relaxing," said Ginsburg. "We chatted the whole time."[9] Ultimately, Warhol made three portraits of her.[10] Ginsburg also owns four of the original Polaroids used for her portrait.

CKC

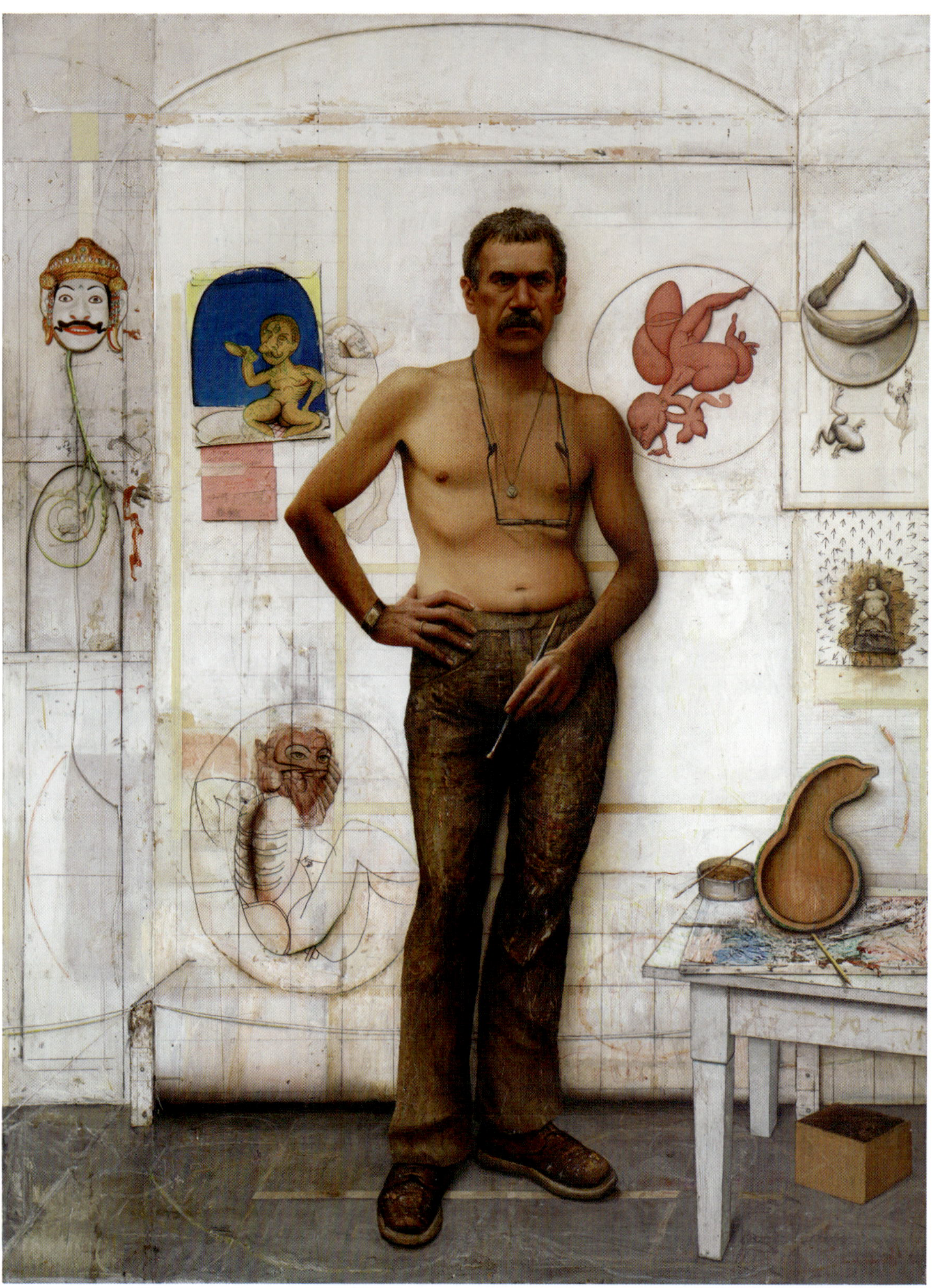

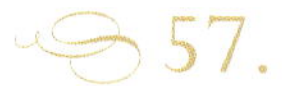

57.

SELF-PORTRAIT WITH SQUASH

By Gregory Gillespie (1936–2000)

Mixed media on panel, 243.8 × 175.3 cm (96 × 69 in.), 1986
Private collection

GREGORY GILLESPIE came of age as a painter during the height of abstract expressionism. Although energized by the work of Willem de Kooning, Franz Kline, and Jackson Pollock, he found that figurative painting captured his interest and excited his imagination.[1] In 1954 he entered Cooper Union School of Art in New York with the intention of becoming a commercial artist, but in 1960 he left to study at the San Francisco Art Institute, where he earned his BA and MFA. Clearly talented, he won a Fulbright Fellowship to Italy in 1962, where he remained for the next eight years, supporting himself with various prestigious fellowships. Represented by the Forum Gallery in New York since 1966, he was given a major solo show at the Hirshhorn Museum and Sculpture Garden in 1977.[2]

Although Gillespie painted landscapes and a variety of figurative works with a strong surrealistic sensibility, self-portraiture looms large in his oeuvre. Some are simple head-and-shoulder portraits; others are elaborate, full-length portraits surrounded by myriad images, as in *Self-portrait with Squash*. Asked in one of the last interviews he gave before his death why he painted himself so often during his forty-one-year career, he mentioned the availability of the subject and the "freedom to take dramatic license," as well as the fact that "the subject (me) and the painter (me) both want to make a strong picture and not flatter anyone's vanity."[3] For Gillespie, his face and his body were "God's work."

Gillespie's response suggests the strong religious content in his work. He called many of his paintings "shrine pieces," and indeed, they have an affinity with Northern Renaissance altarpieces, both in terms of their composition and the incorporation of elements that have symbolic associations. In *Self-portrait with Squash*, Gillespie, who was brought up a Catholic, stands in the center of the composition like a medieval saint. Just as Saint Sebastian was identified by arrows, he holds his paintbrush as a symbol of his martyrdom. Shirtless, he suggests to the viewer that he is revealing the "naked truth about himself."[4] His figure is framed by faintly drawn lines that imply an architectural niche or the center panel of a large altarpiece. The seemingly random selection of objects surrounding him is meant to amplify the narrative of his life. Perhaps most decipherable are the squash and the can of turpentine, placed on the table as if sacred items on an altar. Of similar motifs in another painting, Gillespie said:

> Fruits . . . meant ripening to me, and the ones cut open were a kind of double symbol of death—life sliced. . . . The bowl with the . . . turpentine had always reminded me of holy water, which Catholics use for blessing themselves . . . The visor is part of a uniform along with the bare chest and the paint-spattered pants of the artist.[5]

The painting's exquisitely textured background seemingly harks back to Gillespie's days in Italy, where thick, worn, whitewashed walls, often marked with graffiti, are emblematic of human history and the passage of time.

CKC

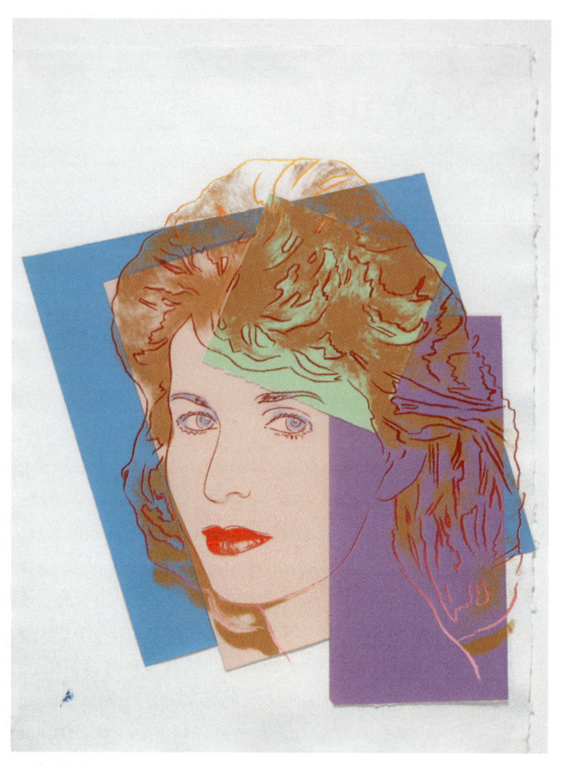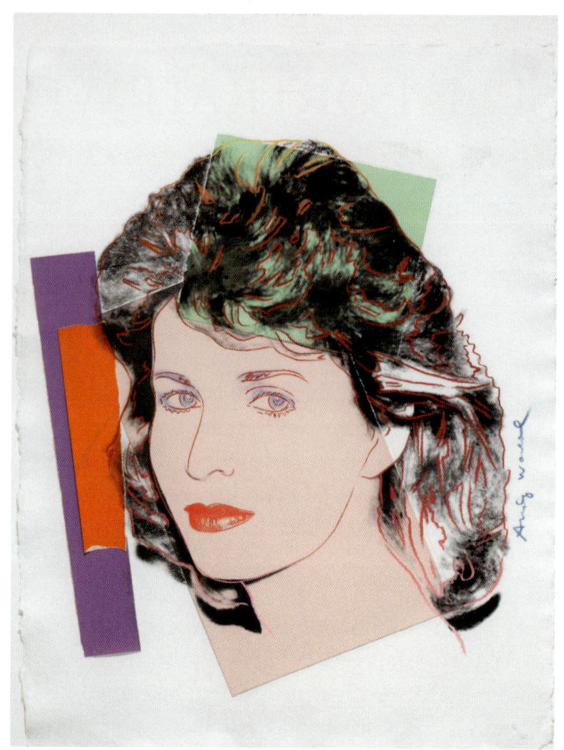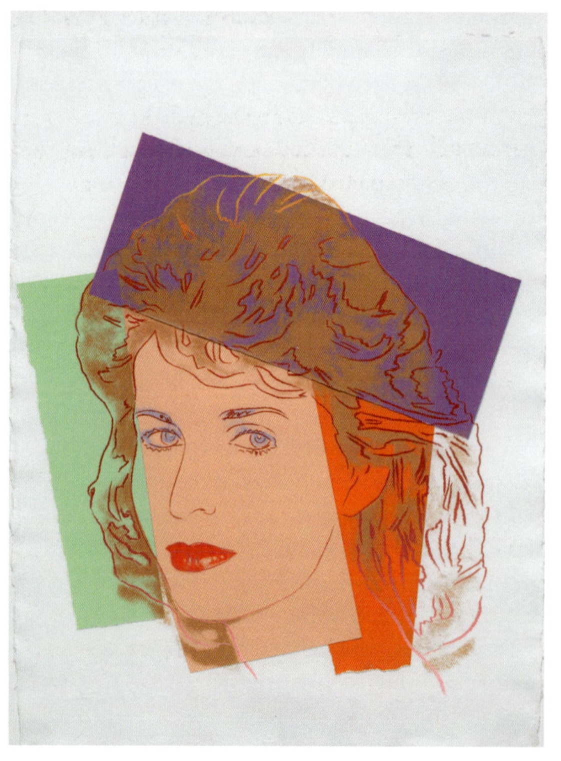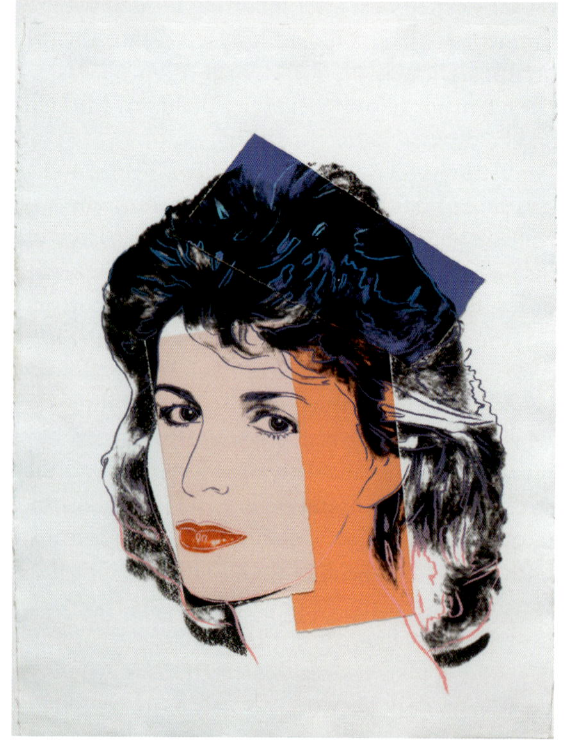

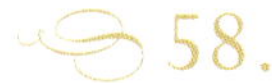 58.

SALLY QUINN
By Andy Warhol (1928–1987)

Each, framed: Serigraph, collage, and mixed media, 91.4 × 71.1 cm (36 × 28 in.), 1986
Sally Quinn

FOR A PORTRAIT of a quintessentially hip Washingtonian of the 1980s, no one was more fit to carry out a commission than Andy Warhol, the quintessentially hip artist of the New York art world. The man who made pop art a household word was happy to accept an assignment from *Washingtonian,* the lifestyle magazine for the national's capital, to make a portrait of Sally Quinn (born 1941) for its August 1986 cover. Portrait fees underwrote the artist's way of life and financed the myriad artistic activities of Warhol Enterprises. Moreover, Warhol, fiscally canny and a keen observer of human behavior, knew that the cover of a prestigious publication could only lead to other requests for portraits from wealthy and prominent individuals and institutions.

Quinn, born in Savannah, Georgia, grew up living the peripatetic life of a child born to a military family. A 1963 graduate of Smith College with a major in theater, her first job in Washington was as social secretary to the Algerian ambassador. In June 1969, Benjamin Bradlee, then executive editor of the *Washington Post*, eager to introduce a less traditional, gushing approach to social reporting, called to ask Quinn if she would be a writer for the *Post*'s style section. Lack of experience—when asked during the interview to show a sample of her writing, she replied, "I've never written anything"—did not deter Bradlee from offering her the job or Quinn from accepting. Her often

acerbic and devastating description of events and people quickly made her reputation.[1] When she entered a room, Quinn later noted, "people would often scatter like cockroaches when you turn on the light."[2]

In August 1973, Quinn headed for New York to co-anchor the *CBS Morning News.* Six months later she returned to the *Post.* Although the general public wasn't a fan, her future portraitist was a devoted viewer.[3] In 1978, Quinn married Bradlee. A stay-at-home mother after her son was born in 1982, Quinn turned her attention to writing a novel. The debut of *Regrets Only,* described by Bob Woodward as a "primer on how people behave at high levels in Washington," occasioned *Washingtonian*'s second profile of Quinn.[4]

For her cover portrait, Quinn went to New York to be photographed by Warhol. As with all his portraits, the artist began the process with a Polaroid photograph of the sitter. In all, six images were subsequently made—two screened "paintings" on canvas—one red (fig. 5), one yellow (selected for the *Washingtonian* cover), and four collages. Quinn never saw the collages, but she was aware of their existence. When Warhol died unexpectedly, Quinn called Fred Hughes, executor of the Warhol estate, and acquired the two paintings and the four remarkable collages.[5] They testify to Warhol's artistry—his inventiveness and his involvement with the process of making art.

CKC

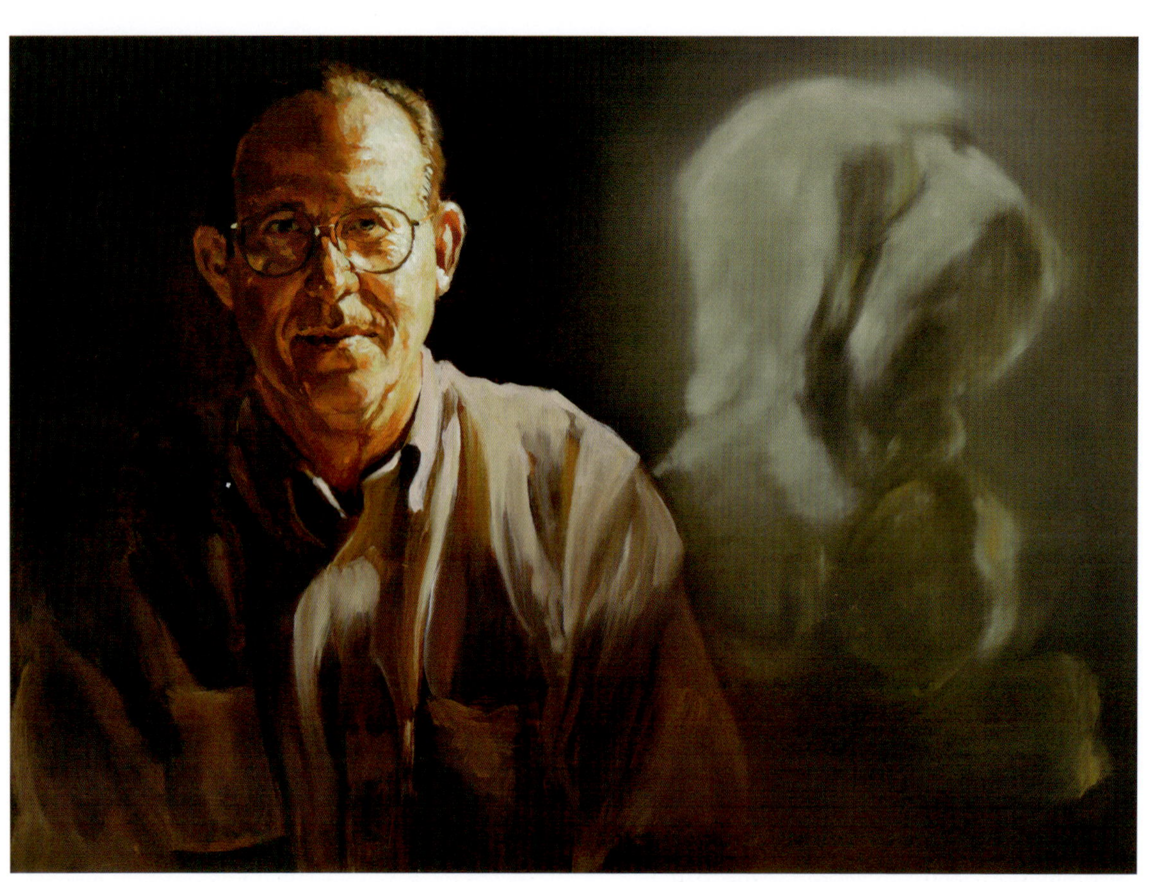

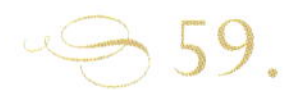

59.

WILLIAM A. HASELTINE

By Eric Fischl (b. 1948)

Oil on canvas, 91.4 × 121.9 cm (36 × 48 in.), 1998
William A. Haseltine

AFTER MORE than a decade in which pop, minimalism, and conceptual art had been the darlings of the critical elite, Eric Fischl made his mark in the competitive New York art world in the early 1980s by challenging the avant-garde's proscription against figurative painting that was both intensely personal and strongly narrative. Known for his disquieting paintings of family psychodramas, Fischl had not considered depicting individuals other than his own relatives until he was approached by William Haseltine (born 1944). Haseltine had seen Fischl's "elegiac paintings done at the time of his father's death" and realized that the artist might be an excellent portrait painter."[1] Having accepted this—his first commission—Fischl found portraiture to be a provocative challenge. Within the next year he had completed likenesses of other friends, among them actor Steve Martin, director Mike Nichols, and dealer Mary Boone.[2]

By asking Fischl to paint his portrait, Haseltine provided the impetus for the artist to expand his subject-matter repertoire. The role of catalyst is characteristic of Haseltine. A molecular biologist by training with an undergraduate degree from the University of California, Berkeley, and a PhD from Harvard, Haseltine began his career as a professor at Harvard Medical School (1976–93). In 1992, building on one of the great scientific discoveries of the late twentieth century, he founded Human Genome Sciences, Inc., for which he served as CEO until 2004. The biopharmaceutical company was one of the first to patent the human genomic sequence for medical use.

Haseltine is currently chairman of Global Health, a virtual pharmaceutical company dedicated to developing new drugs and medical devices.[3]

For this portrait, Fischl made sketches and took photographs in his SoHo studio. "The sittings were pleasant," noted Haseltine. "We had lively conversations while he worked in a quiet, well-lit, peaceful space, filled with his ongoing work and many art and photography books. . . . [Fischl] did no work on the canvas while I was present."[4] As with the portrait of Haseltine, if Fischl wishes to augment the basic image of the sitter, he does so digitally, combining and/or altering photographs on a computer until he arrives at a composition that he wishes to employ as the basis of his painting.[5] For Haseltine's portrait, Fischl juxtaposed a rather straightforward image of the sitter with a somewhat abstract depiction of a classical torso. The incorporation of the classical form was probably a result of Fischl's artistic investigations into sculpture at about the time he turned to portraiture.[6] By coincidence, it also serves as a reference to Haseltine's interest in antiquity and his collection of objects from the Greco-Roman era. This mysterious shape lends a psychological and emotional overtone to the painting, leaving the viewer to speculate about the interior world of the subject. In the horizontal format, relatively unusual for a portrait, Fischl has captured Haseltine's likeness with the sensuous handling of paint that is a hallmark of his style.

CKC

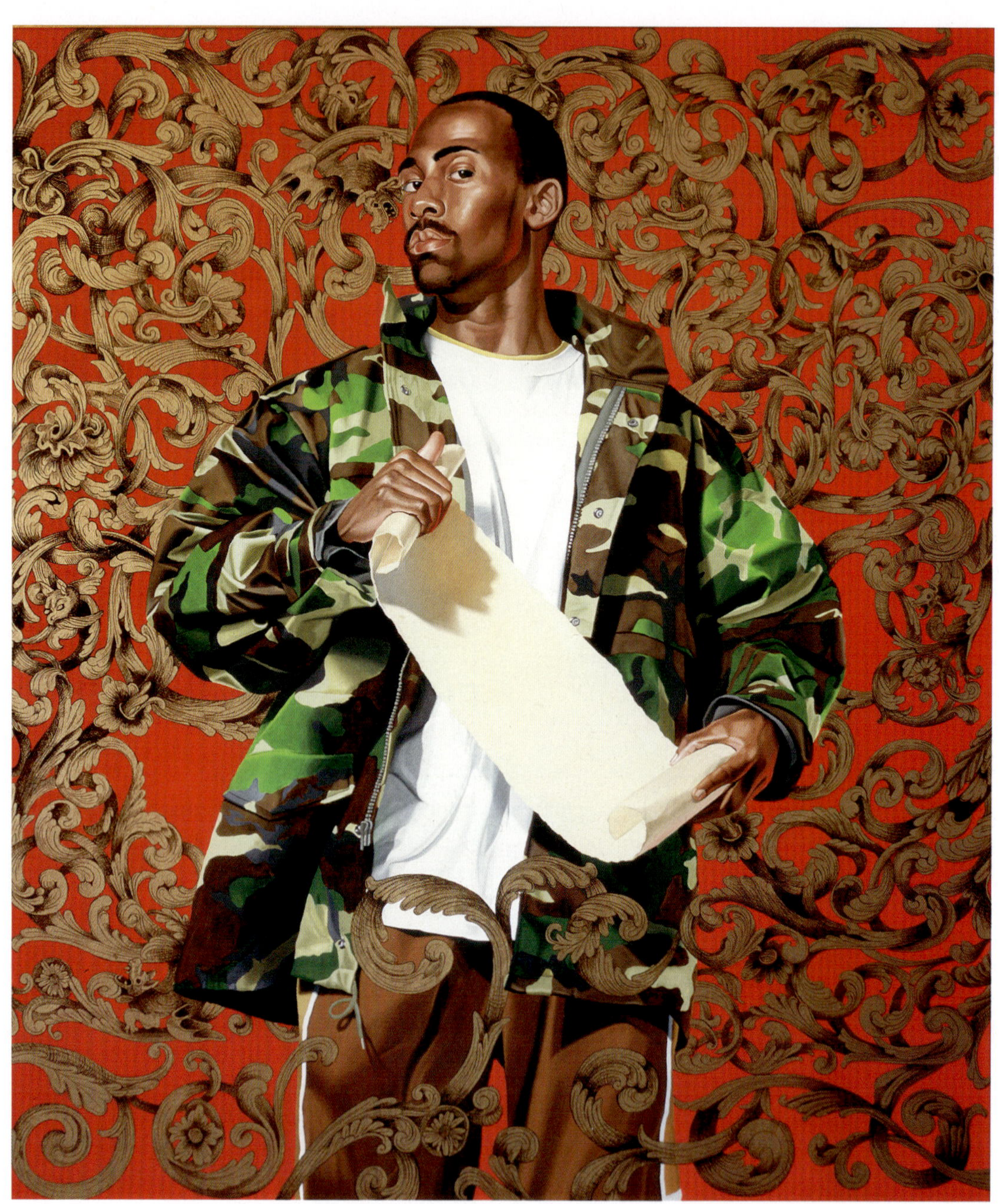

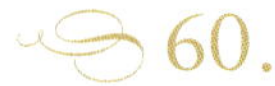 60.

PASSING/POSING (ST. MONACA) (ROBERT REYNOLDS)

By Kehinde Wiley (b. 1977)

Oil on canvas, 210.8 × 182.9 cm (83 × 72 in.) framed, 2005
Henry L. Thaggert III

COMPELLING PORTRAITS that serve to depict specific individuals often also suggest a type. A successful portrait of a president, for example, usually contains within it the concept of "the leader." And while most portraits emphasize the unique rather than generic aspects of a subject, Kehinde Wiley's portraits reverse this set of expectations. His goal is to stress the role of the individual primarily as a type. Thus, while we know the name of Robert Reynolds, who posed for this painting, Wiley was more interested in Reynolds as representing a class of individuals—in this case, the young black man who understands the "bling bling" excesses of hip-hop.[1] Even the title, which contains no hint of the subject's name, underscores his anonymity.[2] One decodes the visual clues in the painting to learn about the attitudes of a group (of which the individual posing is merely a part) as well as other assumptions about art and portraiture.

Wiley, an African American artist born in South Central Los Angeles, came to the attention of the New York art world shortly after he received his MFA from Yale in 2001 and began working on a series of portraits of young black males while an artist-in-residence at the Studio Museum in Harlem. "Passing/Posing: The Paintings of Kehinde Wiley," at the Brooklyn Museum of Art in 2004–5, was his first solo show devoted to his exploration of black identity. His eighteen large-scale paintings, similar to the one featured here, portrayed young black men—whom he had approached on the streets of Harlem and asked if they would sit for him—in urban street clothes posed in front of lushly colored, decorative backgrounds.[3] Wiley, who was profoundly influenced by his first trip to Italy in 2003, begins his painting process by asking each of his subjects to look through monographs on Italian Renaissance and Baroque painting and to select a pose in a historic painting that appeals to him. The subject then assumes that position as Wiley photographs him. For the finished painting, Wiley selects a decorative background, usually a motif appropriated from some historic pattern. As in the Renaissance, assistants generally aid the artist with the application of the patterned area. Wiley either chooses or designs his frames, which are integral to the whole composition. Visually, the pictorial tension between the flat, decorative background; the assertive, sculpture-like three-dimensionality of the figure; and the meticulously crafted face creates a powerful, dynamic, and engaging image. But Wiley's goal is to create more than a handsome artifact. By encapsulating the subject of the portrait in a format used in venerated historical art, Wiley gives dignity and stature to this black youth (and by implication, those like him), something that may not have been available to the subject in his everyday surroundings.

CKC

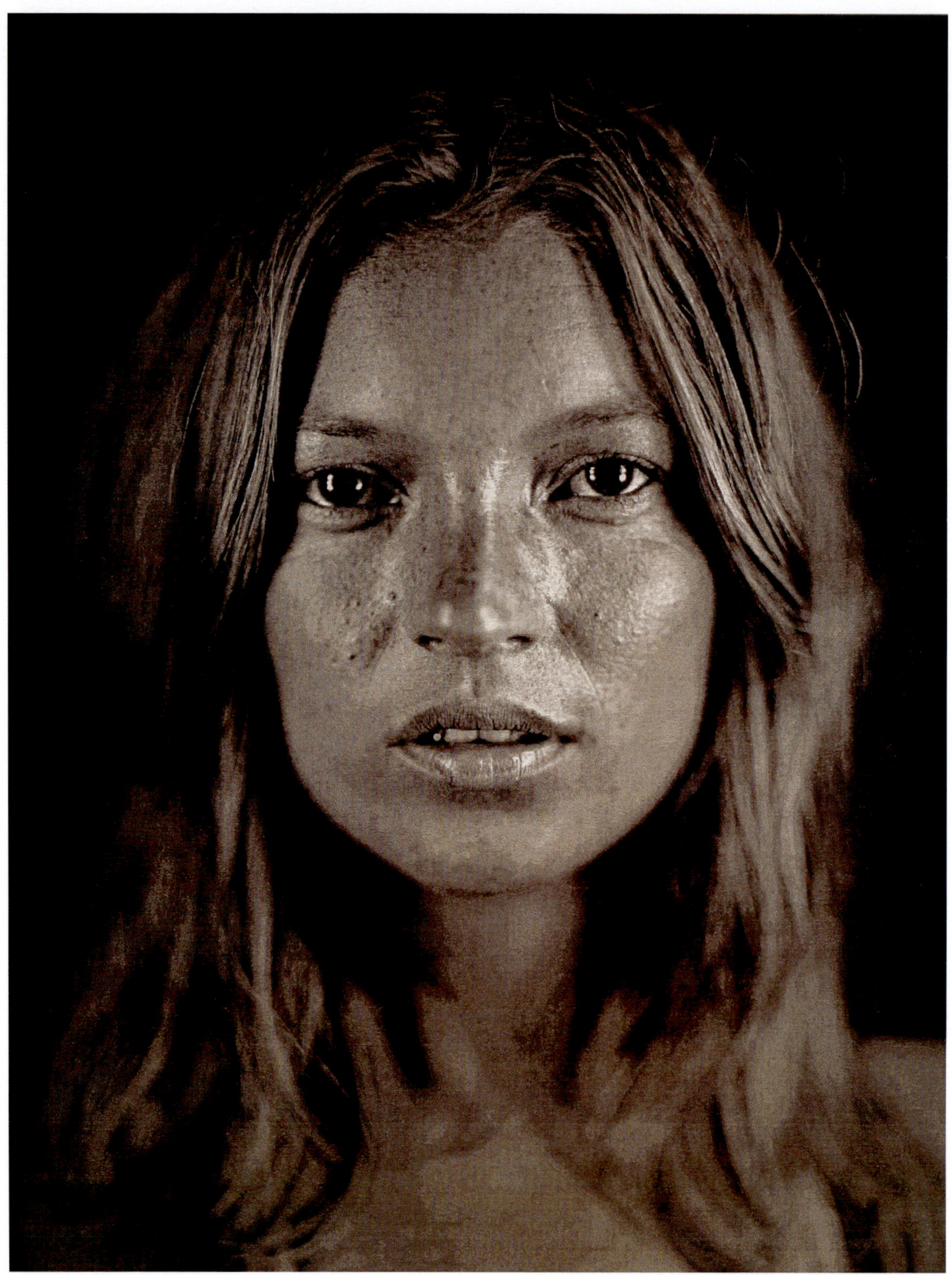

61

KATE (KATE MOSS)
By Chuck Close (b. 1940)

Jacquard tapestry, 261.6 × 200.7 cm (103 × 79 in.), 2007, no. 3 of an edition of 10
Dan Snyder and Tom Breit

ENGLISH SUPERMODEL Kate Moss (born 1974) was only fourteen when, on returning from a vacation in Jamaica, she was spotted in a New York airport by the owner of a modeling agency. Since that serendipitous encounter in 1988, Moss has appeared on more than three hundred magazine covers and has been the key figure in numerous advertising campaigns for such high-end retailers as Dior, Versace, Dolce & Gabbana, and Calvin Klein.[1] In 2003 she was the subject of a forty-page spread in the September issue of *W* magazine, a testament to her fascination for both artists and viewers. Relatively short and thin, the waiflike Moss was (and remains) the antithesis of tall, sexy, and exotic supermodels such as Naomi Campbell. Her appeal at the time seemingly resided in the juxtaposition between the somewhat ordinary aspect of her appearance and the glamour of the objects she was promoting. For an era obsessed by youth, one in which high and low, grunge and luxury were mingled indiscriminately, Moss literally and figuratively served as the model.

Chuck Close was one of the artists commissioned to photograph Moss for *W*'s tribute to her. A daguerreotype that he made of her as part of the assignment is the basis for this tapestry portrait. Invented in 1839 by the Frenchman Louis-Jacques-Mandé Daguerre, that early photographic process appealed to Close, and he began experimenting with daguerreotypes in about 1999.[2] Working with strobe lighting and a short-focal-length lens that permitted only a shallow depth of field, Close produced a highly detailed image of the sitter, capturing every pore, freckle, pimple, and wrinkle on a face that was usually airbrushed to perfection. "I like the warts and all approach," the artist has commented. "The things I like best are the things other people hate the most. I find that stuff interesting . . . because it is a road map of your life."[3]

Close begins all of his work with a photograph, usually, as here, a frontal image, devoid, insofar as possible, of emotional expression. He has recently shown his photographs as art objects, but for the greater part of his career his intent has been to take the information contained in the photograph and transfer it to another medium. In making a painting, Close's process is to grid both the photographic image and the canvas and capture the pictorial data square by square with black-and-white or colored pigments, which are inherently abstract modules. The end result in a painted portrait is an image that hovers between the abstract and the descriptive. At arm's length from the canvas—the position occupied by the artist when he is working on a portrait—the face appears wholly abstract. It is only when the viewer steps back that the portrait coalesces into a recognizable image.

When Magnolia Editions, a printmaking workshop in Oakland, California, approached Close to create tapestries, he realized that weaving—a process of vertical and horizontal warps and wefts—possessed a strong correlation with his painting method. For a tapestry such as *Kate*, which contains thousands of different-colored threads, a proprietary color-matching technique is used to digitally direct electronic looms to replicate the information contained in the original photograph.[4] As with a painting, the image appears either abstract or representational, depending on one's distance from the textile.

CKC

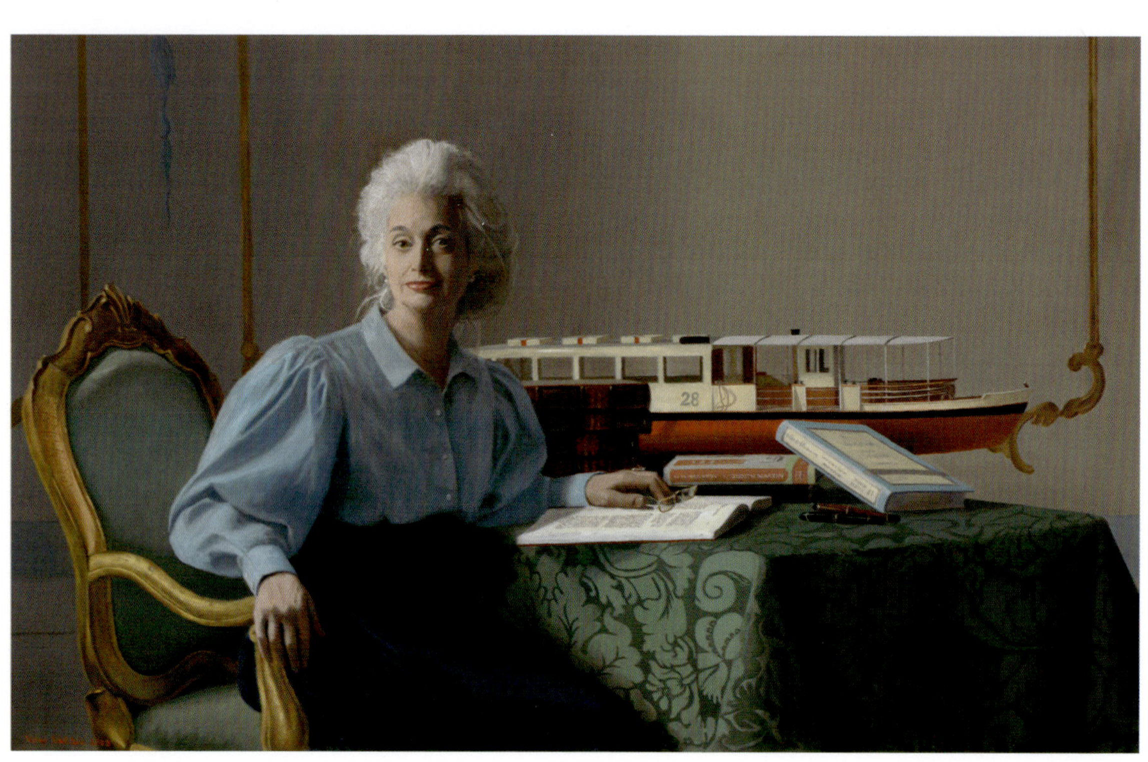

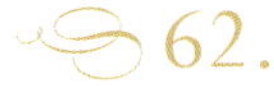

62.

JUDITH MARTIN IN VENICE
By Victor Arnold Edelstein (b. 1946)

Oil on canvas, 101.6 × 157.5 cm (40 × 62 in.), 2008
Private collection

IF YOU CAN'T live the life of those nineteenth-century Bostonians who escaped the snow-laden streets of their native city and acquired palazzos on the Grand Canal in Venice, where they savored leisure and luxury, the next-best option may be to travel to Venice for month-long stays several times a year. Since 1981, this is what Judith Martin—known to all newspaper-reading Americans who care about proper etiquette as "Miss Manners"—and her husband, Robert, have done. Joining others from around the world who revel in traversing the narrow stone byways and elegant bridges of this magical, history-filled city, they have—to use Martin's words—become committed Venetophiles.[1]

Living in apartments in grand historic palazzos, the Martins quickly became part of the fabric of this city. As a gregarious couple who place gourmet meals high on their list of necessities and are known for their intelligent and wide-ranging conversation, the Martins made friends with descendants of families who had lived in Venice for centuries, as well as with other expatriates who shared their romantic dream. Englishman Victor Edelstein and his Italian-born wife, the artist Anna Maria Succi, who moved to Venice in 1997, were among their new friends. Edelstein's initial career was as a couturier. His most famous design is perhaps the blue-velvet evening gown that Princess Diana wore to a White House dinner in 1985, the night she danced with John Travolta. A man of many interests—collecting Renaissance prints and choreographing ballets among them—Edelstein took up painting in 1993.[2]

Robert Martin commissioned Edelstein to paint his wife's portrait as a present for a forthcoming birthday. The artist painted it in Venice just before he moved back to England. The original idea was for a standing portrait, but as all involved wanted show Martin as a writer—in addition to her newspaper columns, she has written numerous books—the decision was made to turn the canvas horizontally, to better incorporate the details seen here in the final composition. The numerous sittings took place over several years in the historic Palazzo Albrizzi, where the Edelsteins maintained a studio and a mezzanine apartment. "Fortunately," said the sitter, "the artist is very amusing, or the process would have been excruciating." Edelstein selected the costume from among the clothes Martin owned—a blouse purchased in Washington, a skirt in New York. On the table beside her are two of the books she authored, *No Vulgar Hotel: The Desire and Pursuit of Venice* and *Miss Manners' Guide to Excruciatingly Correct Behavior*.[3] The model of the vaporetto was made by a well-known Venetian craftsman. A gondola was originally to be included, but Martin, pragmatist that she is, said that she traveled only on the speedier conveyance, not on the historic transport used mainly by tourists.[4] The liveliness and vitality of this elegant portrait is a testament to the value of the artist working directly from the model.

CKC

NOTES

S EVERAL FREQUENTLY cited references are abbreviated in the notes. References to American National Biography Online, a subscription-available resource for a database of biographies, are cited by the Web site address www.anb.org. ProQuest Historical Newspapers, also referenced in the notes by its Web site, www.proquest.com, is a digital archive for newspapers dating back to the nineteenth century; it is also accessed by subscription only. The Smithsonian Institution's Archives of American Art, located in Washington, D.C., is hereafter cited as Archives of American Art.

1. RALPH IZARD

1. For more on the portrait and on Izard, see Margaret Simons Middleton, *Jeremiah Theus: Colonial Artist of Charles Town* (Columbia: University of South Carolina Press, 1953), 141–42; Rosamond Olmsted Humm, *Children in America: A Study of Images and Attitudes* (Atlanta: High Museum of Art, 1978), 15; *Georgia Collects* (Atlanta: High Museum of Art, 1989), 206; and Robert A. Leath and Maurie D. McInnis, " 'To Blend Pleasure with Knowledge,' The Cultural Odyssey of Charlestonians Abroad," in Maurie D. McInnis and Angela D. Mack, *In Pursuit of Refinement: Charlestonians Abroad, 1740–1860* (Columbia: University of South Carolina Press, 1999), 11, 16, 18, 19. For a longer biography of Izard, see Whitfield J. Bell Jr., *Patriot-Improvers: Biographical Sketches of Members of the American Philosophical Society* (Philadelphia: American Philosophical Society, 1999), 2:168–77. Izard was elected a corresponding member of the society in 1768.

2. Two versions of the West portrait exist, the first painted for the Allen family of Pennsylvania (private collection), and the second commissioned by Ralph Izard (1764; The Brook Club, New York).

For portraits of the Izards, see Angela D. Mack and J. Thomas Savage, "Reflections of Refinement: Portraits of Charlestonians at Home and Abroad," in McInnis and Mack, *In Pursuit of Refinement*, 27–29, 31–32. "The Cricketers" is discussed in that volume, 100–103, no. 6, and in Helmut von Erffa and Allen Staley, *Paintings of Benjamin West* (New Haven: Yale University Press, 1986), 571, nos. 726 and 727.

3. For a summation of recent interpretations of Copley's double portrait of the Izards, see McInnis and Mack, *In Pursuit of Refinement*, 116–19, no. 12.

2. ANDREW OLIVER JR. /
3. MARY LYNDE OLIVER

1. For these portraits, see Andrew Oliver, *Faces of a Family: An Illustrated Catalogue of Portraits and Silhouettes of Daniel Oliver, 1664–1732, and Elizabeth Belcher, His Wife . . .* (privately printed, 1960), 11–12, nos. 10, 11. For biographical information on Oliver, see Clifford K. Shipton, *Sibley's Harvard Graduates: Biographical Sketches of Those Who Attended Harvard College in the Classes 1746–1750* (Boston: Massachusetts Historical Society, 1962), 12:455–61; www.anb.org/articles, accessed Feb. 16, 2010.

2. John Adams, "Diary," entry for Dec. 30, 1758, in *Diary and Autobiography of John Adams*, ed. L. H. Butterfield (Cambridge, MA: Belknap Press of Harvard University Press, 1961), 1:66.

3. Ellen G. Miles, "Joseph Blackburn," *Oxford Dictionary of National Biography* (Oxford: Oxford University Press, 2004), 5:930; the letter, dated November 24, 1754, is in the collections of the Rhode Island Historical Society, Newport.

4. For dovecotes in colonial America, see Michael Olmert, "Dovecotes: Food, Feathers, Fertilizer," in his book *Kitchens, Smokehouses, and Privies: Outbuildings*

and the Architecture of Daily Life in the Eighteenth-Century Mid-Atlantic (Ithaca, NY: Cornell University Press, 2009), 173–205; and Therese O'Malley, *Keywords in American Landscape Design* (Washington, DC: National Gallery of Art; New Haven, CT: Yale University Press, 2010), 222–24. For the identification of the structure as a dovecote, I thank John Dixon Hunt of the University of Pennsylvania and his wife, Emily Cooperman. The suggestion that the structure was a circular summer house or dovecote had also been made in 1922 by Lawrence Park in his checklist of Blackburn's work, *Joseph Blackburn, A Colonial Portrait Painter with a Descriptive List of His Works* (Worcester, MA: American Antiquarian Society, 1923), reprinted from *Proceedings of the American Antiquarian Society*, Oct. 1922, 39–40, cat. no. 47; the portrait of Mrs. Oliver is catalogued as no. 48, p. 40. The portraits were included in the exhibition catalogue *Harvard Divided* (Cambridge, MA: Fogg Art Museum, 1976), curated by Linda Ayres; see 80–82, cat. nos. 37, 38.

5. The letter, dated Feb. 25, 1766, is quoted in Peter Oliver's biography, in Clifford K. Shipton, *Sibley's Harvard Graduates: Biographical Sketches of Those Who Attended Harvard College in the Classes 1751–1755* (Boston: Massachusetts Historical Society, 1951), 8:744.

4. PETER OLIVER

1. For Peter Oliver see Clifford K. Shipton, *Sibley's Harvard Graduates: Biographical Sketches of Those Who Attended Harvard College in the Classes 1751–1755* (Boston: Massachusetts Historical Society, 1951), 8:737–63; "Peter Oliver," www.anb.org/articles, accessed Mar. 24, 2010.

2. For Oliver family portraits, see Andrew Oliver, *Faces of a Family: An Illustrated Catalogue of Portraits and Silhouettes of Daniel Oliver, 1664–1732 and Elizabeth Belcher, His Wife . . .* (privately printed, 1960); for Smibert's portraits of the family, see Oliver, *Faces of a Family*, 3–11, and Richard H. Saunders, *John Smibert: Colonial America's First Portrait Painter* (New Haven: Yale University Press, 1995), 162–63, 168–69, 176–78, 181, 183.

3. Oliver, *Faces of a Family*, lists these miniatures by Copley of the two brothers on pp. 5–6, no. 5A–C, and p. 7, no. 8A. Of Andrew Oliver, no. 5A is owned by the Yale University Art Gallery, and 5B is privately owned; the Portrait Gallery's miniature is listed as 5C.

4. Theresa Fairbanks, "Gold Discovered: John Singleton Copley's Portrait Miniatures on Copper," *Yale University Art Gallery Bulletin* (1999): 75–91; Yale's miniature of Peter Oliver is among those painted in oil on gold-leafed copper. For the Olivers as patrons for Copley's miniatures on copper, see Erica E. Hirshler, "Copley in Miniature," in Carrie Rebora et al., *John Singleton Copley in America* (New York: Metropolitan Museum of Art, 1995), 119–21.

5. These family portraits are discussed and illustrated in Oliver, *Faces of a Family,* 6, 11–15, and in Jules David Prown, *John Singleton Copley in America, 1738–1774* (Cambridge, MA: Harvard University Press for National Gallery of Art, 1966), 224–25. For a family tree that identifies Copley's sitters in the Oliver family, see Prown, *John Singleton Copley,* 178–79.

5. JAMES CRAIK

1. *Dictionary of American Biography*, s.v. "Craik, James"; www.anb.org/articles, accessed Mar. 24, 2010.

2. The miniature was described as the work of an unknown artist when it was lent to the exhibition "Our Town" at Gadsby's Tavern in Alexandria, Virginia, in 1956; see *Our Town: 1749–1865: Likenesses of This Place & Its People* (Alexandria, VA: Alexandria Association, 1956), 14, no. 30. The miniature was described by Charles Coleman Sellers in *Charles Willson Peale with Patron and Populace: A Supplement to Portraits and Miniatures by Charles Willson Peale* (Philadelphia: American Philosophical Society, 1969), 58, SP 23, as possibly an early copy of a missing original because it is larger than is typical of Peale's miniatures made during the war.

3. The original was catalogued by Charles Coleman Sellers in *Portraits and Miniatures by Charles Willson Peale* (Philadelphia: American Philosophical Society, 1952), 57, no. 161, as unlocated. Lillian B. Miller, ed., *The Selected Papers of Charles Willson Peale and His Family* (New Haven: Yale University Press, 1983), 1:272, 273, also listed the original as unlocated. This may be the miniature that was recently given to the National Society, Sons of the American Revolution, in Louisville, Kentucky, by Craik's descendants.

4. On the artist, see John E. Kleber, ed., *The Encyclopedia of Louisville* (Lexington: University Press of Kentucky, 2001), 748; and Arthur F. Jones and Bruce Weber, *The Kentucky Painter: From the Frontier Era to the Great War* (Lexington: University of Kentucky Art Museum, 1981), 63–64.

5. The artist's daybooks for the years 1901–34 are in the collection of the Filson Historical Society,

Louisville, Kentucky; we thank James J. Holmberg, curator of special collections at the society, for assistance with the research on this artist and on the Craik family in Louisville. The miniature was reproduced in Margaret Bridwell, "Ramsier: Louisville's Favorite Miniaturist," *Courier-Journal Magazine* (December 18, 1955), 30. On the Reverend Craik, see also the *National Register of the Society, Sons of the American Revolution* (New York: A. H. Kellogg, 1902), 5. For an example of a copy that is signed by Ramsier but is not recorded in his daybooks, see *Kentucky Painter*, 64, no. 82.

6. MYLES COOPER

1. Jules David Prown, *John Singleton Copley,* vol. 2, *John Singleton Copley in England, 1774–1815* (Cambridge, MA: Harvard University Press for National Gallery of Art, 1966), 432, fig. 441. It was then owned by dealer Victor Spark of New York.

2. Prown, *John Singleton Copley,* vol. 1, *John Singleton Copley in America, 1738–1774* (Cambridge, MA: Harvard University Press for National Gallery of Art, 1966), 61, 81, 98, 212, illus. fig. 223. Cooper is listed as Copley's only sitter to attend Oxford University; see p. 123.

3. See www.anb.org/articles, accessed Apr. 8, 2010.

4. A full discussion of the portrait, its technique, and its imagery is found in Carrie Rebora et al., *John Singleton Copley in America* (New York: Metropolitan Museum of Art, 1995), in the entry by Carrie Rebora, 249–52, cat. no. 47. Paul Staiti discusses Copley's technique and the portrait's realism (pp. 41, 56), and Aileen Ribeiro discusses his academic robe (p. 111) and unpowdered hair (p. 113). I thank Dr. Ribeiro for writing that the two portraits appear to represent the same man, in the same gown; e-mail to Ellen Miles, June 11, 2010.

5. For their correspondence, see *Letters & Papers of John Singleton Copley and Henry Pelham, 1739–1776* (1914; reprint, New York: Kennedy Graphics and Da Capo Press, 1970), 70–76.

7. THOMAS AND HENRY SERGEANT

1. *American Paintings in the Museum of Fine Arts, Boston* (Boston: Museum of Fine Arts, 1969), 1:206–7, no. 796, 2:79, fig. 106 (the portrait was on loan to the museum for more than forty years); Charles Coleman Sellers, *Charles Willson Peale with Patron and Populace:*

A Supplement to Portraits and Miniatures by Charles Willson Peale (Philadelphia: American Philosophical Society, 1969), 78, no. 121; Lillian B. Miller, ed., *The Peale Family: Creation of a Legacy, 1770–1870* (New York: Abbeville Press in association with Trust for Museum Exhibitions and National Portrait Gallery, 1996), 48–49.

2. For Jonathan Sergeant, see *Dictionary of American Biography,* s.v. "Sergeant, Jonathan."

3. For these portraits, see Charels Coleman Sellers, *Portraits and Miniatures by Charles Willson Peale* (Philadelphia: American Philosophical Society, 1952), 192–93, nos. 784, 785.

4. Ibid., 193, nos. 786, 787; Lillian B. Miller, *The Selected Papers of Charles Willson Peale and His Family* (New Haven: Yale University Press for National Portrait Gallery, Smithsonian Institution, 1983), 1:517–18, 522–23, 564.

5. For the portrait of Elizabeth Rittenhouse Sergeant, see Sellers, *Charles Willson Peale,* 193, no. 788; and Miller, *Selected Papers,* 1:564.

6. On Thomas Sergeant, see *Dictionary of American Biography;* for their older brother John Sergeant (1779–1852), also an attorney, see www.anb.org/articles, accessed Feb. 23, 2010. Information on Henry Sergeant was generously provided from his alumni file by librarians at the Seeley G. Mudd Manuscript Library, Princeton University, Princeton, New Jersey.

8. MARQUIS DE LAFAYETTE

1. For a succinct biography of the Marquis de Lafayette, see www.anb.org/articles.

2. Anne L. Poulet, *Jean-Antoine Houdon: Sculptor of the Enlightenment* (Washington, DC: National Gallery of Art in association with University of Chicago Press, 2003), 256–62, cat. nos. 45, 46.

3. Ibid., 262, illus. 260.

4. H. H. Arnason, *The Sculptures of Houdon* (New York: Oxford University Press, 1975), 81, 116, n. 199. It is described as "identical to the Versailles version and comparable in quality."

9. JOHN HITE MORTON

1. William Dunlap, *A History of the Rise and Progress of the Arts of Design in the United States* (1834; reprint, New York: Dover Publications, 1969), 1:414.

2. For Trott see Theodore Bolton, "Benjamin Trott: An Account of His Life and Work," *Art Quarterly* 7,

no. 4 (Autumn 1944): 257–77; Theodore Bolton and Ruel Pardee Tolman, "A Catalogue of Miniatures by or Attributed to Benjamin Trott," in *Art Quarterly* 7 (as above): 278–90 (the miniature of Morton is listed on p. 281, no. 24); and www.anb.org/articles, accessed June 18, 2009. For the portrait of Charles Wilkins, see Arthur F. Jones and Bruce Weber, *The Kentucky Painter: From the Frontier Era to the Great War* (Lexington: University of Kentucky Art Museum, 1981), 67, no. 94. The date of Trott's baptism, August 20, 1769, has recently been identified by Isobel Ellis, who located the information on the Web site of the New England Historic Genealogical Society; see "Records of the Hollis Street Church in Boston," www.newenglandancestors.org/database, accessed May 15, 2010.

3. For Morton and his family, see "Descendants of William Morton," in the Morton-Burnett-Bradford Family Genealogy, under the category Family Records/Descendant Charts: William Morton and Elizabeth Hite Smith, http://freepages.genealogy.rootsweb.ancestry.com, accessed Apr. 15, 2010.

4. William Henry Perrin, ed., *History of Fayette County, Kentucky, with an Outline Sketch of the Blue Grass Region by Robert Peter, M.D.* (Chicago: O. L. Baskin, 1882), 65.

5. Obituary for John Hite Morton, *Lexington Observer and Reporter*, August 18, 1830, reprinted in R. Glenn Clift, comp., *Kentucky Obituaries, 1787–1854* (Baltimore: Genealogical Publishing, 1984), 61.

6. *The Medical Recorder* (Philadelphia: James Webster, 1825), 8:440.

7. Dunlap's letter to his wife is included as part of the published *Diary of William Dunlap, 1766–1839: The Memoirs of a Dramatist, Theatrical Manager, Painter, Critic, Novelist, and Historian* (New York: New-York Historical Society, 1931), 2:365–66.

10. ELIZABETH BOWDOIN, LADY TEMPLE

1. Bowdoin College was founded by James Bowdoin III in honor of their father. For these family portraits, see Russell E. Train, *The Bowdoin Family . . .* (Washington, DC: Privately printed, 2000); Richard H. Saunders III, "James Bowdoin III (1752–1811)," in *The Legacy of James Bowdoin III* (Brunswick, ME: Bowdoin College Museum of Art, 1994), 1–31; and Linda J. Docherty, "Preserving our Ancestors: The Bowdoin Portrait Collection," in *The Legacy of James Bowdoin III*, 54–83. For the portraits by Trumbull, see Irma B. Jaffe, *John Trumbull, Patriot-Artist of the American Revolution* (Boston: Little, Brown and the New York Graphic Society, 1975), 56–57, 62–63, 311.

2. For Temple, see www.anb.org/articles, accessed Aug. 6, 2009; Train, *Bowdoin Family*, 27–28; their children are listed on p. 29.

3. The original and the two replicas by Stuart are listed and discussed in Lawrence Park, *Gilbert Stuart: An Illustrated Descriptive List of His Works*, 4 vols. (New York: W. E. Rudge, 1926), as no. 827 (this portrait), no. 828 (oil on canvas, 49 ½ x 35 ½ in., unlocated), and no. 829 (Gibbes Museum of Art). This third portrait is owned with Stuart's copy of Trumbull's portrait of Sir John Temple (Park, *Stuart*, no. 826). The series is summed up in a letter from Dorinda Evans published in Train, *Bowdoin Family*, 173–74.

4. The letter is quoted in Park, *Stuart*, 743, in the text of cat. no. 826, which concerns Stuart's copy of Trumbull's portrait of Sir John Temple.

5. See Jaffe, *John Trumbull*, 57, fig. 37.

6. He also painted her daughter, Sarah Bowdoin Winthrop (undated), and her son, Grenville Temple Winthrop, in about 1824. For these portraits, see Park, *Stuart*, 828–32, cat.nos. 932–33, 935–36.

11. HANNAH SKINNER CHURCH, HER DAUGHTER MARIA CHURCH, AND HER DAUGHTER-IN-LAW ELIZABETH BENTLEY CHURCH

1. Marion Converse Bright, *Early Georgia Portraits, 1715–1870* (Athens: University of Georgia Press, 1975), 34, signed and dated 1809.

2. For details of the family see John A. Church, *Descendants of Richard Church of Plymouth, Mass.* (Rutland, VT: The Tuttle Company, 1913), 99–105, 143–45; "Edward Church" in Clifford K. Shipton, *Sibley's Harvard Graduates: Biographical Sketches of Those Who Attended Harvard College in the Classes 1756–1760 with Biographical and Other Notes* (Boston: Massachusetts Historical Society, 1968), 14:389–93; and "Edward Church (1779–1845)," in *The National Cyclopaedia of American Biography* (New York: James T. White, 1929), 20:52. Hannah Skinner was Edward Church's second wife and the mother of his surviving children.

3. Edward was born on December 9, 1806, and Daniel on July 7, 1810. The dates of his children's

births are given in Church, *Descendants*, 145. The best biography of Church Jr. is in the *National Cyclopaedia* (see above, n. 2).

4. Bright, *Early Georgia Portraits*, 35, signed, lower left "Vallin Pinxit"; dated c. 1806; then owned by Mr. J. C. Hagler III.

5. His descendant Osborne Phinizy Mackie owns a copy of his will.

6. Church, *Descendants*, 143–44.

7. The shipping inventory and the plans are owned by Osborne Phinizy Mackie.

8. Martin Davies, *French School* (London: National Gallery, 1957), 215–16; *French Painting, 1774–1830: The Age of Revolution* (Detroit: Wayne State University Press, 1975), 640–42.

12. SARAH WESTON SEATON WITH HER CHILDREN AUGUSTINE AND JULIA

1. The present owner purchased this portrait at auction at Adam A. Weschler & Son (Washington, D.C.), on Feb. 16, 1975, lot 1468 (where it was dated 1815). The catalogue listed the former owner as Belle M. Johnson of Washington, D.C. The portrait was exhibited at the National Collection of Fine Arts, Smithsonian Institution (now Smithsonian American Art Museum), in 1977–78 and listed in the exhibition brochure *The Paintings of Charles Bird King (1785–1862),* no. 19. It is included in the catalogue of the same title by Andrew J. Cosentino (Washington, DC: Smithsonian Institution Press, 1977), 155, no. 231, dated c. 1835. Oren Andrew Seaton, ed., *The Seaton Family, with Genealogy and Biographies* (Topeka, KS: Crane, 1906), gives the names and dates of the children, pp. 113, 117, 118. The English book *The London Riddler, or The Art of Teasing Made Easy* (London: William Cole, 1825) is not the book he holds, given the probable date of the painting.

2. Joseph P. McKerns, "Seaton, William Winston" in www.anb.org/articles, accessed Feb. 3, 2010; William E. Ames, *A History of the National Intelligencer* (Chapel Hill: University of North Carolina Press, 1972), 104–9.

3. Julia's husband's name and the date of their marriage were found through http://search.ancestry.com. For her date of death, August 7, 1889, see the Web site of the historic Congressional Cemetery (www.congressionalcemetery.org/genealogy/interments/obituaries), "Munroe, Julia Seaton"; the notice of her funeral was in the *Washington Post,* Aug. 10, 1889, 7 (ProQuest Historical Newspapers).

4. For the artist, see Cosentino, *King*; for these portraits, see pp. 115, 134–35, cat. nos. 83–87. A photograph of Eckington is reproduced on p. 39, fig. 22.

13. LATHAM AVERY / 14. BETSEY WOOD LESTER AVERY

1. Biographical information on the Averys was provided by Leslie Evans, director of the Avery-Copp Museum, in an e-mail to Ellen Miles, Apr. 7, 2010, and in Elroy McKendree Avery and Catharine Hitchcock (Tilden) Avery, *The Groton Avery Clan* (Cleveland, OH: Privately printed, 1912), 188, 303–5, 468–69.

2. For Morse, see Paul Staiti, *Samuel F. B. Morse* (Cambridge: Cambridge University Press, 1989), especially pp. 102–7, and William Kloss, *Samuel F. B. Morse* (New York: Harry N. Abrams in association with National Museum of American Art, Smithsonian Institution, 1988), 58, 63, 68–72, 78–86, 88–98.

15. SELF-PORTRAIT (JOHN JAMES AUDUBON)

1. This biography of Audubon is based primarily on Richard Rhodes's *John James Audubon: The Making of an American* (New York: Alfred A. Knopf, 2004). Many of Audubon's drawings and watercolors are illustrated and discussed in the exhibition catalogue *Audubon Watercolors and Drawings* (Utica, NY: Munson-Williams-Proctor Institute, 1965), and in Annette Blaugrund and Theodore E. Stebbins Jr., eds., *John James Audubon: The Watercolors for the Birds of America* (New York: Villard Books and New-York Historical Society, 1993).

2. Mrs. E. C. Walker to R. W. Shufeldt, quoted in Shufeldt's article, "On an Old Portrait of Audubon, Painted by Himself, and a Word about Some of His Early Drawings," *Auk: A Quarterly Journal of Ornithology* 3, no. 4 (October 1886): 417–20, reproduced p. 416.

16. JAMES BOWDOIN SULLIVAN AND GEORGE RICHARD JAMES (SULLIVAN) BOWDOIN

1. The will is published in Russell E. Train, *The Bowdoin Family* (Washington, DC: Privately printed, 2000), 157–62, Appendix C; these references are on pp. 159–61. For the brothers, see Train, *Bowdoin*

Family, 40–47, 176 ("Bowdoin Genealogy"). The younger brother, James Sullivan, is listed on family charts with no death date and no descendants.

2. A good short biography of the artist is found in *Philadelphia: Three Centuries of American Art* (Philadelphia: Philadelphia Museum of Art, 1976), 328–29.

3. James G. Barber, *Andrew Jackson: A Portrait Study* (Washington, DC: National Portrait Gallery, and Nashville: Tennessee State Museum, 1991), 80–82, and Barber, *Old Hickory: A Life Sketch of Andrew Jackson* (Washington, DC: National Portrait Gallery; Nashville: Tennessee State Museum, 1990), 60. Jackson's portrait is signed "R. Street 1824." A testimonial letter to the portrait's accuracy as a likeness, signed by John Eaton and William Neal, is dated April 22, 1824; see "Street, the Artist," in *Catalogue of Robert Street's Exhibition at the Artists' Fund Hall . . . upwards of 200 Oil Paintings . . .* (Philadelphia: J. Young, 1840), 15.

4. "Street, the Artist," 15.

5. For the discussions in the Senate about this claim, which was paid in 1825, see *American State Papers: Documents, Legislative and Executive, of the Congress of the United States* (Washington, DC: Gales and Seaton, 1832–1861), *Class V. Military Affairs,* vol. 3, Senate, 18th Congress, 1st Session, 8–21, no. 275 (Feb. 23, 1824), 93, no. 278 (May 3, 1824); 2nd Session, 104–8, no. 283 (Feb. 22, 1825). Two letters sent by Sullivan and the second commissioner, Joseph H. Peirce, to Secretary of War John C. Calhoun place them in Washington on July 15 and November 10, 1823; see pp. 19, 20. This publication is available online on the American Memory Web site of the Library of Congress: http://memory.loc.gov.

6. A partial paper label attached to the stretcher records the following: "Painted by R. Stree/[paper torn], Washington D/[paper torn], [18?]24 [paper torn]." The label probably records an inscription on the reverse of the canvas that has now been covered by a lining.

7. Francis B. Heitman, *Historical Register and Dictionary of the United States Army* (1903; reprint, Urbana: University of Illinois Press, 1965), 233.

8. His obituary listed his name as George J. Bowdoin; "Obituary," *New York Times,* Mar. 17, 1870, 1. *New York Times* (1851–2006), www.proquest.com, accessed Mar. 2, 2010.

17. PHOEBE CAROLINE ELLIOTT PINCKNEY

1. Thomas Sully, "Register of Paintings," 53, Manuscript Division, New York Public Library (Archives of American Art microfilm N18). Edward Biddle and Mantle Fielding, *The Life and Works of Thomas Sully* (1921; reprint, New York: Kennedy Graphics and Da Capo Press, 1970), 248, no. 1381, which erroneously identifies the sitter as "wife of the prominent Episcopal minister of Charleston, S.C." whereas in fact she was his mother.

2. See Biddle and Fielding, *Life and Works of Sully,* 145, nos. 518–21, for the four portraits of the other members of the Elliott family. For the family, see Stephen B. Barnwell, *The Story of an American Family* (Marquette, MI: 1969), 146–47.

3. Barnwell, *American Family,* 148–49; the portrait by Sully is reproduced on p. 149.

4. Barbara L. Bellows, *A Talent for Living: Josephine Pinckney and the Charleston Literary Tradition* (Baton Rouge: Louisiana State University Press, 2006), 14.

18. CATHARINE PEABODY GARDNER

1. Catharine Peabody to her brother, George Peabody, Salem, Dec. 17, 1825 (collection of the owner of the portrait). For her family and husband, see Betty G. Farrell, *Elite Families: Class and Power in Nineteenth-Century Boston* (Albany: State University of New York Press, 1993), 68, 121–22, 131; and William Richard Cutter, ed., *Genealogical and Personal Memoirs Relating to the Families of Boston and Eastern Massachusetts* (New York: Lewis Historical Publishing, 1908), 1329–30.

2. Sophia Peabody to Maria Chase, Boston, Oct. 8, 1827; Peabody Family Papers, Sophia Smith Collection, Smith College, Northampton, Massachusetts. For Sophia Peabody, who married Nathaniel Hawthorne in 1842, see Megan Marshall, *The Peabody Sisters: Three Women Who Ignited American Romanticism* (Boston: Houghton Mifflin, 2005); I thank the author for her help in locating the letter.

3. Lillian B. Miller, *In Pursuit of Fame: Rembrandt Peale, 1778–1860* (Washington, DC: National Portrait Gallery in association with University of Washington Press, 1992), 149. The portraits of her parents are illustrated as oval images in Walter Muir Whitehill, *Captain Joseph Peabody, East India Merchant of Salem (1757–1844): A Sketch of His Life* (Salem, MA: Peabody Museum, 1962), following p. x, and are dated 1826 (p. vii). Carol Soltis kindly provided the dimensions of these two portraits based on records at the Frick Art Reference Library, New York. On Peabody's portrait at the Athenaeum in 1827, see Robert F. Perkins Jr. and William J. Gavin III, eds., *The Boston Athenaeum Art Exhibition Index, 1827–1874* (Boston: Library of the

Boston Athenaeum, 1980), 108, lent by J. L. Gardiner [*sic*]. Peale painted a similar portrait of Eliza Pickering Gray the following year; see Miller, *In Pursuit of Fame,* 150–51, fig. 79, and 176, color plate 20 (collection of John C. Gray).

4. Farrell, *Elite Families,* 122.

5. For Peale in Boston, see Miller, *In Pursuit of Fame,* 149–55.

19. HOWQUA (WU BINGJIAN)

1. The most thorough recent study of trade with China is Jacques M. Downs, *The Golden Ghetto: The American Commercial Community at Canton and the Shaping of American China Policy, 1784–1844* (Bethlehem, PA: Lehigh University Press; Cranbury, NJ: Associated University Presses, 1997). For a summary, see Margaret C. S. Christman, *Adventurous Pursuits: Americans and the China Trade, 1784–1844* (Washington, DC: Smithsonian Institution Press for National Portrait Gallery, 1984).

2. For Howqua, see Christman, "Houqua," in Christman, *Adventurous Pursuits,* 85–91, and Downs, *Golden Ghetto,* 81–82, 150–57, 181–82, among other references.

3. Downs, *Golden Ghetto,* 154.

4. For the artist, see "Lam Qua—'Handsome Face Painter,'" in Carl L. Crossman, *The Decorative Arts of the China Trade*: Paintings, Furnishings, and Exotic Curiosities (Woodbridge, Suffolk, UK: Antique Collectors' Club, 1991), 72–105, and Patrick Conner, "Lamqua, Western and Chinese Painter," *Arts of Asia* 29, no. 2 (March–April 1999): 46–64. Disassociating Lamqua with the Chinese name Guan Qiaochang (Kwan Kiu Cheong), which Crossman followed, Connor proposed that he is probably the Chinese artist Guan Zuolin, or Kwan Jok Lam (see Conner, "Lamqua," 63), which I have adopted here. This identification also appears at www.oxfordartonline.com/subscriber/article/grove/art, accessed Feb. 1, 2010.

5. Conner, "Lamqua," 47.

6. A portrait of Imperial Commissioner Kiyeng, wearing a similar robe and with a cap having a red stone, is illustrated and described in Christman, *Adventurous Pursuits,* 154.

7. The other known examples were owned by Daniel Nicholson Spooner (Museum of Fine Arts, Boston), Robert Bennet Forbes (Forbes House Museum, Milton, Massachusetts), Augustine Heard (Ipswich Public Library, Massachusetts), William Henry King (Kingscote, Newport, Rhode Island), and Warren Delano, the grandfather of Franklin Delano Roosevelt (private collection). The owner of the likeness once owned by Delano recently described the portrait type as the "Russell and Company portrait." For Russell and Company, its partners, and its extensive business connections with Howqua, see Downs, *Golden Ghetto,* 162–89; for a list of partners, see also pp. 364–65. For biographies of these men, see *National Cyclopedia of American Biography* 34:55–56 (Warren Delano); *Dictionary of American Biography,* s.v. "Forbes, John Murray," "Forbes, Robert Bennet," "Heard, Augustine"; www.anb.org (John Murray Forbes), and the description in Cullen Jay Wilder's paper on Daniel Nicholson Spooner [http://www.umac.mo/fsh/hist/conference/conference_text.html].

For the portraits by Lamqua, see Albert Ten Eyck Gardner, "Cantonese Chinnerys: Portraits of How-qua and Other China Trade Paintings," *Art Quarterly* 16, no. 4 (Winter 1953): 305–24; Crossman, *China Trade,* 83–84; Conner, "Lamqua," 54; Christman, *Adventurous Pursuits,* 86; Museum of Fine Arts, www.mfa.org/collections, accessed Feb. 2, 2010. The portrait owned by William Henry King is illustrated in *A Guidebook to Newport Mansions* (Newport, RI: Preservation Society of Newport County, 1984), 17.

8. *Letters and Recollections of John Murray Forbes Edited by His Daughter Sarah Forbes Hughes* (Boston: Houghton, Mifflin, 1899), 1:98; the letter is dated May 4, 1837.

9. Versions of this small full-length portrait, attributed to Chinnery or Lamqua, include the example sold by Russell's descendants at Sotheby's, London, *Important British Paintings,* June 6, 2007, lot 59, as well as versions at the Metropolitan Museum of Art, New York, and the Redwood Library, Newport, Rhode Island. For the various versions, see Crossman, *China Trade,* 81, and Conner, "Lamqua," 52–55, as well as the very informative entry with extensive bibliography for the version sold at Christies, New York, Jan. 23, 2001, lot 84 (no provenance).

10. Christman, "Howqua," 86, illus.; Robert F. Perkins Jr. and William J. Gavin III, *The Boston Athenaeum Art Exhibition Index, 1827–1874* (Boston, MA: Library of the Boston Athenaeum, 1980), 89.

11. They document physical deformities and external tumors. Most of the more than one hundred surviving examples are now in the Peter Parker Collection, Harvey Cushing/John Hay Whitney Medical Library, Yale University, New Haven, Connecticut. For Parker, see Christman, *Adventurous Pursuits,* 127–40.

20. WILLIAM RUSSELL CONE /
21. REBECCA DAGGETT BREWSTER CONE

1. For the Cones, see Class Secretary [William Russell Cone], *Memorial of the Class of 1830, Yale College* (Hartford, CT: Case, Lockwood and Brainard Press, 1871), 63–64, and *Appendix of 1885*, 135–37; see also William Russell Cone's obituary in John Hooker, *Connecticut Reports: Cases Argued and Determined in the Supreme Court of Errors of the State of Connecticut* (New York: Banks and Brothers for State of Connecticut, 1890), appendix, 58: 94–95. The quote is from Cone, *Memorial*, 63.

2. For a reference to "Mr. Hungerford, of counsel for the Spaniards," see Lewis Tappan, "The Amistad Circuit Court Trial," *New York Commercial Advertiser*, Sept. 23, 1839; "Famous American Trials; Amistad Trials, 1839–1840," at www.law.unks.edu/faculty/projects/ftrials/amistad, University of Missouri–Kansas City School of Law, accessed Mar. 22, 2010.

3. His portrait was painted by Robert McKee in 1889 after a photograph; Elizabeth Mankin Kornhauser, *American Paintings before 1945 in the Wadsworth Athenaeum* (Hartford, CT: Wadsworth Athenaeum; New Haven: Yale University Press, 1996), 2:555, illus.

4. For Philip Hewins, see James G. Barber, *Andrew Jackson: A Portrait Study* (Washington, DC: National Portrait Gallery; Nashville: Tennessee State Museum, 1991), 115–16; Kornhauser, *American Paintings*, 458–60; and Peter Hastings Falk, ed., *Who Was Who in American Art, 1564–1975: Four Hundred Years of Artists in America* (Madison, CT: Sound View Press, 1999), 2:1551. While most sources give the artist's birth as 1806, research by the owner of the portraits indicates he was born in 1808; see Thomas Williams Baldwin, comp., *Vital Records of Sharon, Massachusetts, to the Year 1850* (Boston: Stanhope Press, F. H. Gilson, 1909), 36; and "Families of Early Settlers in Blue Hill, Maine," *Bangor Historical Magazine* 5 (1890): 194. These sources list his birth date as July 25, 1808. For the notice of his death on May 14, 1849, see the *Hartford Daily Courant*, May 15, 1849, 2. For his cousin, Amasa Hewins (1795–1855), who was also a painter, see Kornhauser, *American Paintings*, 2:455–58; Falk, *Who Was Who*, 2:1551. Amasa Hewins's account of his years in Italy is published as Francis H. Allen, ed., *A Boston Portrait-Painter Visits Italy: The Journal of Amasa Hewins, 1830–1833* (Boston: Boston Athenaeum, 1931). The family relationship between the two artists has been identified by the owner of these portraits.

5. Hewins's portraits of members of the Filley family of Bloomfield, Connecticut, provided reliable evidence of his work; see Kathleen Craughwell-Varda, Susan P. Schoelwer, and Sharon Y. Steinberg, "Costume and Portraiture in the 1830s; A Connecticut Case Study," *Dress: The Annual Journal of the Costume Society of America* 29 (2002): 41–58. For the attribution to Hewins and assistance with his career and comparative works, I thank Susan Schoelwer, former director of museum collections at the Connecticut Historical Society, Hartford, and now the curator at George Washington's Mount Vernon, Virginia.

6. Alexander W. Katlan, *American Artists' Materials Suppliers Dictionary*, vol. 1, *Nineteenth Century* (Park Ridge, NJ: Noyes Press, 1987), 18–20, 78, illus. no 13–20, 389–95. Dechaux's stamp changed after 1840, from the use of "Edward" to the abbreviation "EDWD."

22. JAMES BREWSTER CONE

1. The Class Secretary [William Russell Cone], *Memorial of the Class of 1830, Yale College* (Hartford, CT: Case, Lockwood and Brainard Press, 1871), 63–64, and *Appendix of 1885*, 135–37; William Whitney Cone, comp., *Some Account of the Cone Family in America Principally of the Descendants of Daniel Cone, Who Settled in Haddam, Connecticut, in 1662* (Topeka, KS: Crane, 1903), 191; death notice, *New York Times*, Mar. 20, 1918, 13 (www.proquest.com, accessed Mar. 31, 2010); *Obituary Record of Yale Graduates, 1917–1918, Bulletin of Yale University*, 15th series, no. 5 (Feb. 1919): 564–65.

2. See Kathleen Craughwell-Varda, Susan P. Schoelwer, and Sharon Y. Steinberg, "Costume and Portraiture in the 1830s; A Connecticut Case Study," *Dress: The Annual Journal of the Costume Society of America* 29 (2002): 45, figs. 6–7 for illustrations of the portrait, attributed also to Philip Hewins, and the smock.

3. Alexander W. Katlan, *American Artists' Materials Suppliers Dictionary*, vol. 1, *Nineteenth Century* (Park Ridge, NJ: Noyes Press, 1987), 18–20, 78, illus. no. 13–20, 389–95. Dechaux's stamp changed after 1840, from the use of "Edward" to the abbreviation "EDWD."

23. JOHN CLARKE

1. For these bottles, see the Society of Historical Archaeology, http://www.sha.org, under the title "Soda and Mineral Water Bottles," accessed June 15, 2009.

2. For his biography, see James M. Goode, "John Clarke of Saratoga Springs, New York, and His Legacy," unpublished manuscript, 2009. On Saratoga and his role in its development, see also Jon Sterngass, *First Resorts: Pursuing Pleasure at Saratoga Springs, Newport, and Coney Island* (Baltimore: Johns Hopkins University Press, 2001), 7–39; Clarke is discussed on pp. 11–13, 18.

3. This inscription appears to have been transferred from the back of the original canvas, probably during conservation.

4. Cook's very detailed biography can be found at http://www.nelsoncook.com.

5. Andrew Oliver, *Auguste Edouart's Silhouettes of Eminent Americans, 1839–1844* (Charlottesville: University Press of Virginia for National Portrait Gallery, Smithsonian Institution, 1977), xiii–xiv, and catalogue no. 72, illus. (no page numbers). Oliver describes Clarke as "one of the leading physicians at Saratoga early in the century." The same lithograph setting was used for portraits made in Saratoga, Boston, and Washington, D.C.; see nos. 39, 122–23, 149–50, 217, and 243.

24. PORTRAIT OF A YOUNG GIRL

1. "Recent Acquisitions—Samuel Miller," *Bulletin* (Manchester, NH: Currier Gallery of Art, 1977), 27; *American Art from the Currier Gallery of Art* (New York: American Federation of Arts, 1995), 38, no. 10, illus. p. 39, catalogue entry by Carol Troyen. The inscription was recorded before the portrait was lined. Our thanks to the librarian of the Currier Museum of Art, Alison Dickey, for sending this information.

2. Paul S. D'Ambrosio and Charlotte M. Emans, *Folk Art's Many Faces: Portraits in the New York State Historical Association* (Cooperstown: New York State Historical Association, 1987), 111–17.

3. D'Ambrosio and Emans discuss five portraits of children in *Folk Art's Many Faces,* 111–17; Deborah Chotner discusses a similarly painted portrait of a little boy in Chotner et al., *American Naïve Paintings,* National Gallery of Art Systematic Catalogue (Washington, DC: National Gallery of Art; Cambridge: Cambridge University Press, 1992), 448–51.

4. Troyen, in *American Art from the Currier Gallery,* 38.

5. This information is found on his death certificate; see D'Ambrosio and Emans, *Folk Art's Many Faces,* 111.

25. ROBERT WICKLIFFE JR.

1. For both portraits, see Richard P. Wunder, *Hiram Powers: Vermont Sculptor, 1805–1873,* vol. 2, *Catalogue of Works* (Newark: University of Delaware Press; London: Associated University Presses, 1991), 107–8. For that of Wickliffe, see Lynne D. Ambrosini and Rebecca A. G. Reynolds, *Hiram Powers: Genius in Marble* (Cincinnati, OH: Taft Museum of Art, 2007), 56–57. For Wickliffe, see also John Frederick Dorman, *The Prestons of Smithfield and Greenfield in Virginia,* Filson Club Publications, 2d series, no. 3 (Louisville, KY: Filson Club, 1982), 88–89.

2. Wickliffe to Preston, Nov. 22, 1844, Wickliffe-Preston Papers, Special Collections Library, University of Kentucky, Lexington, quoted in *Powers: Genius in Marble,* 56. He is referring to brothers Chester or Horace Harding, two American portrait painters, and to Danish sculptor Bertel Thorwaldsen. In the letter, Wickliffe mentions pictures that he had purchased while he was in Florence.

3. Lester's book on Powers is titled *The Artist, the Merchant, and the Statesman of the Age of the Medici, and of Our Own Times,* 2 vols. (New York: Paine and Burgess, 1845); for a discussion of Lester's publication, see Wunder, *Hiram Powers,* 145–51. Wickliffe's letter to Powers, written from Rome, is dated June 7, 1846 (Archives of American Art; quoted in Wunder, *Hiram Powers,* 1:150).

4. Lester attempted to have Wickliffe removed from his position so that he could be appointed to it. In 1848 Lester lost his diplomatic post when the Sardinian government demanded his recall over the shipment of artwork to America; Wunder, *Hiram Powers,* 1:151

5. According to Richard Wunder, *Hiram Powers,* 1:108, "the marble replica is listed as cut by Ambuchi in 1857." Antonio Ambuchi was one of the two carvers who worked for Powers for many years in Florence (see Wunder, *Hiram Powers,* 1:110).

6. Powers to William Preston, Feb. 6, 1861, William Preston Correspondence, box 54, Jan.–Feb. 1861, Wickliffe-Preston Papers. The letter is quoted in part in Wunder, *Hiram Powers,* 2:108, and in Ambrosini and Reynolds, *Hiram Powers, Genius in Marble,* 57. My thanks go to Rebecca Reynolds for generously lending me her file on this portrait, with copies of the correspondence referred to here.

26. SARAH OSGOOD JOHNSON NEWTON

1. For Johnson's early career, see Teresa A. Carbone, "From Crayon to Brush: The Education of

Eastman Johnson, 1840–1858," in Teresa A. Carbone and Patricia Hills, *Eastman Johnson: Painting America* (New York: Brooklyn Museum in association with Rizzoli International, 1999), 11–47.

2. Ibid., 32, cat. no. 15, illus. p. 34.

3. "Personal [From the Superior Chronicle, Feb 3d]," *Daily (Columbus) Ohio Statesman*, Feb. 27, 1857, 3; America's Historical Newspapers, http://infoweb.newsbank.com, accessed Aug. 12, 2009, by intern Brooks Swett. The article begins: "The many friends of William H. Newton, Esq. and lady, will be pleased to learn of their arrival at St. Paul, on the evening of the 19th ultimo."

4. Carbone, "From Crayon to Brush," 47, n. 98.

27. HANNAH

1. The only marking on the painting is found on the back of the millboard panel, where it is stamped with a French art supplier's stamp: "PANNEAUX et CARTONS/ MULLER/Paris."

2. *Catalogue of Finished Pictures, Studies and Drawings by the Late Eastman Johnson, N.A.* (New York: American Art Association, 1907), unpaginated, no. 22. For a copy of the entry, I thank Sandy Wallace, library assistant, Wilbour Library of Egyptology, Brooklyn Museum, Brooklyn, NY. The description included the size of the painting, which assisted in the confirmation of its identity.

3. For John Davis's important study of the painting, see his article, "Eastman Johnson's *Negro Life at the South* and Urban Slavery in Washington, D.C.," *Art Bulletin* 80, no. 1 (Mar. 1998): 67–92; for Johnson and the painting, see Patricia Hills, "Painting Race: Eastman Johnson's Pictures of Slaves, Ex-Slaves, and Freedmen," in Teresa A. Carbone and Patricia Hills, *Eastman Johnson: Painting America* (New York: Brooklyn Museum of Art in association with Rizzoli International, 1999), 120–65. The identification of Hannah as the model for the figure in *Negro Life at the South* has been suggested by Emeritus Professor Clifford T. Chieffo of Georgetown University.

4. For the story of these paintings, see Patricia Hills, "Painting Race," in Carbone and Hills, *Eastman Johnson*, 131–36.

28. CZAR ALEXANDER II OF RUSSIA

1. For Curtin, see the entry at www.anb.org/articles, accessed Apr. 6, 2010.

2. For their parallel careers, see James Billington, "The Tsar and the President: Alexander II and Abraham Lincoln," in Marilyn Pfeifer Swezey, ed., *The Tsar and the President: Alexander II and Abraham Lincoln, Liberator and Emancipator* (Washington, DC: American-Russian Cultural Cooperation Foundation, 2008), v–vi.

3. The original letter, in French, has been translated with the assistance of Anne Goodyear, associate curator of prints and drawings at the National Portrait Gallery. This part of the short letter reads: «Sa Majesté l'Empereur désirant Vous donner un témoignage particulier de Sa haute bienveillance a voulu qu'en quittant la Russie Vous emportiez Son portrait. Il vient d'être exécuté d'ordre de Sa Majesté Impériale. Elle m'a chargé de vous le transmettre en exprimant le désir qu'il reste a jamais dans Votre famille en mémoire des tous sentiments que Vous avez toujours manifestés envers la Russie et des souvenirs d'estime et d'affection que Vous y laisser.»

4. "A Picture His Inheritance: W. W. Curtin Wanted Nothing More from Father's Estate," *New York Times,* Apr. 16, 1905, 1; from *New York Times* (1851–2006), www.proquest.com, retrieved Apr. 6, 2010.

5. The portrait is signed and dated in the lower left: "G Bothmann St. Petersburg 1872." He is identified in sources as either Gregor or Georg Bothman(n); for a brief biography see Gunter Meissner, ed., *Allgemeines Künstler aller Zeiten und Völker* (Munich: K. G. Saur, 1992–2009), 13:247.

6. For this portrait, see http://www.museo.helsinki.fi/kokoelmat/taidekokoelmat/galleria_academica/Aleksii.htm, accessed June 19, 2009.

7. Swezey, *The Tsar and the President*, 85, cat. no. 58, illus. p. 65; the oval portrait shows the duke in the winter jacket of the Grodno Hussar Life Guards. The portrait was commissioned three years after Nicholas's death by spinal meningitis at the age of twenty-one in 1865, and it hung in Alexander II's study. In this Russian collection, the artist is known by a Russian version of his German name, "Igor Ivanovich Botman"; I thank Alex Dmitriev of the museum staff for information about the artist; his e-mail April 7, 2010.

8. Sold at Christie's London, *Important Russian Pictures Including the Somov Collection*, Nov. 28, 2007, lot 344.

9. Information taken from http://artinvestment.ru/en/auctions/9425/biography.html, accessed Apr. 12, 2010.

29. DELIA SPENCER CATON FIELD

1. Her death in 1937 at age eighty-four is noted in "Marshall Field Widow Victim of Pneumonia,"

Washington Post, July 24, 1937, 1 (www.proquest.com, accessed April 27, 2010). The article notes also that she was fifty-two when she married Field in 1905.

2. Their departure and return on the steamship *Germanic* were noted by the *New York Times*: "Passengers Sailed," May 21, 1876, 12; "Passengers Arrived," Oct. 17, 1876, 10; www.proquest.com, accessed June 11, 2009.

3. Albert J. Beveridge III and Susan Radomsky, *The Chronicle of Catherine Eddy Beveridge: An American Girl Travels into the Twentieth Century* (Lanham, MD: Hamilton Books, 2005), 204.

4. "The Artists' Labors," *Inter Ocean (Chicago)* 5, no. 25 (Apr. 22, 1876): 3; "Art and Its Followers: Studio Notes," *Inter Ocean* 5, no. 49 (May 20, 1876): 9; "America's Historical Newspapers," http://infoweb. newsbank.com, accessed June 19, 2009.

5. The owners of the portrait also own the letter, dated Paris, November 17, 1876, and the invoice of the same date. Healy's address was 64 rue de la Rochefoucauld, Paris. The term "bishop's half length" was used to describe a canvas size that was wider than usual to accommodate the broad sleeves of a bishop's clerical robes.

6. Liza Kirwin, *Lists: To-dos, Illustrated Inventories, Collected Thoughts and Other Artists' Enumerations from the Smithsonian's Archives of American Art* (New York: Princeton Architectural Press, 2010), 38. The replica is briefly listed as in Healy's Paris studio in 1889 (Marie de Mare, *G. P. A. Healy, American Artist: An Intimate Chronicle of the Nineteenth Century* [New York: David McKay, 1954], 7). After his death Healy's family gave it to the Newberry Library in Chicago, but it was later returned to a member of Mrs. Field's family.

7. Brief biographies of Healy are found in Jane Turner, ed. *Encyclopedia of American Art before 1914* (New York: Grove Dictionaries, 2000), 221–22, and www.anb.org.

8. Timothy E. Sullivan, "Marshall Field," www.anb. org/articles, accessed Mar. 23, 2010.

9. "Marshall Field's Handsome Bride," *Olympia (Washington) Record*, published as *Olympia Daily Recorder* 4, no. 130 (Oct. 11, 1905): 5; from *American Historical Newspapers*, http://infoweb.newsbank.com, accessed June 10, 2009.

10. A recent cleaning revealed the overpainted jewelry

11. Beveridge and Radomsky, *Chronicle of Catherine Eddy Beveridge*, 186.

30. SUSAN IN TOQUE WITH ROSES

1. Adelyn Dohme Breeskin, *Mary Cassatt: A Catalogue Raisonné of the Oils, Pastels, Watercolors, and Drawings* (Washington, DC: Smithsonian Institution Press, 1970), 65, cat. no. 105. Breeskin dates this portrait to 1881 and gives the title as *Susan in a Toque Trimmed with Two Roses*. Breeskin also notes that Susan sat for Cassatt numerous times (Breeskin, *Cassatt*, 65–67, nos. 105–8, 111). *Young Girl at a Window* (cat. 111; c. 1883), for which Susan is believed to have been the model, is one of the treasures in the collection of the Corcoran Gallery of Art. Nancy Mowll Mathews, in *Mary Cassatt: A Life* (New York: Villard Books, 1994), 240–41, identifies Susan as a cousin of Cassatt's housekeeper. See also Christie's, *Important American Paintings, Drawings and Sculpture,* sale no. 9006, Dec. 2, 1998, no. 74.

2. Extensive biographical information on Cassatt can be found in Judith A. Barter et al., *Mary Cassatt, Modern Woman* (New York: Art Institute of Chicago with Harry N. Abrams, 1998), 337, and in Mathews, *Cassatt: A Life.*

3. George T. M. Shackelford, "*Pas de Deux*, Mary Cassatt and Edgar Degas," in Barter, *Cassatt, Modern Woman,* 109–43.

31. ALBERT DE BELLEROCHE

1. For the portrait of Mme. Gautreau and related drawings and paintings, see, most recently, Richard Ormond and Elaine Kilmurray, *John Singer Sargent: Complete Paintings*, vol. 1, *The Early Portraits* (New Haven: Yale University Press for Paul Mellon Centre for Studies in British Art, 1998), 112–18, cat. nos. 114–17. The story of the portrait has also been described by Deborah Davis in *Strapless: John Singer Sargent and the Fall of Madame X* (New York: Jeremy P. Tarcher/Penguin Books, 2003).

2. For these paintings and drawings, see Ormond and Kilmurray, *Early Portraits*, 97–100, cat. nos. 96–100 and figs. 44–46; Dorothy Moss, "John Singer Sargent, 'Madame X,' and 'Baby Millbank,'" *Burlington Magazine* 143, no. 1178 (May 2001): 268–75.

3. Albert de Belleroche, "The Lithographs of John Singer Sargent," *Print Collector's Quarterly* 13 (1926): 34, quoted in Moss, "Sargent," 274.

4. Moss, "Sargent," 275.

5. Belleroche, "Lithographs of John Singer Sargent," 42; the lithographs of Belleroche are reproduced on pp. 39, plate IV, and 41, plate V.

6. Count William de Belleroche to Mrs. Stevenson Scott, Apr. 14, 1948, courtesy of the owner of the portrait.

32. PORTRAIT OF MY DAUGHTER (DOROTHY BRÉMOND CHASE)

1. For Chase at Shinnecock, see especially D. Scott Atkinson and Nicolai Cikovsky Jr., *William Merritt Chase: Summers at Shinnecock, 1891–1902* (Washington, DC: National Gallery of Art, 1987).

2. Ronald G. Pisano, completed by D. Frederick Baker, *The Complete Catalogue of Known and Documented Work by William Merritt Chase (1849–1916)*, vol. 2, *William Merritt Chase: Portraits in Oil*, completed by Carolyn K. Lane and D. Frederick (New Haven: Yale University Press, 2006), 150, no. OP. 279, illus. (listed as unlocated).

3. Pisano, *Chase: Portraits in Oil*, 53–54, OP. 106; David B. Dearinger, ed., *Painting and Sculpture in the Collection of the National Academy of Design* (New York: Hudson Hills Press, 2004), 1:98–99, illus., and color plate between pp. 328 and 329.

4. Photographs of Chase family members and their friends in these costumes are included in the exhibition catalogue *William Merritt Chase, 1849 to 1916* (New York: Chapellier Galleries, 1969), and Ronald G. Pisano and Alicia Grant Longwell, *Photographs from the William Merritt Chase Archives at the Parrish Art Museum* (Southampton, NY: Parrish Art Museum, 1992). Betty Fisher's role in these events is also described in the entry on Chase's portrait of her, described in Pisano, *Chase: Portraits in Oil,* 152, OP. 281, illus.

5. Pisano and Longwell, *Photographs*, 30, 34, 35, 38, 40, 44.

6. For portraits painted during these years, see "The Shinnecock Years," in Pisano, *Chase: Portraits in Oil,* 98–189.

7. Pisano *Chase: Portraits in Oil*, pp. 152–53, no. OP.282, illus.; for the photograph of Helen as the infanta, see Atkinson and Cikovsky, *Summers at Shinnecock*, p. 53, and Pisano and Longwell, *Photographs*, p. 45. The Prado now attributes the portrait to Juan Bautista Martínez del Mazo; see http://www.museodelprado.es/coleccion/galeria-on-line, accessed June 18, 2010. The infanta is also represented in *Las Meninas* (Museo del Prado, Madrid), Velázquez's self-portrait with the family of Philip IV of Spain.

8. On this painting see Pisano, *Chase: Portraits in Oil*, 152–53, no. OP. 282, illus., where the observation about Mrs. Porter is quoted from the catalogue of the William Merritt Chase Memorial Exhibition, held in 1917 at the Metropolitan Museum of Art, New York.

9. Butler to William Merritt Chase, January 17, 1916, J. G. Butler Papers, Butler Institute of American Art Archives, Youngstown, Ohio, courtesy of Patrick McCormick, archivist.

10. Pisano, *Chase: Portraits in Oil*, 150.

11. For this painting, see Atkinson and Cikovsky, *Summers at Shinnecock*, 51, 58–59 and pl. 23.

33. ALFRED, LORD TENNYSON

1. For Partridge, see Marjorie Pingel Balge, "William Ordway Partridge (1761–1930): American Art Critic and Sculptor" (PhD diss., University of Delaware, 1982); and Marjorie P. Balge, "William Ordway Partridge," www.anb.org/articles, accessed July 28, 2009.

2. B. O. Flower, "The Soul of Man in Twentieth-Century Sculpture: A Study of Mr. Partridge's Portrait Busts," *Arena* 39, no. 218 (Jan. 1908): 8.

3. For the portraits of Tennyson, see Balge, "Partridge," 333–34, cat. no. 54. She lists four bronzes, three plaster casts and two examples in marble; two additional bronzes are recorded in the art inventories compiled by the Smithsonian American Art Museum; see http://siris-artinventories.si.edu, "Partridge and Tennyson." This example is not recorded in the dissertation or the inventory. The cast owned by the Smithsonian American Art Museum was the gift of the sculptor's widow; see Elizabeth Prelinger, *The Gilded Age: Treasures from the Smithsonian American Art Museum* (New York: Watson-Guptill Publications, 2000), 66, illus. p. 67. I thank George Gurney, deputy chief curator, Smithsonian American Art Museum, for his concise explanation of differences between the various bronze casts.

4. For these works, see William Ordway Partridge, *The Works in Sculpture of William Ordway Partridge, M.A., with Biographical Sketch and Illustrations of Principal Works* (New York: John Lane, 1914), x, xii, and the illustrations on pp. 40, 58, 59, 63, 64; and Balge, "Partridge," 178, 185 , 245, 320, and 346. For Valentine, see *Who Was Who in America* (Chicago: Marquis, 1966), 1:1267.

5. This quote appears with a reproduction of the marble version in Robert Burns Wilson, "William Ordway Partridge," *International Studio* 31 (Mar.–June 1907), lxxii, and in Flower, "The Soul of Man," 8, illus. p. 7.

6. Balge, "Partridge," 91.

7. Flower, "Soul of Man," 5; Wilson, "William Ordway Partridge," lxxii.

34. ETHEL MARY CROCKER (COUNTESS DE LIMUR)

1. In April 1906 the Crocker home on Nob Hill in San Francisco was destroyed by the earthquake and subsequent fire. The Crockers, known for their numerous charitable acts, gave the property to Grace Church as a site on which to build a new cathedral to replace the one that had also been ruined by the earthquake and fire. See Michael Lampen, "Vision, Disaster and Gift: Philanthropy Afloat," part 2, www.Gracecathedral.org/church, accessed Mar. 10, 2010. The Crockers' new home, New Place, was completed in 1917 and was in Burlingame, south of the city. See Porter Garnett, *Stately Homes of California* (Boston: Little, Brown, 1915), 3–12.

2. William H. Gerdts, "The Land of Sunshine," in *Masters of Light: Plein-air Painting in California, 1890–1930* (Irvine: Irvine Museum of Art, 2002), 29–30. Mrs. Crocker maintained a lifelong interest in art and museums and in 1919 served on a committee with J. P. Morgan, Mrs. E. H. Harriman, Herbert L. Pratt, and Robert de Forest to establish a national portrait gallery. See *Annual Report of the Board of Regents of the Smithsonian Institution, 1921* (Washington, DC: Government Printing Office, 1922), 45, and "War Portraits by Eminent Artists," *American Magazine of Art* 12 (Mar. 1921): 77.

3. Allen Sergeant, "Paris," *Harper's Weekly*, Nov. 22, 1897, 294. The most recent assessment of Giovanni Boldini's work is Sarah Lees, *Giovanni Boldini in Impressionist Paris* (Ferrara, It.: Ferrara Arte; Williamstown, MA: Sterling and Francine Clark Art Institute, 2009). For an overview of his oeuvre, see also Carlo L. Ragghianti, *L'opera Completa di Boldini* (Milan: Rizzoli Editore, 1970) and Francesca and Piero Dini, *Boldini: Catalogo Ragionato, 1842–1931,* 4 vols. (Torino: Umberto Allemandi, 2007).

4. "Passenger Lists of Vessels Arriving at New York, New York, 1820–1897, 1894," microfilm serial M237, microfilm roll, M237_634, line 21, National Archives and Records Administration, Washington, DC. I thank Christopher A. Saks for obtaining this documentation.

5. "Ocean Travelers," *New York Times,* Apr. 28, 1906, 5; New York Passenger Lists, 1820–1857 (1906), microfilm serial T715, microfilm roll T715_790, p. 7. I thank Isobel Ellis for the citation from the *Oakland Tribune,* June 23, 1906, that states that the two girls left with their governess and were joined that summer by Mrs. Crocker and their brother Charles, who was at the Groton School in Massachusetts.

6. Ragghianti, *Boldini*. Cat. nos. 418, 469, and 470 reference the three portraits, with illustrations for nos. 418 and 469. Dini, *Boldini*, vol. 3, part 2, no. 924, is the catalogue entry for Ethel's portrait, although she is not identified by name. Her mother's portrait is cat. no. 1000. Helen Victoria's portrait is not mentioned. The family also possesses a small sketch of Ethel done in 1910, when, according to family history, she accompanied her mother to her mother's sitting with Boldini.

7. Passenger List of Vessels Arriving at New York, New York, 1820–1957 (June 17, 1910), microfilm roll T715_1501, p. 114, line 5; (Aug. 1, 1911), microfilm serial T715, microfilm roll T 715_1716, p. 18, line 2; (July 3, 1912) microfilm roll T715_ 1892, p. 19, line 8, all National Archives. See also, "Miss Crocker Ill in Paris," *New York Times*, Mar. 24, 2010, 9. In all likelihood, Mrs. Crocker's portrait and that of her daughter Helen were done while Ethel recuperated. For later prewar trips see "Whitelaw Reid Gives Dinner," *New York Times*, May 13, 1911, 13; "Cheers for a King, an Ascot Surprise," *New York Times*, June 23, 1912, C2; and "London Hotels Sad as Americans Flee," *New York Times*, Aug. 24, 1914, 3.

8. "Miss Crocker Engaged," *New York Times*, Nov. 8, 1917, 15; "Social Season Opens," *New York Times*, Nov. 11, 1917, 75; "Miss Crocker Wed to Count de Limur," *New York Times*, Mar. 28, 1918; "France Honors Americans, *Washington Post*, May 19, 1919, 6; "French Town Rebuilt by American Woman," *Washington Post*, Aug. 1, 1920, 57.

9. "French Nobleman Renounces Title, Swears Allegiance as U. S. Citizen; 55 Naturalized" *Washington Post*, Aug. 5, 1942, 9. More than one hundred entries in the *Washington Post* detail the activities of Countess de Limur and her family from 1942 until her death.

35. HILDEGARDE

1. Hirschl and Adler Galleries, *Lilla Cabot Perry: A Retrospective Exhibition* (New York: Hirschl and Adler Galleries, 1969), cats. 36–39.

2. Meredith Martindale et al., *Lilla Cabot Perry: An American Impressionist* (Washington: National Museum

of Women in the Arts, 1990) contains the most recent and complete information on the artist. Her husband was a descendant of Benjamin Franklin and the grandnephew of Commodore Matthew C. Perry. Perry's older sister was married to artist John LaFarge.

36. SISTER / 37. BROTHER

1. Numerous citations in the *Washington Post*, the *Chicago Daily Tribune*, and the *Boston Globe* from 1907 to 1919 document the contact between the two families. In addition to her home in Chicago, Field maintained a presence in Washington, where her niece had a home for several years. Field had contemplated purchasing property in the nation's capital as early as 1909 (*Washington Post*, June 13, 1909, C1). In 1914 she rented and then in 1923 purchased a home at 2600 Sixteenth Street; see Sue A. Kohler, *Sixteenth Street Architecture* (Washington, D.C.: Commission of Fine Arts, 1988), 2:451–91. William Innes Homer, *Robert Henri and His Circle* (New York: Hacker Art Books, 1988), provides an overview of Henri's life and art.

2. I thank University of Delaware Professor Emeritus William Innes Homer for providing me with the entry on these portraits from his copy of Robert Henri's record books. In the second version of the girl's portrait, she is shown with a fur cap and mittens—which suggests either that Henri augmented the portrait on his own or that she was a willing model and sat again. The boy's second portrait varies little from the first.

3. Delia Spencer Field signed de László's sitter's book on July 3, 1921. I thank Alice Whitehead, coordinating editor for Sandra de László, *The Catalogue Raisonné of Works of Philip de László* (http://www.delaszloarchivetrust.com/) for this information. I also thank Diane Dillon at the Newberry Library for confirming the Newberrys' possession of the portrait and noting that it held a letter from the artist to the sitter, sent from Washington on July 5, 1921.

4. *Bulletin of the Art Institute of Chicago* 32, no. 4 (April–May, 1938): cover, 58. I thank Flavie Durand-Ruel, Durand-Ruel Archives, Paris, for confirming that Mrs. Field purchased the Cassatt painting from the Durand-Ruel Gallery in New York on October 22, 1922. I thank Christine Berry, Spanierman Gallery, New York, with providing me with the provenance of Weir's *Two Sisters*, including the fact that Mrs. Field had purchased this painting—which had been shown at the Knoedler Gallery in New York in 1915—from the Vose Galleries in Boston in 1916.

5. Bennard B. Perlman, *Robert Henri: His Life and Art* (New York: Dover, 1991), 153–56, documents Henri's exhibitions in New York. Henri exhibited at the Art Institute of Chicago almost yearly from 1894 until 1939. See Peter H. Falk, ed., *The Annual Exhibition Record of the Art Institute of Chicago, 1888–1950* (Madison, CT: Sound View Press, 1990), 429–30. "Marshall Fields to Live in the East," *Chicago Daily Tribune*, May 20, 1916, 17, states that Field, who had visited her home on Prairie Avenue before returning to Washington, "has recently had an apartment in New York."

6. *Washington Post*, Oct. 30, 1915, 7; *Chicago Daily Tribune*, June 20, 1915, D2.

7. Jean Redman, "The Two Expositions: Their Differing Charms," *Los Angeles Times*, April 25, 1915, vii.

8. Perlman, *Robert Henri*, 120, states that Field purchased three paintings by Henri in 1915. According to Perlman, the paintings were shown in 1916 at Gertrude Vanderbilt Whitney's portrait exhibition at the Whitney Studio at 8 West Eighth Street. I have been able to locate only two of the three paintings. *Laughing Gypsy Girl* was owned by the Museum of Fine Arts, Boston, until it was sold at Sotheby's on May 24, 2006, cat. no. 130. Both *Laughing Gypsy Girl* and *Imaginative Boy* were illustrated as works from Field's collection in William Yarrow and Louis Bouché, *Robert Henri: His Life and Works* (New York: Boni & Liveright, 1921), 82, 114. I thank John de Feo for confirming the presence of this painting in the New Britain Museum of American Art and for his knowledge of its provenance after the death of Delia Field.

9. Homer, *Robert Henri*, 249, 252.

38. THE PAU HUNT (FREDERICK HENRY PRINCE AND FREDERICK HENRY PRINCE JR.)

1. Alfred J. Munnings, *An Artist's Life*, vol. 2, *The Second Burst* (London: Museum Press, 1951), 159–68. Although Paul Mellon seems improbably young to have developed a large stable of horses, David Cannadine, in *Mellon: An American Life* (New York: Knopf, 2006), 259, notes that Paul's father, Andrew Mellon, "drew the line at foxhunting, which Paul (and later Dick) adored."

2. *New York Times*, Jan. 29, 1933; *Chicago Daily Tribune*, Jan. 29, 1933, G7. In 1947, Princemere was sold to the Gordon College of Theology and Missions. The land was located in multiple districts—Wenham,

Hamilton, Manchester, Essex, and Beverly—and included four ponds and a "large portion of Chebacco Lake" (*Christian Science Monitor*, Dec. 30, 1947). I thank Diana and Frederick Prince IV for providing the names of Prince's estates in southern France.

3. Munnings, *Second Burst*, 338.

4. For a history of the Pau hunt, see C. B. Pitman, "Sport in the South of France," *Baily's Magazine of Sports and Pastimes* 47 (April 1887): 243–47. For Prince's role as master of the hounds, see Harry Worcester Smith, *A Sporting Tour through Ireland England, Wales and France: Master of Foxhounds* (Columbia, SC: State, 1925), 2:262–79, 348; *Washington Post*, May 23, 1926, A3; *New York Times*, Nov. 23, 1926, 5; Jan. 22, 1928, 36; Munnings, *Second Burst*, 101, 102. Prince was known for the quality of his horses, of which he maintained a stable of about sixty. His hounds, who summered at Prides Crossing, were imported from famous packs in West Norfolk, England, and Scotland.

5. Among the works that Munnings painted of the Prince family was a second portrait of F. H. Prince, in profile, astride a horse, with two dogs (1924), *F. H. Prince and the Pau Foxhounds* (sold at Christie's, New York, *Sporting and Wildlife Art*, cat. no. 2055, no. 82, Dec. 3, 2008); *The Ride to the Chateau* (alternatively titled "Mrs. Prince in the Pyrenees" or " Mrs. Prince at Biarritz"); individual portraits of Mr. and Mrs. Prince seated in French chairs on a balcony, started in Biarritz but probably completed in Paris (Munnings, *Second Burst*, 334–39, ill. opposite p. 320); *Mr. and Mrs. Prince Playing Patience* (Munnings, *Second Burst*, 337–39, ill. opposite p. 321); and *Mr. Frederick Prince Jr.* (private collection).

39. PAULINE MORTON SMITH SABIN DAVIS

1. Sheila Cochran to Pie Friendly, May 13, 2010, stated that a conservator at the National Gallery of Art, Washington, D.C., in 1956 reduced this painting in size by removing approximately nine inches across the bottom and slightly more than two inches on the side.

2. See *Bayberry Land Biography*, www.town. southamptonny.gov/FTP/SEQRA/Bayberry/Pauline. In 1936, Sabin married Dwight F. Davis (1879–1945), former secretary of war (1925–29), governor general of the Philippines (1929–32), and during World War II, director general of the Army Specialist Corps. He was also the donor of the international trophy, the Davis Cup. Sabin is featured prominently in Daniel Okrent, *Last Call: The Rise and Fall of Prohibition, 1920–1933* (New York: Scribner, 2010).

3. In 1918 she and her husband began building a large estate near Southampton. See Mary Cummings, www.hamptons.com/Real-Estate/Living-History/330 Bayberry-Land.

4. I thank the Honorable Mrs. Sandra de László, director and editor of the *The Catalogue Raisonné of Works of Philip de László (1869–1937)*, and Alice Whitehead, coordinating editor, for providing me with additional information on the artist and his painting of Pauline Sabin. The Sabin portrait is mentioned in a letter written in London from Philip de László to Sigmund Muenz, May 15, 1926, De László Archive, 0160029; the signature is in Sitter's Book II, f.48, De László Archive, Heinz Archive and Library, National Portrait Gallery, London. Additional information on de László can be found at www.delaszloarchivetrust. com and in Owen Rutter, *Portrait of a Painter: The Authorized Life of Philip de László* (London: Hodder and Stoughton, 1939).

40. VILHJALMUR STEFANSSON

1. Evelyn Stefansson Nef had agreed to lend this artwork to "Capital Portraits" before she died. Her estate and its beneficiaries have honored her wishes that this sculpture and her portrait by Alex Katz be included in this exhibition.

2. Vilhjalmur Stefansson, *Discovery: The Autobiography of Vilhjalmur Stefansson* (New York: McGraw-Hill, 1964*); Evelyn Stefansson Nef, *Finding My Way: The Autobiography of an Optimist* (Washington, DC: Francis Press, 2002), 100–110; "Vilhjalmur Stefansson, 82, Dies," *New York Times,* Aug. 27, 1962, 1.

3. The most complete biographical information on Salemme can be found at www.antoniosalemme.org, accessed July 7, 2010.

4. Stefansson, *Autobiography,* p. 333. In his unpublished memoirs written about 1980, Salemme noted that "I did a first model in fresh clay, which did not satisfy me, so I tore it down and began one in plastilene." He then carved a version in sandstone, which is now in the National Portrait Gallery's collection, a gift of the Salemme Foundation. I thank Joseph Skrapits, president of the Antonio Salemme Foundation, for providing me with entries related to this sculpture from Salemme's unpublished memoirs and additional details about the friendship between the sculptor and the explorer, including the fact that they shared an interest in spiritualism. Stefansson's portrait bust was exhibited at Salemme's first one-man exhibition, at the Faragil Gallery, New York, in November 1939.

5. Stefansson, *Autobiography,* 333–347; Nef, *Autobiography,* 47–51, 121–64. Nef's arctic books include *Within the Circle: Portrait of the Arctic* (1945) and *Here Is the Far North* (1957), both published in New York by Scribner's.

6. Evelyn Stefansson to Antonio Salemme, Mar. 25, 1959, Antonio Salemme Foundation.

41. FREDERICK HENRY PRINCE III

1. Biographical information on Manship can be found in Edwin Murtha, *Paul Manship* (New York: MacMillan, 1957); and John Manship, *Paul Manship* (New York: Abbeville Press, 1989).

2. Paul Manship Papers, Reel N714, Archives of American Art, Smithsonian Institution, Washington, DC (hereafter, Manship Papers).

3. Murtha, *Manship,* 164–66.

4. Eugene V. Thayer to Paul Manship, May 28, 1928, Paul Howard Manship Family Papers, The Margaret Cassidy and John Paul Manship Collection, Boston. I thank Rebecca Reynolds, curator of the collection, and Sharon Spieldenner, archivist of the collection, for permission to quote from this letter.

5. Details of Elizabeth Harding's marriage and divorce from Prince and her marriage to Thayer can be found in the *New York Times,* July 15, 1917, 14; *New York Times,* Mar. 24, 1923, 15; *Boston Daily Globe,* June 3, 1923, 1; and *New York Times,* July 1, 1923, 27. Thayer died unexpectedly in 1937 (*New York Times,* Jan. 2, 1937, 11), and in 1938 Elizabeth married Vadim S. Makaroff, a noted yachtsman (*Chicago Daily Tribune,* Mar. 31, 1938, 18). She died on March 27, 1961 (*New York Times,* Mar. 28, 1961, 35).

6. In 1945, Prince married Helen E. A. Pierce. They were the parents of two children, a daughter (born 1946) and a son (born 1947). After retiring from the Air Force, Prince lived a somewhat peripatetic life, residing in Lausanne, Switzerland; a suburb of Paris; Majorca; Albany, New York; and Princeton, New Jersey. Shortly after he was divorced in the late 1950s, he married Josefa Fay. He died in Vaud, Switzerland, January 2, 1964 (*New York Times,* Jan. 6, 1964, 47). Norman Prince, a graduate of Harvard University and a lawyer who practiced in Chicago, where his father (cat. 38) owned several businesses, died October 15, 1916, while serving in France as a sergeant major in the American Aviation Corps. For his valor, he was awarded a Legion of Honor medal (*New York Times,* Oct. 15, 1916, 4: Oct. 16, 1916, 2; Oct. 17, 1916, 1). Norman Prince's father was a major contributor to the Lafayette Escadrille memorial in France (*New York Times,* June 22, 1927, 33). In 1937, Prince's body was returned for burial in the Washington National Cathedral (*New York Times,* May 7, 1937, 19; Dec. 7, 1937, 7).

42. DORETTE KRUSE FLEISCHMANN

1. Janet Light, "Julius Fleischmann," in Kristin L. Spangenberg, comp., *The Golden Age of Costume and Set Design for the Ballet Russe de Monte Carlo, 1938–1944* (Cincinnati: Cincinnati Art Museum, 2002), 91–101; obituary of Julius Fleischmann, *New York Times,* Oct. 24, 1968, 47; "Dorette Kruse Fleischmann: Civic Leader," *New York Times,* Mar. 4, 1994, B8; Joan Fleischmann Tobin, "Dorette Fleischmann," www.las.iastate.edu/kiosk/plazaContent.aspx?plazaID=1161 (March 31, 1995), accessed Sept. 23, 2009.

2. Ethel Frances Mundy, www.askart.com/AskART/artist/biography, accessed Apr. 4, 2010; Anna Wetherill Olmsted, *Ethel Mundy: Miniatures and Sculptures in Wax* (Syracuse, NY: Museum of Fine Arts, 1938); Claude Bragdon, "The Wax Portraits of Ethel Frances Mundy," *American Magazine of Art* 9, no. 12 (Oct. 1918): 490–93; Anna Wetherill Olmsted, *Ethel Frances Mundy, 1876–1964* (Syracuse, NY: Business Service Bureau, 1960s); "Ethel Frances Mundy Portraitists in Wax," *Mentor World Traveler* 16 (Dec. 1928): 23–35.

43. SEATED FIGURE (LUCILLE CORCOS)

1. Biographical information on Smith and Dehner and their relationship can be found in Joan Marter, *Dorothy Dehner and David Smith: Their Decades of Search and Fulfillment* (New Brunswick, NJ: Jane Voorhees Zimmerli Art Museum, 1983), 23, 51, fig. 45, cat. 37; Rosalind E. Kraus, *The Sculpture of David Smith: A Catalogue Raisonné* (New York: Garland, 1977), 8, n. 50; Garnett McCoy, ed., *David Smith* (New York: Praeger, 1973), 82, 189; Dorothy Dehner, "Reminiscences," in *David Smith of Bolton Landing: Sculpture and Drawing* (Glen Falls, NY: Hyde Collection, 1973), unpaginated. I thank Susan Cooke, associate director of the Estate of David Smith, for permission to read his papers in the Archives of American Art. Likewise, I thank Joel Levy for permission to read the Edgar Levy and Lucille Corcos Papers, 1928–1975, Archives of American Art. The papers of Dorothy Dehner, Archives of American Art, provided additional information on the relationship between the two couples, as did David Levy. An

etching of six portraits in the Archives of American Art further documents the friendship of the two couples as well as their relationship with Adolph and Esther Gottlieb. The etching shows Lucille Corcos drawn by Dorothy Dehner, David Smith by Lucille Corcos, Adolph Gottlieb by Edgar Levy, Edgar Levy by Esther Gottlieb, Dorothy Dehner by Adolph Gottlieb, and Esther Gottlieb by David Smith. Dehner and Smith married in 1927; Corcos and Levy in 1928.

2. Rosalind E. Kraus, *Terminal Iron Works: The Sculpture of David Smith* (Cambridge, MA: MIT Press, 1971), 5–44; Karen Wilkin, *David Smith* (New York: Abbeville, 1984), 1–29.

3. For biographical information on Corcos, see March Michael Epstein, *Jewish Women: A Comprehensive Historical Encyclopedia* (Jerusalem: Shalvi, 2006), http//:jwa.org/encyclopedia/article/corcos-lucille, accessed July 26, 2010 and www.artnet.com/artists. Her *Vanity Fair* cover from 1931 is reproduced on www.condenaststore.com.

4. "Children's Games," *Life*, Aug. 20, 1951, 93; "A Double View of Artists' Lives," *Life*, July 12, 1954, 92.

5. Among the books she illustrated were Deems Taylor, ed., *Treasury of Gilbert and Sullivan: The Words and Music of One Hundred and Two Songs* (New York: Simon and Schuster, 1941); Louis and Bryna Untermeyer, eds., *Grimm's Fairy Tales* (New York: Limited Editions Club, 1962, 1979); and two books of her own writing: *Joel Gets a Dog* (New York: Abelard and Schuman, 1958) and *The City Book* (New York: Golden Press, 1972).

6. The record of Corcos's exhibitions is found, respectively, in the following titles edited by Peter H. Falk and published by Sound View Press, Madison, CT: *The Annual and Biennial Exhibition Record of the Whitney Museum of American Art, 1918–1989* (1991), 125; *The Annual Exhibition Record of the National Academy of Design, 1901–1950* (1990),140; *Record of the Carnegie Institute's International Exhibitions, 1896–1996* (1998), 75–76; *The Annual Exhibition Record of the Art Institute of Chicago, 1888–1950* (1990), 232; *The Annual Exhibition Record of the Pennsylvania Academy of the Fine Arts* (1988), 3:143.

44. HEAD OF A DANCER (HARALD KREUTZBERG)

1. Janet Gail Abbott, "The Barnett Aden Gallery: A Home for Diversity in a Segregated City" (PhD diss., Pennsylvania State University, 2008), 192.

2. "Howard Shows Art of Negro Sculptor," *Washington Post*, Dec. 14, 1940, S13; "Howard Shows

Contemporary American Art," *Washington Post*, Apr. 7, 1940, L7. See also Abbott, "Barnet Aden Gallery," 8, 44, 46–47.

3. Beginning in 1929 and throughout the 1930s, Barthé's work gained notice in the *New York Times* on Jan. 7, 1929, 9; Feb. 17, 1931, 29; Dec. 18, 1931, 28; May 1, 1934, 21; Apr. 23,1935, 19; Apr. 28, 1935, X7; Mar. 29, 1936, X9; Dec. 3, 1937, 26; May 22, 1938, 157; Mar. 12, 1939, 158; June 4, 1939, X7. In addition, references to his display in the permanent collection of the Whitney Museum of American Art are cited in the *New York Times,* May 16, 1937, 1, and May 18, 1938, 18, 173. Barthé also received a positive review for his exhibition in 1930 at the Woman's City Club in Chicago (Eleanor Jewett, *Chicago Daily Tribune,* June 14, 1930, 10). Perhaps the most important article for his early career was Winslow Ames, "Contemporary American Artists: Richmond Barthé," *Parnassus* 12, no. 3 (Mar. 1940): 10–17. Barthé was a Rosenwald Fellow, 1930/31, and received a Guggenheim Fellowship, 1940/41.

4. Margaret Rose Vendryes, *Barthé: A Life in Sculpture* (Jackson: University of Mississippi Press, 2008), 183–85.

5. "Harald Kreutzberg," *International Encyclopedia of Dance*, ed. Selma J. Cohen (New York: Oxford University Press, 1998), 4:60–61.

6. Kreutzberg's presence in New York between 1932 and 1939 is documented in the *New York Times*; see, for example, Jan. 30, 1930, 16; Mar. 1, 1930, 15; Jan. 12, 1932, 28; Apr. 25, 1932, 18; Jan. 8, 1933, 13; Apr. 5, 1933, 23; Mar. 18, 1935, 15; Mar. 10, 1935, X6; Mar. 17, 1935, X9; Mar. 31, 1935, X9; Jan. 31, 1936, 15; Feb. 3, 1936, 21; Feb. 10, 1936, 14; Sep. 26, 1937, 183; Oct. 18, 1937, 14; Feb. 26, 1939, 130.

7. Ames, "Contemporary American Artists: Barthé," 13.

8. *New York Times*, Mar. 12, 1939, 158. This exhibition also included portraits of Maurice Evans as Richard II, and John Gielgud as Hamlet.

9. "Howard," *Washington Post*, Apr. 7, 1940, L7.

45. SELF-PORTRAIT AS A YOUNG MAN WITH MIRROR (JOHN N. ROBINSON)

1. Biographical information can be found in *John Robinson: A Retrospective* (Washington, DC: Smithsonian Institution Press for Anacostia Neighborhood Museum, 1976), 13–15, for an exhibition June 18– July 30. Additional details of Robinson career can be

found in Paul Richard, "Mr. Robinson's Neighborhood," *Washington Post*, Sep. 17, 1993, D1; "John Robinson, Noted Artist, Dies," *Washington Post,* Oct. 19, 1994, B1; as well as Jeffrey C. Stewart, *Selections from the Barnett-Aden Collection: A Homecoming Celebration* (Washington, DC: Hemphill Gallery, 2009), 40–42.

2. Janet Gail Abbott, "The Barnett Aden Gallery: A Home for Diversity in a Segregated City" (PhD diss., The Pennsylvania State University, 2008), 192–97.

3. Richards, "Robinson," *Washington Post*, Oct. 19, 1994, B7. Robinson also exhibited at the Anacostia Neighborhood Museum from November 1982 to February 1983 (*Washington Post,* "Museums," Dec. 10, 1982, W43), and he was part of a group exhibition at the Washington Project for the Arts in 1985. See Keith Morrison, *Art in Washington and Its Afro-American Presence, 1940–1970* (Washington, DC: Washington Project for the Arts, 1985), 102, on the exhibition April 2–May 11; Paul Richard, "The Black Presence, Art and Integration," *Washington Post,* Apr. 7, 1985, B1. This self-portrait has been included in several exhibitions after Robinson's death, among them "Self-Portrait: Renaissance to Contemporary," National Portrait Gallery, London, October 20–January 29, 2006, which traveled to the Art Gallery of New South Wales, Sydney, Australia.

46. SELF-PORTRAIT (FREDERICK C. FLEMISTER)

1. The most complete biographical information on Flemister can be found in Theresa Dickason Cederholm, ed., *Afro-American Artists: A Bio-bibliographical Directory* (Boston: Trustees of the Boston Public Library, 1973), 94. See also Richard J. Powell and Jock Reynolds, *To Conserve a Legacy: American Art from Historically Black Colleges and Universities* (Cambridge, MA: MIT Press, 1999), 196, and Jeffrey Stewart, *Selections from the Barnett-Aden Collection: A Homecoming Celebration* (Washington, DC: Hemphill Gallery, 2009), 31. Flemister's military record given on ancestry.com shows that he was born February 5, 1917; entered service as a private on May 22, 1942, at Fort Benning, Georgia; and left December 11, 1944. He died on February 29 and was buried at Long Island National Cemetery, Farmington, New York, on March 4, 1976. Morehouse was—and is—part of a six-institution consortium now known as the Atlanta University Center; the John Herron Institute is now known as Herron School of Art and Design; and Atlanta University is now Clark Atlanta University.

2. Janet Gail Abbott, "The Barnett Aden Gallery: A Home for Diversity in a Segregated City" (PhD diss., The Pennsylvania State University, 2008), 192. For a history of black art during the gallery's existence, see David C. Driskell, "The Evolution of a Black Aesthetic, 1920–1950," in Driskell, *Two Centuries of Black American Art* (1976; reprint, Los Angeles: Los Angeles County Museum of Art; New York: Knopf, 2003), 59–79 and Richard J. Powell, *Black Art: A Cultural History* 2d ed. (London: Thames and Hudson, 2003), 86–120.

3. Abbott, "Barnett Aden," 46. This exhibition served in part for as the basis for Alain Locke, ed., *Negro in Art: A Pictorial Record of the Negro Artist and the Negro Theme in Art* (1940; reprint, New York: Hacker Art Books, 1971). On pages 113–14 this book reproduces three paintings by Flemister, including *Man with a Brush.* See also "Urban League Bulletin," *Atlanta Constitution,* Aug. 25, 1940, 16A.

4. Abbott, "Barnett Aden," 192. In addition to Woodruff, others showing in Aden's exhibition of February 1944 included Alice Acheson, Richmond Barthé, William Carter, Elizabeth Catlett, Tony Cornetti, Eldzier Cortor, Allan Rohan Crite, Aaron Douglas, Margaret Goss, Lois Mailou Jones, Edward Loper, Frank Neal, James A. Porter, Charles White, and Andrea de Zerega.

5. Donald F. Davis, "Hale Woodruff of Atlanta: Molder of Black Artists," *Journal of Negro History* 69, no. 3–4 (Summer–Autumn 1984): 152. *The Mourners* was again exhibited January 3–February 11, 1945, at the Institute of History and Art. See *The Negro Artist Comes of Age: A National Survey of Contemporary American Artists* (Albany, NY: Institute of History and Art, 1945), unpaginated.

6. Cederholm, *Afro-American Artists,* 94.

47. FIRST GALLERY (ALONZO J. ADEN)

1. For a history of the gallery and biographical information on Aden and Herring, see Janet Gail Abbott, "The Barnett Aden Gallery: A Home for Diversity in a Segregated City" (PhD diss., The Pennsylvania State University, 2008). See also Jeffery C. Stewart, *Selections from the Barnett-Aden Collection: A Homecoming Celebration* (Washington, DC: Hemphill Gallery, 2009), for an exhibition January 31–March 7, 2009. For reviews of exhibitions at the Barnett Aden Gallery and a sense of its place in the Washington Arts Community, see *Washington Post,* Oct. 31, 1943, L8;

Sep. 7, 1947, 5; Dec. 14, 1947, L5; Aug. 15, 1948, L3; Nov. 22,1953, L6; Aug. 29, 1954, SA11; Mar. 16, 1958, E7; June 29, 1958, E7; Oct. 19, 1958, E7; Dec. 18, 1960, G7; Oct. 14, 1960, C6: Oct. 23, 1960, G6; Mar. 9,1961, D2. After Aden's death, David Driskell initially served as gallery director under Herring's supervision (*Washington Post*, Feb. 25, 1962, G6). Driskell's connections to Aden and Herring are detailed in Julie L. McGee, *David C. Driskell, Artist and Scholar* (San Francisco: Pomegranate, 2006), 31–35. Artists shown at the Barnett Aden Gallery included African Americans such as Robinson, Richmond Barthé, Romare Bearden, Elizabeth Catlett, and Jacob Lawrence, as well as Lois Mailou Jones and David Driskell, who both had their first exhibition at that gallery. The work of Washington artists such as Jack Perlmutter and color field painters Morris Louis, Gene Davis, Kenneth Noland, and Jacob Kainen was featured by the gallery as was that of non-Washingtonians Theodore Stamos, Marguerite Zorach, and Irene Rice Pereira. The diversity of art shown is suggested by the February 1944 exhibition of Mexican watercolors and the October 1944 exhibition of the work of Brazilian artist Candido Portinari, who had done murals for the Hispanic Reading Room at the Library of Congress ("Art Calendar," *Washington Post*, Feb. 9, 1944, 12, and Oct. 8, 1944, S5).

2. Jane Watson, "Pacific, Canada, Latin America Exhibits Now Merit Attention," *Washington Post*, June 3, 1945, B6.

3. After Herring's death, the collection was shown at the Anacostia Neighborhood Museum (now Anacostia Community Museum), Smithsonian Institution, in 1974 and at the Corcoran Gallery of Art in 1975 (Adrienne Manns, "Ebony Reflections on Art," *Washington Post*, Jan. 21, 1974, B9; Paul Richard, "Of Art and Artist, Past and Present," *Washington Post*, Jan. 11, 1975, B2). The collection was sold in 1989 to the Florida Education Fund of Tampa, Florida, and purchased from them in about 1998 by Robert L. Johnson (Jacqueline Trescott, "Black Art Nets $6 Million," *Washington Post,* Dec. 4, 1989; Stewart, *Barnett-Aden Collection*, 6).

4. Abbott, "Barnett Aden Gallery," 11; "New Gallery Emphasizes Negro Art," *Washington Post*, Oct. 31, 1943, L8.

48. GWENDOLYN DETRE CAFRITZ

1. Marjorie Williams, "The Philanthropist (Gwendolyn Cafritz)," in Williams, *The Woman at the Washington Zoo: Writings on Politics, Family, and Fate,* ed. Timothy Noah (New York: Public Affairs, 2005), 22.

2. "Licensed to Marry," *Washington Post*, July 12, 1929, 20; photo, 7.

3. Williams, *Woman*, 12–29; Hope Ridings Miller, *Great Houses of Washington, D.C.* (New York: C. N. Potter, 1969), 167.

4. "The Capital: Life Among the Party Givers," *Time*, July 11, 1949; "Gwendolyn Cafritz Makers Her Bid," *Life*, Aug. 1, 1949, 81.

5. "Gwendolyn Cafritz, 78, Washington Hostess," *Washington Post*, Nov. 30, 1988, D4; Sarah Booth Conroy, "The Cafritz Largesse," *Washington Post*, Nov. 30, 1988, C1.

6. Stéphane-Jacques Addade, *Bernard Boutet de Monvel* (Paris: Amateur, 2001).

7. Boutet de Monvel completed "Folie Monvel" in January 1937. In May 1939 he returned to France for the duration of World War II, and the house remained unoccupied (Addade, *Boutet de Monvel*, 288, 292). Cafritz may have also seen "Who Will Paint Your Portrait?" *Town and Country*, Dec. 1939, 62–71, in which the artist was favorably discussed as a society portrait painter. During the 1930s, Boutet de Monvel was a frequent participant in the Carnegie Museum International exhibitions in Pittsburgh, Pennsylvania; see *Carnegie International* (Pittsburgh: Museum of Art, Carnegie Institute, 1934, 1935, 1936, 1937, 1939).

8. Agnes K. Gray, "Washington Possesses Rare Masterpieces in the Clark Collection," *Sunday (Washington) Star,* May 27, 1928, 7. Coincidentally, in 1948, the year of the Cafritz portrait, Boutet de Monvel painted a portrait of Ingrid Bergman in costume for her role as Joan of Arc, which together with her costume from the film was exhibited at the Metropolitan Museum of Art, New York ("Armour Suit to Be Shown," *New York Times*, Sep. 1, 1948, 33).

9. Addade, *Boutet de Monvel*, 301, states that after World War II ended, Boutet de Monvel first returned to New York in 1946. A review of the artist's show at Knoedler's November 10–29, 1947, appeared in *ARTnews* 46 (Dec. 1947): 59. I thank Mr. Addade for his gracious responses to my numerous requests for documentation related to the Cafritz portrait (Addade to Carr, Jan. 1, 24, and 29 and Apr. 4, 2010). Regrettably, other than a photograph of the portrait, no correspondence between the artist and the sitter exists (Addade to Carr, Jan. 1, 2010). According to Mr. Addade, Boutet de Monvel occasionally used the studio of his close friend, Russian painter Saveli Sorine (1878–1953), when painting in New York, although

Addade indicates that the artist did the Ingrid Berman portrait at Hampshire House, where he was residing while in New York (Addade to Carr, Jan. 24 and Apr. 4, 2010).

10. Mary van Rensselaer Thayer, "Whitey Finds Easter Laurels Rather Thorney," *Washington Post*, Apr. 4, 1948, S1.

11. "Forty-eight Killed in Azores Crash," *New York Times*, Oct. 29, 1949, 1.

49. WARREN ZIMMERMANN

1. The Zimmermann family bases the date of the medallion portrait on a photograph taken in 1948, which is similar in appearance to the medal and coincides with the family's memory of Waggoner's rental of their summer house in the Hamptons. I thank Teeny Zimmermann, widow of Warren Zimmermann, for communicating with her husband's siblings about the date of the portrait.

2. Florence S. Berryman, "The Art World: Works of Electra Waggoner Given First Washington Showing at Corcoran," *(Washington) Sunday Star*, Nov. 4, 1945, C6.

3. Genevieve Reynolds, "Heiress Lives in Capital Unheralded: Sculpture and Baby Require Her Time," *Washington Post*, Feb. 11, 1945, S3, notes that by the time of his death, W. T. Waggoner "had created the largest fortune ever amassed west of the Mississippi River." See also, www.waggonnerranch.com. Electra's father, E. Paul Waggoner (1889–1957), was one of W. T. Waggoner's three children.

4. F[lorence] S. B[erryman], "Electra Waggoner, Noted Sculptress Is Talented Newcomer to Washington," *Washington Star*, Aug. 12, 1945. The sculptor named in the article as M. Giovanelli is possibly Jean-Pierre Giovannetti. See Société des Artistes Français, *Le Salon de 1928* (Paris, 1928),163.

5. *New York Times*, June 15, 1933, 14; May 4, 1935, 5

6. "Young Sculptress Visits Capital," *Washington Times*, Mar. 30, 1936, 10. The bust was originally created for the 1936 Texas Centennial Exhibition, the same exposition that saw an exhibition of Negro Life organized by Alonzo Aden (cat. 47). It is at Texas Technical College (now University), Lubbock. About this time, Waggoner also made a large sculpture of Will Rogers on his horse Soapsuds, originally given to Fort Worth, Texas, in the mid-1930s. She also received a commission from Consolidated Edison Company for a series of bas-reliefs to represent them in the 1939 New York World's Fair.

7. "Sculpture Exhibition by Electra Waggoner," Apr. 19–May 7, 1938. The exhibition included thirty-one life-size busts, among them the portrait of Vice President Garner. See "Electra Waggoner," *Art Digest* 12 (May 1, 1938): 21; *ARTnews* 36 (Apr. 23, 1938): 15.

8. "Young Sculptress Visits Capital," *Washington Times*, Mar. 30, 1936, 10; Berryman, "Electra Waggoner," *(Washington) Sunday Star*, Nov. 4, 1945, C6.

The Truman sculpture was begun in May 1945 and completed in time for Waggoner's Corcoran opening. See Eva Hinton, "Town Talk," *Washington Post*, May 22, 1945, 10; "John Biggses to be Hosts," *Washington Post*, Sept. 22, 1945, 8; Katrina van Hook, "New Art Exhibitions Varied," *Washington Post*, Oct. 28, 1945, B6.

9. See www.redrivervalleymuseum.org. For information on Waggoner after she returned to Texas, including the fact that in 1958, her brother-in-law— then president of the Buick Division of General Motors—named the Buick Electra after her, see "The Texas One Hundred: Money Becomes Electra," *Texas Monthly*, Sept. 1992, and also *Texas Monthly*, Jan. 2004, both at www.texasmontly.com.

10. Berryman, "Electra Waggoner," *(Washington) Sunday Star*, Nov. 4, 1945, C6.

11. The first book was published New York by Times Books, the second in New York by Farrar, Straus and Giroux. See www.nndb.com/people; *New York Times*, Feb. 5, 1964; and www.guardian.co.uk/news/2004/feb/10/guardianobituaries.

50. MAMIE GENEVA DOUD EISENHOWER

1. The initial conversation at Fort Myer is recalled in Harold E. Stassen and Marshall Houts, *Eisenhower: Turning the World Toward Peace* (St. Paul, MN: Merrill/Magnus, 1990), 225–27. This 1947 portrait now belongs to the National Portrait Gallery (NPG. 65.63).

2. Stephens's portrait of Mamie Eisenhower is now at the Eisenhower National Historic Site, Gettysburg, Pennsylvania.

3. Dwight David Eisenhower, *At Ease: Stories I Tell to Friends* (Garden City, NY: Doubleday, 1967), 340–41. Memories are selective, and precisely when Eisenhower took up painting is a bit in dispute. In contrast to her husband, Mamie Eisenhower recalled that it was at Fort Myer, as Stephens was working on a portrait of her in early 1948, that her husband took up painting; see "Wife Likes Eisenhower's Cooking but His Portrait Painting Misfires," *Los Angeles Times*, July 13, 1953, 1. Travis Beal Jacobs, *Eisenhower at*

Columbia (New Brunswick, NJ: Transaction, 2001), 211, also states that Mrs. Eisenhower gave him paints for Valentine's Day 1948. In a review of the exhibition "Ike's Paintings," in the *Topeka (KS) Capital-Journal*, September 19, 2004, the date of February 1948 is also given as the time when Eisenhower launched his new hobby and painted a portrait of his wife.

4. Leonard Lyons wrote in the *Washington Post*, June 10, 1948, B14, three days after Eisenhower was appointed president of Columbia University, that he contributed a painting to the Urban League fundraiser. The painting of an Indian that he submitted was copied from a painting by Henry C. Balink and sold for $2,600 ("Eisenhower's Painting Is Sold for $2,600 after Spirited Bidding at Benefit Show," *New York Times*, Oct. 14, 1948, 31).

5. Eisenhower, *At Ease*, 34.

6. I thank Lou Molnar, painting conservator at the National Portrait Gallery, for unframing and photographing the back of this work, which has enabled the secure dating of this portrait. The back of this painting is signed "By DDE." Below the signature is "Mamie 41." In the upper left corner, in pencil, is the number 52. The artist board is stamped "Papiers a Dessign, Couleurs Fines pour Artistes, R. C. Bon, 19 Rue de la Paroisse, VERSAILLES." The purchase price was two francs. Dwight and Mamie Eisenhower moved to Versailles in February 1951, staying at the Hotel Trianon Palace until he moved into the nearby villa at Marnes-la Coquette in September 1951. On June 1, 1952, Eisenhower returned to the United States to begin his campaign for president (*New York Times*, "Eisenhower Gets Suite," Feb. 17, 1951, 5; "Be It Ever So Humble, It's Ike's Home," *New York Times*, Sep. 30, 1951, 5; Henry Wales, "Eisenhower to Leave France for U.S. May 28," *New York Times*, May 13, 1952, 3).

7. It was customary for Eisenhower to paint from photographs. A photograph from Dwight D. Eisenhower Library, reproduced at www.whitehousehistory.org, in an article by Sister Wendy Beckett, "President Eisenhower: Painter," accessed July 26, 2010, shows him painting with a photograph before him.

8. Susan Eisenhower, *Mrs. Ike: Memories and Reflections on the Life of Mamie Eisenhower* (New York: Farrar, Straus and Giroux, 1966), 4, 91, 109–10, 136–38, 176, 210.

51. DOLORES SUERO

1. Fleur Cowles, *The Case of Salvador Dali* (London: William Heinemann, 1959), 245. Dali's full name was Salvador Domingo Felipe Jacinto Dalí i Domènech, first Marquis of Púbol).

2. *ARTnews* 42 (Apr. 1943): 11. The exhibition also merited a review in *Time*, Apr. 26, 1943, 79. Among the portraits shown were those of Dorothy Spreckels, Mrs. Harrison Williams (later Princess Bismarck), Mrs. Louis Green, Mrs. Charles Swift, Mrs. Ortiz de Linares, and Lady Louis Mountbatten. Dalí's portrait of Helena Rubinstein was probably painted in 1943.

3. Cowles, *Dali*, 245.

4. Cowles, *Dali*, 244.

5. *ARTnews* 53 (Jan. 1955): 49; *ARTnews* 55 (Jan. 1957): 22; R. M. Coates, "Exhibition at Carstairs Gallery," *New Yorker*, Dec. 15, 1956, 129–30; "Museum Acquires Its First Dalí; 'Crucifixion' to Be Shown Today," *New York Times*, Jan. 14, 1955, 23; Jean White, "Gallery Puts on Exhibit Its First Dalí Painting," *Washington Post and Times Herald*, Apr. 1, 1956, A15. While in town for the opening at the National Gallery of Art, Dalí attended a party given by Gwendolyn Cafritz (cat. 48). See Mary V. R. Thayer, "Dalí's Mustache Is Worth the Bother," *Washington Post and Times Herald*, Mar. 23, 1956, 66; George Dixon, "Washington Scene: Happy Easter Had by All," *Washington Post and Times Herald*, Apr. 6, 1956, 19. Dale gave *The Sacrament of the Last Supper* to the National Gallery in 1963.

6. Dolores Suero y Falla was the daughter of Isabel Falla y Bonet (Cuba 1890–Spain 1976) who married David Suero y Balbin (born Asturia, Spain; died Cuba, 1940). Suero y Falla married Manuel de la Cruz y Obegron (Cuba 1917–Miami 1976) and divorced him in the late 1940s. The family home in Cuba is now the House of the Friendship of the People (Casa de la Amistad de los Pueblos). During the time that Dolores Suero lived in the United States, her son and only child was born in 1941. He attended the Harvey School in Katonah, New York, beginning in 1949; Phillips Academy, Andover, Massachusetts, from 1955 to 1959; and the Wharton School, University of Pennsylvania. I thank Carlos M. de la Cruz, Dolores Suero's son, and his daughter, Isabel Ernst, for this information.

7. "Tea Dance April 24 to Assist Nursery," *New York Times*, Mar. 19, 1952, 36; "Boys Club to Gain by Dinner Dance," *New York Times*, Mar. 2, 1954, 21.

8. Carlos M. de la Cruz to Carolyn K. Carr, e-mail, Apr. 7, 2010.

9. Isabel Ernst to Carr, Feb. 23, 2009.

10. De la Cruz to Carr, e-mail, Apr. 7 and 8, 2010.

52. NAT (NAT ROSE)

1. Anita Reiner to Carolyn K. Carr, Apr. 25, 2010. Soon after the close of Close's solo exhibition at the Bykert Gallery (Dec. 4, 1971–Jan. 5, 1972), the painting was loaned to Whitney Annual exhibition (Jan. 25–Mar. 19, 1972). Mr. and Mrs. Reiner also own photographic separations related to the work.

2. Several catalogues and monographs provide insight into the work of the artist, among them, Robert Storr, *Chuck Close,* with essays by Kirk Varnedoe and Deborah Wye (New York: Museum of Modern Art, 1998); Martin L. Friedman, *Close Reading: Chuck Close and the Artist Portrait* (New York: Harry N. Abrams, 2005); Christopher Finch, *Chuck Close: Work* (Munich: Prestel, 2007).

3. Storr, *Close,* 205. This description of his technique was first published in a brochure for an exhibition of nine paintings by Close at the Los Angeles County Museum of Art (Sep. 21–Nov. 14, 1971).

53. EVIE (EVELYN STEFANSSON NEF)

1. Evelyn Stefansson Nef, *Finding My Way: The Autobiography of an Optimist* (Washington, DC: Francis Press, 2002). After she completed her autobiography, she was awarded honorary doctorates from the University of Alaska (1998); the Corcoran School of Art (2000); and Dartmouth College (2002). See "Evelyn Stefansson Nef," *Washington Post,* Dec. 11, 2009, B7; Adrian Higgins, "Life of Arts Patron and Author Marked by Intriguing Events," *Washington Post,* Dec. 16, 2009, B5. Evelyn Nef's enthusiasm for life and her pleasure in participating in the cultural life of Washington is reflected in her signing, while she was terminally ill, the forms to loan the portraits of herself and her second husband to this exhibition. She died four days later.

2. Arthur Molella, "John U. Nef," *Technology and Culture* 31, no. 4 (Oct.1990): 916–20. Nef's first wife, Elinor Henry Castle, died in 1953 (Wolfgang Saxon, "John U. Nef, Economic Historian at Chicago University, Dies at 89," *New York Times,* Dec. 27, 1988, A19.)

3. Higgins, "Life of Arts Patron," B5, notes her support of the National Symphony Orchestra, the Washington Opera, and the Corcoran Gallery of Art. At the Corcoran Gallery of Art, Eveyln Nef served on the board, underwrote an exhibition series for regional artists over seventy years old, endowed the position of associate curator of American art, and bequeathed her portrait by Katz to the museum.

4. Meryle Secrest, "I Am an Ordinary Man . . . ," *Washington Post,* Nov. 14, 1968, E1; "Evelyn Stefansson Nef," *Washington Post,* Jan. 23, 1972, PO16; Siobhan Morrissey, "Chagall's Thank You," *Washington Post,* May 7, 1985, B7.

5. The selection of Katz may have been inspired by the favorable review he received for his recent exhibition at New York's Marlborough Gallery. See Hilton Kramer, "The World of Alex Katz: 'Big Numbers, Fast Moves,'" *New York Times,* Dec. 16, 1973, 177.

6. The estate still possesses the dress that she wore for this painting.

7. Evelyn Nef to Carolyn K. Carr, Jan. 8, 2009. Most likely, they saw the drawing in the Katz exhibition at the Galerie Marguérite Lamy, May 29–July 12, 1975. In her will, Mrs. Nef left the drawing to the National Gallery of Art. A small study 8¼ × 12 in.) for the portrait is in the collection of the Hirshhorn Museum and Sculpture Garden, acquired as part of the Joseph H. Hirshhorn bequest.

54. DIANA #3 (DIANA MOORE BECKMAN)

1. William Beckman, "Artist's Statement," in *Portraiture Now,* Series 1: *William Beckman, Dawoud Bey, Nina Levy, Jason Salavon, Andres Serrano* (Washington, DC: National Portrait Gallery, 2006), 7.

2. For the range of his portraits featuring Diana, see Carl Belz, *William Beckman* (Seattle: Frye Art Museum in association with the University of Washington Press, 2002), 18–41.

3. Penelope Hunter-Stiebel, *William Beckman: Dossier of a Classical Woman* (New York: Stiebel Modern, 1991), 47–53, contains a chronology that includes Beckman's activities before he moved to New York.

4. Belz, *Beckman,* 10–17.

5. James K. Monte, *Twenty-Two Realists* (New York: Whitney Museum of American Art, 1970), 26, 42.

6. Erwin Panofsky, *Early Netherlandish Painting: Its Origins and Character* (1953; reprint, New York: Harper & Row, 1971), 2: pl. 109.

55. SELF-PORTRAIT (GENE DAVIS)

1. Among the monographs that provide biographical details are Steven W. Naifeh, *Gene Davis*

(New York: Arts Publisher, 1982) and Jacquelyn Days Serwer, *Gene Davis: A Memorial Exhibition*, with essays by Douglas Davis and Donald Kuspit (Washington, DC: Smithsonian Institution Press, 1987). His early amateur status is detailed in Sonia Stein, "Workshop Turns Reluctant Novices into Artists," *Washington Post*, May 14, 1950, S10; his growing importance is reflected in Leslie Judd Ahlander, "An Artist Speaks: Gene Davis," *Washington Post/Times Herald,* Aug. 26, 1962, G7.

2. Paul Richard, "Between the Stripes," *Washington Post*, Feb. 26, 1983, C3.

3. Ahlander, "Davis," *Washington Post,* C3. Davis also liked to work on an exceptionally small scale, and some heads were merely less than two inches square, a format that he also used in his "Micro-paintings" of 1968.

4. Naifeh, *Davis*, 110.

5. Pam Kessler, "Gene Davis: Paint, Paint, Paint," *Washington Post,* Nov. 26, 1982, W33.

6. Anne Collins Goodyear and James W. McManus, eds., *Inventing Marcel Duchamp: The Dynamics of Portraiture* (Washington, DC: National Portrait Gallery, 2009), 174–75, 222–23; Francis M. Naumann and Bradley Bailey, *Marcel Duchamp: Chess Master* (New York: Ready Made Press, 2009).

7. Benjamin Forgey, "Gene Davis, Noted Artist, Dies Here," *Washington Post*, Apr. 7, 1985, C7. For a sampling of the artist's thoughts about art, see Gene Davis, "Random Thoughts about Art," *Art International* 15 (Nov. 20, 1971): 39.

8. Quoted in Naifeh, *Davis*, 115.

56. INA GINSBURG

1. Monographs on Andy Warhol are as numerous as his portrait commissions. For insights into the Warhol art and publishing empire, I have relied on books by those who worked for him, including Victor Bockris, *The Life and Death of Andy Warhol* (New York: Bantam Books, 1989); Bob Colacello, *Holy Terror: Andy Warhol Up Close* (New York: HarperCollins, 1990); Pat Hackett, ed., *The Andy Warhol Diaries* (New York, Warner Books, 1989). *Interview*'s focus on luxury in every arena of life made it a progenitor of the "lifestyle" journals that have since become ubiquitous.

2. Warhol quoted by Ina Ginsburg to Carolyn K. Carr, Jan. 14, 2009.

3. Beginning in the 1960s, Ginsburg's name showed up repeatedly in the *Washington Post*'s reports of major social events. Ginsburg served on the board of the American Film Institute from the early 1970s until 2009 and is now trustee emerita. In 1977 she chaired the Opera Ball (*Washington Post*, June 11, 1977, B1, 2), and later that year, the American Film Institute gala at the Kennedy Center, attended by an ample number of celebrities in the more than twelve hundred guests (*Washington Post*, Nov. 19, 1977, C1, 2). Among other honors, she received the Decoration of Honour in Silver for Services Rendered to the Republic of Austria in September 2004, and the Chevalier dans l'Ordre des Arts et des Lettres from the Republic of France in May 2009.

4. One of Warhol's more well-recorded visits was on November 15, 1979, when he came to town to promote his new book, *Andy Warhol's Exposures* (New York: Grosset and Dunlap, 1979). In Hackett, *Diaries,* Tuesday, Dec. 4, 248, he wrote "The tour began so chicly in Washington when I sat in President Carter's box at Kennedy Center." Colacello, *Holy Terror,* 433–34. Two articles appeared in the *Washington Post*: Paul Richard, "Mirror of the Glitterati, High Judge of Pop Society," and Donnie Radcliffe, "Warhol's Contagious Celebration," *Washington Post,* Nov. 13, 1979, F1, F10, F19. For the Reagan inauguration on January 20, 1981, Ginsburg got VIP tickets for Warhol and Colacello on the lawn in front of the podium (Hackett, *Diaries*, 355).

5. "A Visit to the Saudi Embassy; from the Camel to the Concorde in Ten Years," *Interview* 10 (Feb. 1980): 37–39.

6. A partial list of the more than fifty articles and interviews by Ina Ginsburg includes: "Alexander Godunov," *Interview* 10 (July 1980): 21–22; "Werner Fassbinder," *Interview* 10 (Sept. 1980); "Muffy Brandon," *Interview* 11 (May 1981): 20–21; "William French Smith," *Interview* 12 (Jan. 1982): 25–26; "Alan Cranston" *Interview* 12 (Feb. 1982): 46–47; "Alexander M. Haig," *Interview* 12 (July 1982): 38–39; "Dr. Osvaldo Hurtado Larrea," *Interview* 12 (Oct. 1982): 35–36; "Sherrye Henry,*" Interview* 12 (Nov. 1982): 68–69; "Baron Thyssen-Bornemisza," *Interview* 12 (Dec. 1982): 88–89; "Nancy Thurmond," *Interview* 13 (Jan. 1983): 22–24; "Donald Sutherland," *Interview* 13 (Mar. 1983): 33–35; "Jeane Kirkpatrick," *Interview* 13 (Apr. 1983): 41–43; "President Ferdinand Marcos," *Interview* 13 (May 1983): 58–60; "Imelda Marcos," *Interview* 13 (Aug. 1983): 32–33; "Robert S. McNamara," *Interview* 13 (Nov. 1983): 72–73; "Casper W. Weinberger," *Interview* 14 (July 1985): 60–66; "Paul Volker," *Interview* 17 (June 1987): 52–54; "Warren Christopher," *Interview* 24 (Nov. 1994): 42–44.

7. Bob Colacello to Carr, April 20, 2010.

8. Warhol moved to 860 Broadway in 1974. Not long after Ginsburg's sitting in 1982, he moved to a five-story block-sized building between Thirty-second and Thirty-third Streets and between Madison and Fifth Avenues. See Bockris, *Warhol*, p. 327. Warhol doesn't document the initial sitting in his diaries, but he does mention her return visit in his new location. She came on March 25, 1983, with her son Mark, who also wrote for *Interview*, to talk about the portraits, see Warhol, *Diaries*, 492.

9. Ginsburg to Carr, January 29, 2010, and Ginsburg to Friendly, April 20, 2010.

10. Ginsburg's portrait is published in Tony Shafrazi, ed., *Andy Warhol: Portraits* (London and New York: Phaidon, 2007), 262.

57. SELF-PORTRAIT WITH SQUASH (GREGORY GILLESPIE)

1. Donald D. Keyes et al., *Unique American Vision: Paintings by Gregory Gillespie* (Athens: Georgia Museum of Art, University of Georgia, 1999), 50.

2. Sources for Gillespie's life include Abram Lerner, *Gregory Gillespie* (Washington, DC: Smithsonian Institution Press for Hirshhorn Museum and Sculpture Garden, 1977); Donald Kuspit, "Gregory Gillespie's Consciousness of Self," in *Gregory Gillespie: Self-Portraits, 1969–1991: A Comprehensive Survey* (New York: Forum Gallery, 1992); and Keyes et al., *Unique American Vision*.

3. Quoted in Keyes et al., *Unique American Vision*, 36.

4. Kuspit, "Gregory Gillespie's Consciousness of Self," unpaginated.

5. Ibid.

58. SALLY QUINN

1. *Washingtonian* magazine first profiled Quinn in 1972. Quoted in Richard Lee, "Brenda Starr Lives: An Intimate Look at Sally Quinn," *Washingtonian*, Nov. 1972, 82

2. Quoted in Richard Lee, "The Return of Sally Quinn," *Washingtonian*, Aug. 1986, 100

3. Quinn to Pie Friendly, e-mail, June 2, 2010.

4. Quoted in Lee, "Return," *Washingtonian*, Aug. 1986, 102.

5. Quinn in conversation with Carolyn K. Carr, June 10, 2009.

59. WILLIAM A. HASELTINE

1. William Haseltine to Pie Friendly in response to questions from Carolyn K. Carr, Apr. 29, 2010; Fischl to Carr, Dec. 22, 2009. I thank William Haseltine for information regarding his friendship with Fischl, his admiration of the artist's work, and his recollections of sitting for this portrait. Likewise, I thank Eric Fischl for his recollections regarding the making of this portrait.

2. *Portraits* (New York: Mary Boone Gallery, 1999); Robert Enright, "The Former 'Bad Boy' of Painting Turns to Portraits," *Globe and Mail,* May 29, 1999, C22; Donald Kuspit, "Eric Fischl," *Artforum* 38, no. 2 (October 1999): 144.

3. "William Haseltine," www.futureinrerview.com, accessed 2008; Ann Graham, "William Haseltine: The Thought Leader Interview," www.strategy-business.com/press, accessed spring 2009.

4. Haseltine to Friendly and Carr, Apr. 29 2010.

5. Quoted in Eric Tuten, *Eric Fischl: The Bed, the Chair . . . New Paintings* (New York: Gagosian Gallery, 2000).

6. Eric Fischl and Elan Wingate, *Eric Fischl: Sculpture* (New York: Gagosian Gallery, 1998), 4. Given that Fischl has been a fellow at the American Academy in Rome, the image of the torso could have been based on the Belvedere torso in Vatican, although most likely it is derived from the *Statue of Herakles Seated on a Rock* (Metropolitan Museum of Art).

60. PASSING/POSING (ST. MONACA) (ROBERT REYNOLDS)

1. "Tumelo Mosaka, "Beyond Likeness: Portraits by Kehinde Wiley," in *Kehinde Wiley, Passing/Posing: Paintings and Faux Chapel* (New York: Earth Enterprise, 2004), 3–6; Franklin Sirmans, "Kehinde Wiley: The Paintings of My Familiar," in *Passing/Posing*, 7–12; Dereck Conrad Murray, "Kehinde Wiley: Splendid Bodies," *Nka: Journal of Contemporary African Art* 21 (Fall 2007): 90–101. I thank those at the studio of Kehinde Wiley for providing the name of the young man who posed for this portrait. As scholars have noted, Wiley's paintings incorporate the hip-hop ethos of sampling, mixing, and remixing. See Krista Thompson, "The Sound of Light: Reflections on Art History in the Visual Culture of Hip-Hop," *Art Bulletin* 91 (Dec. 2009): 481–505. This aspect of Wiley's work was reflected in the exhibition

"Recognize! Hip-Hop and Contemporary Portraiture," National Portrait Gallery, Feb. 8–Oct. 6, 2008.

2. *Passing/Posing (St. Monaca)*, the title on the owner's invoice, has also been titled *Passing/Posing (St. Monica)* in Alexa Gotthardt to Henry Thaggert, e-mail Jul. 8, 2010. Whether or not Monaca is the misspelling of Monica, a fourth-century saint who was the mother of Saint Augustine and was venerated by mothers, the important point is that Reynolds's pose was based on an Italian Renaissance source.

3. "Passing/Posing: The Paintings of Kehinde Wiley," was exhibited at the Brooklyn Museum of Art from October 8, 2004, to February 5, 2005; Sarah Lewis, "De(i)fying the Masters," *Art in America* 92 (Apr. 2005): 120–25; Mia Fineman, "The History of Art, in Baggy Jeans and Bomber Jackets," *New York Times*, Dec. 19, 2004, AR39.

61. KATE (KATE MOSS)

1. For a recent biography, see Angela Buttolph, *Kate Moss: Style* (London: Century, 2008).

2. Christopher Finch, *Chuck Close: Work* (Munich: Prestel, 2007), 280; Martin L. Friedman, *Close Reading: Chuck Close and the Art of the Self-Portrait* (New York: Harry N. Abrams, 2005), 157.

3. Quoted in Alastair Sooke, "Chuck Close: Capturing the Clinton Charisma," *Telegraph*, Oct. 6, 2007, reproduced at www.telegraph.co.uk/culture/art.

4. Lily Wei, *Chuck Close: Selected Paintings and Tapestries, 2005–2009* (New York: Pace Wildenstein, 2009); for a history of Magnolia Editions and a discussion of its proprietary weaving technique, see www.MagnoliaEditions.com.

62. JUDITH MARTIN IN VENICE

1. Judith Martin, *No Vulgar Hotel: The Desire and Pursuit of Venice* (New York: W. W. Norton, 2007), 15–54.

2. Elizabeth Sleeman, ed., "Victor Arnold Edelstein," *International Who's Who 2004* (London: Routledge, 2003); "The Fountains of Rome: Recent Pastels by Victor Edelstein," May 5–June 18, 2004, Didier Aaron Gallery; see www.didieraaron.com.

3. Martin, *No Vulgar Hotel*; Martin and Gloria Kamen, *Miss Manners' Guide to Excruciatingly Correct Behavior* (1982; reprint, New York: W.W. Norton, 2005).

4. Martin, in a telephone interview by Carolyn K. Carr, Jan. 27, 2010, provided background information on her trips to Venice, a description of the painting process, and its iconographic details.

ACKNOWLEDGMENTS

AN EXHIBITION occurs with the support of numerous individuals, and we are indebted to all who have contributed to the success of "Capital Portraits: Treasures from Washington Private Collections." Foremost among these individuals are the lenders. Without their extraordinary generosity, this exhibition would not have happened. Often with only a telephone call, they invited us into their houses and then agreed to let us borrow portraits of their own images, their ancestors, or portraits they had acquired as part of a more extensive collection of art, leaving their walls bare for some five months. In addition, these owners provided family documents and relevant publications as well as stories related to the portraits in their possession. We learned, too, what it has meant to them to be the stewards of such portraits. We are also grateful to those who showed us other remarkable portraits that, because of limited space, are not included in this exhibition. We thank Osborne Mackie and Dodge Thompson, lenders to the exhibition, for suggesting additional collectors we might contact. Mr. and Mrs. Jay P. Moffat, Dan Okrent, Dorothy Moss Williams, and Toby Chieffo-Reidway also made valuable suggestions that led to loans for the exhibition.

Several volunteers and interns undertook crucial research at all stages of the exhibition. Most of all, we would like to thank Pie Friendly, who has worked with us from the start of this project to its completion. We are particularly grateful for her enthusiasm, which has paralleled our own in the shaping of this exhibition. Her contributions are myriad. She made appointments to visit owners, collected and verified the historical information they possessed, and even helped them fill out loan forms. In addition to identifying published research, she contacted artists, scholars, and foundation administrators to elicit unpublished information. We also wish to thank Brooks Swett, Madeleine Morgan, Michelle Pollak, Jenna Kloeppel, and Sarah Ickow, a group of talented interns who assisted at various stages of the project, researching collectors, artists, and sitters.

We are fortunate in having remarkable colleagues to whom we owe a debt of gratitude. For their special knowledge regarding individual loans, we wish to thank Stéphane-Jacques Addade, author and expert on Bernard Boutet de Monvel, Paris; Carol Aiken, scholar and conservator of miniatures, Baltimore; Christine Berry, Spanierman Gallery, New York; Clifford T. Chieffo, Distinguished Research Professor of Art emeritus, Department of Art and Art History, Georgetown University, Washington, D.C.; Bob Colacello, former editor of *Interview* magazine, New York; Emily T. Cooperman, principal, Architectural Research and Cultural History Consulting, Philadelphia; Richard Cote, curator, Department of the Treasury, Washington, D.C.; John de Feo, curator, New Britain Museum of American Art, Connecticut; Rosemary DeRosa, formerly with the Barnet Aden Collection, Washington, D.C.; Alison Dickey, librarian, Currier Museum of Art, Manchester, New Hampshire; Diane Dillon, assistant director of research and education, Newberry Library, Chicago; Alex Dmitriev, State Museum, Tsarskoye Selo, St. Petersburg; Linda J. Docherty and Laura Latman, Bowdoin College, Brunswick,

Maine; Leslie Evans, director, Avery-Copp House, Groton, Connecticut; Martha Fleischman, director, Kennedy Galleries, Inc., New York; James Goode, independent historian, Washington, D.C.; Anne Halpern, Department of Curatorial Records, National Gallery of Art, Washington, D.C.; Patricia Hills, professor of art history, Boston University; James J. Holmberg, curator of special collections, Filson Historical Society, Louisville, Kentucky; William Innes Homer, professor emeritus, University of Delaware, Newark; John Dixon Hunt, professor emeritus of the history and theory of landscape, University of Pennsylvania, Philadelphia; Jan Ivie, adjunct professor of the history of art, College of Southern Maryland, La Plata; John A. Limpert, editor at large, *Washingtonian*, Washington, D.C.; Carrie Mackin and Kevin Cyr, assistants to Kehinde Wiley, New York; Megan Marshall, assistant professor of writing, literature, and publishing, Emerson College, Boston; Patrick McCormick, archivist, Butler Institute of American Art, Youngstown, Ohio; Estill Curtis Pennington, independent scholar, Paris, Kentucky; Mary Ann Rea, Los Angeles, assistant to James Garner, longtime friend of Richmond Barthé; Rebecca Reynolds, curator, the Margaret Cassidy and John Paul Manship Collection, Boston; Aileen Ribeiro, professor emeritus, Courtauld Institute of Art, London; Susan Schoelwer, curator, George Washington's Mount Vernon, Virginia; Lucy Silberman, assistant managing editor, *Interview*, New York; Joseph Skrapits, director, Antonio Salemme Foundation, Allentown, Pennsylvania; Carol Eaton Soltis, associate curator, American Art Department, Philadelphia Museum of Art; Alexandra Tice, conservator, Chevy Chase, Maryland; Alice Whitehead, coordinating editor, Philip de László Catalogue Raisonné, London; Christine M. Sullivan, director, Forbes House Museum, Milton, Massachusetts; Karina H. Corrigan, H. A. Crosby Forbes Curator, Peabody Essex Museum, Salem, Massachusetts; Paul Elias, Boston; Frederic D. Grant Jr., Milton, Massachusetts; Cullen Jay Wilder, Healdsburg, California; John D. Wong, Harvard University, Cambridge, Massachusetts; and Andrea Forbes Schoenfeld, Washington, D.C.

Exhibitions presented in an institution reflect the dedication of all of its staff. In addition to the encouragement and support of Director Martin E. Sullivan, we particularly wish to acknowledge the research assistance of Lauren Johnson; Anne Collins Goodyear; Linda Thrift and the staff of the Center for Electronic Research and Outreach Services, notably Patricia Svoboda, Susan Garton, and Benjamin Bloom; Cindy Lou Molnar, senior conservator; Dru Dowdy, head of publications; Beverly Cox, Claire Kelly, Kristin Smith, and Molly Grimsley of the Department of Exhibitions and Collections Management; Tibor Waldner and his staff in the Office of Design and Production; Sherri Weil and her staff in the Office of Development and External Affairs; contract photographer Alex Jamison, whose work provided the essential illustrations for the catalogue; and research volunteer Christopher A. Saks. In addition, colleagues from other Smithsonian Institution bureaus merit our gratitude, particularly Doug Litts, supervisory librarian, Smithsonian American Art Museum/National Portrait Gallery Library, and staff members Alice Clarke, Stephanie Moye, and Courtney Shaw; Liza Kirwin, curator of manuscripts, and Marisa Bourgoin, the Richard Manoogian Chief of Reference Services, Smithsonian Archives of American Art; Richard Stamm, curator, Smithsonian Institution Castle Collection; and George Gurney, deputy chief curator, Smithsonian American Art Museum.

The exhibition and the catalogue would not be possible without the generosity of our donors. We are deeply grateful to our friend the late Robert Lincoln McNeil Jr., a former commissioner of the National Portrait Gallery, for his respect for our scholarship and curatorial work. His extraordinary gift in the planning stages of this exhibition gave us the confidence and ability to proceed. We were pleased, too, that he agreed to let us dedicate this catalogue to him. We also wish to thank the Mr. and Mrs. Raymond J. Horowitz Foundation for the Arts, Inc., for additional funding of the publication and the exhibition. And we thank Isobel Ellis for her donation as well as for her research and her enthusiasm.

IMAGE CREDITS

Photographers

Matt Flynn: cat. 54

Alex Jamison Photography: figs. 1, 2, 3, 4, 5, 6, 7, 8, 9, 11, 13, 14, 15; cats. 1, 2, 3, 4, 6, 7, 8, 10, 11, 13, 14, 16, 17, 18, 19, 23, 24, 25, 26, 27, 28, 29, 31, 32, 33, 34, 35, 36, 37, 38, 39, 40, 41, 43, 48, 51, 56, 57, 58 a-d, 59, 62

Arthur Page Conservation: cat. 20-1

Gene Young: fig. 10

Copyrights

Art © Estate of Robert Arneson / Licensed by VAGA, New York, NY: fig. 15

© 2010 Artists Rights Society (ARS), New York, ADAGP, Paris: cat. 48

© William Beckman, courtesy of Forum Gallery, New York, NY: cat. 54

© Chuck Close, courtesy the artist (in collaboration with Magnolia Editions, Oakland) and The Pace Gallery: cat. 61

© Chuck Close, courtesy the artist and The Pace Gallery: cat. 52

© Salvador Dalí, Fundació Gala-Salvador Dalí / Artists Rights Society (ARS), New York 2010: cat. 51

© The Estate of Gene Davis, Smithsonian American Art Museum: cat. 55

© Eric Fischl: cat. 59

Art © Alex Katz / Licensed by VAGA, New York, NY: fig. 16; cat. 53

Art © Estate of David Smith / Licensed by VAGA, New York, NY: cat. 43; back cover

©2010 The Andy Warhol Foundation for the Visual Arts, Inc. / Artists Rights Society (ARS), New York: figs. 4, 5; cats. 56, 58 a-d

© Kehinde Wiley: cat. 60